# Migration Con
# North Atlant

# Migration Control in the North Atlantic World

*The Evolution of State Practices in Europe and the United States from the French Revolution to the Inter-War Period*

Edited by Andreas Fahrmeir, Olivier Faron, Patrick Weil

*Berghahn Books*
New York • Oxford

First published in 2003 by **Berghahn Books**
www.berghahnbooks.com

©2003 Andreas Fahrmeir, Olivier Faron, Patrick Weil

First paperback edition published in 2005.

**The Library of Congress has previously cataloged a hardback edition as follows:**

Migration control in the North Atlantic world: the evolution of state practices
in Europe and the U.S. from the French Revolution to the inter-war period /
edited by Andreas Fahrmeir, Olivier Faron, Patrick Weil.
   p. cm
Includes bibliographical references and index.
ISBN 1-57181-812-X (cloth : alk. paper)
   1. Europe, Western--Emigration and immigration--Government policy--
History. 1. Fahrmeir, Andreas. II. Faron, Olivier. III. Weil, Patrick, 1956-
JV7590 M5243 2002
325.4'09'034--dc21

               2002018427


British Library Cataloguing in Publication Data
A catalogue record for this book is available from the British Library


ISBN 1-57181-812-X hardback
ISBN 1-57181-328-4 paperback

# Contents

# List of Illustrations

## Tables

## Figures

# Acknowledgements

The contributions in this volume are loosely based on papers first presented at a workshop at the Centre d'Histoire Sociale du 20$^{\text{ème}}$ Siècle, in the University of Paris I - Sorbonne on 25 and 26 June 1999. This event was made possible by generous financial contributions from the German Marshall Fund of the United States, the German Historical Institute London, and the University of Paris I. It would have run much less smoothly had it not been for Stéphane Dufoix's superb organisational skills. The editors are very much indebted to the contributors, to all participants in the workshop, to Dr Marion Berghahn and Dr Sean Kingston of Berghahn Books for taking this project on board and seeing it through to completion, and to the publisher's anonymous reader for many invaluable suggestions.

# Notes on Contributors

**Birgitta Bader-Zaar** is assistant professor at the Department of History of the University of Vienna, Austria. Her publications include the history of women's suffrage in a comparative perspective, women and politics as well as electoral systems in Austria. She is currently engaged in research on the legal status of foreigners. She has recently published *Das Frauenwahlrecht: Vergleichende Aspekte seiner Geschichte in Großbritannien, den Vereinigten Staaten von Amerika, Österreich, Deutschland und Belgien, 1860-1920*. Vienna: Böhlau, 2000.

**Frank Caestecker** is a Doctor in history. He read history at the University of Ghent, and after his undergraduate studies he worked at the University of Brussels, Warsaw, Osnabrück and Madison (Wisconsin-USA). He completed his graduate studies at the European University Institute in Florence where he defended his Ph.D. entitled "Belgian Alien Policy, 1840-1940. The Creation of Guest Workers, Refugees and Illegal Aliens". He is now affiliated with SOMA, a Brussels based research Institute and pursuing comparative research on alien policy in nineteenth- and twentieth-century Europe. He has published extensively on alien policy. His latest publication is *Alien Policy in Belgium, 1840-1940. The Creation of Guest Workers, Refugees and Illegal Aliens*. Oxford-New York: Berghahn Books.

**K.M.N. Carpenter** received her Ph.D. in European history from Georgetown University in 1998. Her dissertation examined beer riots in mid nineteenth-century Bavaria. As an independent scholar, she has published several articles in various academic journals and texts. Her research areas also include feminism and motherhood in 1950s West Germany.

**Catherine Collomp** is professor of American history at the Université Paris VII. Her book, *Entre classe et nation, mouvement ouvrier et immigration aux Etats-Unis, 1880-1920*, Paris, Belin, 1998, explores the relationship between labor and immigration at the most classic time of working class formation in US history. Her research now bears on American labor reactions to nazism and fascism.

**Laurent Dubois** is an Assistant Professor of History at Michigan State University. He received his PhD in 1998 from the Interdisciplinary Program in Anthropology and History at the University of Michigan. In 1996-7 he was the recipient of a Fulbright Grant to study in France, and was a fellow at CEPIC. His publications include *Les Esclaves de la République: l'Histoire oubliée de la première émancipation*. Paris, Calmann-Lévy, 1998.

**Andreas Fahrmeir**, a former fellow of the German Historical Institute London, is now a consultant with McKinsey & Company and Privatdozent at Frankfurt University. He is the author of *Citizens and Aliens: Foreigners and the Law in Britain and the German States, 1789-1870*, Berghahn Books, 2000, of articles on migration history, aspects of nationalism and historiography, and co-editor, with Sabine Freitag, of *Mord und andere Kleinigkeiten: Ungewöhnliche Kriminalfälle aus sechs Jahrhunderten*, Munich: C.H. Beck, 2001. He has just completed a history of the Corporation of the City of London from 1688 to 1900, which was accepted as a *Habilitationsschrift* in December 2001.

**Olivier Faron** is professor at the Université de Lyon II and the Institut d'études politiques de Paris. His research interests include urban history and family history. He is the author of *La ville des destins croisés. Recherches sur la société milanaise du XIXᵉ siècle (1811-1860)*, Bibliothèque de l'école français de Rome, 1997. His most recent publication is *Orphelins et pupilles de la nation de la première guerre mondiale (1914-1941)*, Editions La Découverte, 2001.

**David Feldman** is Reader in History at Birkbeck College, University of London. He is the author of *Englishmen and Jews: Social Relations and Political Culture, 1840-1914*, Yale UP, 1994. He has published a number of essays on migrants and immigrants in modern Britain and is currently writing a book titled 'The Rights of Strangers: Migrants, Immigrants and Welfare in Britain since 1660'.

**Cyril Grange** received his PhD from the Ecole des Hautes Etudes en Sciences Sociales. He is a researcher at the CNRS (Centre Roland Mousnier, UMR 8596, Université de Paris IV). His research interests centre on the social history of the Jewish bourgeoisie under the Third Republic and the formation of the Parisian population at the end of the eighteenth century. In 1996, he published *Les gens du Bottin Mondain, 1903-1987. Y être c'est en être*, Fayard.

**Andrea Komlosy**, Dr. phil, is professor for economic and social history at the University of Vienna. Her research covers European economic and social history, history and theories of uneven development on a global, a European and a regional scale, concentrating on questions of border, migration and cross-border cooperation in Central Europe. Her recent publications include articles on the Marshall plan, economic frontiers, capital accumulation in Eastern Europe, and regional inequalities in the Habsburg monarchy.

**Leo Lucassen** is associate professor at the History Department of the University of Amsterdam, where he directs the research programme 'Immigration in the Netherlands 1860-1960'. He has published extensively on gypsies, itinerant groups and more recently on migration and integration. Among his recent publications are *Migration, Migration History: Old Paradigms and New Perspectives* (ed. with Jan Lucassen, 1997) and *Gypsies and other Itinerant Groups. A Socio-Historical Approach* (with Annemarie Cottaar and Wim Willems, 1998).

**Gerald L. Neuman** is the Herbert Wechsler Professor of Federal Jurisprudence at Columbia Law School. He is the author of *Strangers to the Constitution: Immigrants, Borders, and Fundamental Law* (Princeton University Press 1996), and has written numerous articles on immigration and nationality law and United States constitutional law.

**Peter Sahlins** is Professor of History at the University of California, Berkeley. He has extensively worked and published on nation, foreigners and boundaries in eigteenth and nineteenth-century France. He is the author of *Boundaries: The Making of France and Spain in the Pyrenees*. Berkeley, University of California Press, 1989, and *Et si on faisait payer les autres? Louis XIV, les immigrés et quelques autres* (with Jean-François Dubost). His latest book, *The Naturalization of Foreigners: France in the Old Regime and After* is about to appear.

**Margrit Schulte Beerbühl** is lecturer in social and economic history at the University of Düsseldorf. She is author of *Vom Gesellenverein zur Gewerkschaft. Entwicklung, Struktur und Politik der Londoner Gesellenorganisationen 1550-1825* (1991) and has since published several articles on the development on a consumer society in Britain, on immigration and German merchants in Britain in the seventeenth and eighteenth centuries. Currently she is working on a research project on *Nationality and Commerce in Eighteenth-Century Britain*.

**John Torpey** is author of *The Invention of the Passport: Surveillance, Citizenship, and the State* (Cambridge University Press, 2000) and co-editor, with Jane Caplan, of *Documenting Individual Identity: The Development of State Practices in the Modern World* (Princeton University Press, 2001). He teaches sociology, history, and European studies at the University of British Columbia in Vancouver.

**Patrick Weil** is Director of Research at CNRS in the Center d'histoire sociále du XX^e siècle (Université Paris I – Panthéon Sorbonne). He is the author of a report to the French Prime Minister on French nationality and immigration law, presented in July 1997. He is also a member of the French Consultative Commission on Human Rights. His area of interest primarily concerns the comparative history of nationality and immigration laws and policies. His most recent publications include *La France et ses étrangers: L'aventure d'une politique de l'immigration 1938-1991*. Paris: Calmann-Lévy, 1991; *The State Matters. Immigration Control in Developed Countries*. New York: United Nations, 1998 and *Qu'est-ce qu'un Français? Histoire de la nationalité française depuis La Révolution*. Paris, 2002. He is co-editor, with Randall Hansen, of *Nationality Law in Europe*. Basingstoke: Macmillan, 2000, and *Reinventing Citizenship: Dual Nationality, Social Rights and Federal Citizenship in Europe and the United States*, Berghahn Books.

**Katja Wüstenbecker** studied History and English at the Universities of Heidelberg, Ohio/USA and Marburg. In 1996 she received her M.A. with a thesis on Jewish emigration to America in the nineteenth century. Since then she has been a research assistant at the Department for Modern History at the University of Marburg, Germany. She is currently working on a PhD thesis entitled 'Americanization in times of crisis: German-Americans and World War I'.

**Aristide Zolberg** is University-in-Exile Professor at the Graduate Faculty of the New School for Social Research in New York City and Director of its International Center for Migration, Ethnicity and Citizenship. He served twice as Chair of the Department of Political Science and is a member of the Committee on Historical Studies as well as Chair of the New School component of the New York City Consortium on European Studies. A member of the Social Science Research Council's Committee on International Migration and of the editorial board of *International Migration Review,* he has written extensively in the fields of comparative politics and historical sociology, on ethnic conflict and immigration and refugee issues, in both English and French. His most recent publications include *The Challenge of Diversity: Integration and Pluralism in Societies of Immigration* (co-editor with Rainer Bauboeck and Agnes Heller), Avebury, 1996. He is currently completing a book on the role of immigration policy in American political development, tentatively titled *Fashioning an Immigrant Nation: American Projects and Policies, 1750-2000.* Another pending research concerns the emergence of anti-immigrant parties in Europe (with Martin Schain and Patrick Hossay).

# Introduction

*Andreas Fahrmeir, Olivier Faron and Patrick Weil*

International public opinion has recently been traumatised by the horrific death of almost sixty Chinese migrants in the back of a lorry headed for Britain. This example demonstrates that, even in an apparently close-knit community like the European Union, there exist different national systems of migration control which encourage migrants to continue their journey at great personal risk to reach a country they consider either more welcoming or less closely regimented. Studying the origins of such systems of migration control is an important task. The question of whether or not it is possible to identify different systems of migration control with deep historical roots is one that deserves detailed study. This is all the more true as, in a historical context, systems of migration control have been identified much more frequently within states (poor relief systems and the control of vagrancy, for example) than at their borders. Yet, it is at frontiers, both at those between territories and the more intangible ones between citizens and foreigners, that essential conditions for the movement of individuals and of populations were laid down.

The nineteenth century has always been considered a key period in the creation of nation-states. However, as far as the study of migration is concerned, there is a central paradox. The various processes through which the emerging nation-states gained increasing control over their population and territory have been traced in some detail. It has also been noted that the nineteenth century was an age of substantial and increasing migration over both short and long distances. But, until very recently, migration historians have been concerned above all with establishing the facts of migration movements. This has caused them to concentrate on the quantitative and qualitative aspects of migration and to neglect the question of migration control. The nineteenth century has thus appeared – implicitly rather than explicitly – as an age of minimal state intervention in cross-border migration. It appeared that largely unrestricted freedom of movement was the norm throughout much of Western Europe at least during the second half of the nineteenth century, and that ethnic and cultural criteria should thus be paramount when

classifying migrations as either 'internal' or 'international'
(Hoerder 1985: 11; Page Moch 1992: 107; Cohen 1995). In this
view, the nineteenth century was characterised by states which
were interventionist in their domestic policies, but adopted a
hands-off approach to migration. They thus allowed (if not
encouraged) massive emigration from Europe to North America,
and enormous numbers of migration movements within Europe,
until the First World War led to drastic restrictions on international travel as well as on the communities of 'enemy aliens' in
the belligerent states.

However, this picture is far too simple. The extent of migration in the nineteenth century does not indicate the absence of
regulation, but merely that regulation was not designed to (and
in any case could not) put a stop to migration. States took an
active interest in 'their' emigrants and in the immigrants who
crossed their borders, and used various means of classifying
international migrants as 'desirable' or 'undesirable'. The detailed
studies of migration control in various places at various times
contained in this volume demonstrate that in the field of migration control, the nineteenth century was an age of
experimentation. Regulations of cross-border travel were
imposed in a variety of ways by a great number of different agencies – localities, central governments, and regional governments,
even private charitable associations – and were influenced by,
often short-term, political and economic considerations. Various
systems of immigration control were imposed, tested, and later
modified or repealed. Bureaucratic mechanisms designed to
trace the movement of all travellers were installed in many countries (France, the Netherlands, Belgium, and the German states)
but not others (Britain or the United States). Some states
preferred to check and reject immigrants at borders, others
thought it more sensible to allow free immigration while removing foreigners who had proven to be troublesome or a burden on
public funds, and others tried both systems at different times.
Control was often placed in the hands of local officials, who were
given sweeping powers, and who sometimes actively contravened
the orders of central governments. The picture that emerges from
the detailed study of migration control in the nineteenth century
is one of extreme diversity, and at this stage it is scarcely possible to present more than provisional conclusions in a quite new
but rapidly progressing field. However, all studies indicate that
state control and state intervention in migration were present
everywhere. Along with economic incentives and cultural barriers or attractions, state migration control must be considered to

be a one of the major factors that determined the character and direction of migration flows in the nineteenth century.

Even though – as the concluding essay by Andreas Fahrmeir emphasises – a substantial number of questions remain, the essays in this volume do allow the description of certain trends in migration control. Before the beginning of the 'long nineteenth century' commencing with the French Revolution, legislation concerning citizenship and international migration was characterised by immense fragmentation. There was uncertainty about the precise status of foreigners, travellers, foreign residents and naturalised aliens and about the right to emigrate. Various regulations introduced during the age of mercantilism had prohibited emigration or introduced financial penalties for it. Generally speaking, such penalties became more stringent the farther eastwards one moved. However, even by the end of the eighteenth century, these regulations were being only haphazardly enforced, as some states wished to encourage their neighbours' subjects to emigrate. It seemed advisable to allow certain groups of people to emigrate, not least because emigration was impossible to prevent. Certain groups, such as journeymen and students, even possessed rights to travel that were based on their social position and were largely independent of their 'nationality' or the places they wished to visit.

While it is possible to trace a European political model of society to the city-states of fourteenth-century Italy, where citizens were defined primarily in opposition to foreigners, and even though the territorial element in this definition gained crucial importance over time, foreigners were subdivided into different groups and clearly set apart from a community of citizens in administrative practice only much later. Based on an 'eighteenth-century revolution of citizenship' described here by Peter Sahlins and alluded to by Birgitta Bader-Zaar, the French Revolution proved to be a major turning point. Its effects were not necessarily universal or enduring even within French territories. As Laurent Dubois shows, blacks in the French Antilles, for instance, experienced various processes of inclusion in and exclusion from the community of citizens. The code of 1685 had postulated that liberation amounted to naturalization. The French Revolution introduced an emphatic concept of 'fraternity', which was replaced by an all the more brutal reversal in 1802, when blacks were prohibited from entering the territory of the French republic in Europe, re-introducing de facto slavery until 1848. At least as important as the reformulation of concepts of citizenship was the way in which the French Revolution

encouraged the formulation of immigration laws and the introduction of novel techniques for migration control. In the British
case, examined by Margrit Schulte Beerbühl, the 1793 Alien Act
was both a reaction to, and a copy of, the decisions of the French
revolutionaries. Fear of spies and agents dispatched by revolutionary France encouraged states to require mechanisms for
expulsions as an indispensable precaution, while mounting
suspicion against foreigners caused Britain to make her naturalization policies between 1806 and 1820 even more restrictive
than previsouly.

The French Revolution also appears to have set in motion a
multiplication and uniformisation of identity documents such as
passports, and of registers detailing the native and foreign population of cities. Olivier Faron's and Cyril Grange's analysis of the
*cartes de sûreté* issued in Paris illustrates both the impact of the
new technique and the value of the resulting files for migration
historians. More generally, having a fixed and bureaucratically
recognised domicile became a condition for one's identification
as a citizen, but also of access to social assistance. Under the
nineteenth-century Habsburg monarchy, Austrian citizenship
was taken to be acquired after ten years of effective residence (as
shown by Birgitta Bader-Zaar and Andrea Komlosy), whereas in
the Netherlands only six years were required in order to obtain
a passport, as is spelled out in Leo Lucassen's analysis.

However, neither all European states nor the United States
managed to impose a matrix of effective and coherent migration
controls immediately after the French Revolution. The evolution
of the system of control remained contested and complex.

In most states under consideration – the great cities of the
eastern United States and the city-states of the German Confederation were the main exceptions – the numbers of foreigners
remained extremely modest during the first part of the nineteenth century. In late eighteenth-century Paris, foreigners only
accounted for a small percentage of the inhabitants, and in mid-
and late-nineteenth-century Britain they were less than one
percent of the total population. In Britain, nationality was not
considered of primary importance for much of the nineteenth
century, as persons who were not British citizens attracted less
government attention than internal migrants, particularly Irish
migrants to England. The improvement of the transport infra-
structure and the declining cost of travel led to a spectacular
increase in migration flows – particularly those across the
Atlantic – in the second half of the nineteenth century.

The relatively small number of foreigners explains how the legal framework for migration control could continue to be composed of a number of ad hoc measures which hardly amounted to a coherent system informed by specific policy goals or recognisable ideological predilections. The question of how laws were applied and which institutions – local government, a centralised police force, the judiciary, or voluntary associations – were effectively responsible for determining migration control was of paramount importance. The case studies of Austria (Andrea Komlosy), Bavaria (Kim Carpenter), Britain (David Feldman), the Netherlands (Leo Lucassen), and the United States (Gerald Neuman) as well as John Torpey's general essay on the evolution of the system of control in the North Atlantic World and Frank Caestecker's examination of expulsion policies, demonstrate both the importance of local actors and the substantial variations even between neighbouring countries. Whatever location and time one picks, one will find a succession of liberalisation and restriction, a short-term procedure of trial and error. These essays also show how short-term variations in the economic climate had immediate repercussions on the parameters of migration control; in Munich, an economic downturn immediately led to the tightening of the conditions for residence permits in the 1830s.

Fear of contagion was also a powerful factor influencing migration control, sometimes in irrational ways. Even as renowned a doctor as Koch incorrectly attributed the outbreak of the 1892 cholera epidemic in Hamburg to Russian immigrants, which led to the decision to close Germany's eastern border, at least to poor immigrants. The situation in late nineteenth-century Hamburg, examined by Katja Wüstenbecker, also indicated some changes in the balance between the influence of local government, central government and economic actors on migration control. When Germany's eastern border was re-opened, control of migrants was effectively handed over to steamship companies, which emerged as major players in the debate about immigration policy. They undertook to organise the transfer of migrants from the borders to the ports, and to ensure that migrants were free of infectious diseases. However, this sort of migration control also clearly discriminated on the basis of class: wealthy migrants were exempt from it.

Another change which occurred at the end of the nineteenth century was a shift in the way immigration was perceived and discussed. In terms of the enforcement of migration restrictions, there was a clear tendency towards 'nationalisation'. This trend, coupled with the growing interest in statistics around the turn of the nineteenth to the twentieth century, encouraged a more general and abstract monitoring of migration than before and reinforced the inclination to frame immigration issues according to the treatment of certain 'categories' rather than the individual 'cases' dealt with according to qualitative rather than quantitative criteria. At the same time, the influence of more or less organised interest groups (shipping companies, trade unions) was on the rise, leading to a more intense and public debate about immigration. While these developments were noticeable in Europe, they were more apparent in the American system. This was due to a more open debate about immigration issues in a democratic system of government at a time of systemic reform through the 'federalisation' of immigration control. Aristide Zolberg shows how the electoral concerns of political parties, states' interests, and the economics of shipping shaped American immigration policy in the mid-nineteenth century. Catherine Collomp and Michael Berkowitz deal with the input of labour unions on the structure of immigration. But whereas the United States increasingly opted for remote control through consuls, in Europe these processes had the opposite effect. Whereas previously a considerable part of migration control had taken place at or close to frontiers in the framework of a system designed to register and control all migration movements, the focus shifted to control within the national territory itself through the deportation of foreigners who had turned out to be 'undesirable'. The control of travel was relaxed considerably from the 1860s onwards. The emergence of the welfare state – still in its early beginnings, but nevertheless noticeable – caused a new sort of distinction between citizens who were entitled to benefits and foreigners who were not entitled to them. In Europe, at the beginning of the twentieth century, migrants had more rights to circulate than they had enjoyed at the beginning of the nineteenth century, but far fewer social rights while they remained on the territory of a state whose citizenship they did not possess.

It was at this point that the United States entered the process of Atlantic migration control more forcefully. Throughout the nineteenth century, improvements in transport links and declining fares had made the United States ever more accessible to European migrants, who were driven to emigrate by political or economic considerations, while the development of an industrial economy on the East Coast made the port areas progressively less keen to accept all immigrants. As the Atlantic became less of a barrier, and America became less eager to attract potential settlers, the issues raised by migration control in the U. S. became less distinguishable from those faced by European governments. American authorities began to experiment with systems of control similar to those of their counterparts across the Atlantic, which were first implemented at the state level. However, several factors caused developments in the United States to progress more swiftly than they did in Europe. First, because of the conflict of interest between coastal states, where immigrants landed, and those of the interior, which continued to seek them, a national solution was required. Second, because of the greater degree of democratization, effective interest groups could exercise more public influence on developments than they appear to have done in Europe. This is perhaps most apparent in the different significance which race assumed as a category for immigration control in many European countries (Germany being the obvious exception) and the United States. Patrick Weil shows how a quantitative immigration policy explicitly determined by racial considerations took shape in the United States from the 1880s onwards. In this respect, the First World War was no turning point. Policies developed before it were implemented, sometimes in a more radical fashion, after its end, aided by the passport and visa requirements introduced almost everywhere. However, as Weil demonstrates, the different paths of European and American immigration policies were not predetermined, but influenced by short-term factors which led to race being excluded as a key element only after the Second World War.

## References

Cohen, Robin, 1995, 'Prologue', in *The Cambridge Survey of World Migration*, ed. idem. Cambridge, pp. 1-9.

Hoerder, Dirk, 1985, 'An Introduction to Labor Migration in the Atlantic Economies, 1815-1914', in *Labor Migration in the Atlantic Economies: The European and North American Working Classes during the Period of Industrialization*, ed. idem, Westport, Conn., pp. 3-31.

Page Moch, Leslie, 1992, *Moving Europeans: Migration in Western Europe since 1650*. Interdisciplinary studies in history. Bloomington, Ind.

# Part I

---

# Beyond the French Revolution

*New Concepts of Citizenship:*
*New Methods of Control*

# Chapter 1

# The Eighteenth-Century Citizenship Revolution in France

*Peter Sahlins*

The birth of modern citizenship in France is conventionally attributed to the political revolution of 1789. According to Rogers Brubaker (1992: 39), in a restatement of the received wisdom:

By sweeping away the tangled skein of privilege – regional liberties and immunities, corporate monopolies, fiscal exemptions, vestigial seigneurial rights, and so on – the Revolution created a class of persons enjoying common rights, bound by common obligations, formally equal before the law. It substituted a common law for privilege (etymologically, private law), *citoyens* for *privilégiés* [sic].[1]

In this narrative, the French Revolution, in global terms, marks the passage from the 'ancient' citizenship to the 'modern'. The 'ancient', or 'first citizenship' on which Peter Riesenberg has recently reflected,[2] was a set of economic and political privileges held by a small and wealthy minority of the population, whether in small city-states or larger monarchies. It was fundamentally hierarchical and exclusive. The Italian city-states of the thirteenth and fourteenth century developed the most elaborate example of an 'ancient' citizenship, inspired by the classical examples of Greece (following the rediscovery of Aristotle in the twelfth century) and Rome (founded on the commentary of the sixth-century *Institutes* and the *Corpus juris civilis* of Justinian). As the concept and practice of the 'citizen' spread to the 'New Monarchies' (France, Spain, and England) in the late fifteenth and sixteenth centuries, the citizen became, in this traditional view, no more than a mere subject.[3] The first citizenship was thus fundamentally hierarchical and exclusive, amounting to at most a bundle of privileges held by local and national ruling elites.

The new citizenship, that of Rousseau and the French Revolution, was more inclusive and democratic, founded on subjective and universalist principles, requiring a formal equality of its members or 'associates', and representing itself as the source of national sovereignty and state legitimacy.

This evolution of the citizen recapitulates the classically stated and restated principles of social organisation: from status to contract (to follow Sir Henry Maine [1878: 170]), from hierarchy to equality, and from ascription to achievement. Yet this passage was not strictly speaking a revolutionary invention. The dramatic and abrupt rupture of 1789 had been prepared by a political and philosophical 'revolution' of citizenship in the decades of the 1760s and 1770s. That citizenship revolution was the conjuncture of three discrete political and ideological processes that restructured fundamentally the 'absolutist' model of citizenship, perfected by Louis XIV, but still vital until the 1760s, when:

First, the French monarchy undertook a piecemeal but consistent abolition of the right of escheat (*droit d'aubaine*), the king's right to seize the property of a dead foreigner without French heirs, thus formally abolishing the principal legal distinction of French citizens (*citoyens, naturels français)* and aliens (*aubains*) on which the practice of absolutism rested.

Second, the foreign ministry and the Paris police perfected an administrative and political mechanism of registering the movement of foreigners into and within the capital city, creating a specialized administration for the surveillance of foreigners, a policed state (albeit primitive by contemporary standards).

Third, lawyers and men of letters invented a new kind of participatory citizenship. Among men of letters, citizens were defined less in relation to sovereignty than to utility and public service, oriented toward the public good. Among barristers and magistrates in the *parlements* and other opponents of royal 'despotism', the citizen gained an increasingly political identity. At its most radical, this result was a renovated and democratized republicanism that went from Rousseau's *Du contrat social* (1762), to Saige's *Cathécisme du citoyen* (1775).

Together, these three transformations redefined the nature of citizenship and 'nationality' (although the word did not yet exist) in France before the Revolution. Occurring nearly simultaneously in the 1760s and 1770s, these transformations together enunciate a shift in the discursive fields and administrative practices of 'citizenship'. In France, the transition toward a modern form of citizenship involved a displacement of the discourse and practice of the citizen from a narrow and highly technical legal sphere to a literate public (or series of public) and political ones. In 'classical times', this was the distinction between the Aristotelean idea of *zoon politikon* (the political being who 'rules and is ruled in turn',) and the later Roman notion of *legalis homo* (legal subject) (Pocock 1998). The eighteenth century reversed this movement, shifting the field of the 'citizen' from law to politics, preparing for the political citizenship of the French Revolution. At the same time, the citizenship revolution of the 1760s and 1770s already reveals what historians of the Revolution have increasingly emphasised: how a 'modern' citizenship in fact excluded a large part of the 'nation' (Waldinger, Dawson, Woloch 1993; Le Cour Grandmaison 1992). Political citizenship, unlike legal citizenship (what we call today 'nationality'), was a limited membership category that created an entire class of 'passive citizens' with civil rights ('nationals') but without political rights. Formally stated in the Napoleonic Code, this definition was anticipated long before: I will argue how the 1760s and 1770s were the crucible of modern citizenship in France.

There is, perhaps, no better place to begin than with Jean Bodin and the 'absolutist' model of citizenship that took shape in France between the sixteenth and mid-eighteenth century. Jean Bodin's *Six livres de la république* (first published in 1576) is known, most famously, for offering a durable justification of absolute sovereignty, but it was also the most elaborated and theoretically sophisticated treatment of the citizen in the public law during the early modern period (Goyard-Fabre 1989, Kim 1998).[4] Like his contemporaries, Bodin adapted the metaphor of the city (*civitas*), perfected in the Italian city-states of the fourteenth century, to the level of the kingdom (Wells 1995: 1–15). But the adaptation involved a fundamentally anti-Aristotlean claim that divorced citizenship from a public role, and placed the citizen at the receiving end of sovereignty: the definition of *citoyen*, repeated three times in book I, chapter VI, was 'the free subject of another's sovereignty' (*'le franc sujet dependant de la souveraineté de l'autrui'*) (Bodin 1583 [1576]: 70–1, 76). Bereft of a political role, the *citoyen* was conceived, in social terms, as a general membership category: it included 'women and children who are free of all servitudes, even thought their rights and liberties, and the power to dispose of their goods, are never exercised under [the] domestic authority [of the family]'. Every man, woman, and child, noble and commoner alike, was considered a *citoyen*, unless he or she was either a slave (and thus not a 'free subject') or a foreigner.

Bodin's treatment thus ran counter to the Aristotlean notion of a *zoon politikon*, classically defined as one who rules and is ruled in turn, and substituted for it the idea of a *legalis homo*, which, following the Roman jurist Gaius, turned the citizen into a legal being, existing in a world of persons, actions, and things regulated by law. Gaius had defined a 'fundamental division' between the citizen and the slave (Ducos 1996: 32). Bodin, in turn, defined the citizen less in opposition to the slave than to the 'foreigner', much as did the lawyers and magistrates of the sovereign courts during the early modern period. For in the absence of a statutory definition at the level of the kingdom, these jurists, confronting a wide sample of contested inheritances between citizens and foreigners, became the arbiters of citizenship.

At the centre of the debate were not the 'rights, privileges, duties, franchises, liberties' of the French native that were promised, stereotypically, in letters of naturalization, but rather the opposite qualities of the citizen, those of the foreigner. 'A *regnicole* is the opposite of an *aubain*; and as opposites ought to define one another, in defining the *aubain* we will know the full meaning of the *regnicole*' (Daguesseau 1942: vol. 6, 131). Chancellor Daguesseau's reasoning used the technical terms ('terms of chancellery and court' as the *Encyclopédie* was to call them) in his Paris *parlement* decision of a highly complicated inheritance dispute in 1694. The *aubain* was largely what it had been to the sixteenth-century jurist Jean Bacquet, royal attorney of the treasury court: 'any person not born in the kingdom, country, lands, and seigneuries of the obedience of the French king'. A *regnicole* was a native-born and resident subject of the French crown, largely synonymous with a *naturel français* or a *citoyen* (Bacquet 1742: vol. 2, 1–144). This specialized legal vocabulary was organized specifically around the juridical incapacities of foreigners. At the center of these was the right of escheat, the privilege by which the monarch could confiscate the property of a foreigner deeded to another foreigner upon his death. The jurisprudence of case law came to rest on Jean Bacquet's *Traité du domaine*, written in the 1570s, and widely cited into the eighteenth century. By that time, according to one of the crown's ardent apologists, Lefèvre de la Planche, the *droit d'aubaine* was a 'domanial right inherent to sovereignty, so ancient that one cannot locate its origins, as with other fundamental laws of the monarchy' (Lefèvre de la Planche 1764–65: vol. 2, book 16).

In fact, the strict definition of the *droit d'aubaine* had been by its origins a Germanic, "feudal" inheritance practice of customary and seigneurial law that the monarchy wrestled from the nobility from the twelfth to the fourteenth century (d'Alteroche 2000), although the process was not yet fully completed at the time Bodin wrote. But this testamentary disability was only the beginning of the crown's reworking of the right of escheat. Beginning in the early sixteenth century, the monarchy was to add to this inheritance disability a whole series of other incapacities that culminated in the robust, absolutist version of the *droit d'aubaine*, a royal right extended to the entire kingdom, even in provinces (Languedoc, Provence, Alsace) that had historically been exempt. Such a totalizing process culminated in the 1697 tax on naturalizations, and the monarchy's absolutist amalgamation of inheritance disabilities with the incapacity to hold office or benefice, or to exercise certain professions, as it tried to tax all foreigners and descendants of foreigners in France (Dubost, Sahlins 1999: esp. 64–96). This 'robust' or 'muscular' version of the right of escheat, extended to the entire kingdom (and even to French-born descendants of immigrants who had arrived in the kingdom after 1600), was part of the crystallization of a specifically 'French' civil law under absolutism, that continued under the mentorship of Chancellor Daguesseau (who undertook to reform civil law and specifically inheritance disabilities) in the 1730s (Folain-le-Bras 1941).

This 'absolutist' model of citizenship was interrupted in a dramatic fashion during the 1760s and 1770s.

First, the crown itself turned against this model when it began to systematically dismantle the inheritance disabilities of foreigners by abolishing (or exempting groups of foreigners from) the *droit d'aubaine* in a series of collective naturalizations and international treaties.

In point of fact, this effort had begun with the piecemeal abolitions and exemptions early in the eighteenth century, in the wake of the naturalization tax of 1697. With the declaration of March 1702 in favour of the Lorrains, the monarchy began a new phase – but not yet the final one – in the abolition of the *droit d'aubaine* (Dubost, Sahlins 1999: 372–7). But it was only after 1762, date of the 'Family Compact' between the French and Spanish Bourbons (reciprocally abolishing the *droit d'aubaine*) that a series of treaties was signed between France and most of the existing European powers. In the last three decades of the Ancien Régime, France signed 66 such conventions, treaties, or letters patent, benefitting a diverse series of national and political groups that reproduced the political map of the time: the sample goes from the minuscule bordering principality of Liège (1768) to the vast and distant Poland (Convention of 1777). France engaged in diplomatic negotiations, not with Vienna, but with the constituent states of the Holy Roman Empire: yet another index of the dissolution of Imperial power. In addition to the Hanseatic Cities, the crown treated directly the requests of the nobility of the Equestrian Circles of Swabia, Franconia, and the Rhine. The resulting conventions either abolish outright the *droit d'aubaine* or mutually exempt subjects from its application, under conditions of reciprocity. Indeed, they amount to a series of collective naturalizations, contingent on the reciprocal treatment of French natives in foreign countries.[5]

This increasing rhythm of reciprocal abolitions after 1760 was radically different from the challenges to and exemptions from the *droit d'aubaine* of the seventeenth century. For one, the initiative came in part from the office of the Comptroller-General, and the resulting treaties (although limited by reciprocal clauses) were inscribed in an Enlightenment critique of 'barbarous' practices. As such, the foreign policy of the crown was grounded in an essentially cosmopolitan spirit that celebrated the freedom of movement, both for goods and for peoples. In 1748, Montesquieu decried this 'insane right' while Necker, who proposed a general abolition in 1780, called it 'unwise and cruel' ('impolitique et sauvage'). Necker invoked the 'principles of an enlightened administration' that he founded in the principles of political economy and the interests of the nation:

> All that would prevent foreigners from coming to spend their wealth in the kingdom, from exchanging their money for the products of our industry, seems such an unreasonable disposition as a law that would directly prohibit the export of these products. The *droit d'aubaine* is even more detrimental to the nations that exercise it than it is to foreigners whose fortunes have been usurped (Necker 1780: 271).

To this economic rationale, the reformer and early populationist Moheau added the demographic argument:

> the French were emigrating more than immigrants were arriving in the kingdom. According to Moheau, there was never a more savage, barbarous, and absurd right than the *[droit d']aubaine* which repels foreigners from our midst and places, in the name of the king, obstacles to the increase of his subjects. Fortunately, this right that the ancient jurisconsults thought was one of the columns of the throne has lost much of its reputation (Moheau 1778: 113).

The rejection of the *anciens jurisconsultes* even went as far as Vergennes, the otherwise deeply conservative minister of foreign affairs under Louis XVI. He denied (on 11 December 1785) to the Council of State that the *droit d'aubaine* contained 'the very essence of our constitution. Some light was shed on this matter during the reign of Louis XIV, but the few exceptions admitted by this king were only temporary ... Louis XV gave a greater development to these principles ... this king accorded exemptions to the *droit d'aubaine* to all the nations that asked for it'. The rhetoric of Enlightenment and the politics of the monarchy converged to discredit the absolutist model, long before the National Assembly abolished (but not definitively) the right of escheat by its law of 6 August 1790.[6]

The abolitions and exemptions beginning in the 1760s undercut the absolutist model of citizenship upheld by the jurists, as they effaced what had been the most important legal distinction of citizen and foreigner, native French and alien. Thus the reaction of some of the jurists, more royalist than the king, such as Lefèvre de la Planche, who continued to distinguish 'foreigners' from 'citizens' by invoking Roman law and underscoring the incapacity of foreigners to inherit property in France, 'an entirely different thing than the right of escheat' (Lefèvre de la Planche 1764–65: 68). Clearly, in these decades, enlightened and unenlightened France were seeking a new definition of the foreigner ... and of the citizen.

Second, the administrative monarchy was to contribute a more practical definition of foreigners based on the notion of *police*.[7]

Indeed, the second half of the eighteenth century witnessed a renewed emphasis on the 'police' of the foreign population. This was especially the case of Paris, at a time when a large proportion of the capital, perhaps two-thirds, were born 'foreigners' (from the provinces and beyond). At the center of this foreign population were the diplomatic milieux so closely watched by the spies and informants of the Lieutenant General of Police in Paris, the archival traces of which date back to the 1720s.[8] But the monarchy's administrative gaze extended beyond such milieux, to the monitoring of all foreigners *de passage* in the capital city. Of course, this was a long-standing preoccupation: The registers of the Paris *bureau de la ville* reveal the collaboration of the municipal elite with the crown in registering foreigners from the early fourteenth century onwards. Presumably such practices existed, at least sporadically, throughout the early modern period (although no records survive). But the middle of the eighteenth century witnessed a renewed attention to the policing of foreigners, especially in the capital, less for political than for economic reasons. The decades after the wars of Louis XIV had been marked by a resurgence of anti-foreigner propaganda among French elites, culminating in the anti-English sentiment during the Seven Years War (1757–1763) (Bell, 2001). This xenophobic wave coincided with an administrative reform of the *police des étrangers*.

The administrative history of policing foreigners in the capital city was one of increasing specialization: a gradual attribution of the responsibility for policing the foreign population, first to the lieutenant general of police under Louvois (1667), then to *an inspecteur de police* with other responsibilities, such as the *police des moeurs* (1708), and then by the initiative of *lieutenant de police* Berryer, to the charge of an inspector whose only task was to 'police all the foreigners, especially the ambassadors and ministers, to arrest undesirables and suspects, and to keep the seals placed on all their papers and effects'. Officially called an *inspecteur de police chargé de la partie des étrangers*, he took responsibility for the administrative police of boarding houses and rented rooms, but also for the surveillance of the ambassadorial milieu, in which a large network of his own spies and informants (*mouches*) were employed (Dubost 2000: 251–5).

This administrative history of policing foreigners came to fruition in the 1770s, during the last years of the reign of Louis XV (who died in 1775). The surviving registers of the *contrôle des garnis* and of the *surveillance des étrangers par quartiers* date precisely from this period, with bi-weekly reports on all the foreigners lodged in Paris, sent directly to the Minister of Foreign Affairs. Jean-François Dubost has presented the complete portrait of the foreign population in Paris during the 1770s and 1780s based on these registers. But what is important here is the timing. Was it a mere coincidence that this paper trail begins only in the 1770s? Perhaps, but the 1770s were critical in all sorts of ways: at the moment that the principal *legal* distinction of foreigner and national was being effaced, the *administrative* apparatus of identifying foreigners in the capital became fully functional.

Third, it was during this period of increased surveillance that the *political* referent of citizenship exploded in both philosophical texts and public contexts.

Rousseau's *Du contrat social* (1762) was of course the most dramatic and self-conscious break with the absolutist definition of a *citoyen-sujet*. In a famous footnote in Chapter 6 of Book I, Rousseau positioned himself outside of common usage: 'For the French ... the name citizen expresses a virtue and not a right'. He dismissed in particular Jean Bodin (who committed a 'terrible blunder' in his linking of 'citizens' and 'bourgeois') and other French authors who 'denatured' citizenship by ignoring its active, participatory, and political character.[9] Rousseau believed that he was breaking with the model of a subject-citizen as defined by the absolute monarchs and their apologists. Citizens, he continued in the text, are the individual designations of the 'people' who participate in the sovereign authority; but these citizens are also subjects, 'insofar as they are subjected to the laws of the state' (Rousseau 1762: 54f.). But despite Rousseau's claims of originality, this radical reversal of the absolutist model was partly a retrieval of an ancient citizenship, modeled on his native Geneva, where, as he approvingly noted in the same footnote, his colleague d'Alembert had clearly seen that of four distinct classes of inhabitants (five, including foreigners), only two 'composed the Republic' – that is, belonged as citizens to the *res public*, the public thing (Brubaker 1992: 42; Krafft 1964: 219–27; Eisenmann 1964: 192–226).

Rousseau, in this sense, was less original than he thought himself to be. His rethinking of the 'citizen' drew in direct and indirect ways upon the explosion of political and philosophical debate in a nascent public sphere, where the citizen was socially restricted, even if the public sphere were universalized (although not yet the source of sovereignty). As ideas of the Enlightenment were gradually diffused, 'public law' was reborn, the 'public sphere' made its appearance, the ideas of 'publicity' and 'public opinion' became legitimating principles of politics (Van Horn Melton 2001: esp. 1–16). In this context, the language of the citizen passed from the narrow discourse of legal specialists to broader arenas of political debate, where it intersected with a growing political language of 'rights'. The rhetorical and political construction of the 'citizen', in the last decades of the Ancien Régime, then spread much more widely than the Enlightenment itself. Used by the enemies of the Enlightenment as well as its friends, the concept of the 'citizen' lost its inclusive, juridical frame and became a keyword for political debate throughout governmental institutions (the law courts, the royal council), and throughout a nascent civil society: in provincial academies, in cafes, and in a vast pamphlet press, in the second half of the eighteenth century.

An important context of this passage of the citizen from law to politics was the crisis of the absolute monarchy, a crisis occasioned principally in the confrontation of the French *parlements* and the monarchy during the years surrounding *Du contrat social*. The role of religion in the public order stood at the center of this debate: in a series of politico-religious struggles ranging from the Jansenist *billets de confessions* in the 1720s to the expulsion of the Jesuits in 1764. It centered thereafter on questions of toleration for the Protestants, where in the *parlements* and a vast pamphlet literature deployed the term *citoyen* in opposition to

royal authority (Merrick 1990). At the same time, the monarchy
itself, following the lead given decades earlier by Chancellor
Daguesseau, increasingly relied on notions of the *citoyen* in its
elaboration of an official discourse of patriotism. Increasingly,
the citizen became defined as the subject of rights, including the
right to the security of their persons and their property: such
rights 'make of a man a citizen', declared the Paris magistrates
in a *remonstrance* of 1770 over clerical taxation, 'and of all citizens a state'.[10] The subsequent Maupeou 'revolution' of 1771 that
abolished the venality of parliamentary offices produced a
further politicization of the notion of citizenship, most radically
when Guillaume Joseph Saige, a Bordeaux magistrate, penned
his classical republican text, *Le catéchisme du citoyen* (Baker
1990: 128–520). More broadly, as Pierre Rétat has shown,

> The concept *'citoyen'* was integrated into the conceptual field of the
> neighboring terms *'patrie'*, *'patriotisme'*, *'intérêt'*, *'vertu'*, and *'bonheur'*,
> where it took on a new meaning and centrality. With this new meaning
> the *'citoyen'* became a fixture of social theory in the second half of the
> eighteenth century, and was revalorised, elevated to the level of the
> socialized individual (Rétat 1988: 83).

In this brave new world, the citizen became clearly distinguished
from the subject: identified as a useful individual, the citizen
organizes his ethical and political life around the social good, not
his private interest. The citizen, however, was not everyman (or
woman): sociologically, citizenship shrank from a general
membership category to a limited one. The Enlightenment thus
hesitated, not so much between an ancient and a modern definition of citizenship, but between the Aristotlean idea of *zoon
politikon* and the Roman notion of a legal subject. D'Alembert's
entry *'citoyen'* in the *Encyclopédie* expressed some of this ambiva-
lence concerning the exclusion of non-adult males from the
rights of the citizen: 'The title [of citizen] is not given to women,
to young children, or to servant except as members of a citizen's
family properly speaking; but they are not truly citizens'. Indeed,
Diderot like Rousseau believed in a restricted notion of citzen-
ship: if the latter was partly inspired by his native Geneva, the
former favored the Athenians, who preserved the dignity of the
*citoyen*, over the Romans, who gave away the 'privilege' too freely
(Diderot, d'Alembert 1751–1772: vol. 1, 488f.).

In the broader discursive outpouring of the 1760s and 1770s,
the citizen was constructed as a political subject, an increasingly
political actor, with positive and statutory 'rights' that stood
opposed to the 'privileges' conferred by the absolute monarchy.
The term denoted a limited membership category: only a portion

of the population would be citizens, and among them, even fewer would be 'good citizens'. This rupture with the absolute model was also a rejection of the jurisprudential definition that had dominated the language of citizenship since Bodin: as the notion of citizen passed from the more technical and arcane language of the law to the broader philosophical and literary discourse of the public sphere, it entered the world of politics. Citizens were political beings, even if the exercise of sovereignty was not yet consistently invoked as one of the 'rights of the citizen'.

Once the principal legal distinction of foreigner and national was effaced by the dismantling of the right of escheat, once the administrative distinction of foreigner and national was (re)instituted, and once the citizen became the carrier of a political charge, what distinguished foreigners from citizens? The boundaries of 'nationality' and 'citizenship' remained contested and negociated concepts before the Revolutionary reformulations of the 1790s. Only during the French Revolution was the *droit d'aubaine* to be abolished (not once, but three times) in 1790 and 1791; even if it was to reappear within Napoleon's Civil Code of 1804, not to be eliminated completely until 1819. More importantly, in 1790, the French revolutionaries made the acquisition of citizenship (as nationality) an automatic condition (once the resident foreigner had fulfilled a series of requirements testifying to his social integration in a local community) but spent great political energy arguing about the restriction of the political franchise (Weil 2002: ch. 1). Indeed, the French Revolution's legacy to the modern world rests on its struggles to delineate the *political* boundaries of 'citizens' and 'foreigners'. At the height of the Revolution, the latter came to include not just geographical foreigners, those individuals born elsewhere (appropriating in political terms the legal definitions of the Ancien Régime) but also émigrés, ex-nobles, priests who refused to swear allegiance to the Republic, and other political enemies of the revolution. Citizenship remained principally, although not exclusively, a political and discursive category, epitomized by Tallien's remark: 'the only foreigners in France are bad citizens' (Brubaker 1992: 47). Legal and political foreigners – émigrés, refractory priests, aristocrats, and geographical foreigners – were eventually lumped together as enemies of the French Revolution, and citizenship became a category of political loyalty (Weil 2002; Rapport 2000).

The confounding of 'nationality' and 'citizenship', of law and politics in the definition of foreigners during the 1790s, was clarified in the redaction of the Civil Code that re-instated the condition of reciprocity in the abolition of the right of escheat, and formally distinguished between a general membership category ('nationality', although the term was not to come into use until later) and a limited one ('citizenship'). In a rights-based discourse, this distinction between 'civil' and 'political' rights was fundamental to the nineteenth-century Francophone and Anglo-Saxon worlds. Although formalized through the revolutionary process, it was already at the core of the eighteenth-century citizenship revolution. After the 1760s the absolutist model was overturned, the principal distinction between citizens and foreigners was abolished, and the French state put into place administrative and political modalities for defining and policing citizenship.

## Notes

Research for this paper was generously funded by the National Endowment for the Humanities, the Guggenheim Foundation, and the University of California, Berkeley, which are gratefully acknowledged. Thanks to Jim Amelang, David Bell, Daniel Gordon, and especially, as always, Ramona Naddaff for their critical comments on earlier versions. All translations are my own unless otherwise noted. Material in this paper is amplified in my forthcoming book, *The Naturalization of Foreigners: France in the Old Regime and After*.

1.  See also G. Bossenga's (1997) review of recent literature, most of which underscores the dramatic mutation of 1789.
2.  Riesenberg 1992. For some interesting reflections on the 'Ancient' and the 'Modern', see Balibar 1996: esp. 358.
3.  But cf. Wells 1995, which is unfortunately marred by a limited source base, an inattention to terminology and conceptualization, and an excessive emphasis on the 'modernity' of the sixteenth century.
4.  Bodin 1583 [1576], bk. I, ch. 6. Seventeenth and eighteenth-century French jurisprudence cited Bodin less often than his fellow jurists Bacquet and Choppin who, also in the 1570s, fixed a model of the citizen between 'public' and 'private' law. These, and other ancillary points, are fully elaborated in my forthcoming book, *The Naturalization of Foreigners. France in the Old Régime and After*.
5.  Because the droit d'aubaine was unique to France, the process entailed the systematic misapprehension of a right known as the *"droit de détraction"* as its formal equivalent. The movement of abolishing the droit d'aubaine has not yet received an adequate treatment, but see Dubost, Sahlins 1999, and J.-B. Gaschon's excerpts of and commentaries on these treaties (especially informed by his belief that the *droit d'aubaine* ought to be maintained), in Gaschon 1818.
6.  Dubost, Sahlins 1999: 376f. After being revived conditionally (dependant on reciprocity) by the Napoleonic Code in 1803 and partially reinstated after the settlement of Vienna in 1815, the right of escheat was definitively abolished in France in 1819.
7.  On 18th century notions and practices of "police," see Napoli 1994–5 and Williams 1979: esp. 5–16. The following account of administrative changes is largely drawn from Dubost 2000.

8. Bibliothèque de l'Arsenal, Archives de la Bastille 10283–10293, *Surveillance des étrangers* (1725, 1729–48), 1750, 1753–4, 1761, 1767, and other undated pieces.
9. The accusation is unfair: Bodin had deliberately distinguished the *ville* (its inhabitants) from the *cité* : 'car la ville ne fait pas la cité ; ainsi que plusieurs ont escrit ; non plus que la maison ne fait pas la famille', Bodin 1583 [1573]: 72. On Rousseau's otherwise unacknowledged dialogue with Bodin, see Quaglioni 1996.
10. Merrick 1990: 134. On the development of a language of 'rights' in the second half of the 18th century, see Hunt 2000.

## References

Alteroche, B. d', 2000, *De l'étranger à la seigneurie à l'étranger au royaume, XI^e XV^e siècle*, Thèse de droit, Université de Paris II.

Bacquet, Jean, 1742, 'Traité du droit d'aubaine', in *Les oeuvres de Messire Jean Bacquet*, Lyon.

Baker, K., 1990, *Inventing the French Revolution*, Cambridge.

Balibar, E., 1996, 'Is a European Citizenship Possible?', *Public Culture*, 8: 355–76.

Bell, D., 2001 *The Cult of the Nation in France: Inventing Nationalism, 1680–1800*, Cambridge, Ma.

Bodin, Jean, 1583 [1576], *Les Six livres de la République*, Paris.

Bossenga, G., 1997, 'Rights and Citizens in the Old Regime', *French Historical Studies* 20/2: 217–43.

Brubaker, R., 1992, *Citizenship and Nationhood in France and Germany*, Cambridge, Mass.

Daguesseau, H., 1942, *Oeuvres complètes*, 13 vols, Paris.

Diderot, D., J. Le Rond d'Alembert, eds, 1751–1772, *Encyclopédie ou dictionnaire raisonné des sciences, des arts et des métiers*.

Ducos, M., 1996, *Rome et le Droit*, Paris.

J.-F. Dubost, J.-F., 2000, 'Les étrangers à Paris au siècle des lumières', in *La ville promise : mobilité et accueil à Paris (fin XVII^e – début XIX^e siècle). Étrangers et provinciaux à Paris, XVII^e–XIX^e siècle*, ed. D. Roche, Paris : 221–289.

Dubost, J.-F., P. Sahlins, 1999, *Et si on faisait payer les étrangers? Louis XIV, les immigrés, et quelques autres*, Paris.

Eisenmann, C., 1964, 'La Cité de Jean-Jacques Rousseau', in *Etudes sur le contrat social de Jean-Jacques Rousseau*, Paris: 191–201

Folain-le-Bras, M., 1941, *Un projet d'ordonnance du chancelier d'Aguesseau; Etude de quelques incapacités de donner et recevoir sous l'Ancien Régime*, Paris.

Gaschon, J.-B., 1818, *Code diplomatique des aubains ...*, Paris.

Goyard-Fabre, S., 1989, *Jean Bodin et le droit de la République*. Paris.

Hunt, Lynn, 2000, 'The Paradoxical Origins of Human Rights', in *Human Rights and Revolutions*, eds J. Wasserstrom, M. Young, L. Hunt, Lanham.

Kim, K., 1998, 'L'étranger chez Bodin, l'étranger chez nous', in *Revue de l'histoire de droit* 76 (98): 75–92

Krafft, O., 1964, 'Les classes sociales à Genève et la notion de citoyen', in *Jean-Jacques Rousseau et son oeuvre. Problèmes et Recherches*. Commémoration et Colloque de Paris (16–20 octobre 1962), Paris: 219–27.

Le Cour Grandmaison,, O., 1992, *Les Citoyennetés en Révolution, 1789–1794*, Paris.

Lefèvre de la Planche, ?, 1765–65, *Mémoire sur les matières domaniales ou Traité du domaine*, 3 vols, Paris.

Maine, Sir Henry, 1878, *Ancient Law*, London.

Merrick, J., 1990, *The Desacralization of the French Monarchy in the Eighteenth Century*, Baton Rouge.

Moheau, 1778, *Recherches et considérations sur la population de la France*, Paris.

Napoli, P., 1994–5, »Police » : la conceptualisation d'un modèle juridico-politique sous l'ancien régime, in *Droits*, 1994 : 151–160; 1995: 183–196.

Necker, J., 1780, *De l'Administration des finances de la France*, Paris.

Pocock, J.G.A., 1998, 'The Ideal of Citizenship since Classical Times', in *The Citizenship Debates: A Reader*, ed. G. Shafir, Minneapolis, pp. 31–41.

Quaglioni, D., 1996, 'Les citoyens envers l'Etat: l'individu en tant que citoyen de la *République* de Bodin au *Contrat social* de Rousseau', in *L'individu dans la théorie politique et dans la pratique*, ed. J. Coleman, trans. M.-A. Kisch, Paris: 310–21.

Rapport, M., 2000, *Nationality and Citizenship in Revolutionary France: the Treatment of Foreigners, 1789–1799*, Oxford.

Rétat, Pierre, 1988, 'Citoyen-Sujet, Civisme', in *Handbuch politisch-sozialer Grundbegriffe in Frankreich 1680–1820*, eds R. Reichardt, E. Schmitt, Munich.

Riesenberg, Peter, 1992, *Citizenship in the Western Tradition: Plato to Rousseau*, Chapel Hill.

Rousseau, J.-J., 1762, *Du Contrat Social*.

Saige, 1775, *Le cathécisme du citoyen*.

Sahlins, Peter, forthcoming, *The Naturalization of Foreigners. France in the Old Régime and After*.

Van Horn Melton, J., 2000, *The Rise of the Public in Enlightenment Europe*, Cambridge.

Waldinger, R., P. Dawson, and I. Woloch, eds, 1993, *The French Revolution and the Meaning of Citizenship*, Westport, Conn., and London.

Weil, P., 2002, *Qu'est-ce qu'un Français? Histoire de la nationalité française depuis La Révolution*, Paris.

Wells, C., 1995, *Law and Citizenship in Early Modern France*, Baltimore.

Williams, A. 1979, *The Police of Paris*, Baton Rouge.

# Chapter 2

## 'African Citizens'
## *Slavery, Freedom and Migration during the French Revolution*

*Laurent Dubois*

In September of 1801, two former slaves appeared in front of a notary in Basse-Terre, Guadeloupe, to tell the story of how they had gained their freedom. In February of 1794, when the National Convention abolished slavery throughout the French Republic, both Geneviève Labothière dite Mayoute and her brother Joseph Labothière were slaves. But while Geneviève was in Guadeloupe, where the decree was instituted in June of 1794, Joseph was in Martinique, which was occupied by the British, and therefore he 'did not enjoy the benefit of general liberty pronounced by the laws of the French Republic'. As many slaves had throughout the preceding centuries, Joseph, who was a tailor, managed to earn money through his 'active work' and 'honest industry' until he finally had enough to buy his freedom. His master, however, refused to sell him his freedom. Desperate, Joseph wrote to his free sister in Guadeloupe, who by then was working as a merchant, and asked her to help him. She could not, of course, travel to Martinique herself without endangering her freedom, and so she arranged for a white man named Jacques Dupuy to go to Martinique and buy Joseph. In October of 1796, Dupuy found Joseph and purchased him as his own slave. Both men then travelled to St. Thomas, where two years later Geneviève was able to meet with them. She reimbursed Dupuy for the money he had paid for her brother, and therefore became his legal owner. Soon afterwards, Joseph paid back his sister and they returned to Guadeloupe, both of them free[1].

In registering this series of events, the siblings had to confront a complicated legal problem. Because Joseph was in Martinique, where slavery had not been abolished, it was necessary, and legal, for him to buy his freedom. But Geneviève, as a resident of Guadeloupe and therefore a subject of the laws of the Republic, had broken the law by participating in the purchase of slave. To justify this transgression, Geneviève invoked both the legal and natural rights she and her brother had as human beings and as citizens of the French Republic. She declared that while her brother had the right to be 'taken out of slavery by the laws of the Republic', he had been 'forced by circumstances, because he was in a colony which had been usurped by the enemies of France, to re-conquer his liberty with his own money'. Therefore in helping him free himself, she had 'purely and simply committed a benevolent and fraternal act, based on the laws of nature, without hurting the laws of the Republic'. Geneviève and Joseph's declaration, while sensitive to the fact that Geneviève had broken the law by purchasing a human being, claimed broadly that the Republican decree of emancipation, and the natural rights on which it was based, gave the right to all people, even those in occupied territory, to fight for their freedom in whatever way they found necessary.

Geneviève and Joseph were applying, and further developing, the legal principles that had become the basis of France's colonial policy in 1794. They did so in describing a history of migration, and naturalization, which was also a story of the move from being enslaved under the British to being free in the French Republic. Their story is one example of the broad transformations in the laws concerning citizenship, and migration, in the colonies of the Caribbean during the French Revolution. This transformation represented a complete overturning of the previous colonial system, for whereas before 1794 the majority of the island's populations were slaves, with no civil rights and the legal status of objects, after emancipation these slaves became free citizens with access to many new rights. Among these was the right to move freely within the bounds of a legally homogenous French empire. In this paper, I examine how the transformation in colonial policy during the French Revolution created both new patterns of movement and new policies regarding migration and citizenship for individuals of African descent from the Caribbean. I do so in order to suggest the important precedents set by both pre-Revolutionary and Revolutionary policies regarding the colonies for the broader development of the history of migration, and its control, in modern France.

The transformations of the Revolution depended, of course, on the foundation of what had come before, and there were certain continuities in the way those who administrated the colonies thought about the question of citizenship. The *Code Noir* of 1685, which had set forth by royal decree the laws governing slavery in the French colonies, explicitly made emancipation equivalent to naturalization. 'We declare that an emancipation which takes place in our islands will take the place of birth in our islands', read Article 57 of the *Code*, 'and that the emancipation slaves will not need our *lettres de naturalité* to enjoy the advantages of our natural subjects ... even if they were born in foreign countries'. Emancipated slaves were also to have the same rights as those born free. In reality, of course, the laws and administrative practices in the colonies themselves profoundly limited those rights, and put in place a long series of exclusions which made the *gens de couleur* a separate, and unequal, social and political category. Still, the principle that emancipation was the equivalent of naturalization set the important precedent of making clear that even those who were African-born, as many slaves were, could come to be French subjects once they were free[2].

By the late eighteenth century, slavery was booming in the Caribbean, propelling France's economy through the production of colonial commodities, most importantly sugar, which were both consumed in the country and exported throughout Europe. As slavery expanded, the number of planters who travelled to France with their slaves also increased. In collaboration with sympathetic lawyers of the *Parlement de Paris*, certain slaves in metropolitan France used the opportunity to contest their enslavement. Through a series of cases, notably during the 1760s, these lawyers and their slave clients contributed to the creation of a common law tradition that argued that slavery was illegal within the territory of metropolitan France. Explaining that during medieval times slavery was slowly eliminated from the Kingdom of France, those who argued these cases often succeeded in winning the freedom of slaves who had come to France with their masters (Peabody 1996: ch. 6).

Yet during the late 1770s and 1780s certain royal officials became alarmed at the presence of both slaves and former slaves in Paris, and sought to institute a precocious form of identity controls as a way of excluding them from the territory of France. A 1778 royal decree outlawed interracial marriages in France. In the 1780s, one official used the spectre of interracial marriages to advocate the removal of all 'Africans' from France, arguing that their presence led to a situation in which 'the public houses are infected; the colours mingle together; the blood degenerates'. He declaimed about 'bizarre marriages of black men with white women and white men with negresses, monstrous unions of slave with free, by which are graced creatures of neither one or the other species, forming an oddity which will soon disfigure the children of the state'. The *Police des Noirs* was instituted, requiring those identified as 'blacks' who lived in France to carry identity papers (*cartouches*) proving their status and right to be in the country; they could be stopped and questioned on the streets, and deported to the colonies if they lacked papers[3].

By then, of course, the question of slavery was increasingly the subject of debate both in Britain and in France. In the *Histoire des Deux Indes*, edited by the Abbé Raynal and written by Denis Diderot among others, a powerful indictment of slavery was delivered along with a prophetic threat:

> Your slaves do not need your generosity or your advice, to shatter the sacrilegious yoke that oppresses them. Nature speaks louder than philosophy or interest. ... [A]ll that the negroes lack is a leader courageous enough to carry them to vengeance and carnage. Where is he, this great man, that nature owes to its vexed, oppressed, tormented children? Where is he? He will appear, do not doubt it. He will show himself and will raise the sacred banner of liberty. This venerable leader will gather around him his comrades in misfortune. More impetuous than torrents, they will leave everywhere ineffaceable traces of their just anger. Spanish, Portuguese, English, French, Dutch, all their tyrants will fall prey to iron and flame. The American fields will be transported with drunkenness from the blood that they have been awaiting for so long, and the bones of so many unfortunates, piled up for three centuries, will shake with joy. The Old World will join its applause to that of the New. Everywhere people will bless the name of the hero who re-established the rights of the human species, everywhere monuments will be erected to his glory. Then the *Code Noir* will disappear, and the *Code Blanc* will be terrible, if the victors consult only the law of revenge![4]

Within a decade, the prophesy had come true, with massive slave insurrections in St. Domingue propelling the destruction of the old colonial system and the creation of a new one in its place. During the early 1790s, slaves throughout the French Caribbean organized insurrections, often mobilizing around rumours that the metropole had decreed emancipation but that local officials were resisting its application. Ultimately, these insurrections made conceivable, and necessary, the alliance between slave insurgents and Republican officials. In St. Domingue, starting in 1791, with an organisation that bewildered the whites who had become its victims, slaves had destroyed nearly a hundred plantations across the most prosperous section of France's most prosperous colony.

They defeated the confident attempts to end their insurrection, and transformed themselves into a credible military force that ultimately became the salvation of the Republic in St. Domingue. A parallel process took shape in Guadeloupe. In April of 1793, when hundreds of slaves rose up in Trois-Rivières and killed twenty-three whites, they presented their actions to the officials of the island as an attack against the royalist conspiracies of their masters. 'We have come to save you', they told the whites, 'we want to fight for the republic, the law, the nation, order'. Instead of punishing them, Republican whites and *gens de couleur* accepted their version of the events, and called for the formation of a slave army to defend the island from attack[5].

Such alliances ultimately formed the foundation for the abolition of slavery. In St. Domingue in June of 1793, pressured by slave insurgents, many of them allied with Spain, and threatened by an English invasion made more likely by the increasing defection of white planters from the Republic, the Republican commissioner Légér Félicité Sonthonax offered liberty and citizenship to those slaves who would serve as soldiers of the Republic. Strengthened by these new recruits, Sonthonax was able to hold off the royalists on the island, and in August 1793 he broadened his offer for individual liberty into a blanket emancipation. In February of 1794, representatives elected in St. Domingue brought news of the successes of Sonthonax's decrees to the National Convention. One of them, Dufay, eulogized the slaves-turned-soldiers who presented themselves to the commissioners and announced: 'We are black, and French ... we will fight for France, but in return we want our freedom'. He argued that it was sound policy 'to create new citizens for the Republic in order to oppose our enemies'. Moved by his speech, another deputy demanded the immediate abolition of slavery, and the National Convention quickly voted a law decreeing 'that slavery is abolished throughout the territory of the Republic; in consequence, all men, without distinction of colour, will enjoy the rights of French citizens'. A year later, Sonthonax warned that if France abandoned St. Domingue, 'the last place where the flag of the Republic would fly would be that defended by an army of blacks'. He continued: 'The blacks are the true *sans-culottes* of the colonies, they are the people, and only they are capable of defending the country'.[6]

One of those who entered the National Convention to applause in February of 1794 was Jean-Baptiste Belley, who had been born in West Africa in 1747 before being enslaved and brought to St. Domingue. He had acquired his freedom before the Revolution through military service, before being elected to represent St. Domingue in 1793. In 1796, Anne-Marie Girodet immortalized Belley wearing the dress of a parliamentarian, a tricolour sash wrapped around his waist, the symbol of the 'new citizens' of the Caribbean. In the painting, Belley leans comfortably on a bust of Raynal. Out of the irredeemable past of slavery came the force that had eliminated, at least for a time, the stain of slavery from the French empire.[7]

The 1794 abolition of slavery brought with it a new colonial order, one in which the same law was to be applied in the metropole and the colonies. This policy of integration of course meant that there was free and untrammelled circulation of all citizens between France and the Caribbean. Policies such as the *Police des Noirs* could have no place in a context in which all citizens of all countries were equal. The Republican army was one of the primary institutions through which this new equality, as well as the movement that came with it, was practised. In the Caribbean, administrators recruited ex-slaves into the army, and soon they were a majority in the important campaigns against the English. Captured officers, many of them *gens de couleur* who were free before emancipation, were often taken as prisoners to England, and then released to France, from where they were re-organised into regiments to be sent to the Antilles.[8]

In 1798, one of the leading defenders of the policy of emancipation, Etienne Laveaux, described it as a 'System of Absolute Unity'. At the time, Laveaux sought to solidify the juridical assimilation of the colonies into the metropole through a new law containing a number of stipulations on the citizenship of the ex-slaves. The 1795 Constitution of France had declared that all those who had participated in military campaigns for the 'establishment of the Republic' were automatically citizens with full political rights. This regulation was reiterated in the law on the colonies, which stipulated that a citizen who wanted to vote in a primary assembly could either pay an electoral contribution or present a certificate attesting to the fact that he had been part of 'one or more campaigns against the enemies of the Republic'. This meant that the huge number of ex-slaves who had served in the army and navy would potentially have access, for the first time, to the right to vote.[9]

During the debates leading to promulgation of the law on the colonies, Laveaux argued for the need to expand the rights of citizenship even further. A strict reading of the stipulation that those who fought for the Republic should be citizens would result in the assumption that 'the black *cultivateurs* were not

French citizens'. Yet the *cultivateurs*, Laveaux argued, were a vital part of the military campaigns of the Republic, and their citizenship would be a crucial foundation for the establishment of "peace and internal tranquillity" in the colony. 'Hasn't the *cultivateur* made himself as useful as the *Noir* who has carried weapons? How would we have fed the army, if they had not wanted to cultivate the soil? France sent nothing to the colony of St. Domingue'. Citizenship, Laveaux concluded, could be a reward for labour: 'if we agree that the state of the *cultivateur* is pernicious for Europeans, let us honour this state to encourage the *Noirs* to continue'. Ultimately, this provision was not passed, although in Guadeloupe in 1799 it seems that a number of ex-slave soldiers did in fact vote in the election of electors, the latter of who were nevertheless mostly white.[10]

Laveaux's 1798 law also re-asserted the radical, and internationalist, significance of the French emancipation. 'All black individuals, born in Africa or in foreign colonies, brought to the French islands, will be free as soon as they set foot on the territory of the Republic'. They would have the same rights as those born in France. 'Individuals who are black or *de couleur*, who were abducted from their homeland [*patrie*] and transported to the colonies, will not be considered foreigners; they enjoy the same rights as a person born of the French territory, if they are attached to cultivation, serve in the army, or exercise a profession or trade'. The law also made particular provisions that made it easier for those born into slavery to have access to forms of documentation such as the *état civil*, and to the possibilities that flowed from them. For those 'for whom the birth was not recorded in the public registers which serve to certify the state of citizens', the declaration of four citizens from the *commune* could serve as a replacement for a birth certificate.[11]

This last stipulation was a testament to the fact that Laveaux understood how important the rituals of documentation had become for the ex-slaves. Although in many ways their political rights were restricted, ex-slaves had full access to the *état civil* and the notary registers through which births, marriages, deaths, and property dealings were registered. They used this new right to legitimise old relationships through marriage and assure their hold over property and its transfer to their children. Ex-slaves on plantations also used these documents to assimilate new arrivals from Africa – human "cargo" from English ships captured by French corsairs – placed on their plantations. In groups of three or four, they brought these Africans to the municipal offices of Basse-Terre and gave them new, French, names. They did so in registers of births, marking their social existence, their 'rebirth' into the Republic. And in so doing they described the new arrivals as 'from the coast of Africa', marking their origin instead of their 'race'. In certain cases they called them 'African citizens'.[12]

Documentation, however, was also used to control the movement of the ex-slaves turned *cultivateurs* on the plantations. Although legally free, the *cultivateurs* in both Guadeloupe and St. Domingue were ordered, unless they joined the army, to keep working on the plantations where they had lived before emancipation. Of course, many refused to do so, leaving the sites of their previous enslavement and seeking opportunities in port towns booming in the context of war. In 1795 one local official in Guadeloupe complained that many *cultivateurs* were ignoring his injunctions and leaving their plantations. 'Yesterday, again, five or six from this plantation left without permission, carrying baggage and weapons and heading for Port de la Liberté, or the *bourg* of Abymes. All of the *ateliers* (workers) disperse when we talk to them of work, and each day a considerable number are missing'. In the same month, in Basse-Terre, officials stopped a 'mass of *citoyennes* who were watching the troops march' and others who had taken up residence with the garrison of the town, and brought them back to their plantations, which they once again immediately abandoned. A survey of the changes in the populations on plantations in Guadeloupe between 1793 and 1796 confirms that a massive exodus among ex-slaves was underway.[13]

Counteracting this process necessitated gathering information about who was supposed to live where. In 1796 and 1797, Victor Hugues, the commissioner in charge of Guadeloupe, ordered local administrators to draw up lists of all of the citizens in their respective *communes* throughout the island. Each citizen, including the ex-slaves who were the majority on the island, was listed by name with their age, race, and profession duly noted. Hugues's administration had taken over a task that had previously always been the responsibility of slave masters themselves, who in various private inventories had listed their slaves noting their names, their market value, and often their African nation of origin or else the description 'creole'. As the state took over the task of managing and disciplining the labourers of the island, they also took on the task of accounting for them, highlighting the important connection between documentation and control. Although the terms of the census were different in some ways than what had come before the notation

of African or 'creole' origins was replaced with a system of identification of 'colour', that divided people into the categories
'white', 'black', and 'red' (which replaced the category of the free
*gens de couleur*) there were also important continuities. The
census forms included a column for 'observations', and certain
of those termed *cultivateurs*, were described as *divaguant*
(meaning 'rambler') – a new term for an old practice which
remained a mechanism for resistance: running way from the
plantation.[14]

By seeking in various ways to control the aspirations of the
ex-slaves in Guadeloupe, and by trumpeting his success in doing
so, Hugues contributed to a broader attack on the policy of
racial equality and emancipation. When Laveaux passed his law
on the organisation of the colonies in 1798, there were already
many critics of the policy, despite its being affirmed in the law.
Echoing Hugues's opinions, one former planter from French
Guiana suggested that it was a folly to attempt to assimilate the
colonies as departments of France without making modifications to the Constitution. 'Shouldn't the right to citizenship be
more difficult to acquire in these countries than in France?' he
asked. 'The easy attribution of this right degrades it and takes
away the force that makes it the basis of public order. The exercise of this right requires great discernment, acquired knowledge
and many moral qualities'. Soldiers, sailors and servants were
all restricted to a state of servitude; why shouldn't the blacks be,
'at least until they have shown themselves worthy of escaping
from it?' Practically speaking, immediately removing the rights
of citizenship from all of the *noirs* (whose vanity had been flat-
tered by this status) might cause problems. The solution, stated
plainly by St. Elaire, was 'to leave them the right to become a
citizen, but to make its acquisition difficult, basing this difficulty
on the wider good'.[15]

Daniel Lescallier, a colonial administrator and one-time advocate of gradual emancipation, also argued that emancipation had
been a disaster in the Caribbean. Like St. Elaire, he argued for
limiting the rights of certain citizens, particularly the *nègres
nouveaux* who arrived from Africa. '[I]t must be admitted that
the *nègres nouveaux*, those who are not yet accustomed to the
language and the customs of Europeans, cannot, without endangering the plantations and without causing problems for
themselves, be given liberty, instantly and without precautions'.
Reiterating his vision of a gradual path to citizenship, Lescallier
wrote: 'In the same way that eyes, weakened by a long obscurity,
cannot suddenly see the light, without being blinded: one has to

give it to them carefully, and by degrees'. Such proposals, of course, went directly against Laveaux's laws and its stipulations on the citizenship of those who had been born in Africa but were now living in the French Republic (Lescallier 1799: 84).

In the middle of 1798, the Minister of the Colonies, a planter from St. Domingue named Baron de Bruix, took a threatening action that sought to carry out the dismantling of one of the key effects of emancipation: the integration of the armed forces. He ordered the creation of a segregated military unit that would regroup all of the 'black or coloured' soldiers in metropolitan France. All such soldiers in metropolitan France were told to leave the units in which they were posted and travel to the island of Aix, near La Rochelle, to await the formation of this new company. Most of these were from the Caribbean, but included in the order were men of African descent who had been born in metropolitan France. At Aix, the soldiers found themselves hungry and ill-treated. Etienne Mentor, one of the representatives for St. Domingue in the *Conseil des 500*, sharply attacked Bruix's order, which he argued set up a situation in which these soldiers were 'isolated from their European comrades, so that it seems that they are being punished for having supported, in the New World, the principles of the Republic'. How could governors dare 'to re-establish such insulting distinctions'? 'The time has come to right all wrongs, to redress all grievances', he declared. 'Show yourselves once again to be the defenders of the Republicans of the Antilles, pursued by their old tyrants, by ending the exile which degrades them and which isolates them from the rest of the French. These courageous soldiers wish only to die fighting for the French Republic'. Mentor's intervention was convincing to the other representatives; his proposition to retract the order was 'unanimously adopted'.[16]

Yet ultimately the idea that emancipation should be reversed, and that it had been a mistake to grant full citizenship to ex-slaves, took hold, especially in Bonaparte's administration. Bonaparte's 1800 Constitution explicitly abandoned the policy of integrating metropole and colony under one set of laws in favour of a return to the idea of implementation of 'particular' set of laws for each colony. Toussaint Louverture reacted by creating his own local Constitution in St. Domingue, which infuriated Bonaparte. In March of 1802, after the Treaty of Amiens ended the war between Britain and France (for the time being), Bonaparte decreed that in those colonies that were being returned to France, notably Martinique, slavery would be maintained. He also sent missions to St. Domingue and Guadeloupe with the goal of re-establishing slavery there, although these missions were to be silent about this mission in order to better accomplish it. Slave trading was once again allowed on French ships. Two months later, another law was passed which ruled that 'noirs, mulâtres, or other gens de couleur' could not enter the 'continental territory of the Republic' without explicit authorization from the tribunals of the colonies or the Minister of the Colonies himself. All those who illegally entered the territory after the publication of the law would be arrested and imprisoned until their deportation.[17]

In the wake of the independence of Haiti and the resistance to the re-establishment of slavery in Guadeloupe, the new regime of juridical separation was strengthened, as were the provisions meant to prevent those of African origin who had not been re-enslaved, because they were free before the abolition of slavery, to travel freely in France. Once again, the metropole and the colonies were separated, and the legal regime of the colonies was dictated from Paris. The return to slavery was sharply illustrated in the way those Africans who had been captured by French corsairs and freed in Guadeloupe were treated. In Basse-Terre, government administrators examined all of them, registering their characteristics as slave traders had always done, and sold them as slaves to plantation owners in Guadeloupe. Having once been registered as 'African citizens', the Africans were now re-registered as human property.[18]

Geneviève and Joseph Labothière had, in 1801, understood that France might in fact seek to return them to slavery, and that is why they decided to explicitly register Joseph's freedom in order to provide him with an individual freedom that might outlive that granted by the Republic. Their traces disappear from the archives, but the legal transformations they participated in left broader traces on the political culture of France. The nineteenth century would see the continuation of the struggle to end slavery, and it would be with the return of a Republic in 1848 that emancipation was finally declared, this time permanently. As had been the case in 1794, administrators sought to control the movement of former slaves within the colonies in various ways; the abolition of slavery was only the first step in a long struggle against political and economic exclusion that ultimately led to departmentalization in 1946.[19] Today, nearly a third of those who are from France's Caribbean Départements d'Outre-Mer live in metropolitan France, while an increasing number of wealthy Europeans are buying land in the departments themselves, inciting anger against these new 'immigrants'.

In the midst of these new forms of migration, and the profound social and economic problems linked to them, the legacy of slavery and the struggle for freedom and citizenship remains alive.

## Notes

I would like to thank Mickaëlla Périna and Jean-Michel Duboist for their comments on earlier drafts of this paper. All translations are by the author.

1. ADG Dupuch 2E2/27, 6 Vendémiaire An 10 (28 September 1801).
2. See Sala-Moulins 1987: esp. 196f.; on the *gens de couleur* of St. Domingue see Garrigus 1988.
3. Peabody 1996: 119, 129; Debien 1974: 389.
4. Raynal 1780: vol. 3, 204f. There are many versions of this text, and this is the most extreme example of this passage, which nevertheless appears in most of the editions from the mid 1770s onwards.
5. I explore in detail the revolt of Trois-Rivières, and put forth the argument that slave insurgents in Guadeloupe and throughout the Caribbean gave new content to the universal language of rights, in Dubois 1998b. The most detailed history of the political conflicts between whites, *gens de couleur*, and slaves in Guadeloupe during the period from 1789–1794 is Pérotin-Dumon 1984.
6. Fick 1990: esp. 159–63. For the abolition of slavery in the National Convention, see *Archives Parlementaires*, vol. 84: 276–85 and Gauthier 1995. For Sonthonax's speech, see 'Sonthonax, ci-devant Commissaire Civil, Delegué a St. Domingue, à la Convention Nationale', 2 Fructidor an II, AN, AD VII, 20A.
7. For an excellent discussion of Girodet's painting, on which I have drawn here, see Weston 1994.
8. For more on the military aspects of emancipation, see Dubois 1998a.
9. For the phrase 'System of Absolute Unity', see the 'Discours prononcé par Laveaux, sur l'anniversaire du 16 Pluviôse An 2', Corps Législatif, Conseil des Anciens; for the law see 'Loi concernant l'organisation constititionale des colonies', 12 Nivôse An 6 (1 January 1798), Titre III 'Sur l'état des citoyens', Bulletin des Lois #177 and 178, in AN AD VII 20 A. See also Bernard Gainot, 'La constitutionalisation de la liberté générale sous le Directoire', pp. 213–229 in Dorigny 1995.
10. See Gainot 1995: 223; 'Procès verbal de l'assemblée électorale du départment de la Guadeloupe', 20 Germinal An 7 (9 April 1799), AN C577, #102. This was the first election that took place in Guadeloupe in the wake of emancipation, since Victor Hugues, who had administered the island, had refused to organize any elections. There is no direct proof of ex-slaves voting in the documents, but the numbers of those who voted (according to the number of electors chosen) exceeds by several thousand the number of whites and *gens de couleur* who were in the colony a few years before.
11. 'Loi concernant l'organisation constititionale des colonies', 12 Nivôse An 6 (1 January 1798), Titre III 'Sur l'état des citoyens', Bulletin des Lois #177 and 178, in AN AD VII 20 A.
12. For the naming of the new arrivals from Africa, see for example Archives Nationales, Section Outre-Mer (ANSOM), EC Basseterre 10 (Births, 1797), Numbers 64, 65, 71–73.

13. Lacour 1857/58: vol. 2, 390–2; for a detailed account of Hugues regime, see Dubois 1999.
14. The censuses are located in ANSOM G1 501–504.
15. 'Mémoire sur les moyens de rétablir l'ordre, la culture et l'industrie dans les colonies françaises', by Marie St. Elaire, 14 Messidor An 5 (2 July 1797), AN AF III 208, Dossier 947, #29.
16. See the law, from 3 Prairial An 6 (22 May 1798), in AN ADVII 20B and the "Motion d'ordre faite par Mentor," AN AD VII 21A, #52.
17. 'Loi relative à la traite des noirs et au régime des colonies', 30 Floréal An X (20 May 1802) in AN ADVII 21A #54; 'Arrêté portant défense aux noirs, mulâtres ou autres gens de couleur, à entrer sur le territoire continental de la République', 13 Messidor An X (2 July 1802), AN ADVII 21A #55. For St. Domingue and the war for independence, see Fick 1990; on Guadeloupe see Adélaide-Merlande: 1986.
18. See the register of these transactions in ANSOM C7A 81.
19. For a study of this process see Périna 1997.

## References

Adélade-Merlande, Jacques, 1986, *Delgrès: La Guadeloupe en 1802*, Paris.
*Archives Parlementaires de 1787 à 1860, première série (1787–1799)*, eds M.J. Mavidal, and M.E. Laurent. Paris 1962.
Debien, Gabriel, 1974, *Les esclaves aux Antilles françaises*, Basse-Terre.
Dorigny, Marcel, ed., 1995, *Les abolitions de l'esclavage de L.F. Sonthonax à V. Schoelcher, 1793, 1794, 1848*, Paris.
Dubois, Laurent, 1998a, 'A Colony of Citizens: Revolution and Slave Emancipation in the French Caribbean, 1789–1802', Ph.D. diss, University of Michigan.
Dubois, Laurent, 1998b, *Les Esclaves de la République: l'histoire oubliée de la première émancipation*. Paris.
Dubois, Laurent, 1999, 'The Price of Liberty: Victor Hugues and the Administration of Freedom in Guadeloupe, 1794–1798', *William and Mary Quarterly*, 46:2 (April): 363–92.
Fick, Carolyn, 1990, *The Making of Haiti: The San Domingo Revolution From Below*. Knoxville.
Gainot, Bernard, 1995, 'La constitutionalisation de la liberté générale sous le Directoire', in *Les abolitions de l'esclavage de L.F. Sonthonax à V. Schoelcher, 1793, 1794, 1848*, ed. Marcel Dorigny, Paris, 213–29.
Garrigus, John, 1988, 'A Struggle for Respect: The Free-Coloreds of Pre-Revolutionary St. Domingue, 1760–69', Ph.D. diss., Johns Hopkins University.
Gauthier, Florence, 1995 'Le rôle de la députation de Saint-Domingue dans l'abolition de l'esclavage', in *Les abolitions de l'esclavage de L.F. Sonthonax à V. Schoelcher, 1793, 1794, 1848*, ed. Marcel Dorigny, Paris, 200–11.
Lacour, Auguste, 1857–58, *Histoire de la Guadeloupe*. 3 vols. Basseterre, Guadeloupe: Imprimerie du Gouvernement.
Lescallier, Daniel, 1799, *Notions sur la culture des terres basses dans la Guiane. Et sur la cessation de l'Esclavage dans ces Contrées. Extrait du Voyage à Surinam et dans l'intérieur de la Guiane du capitaine J.G. Stedman*. Paris.
Peabody, Sue, 1996, *'There Are No Slaves in France': The Political Culture of Race and Slavery in the Ancien Régime*, Oxford.
Périna, Mickaëlla, 1997, *Citoyenneté et sujétion aux Antilles francophones: Post-esclavage et aspiration démocratique*, Paris.
Pérotin-Dumon, Anne, 1984, *Etre patriote sous les tropiques*, Basseterre.

Raynal, Guillaume Thomas, 1780, *Histoire Philosophique et Politique des tablisse-ments et du Commerce des Européens dans les Deux Indes*, Geneva.

Sala-Moulins, Louis, 1988, *Le Code Noir, ou le calvaire de Canaan*, Paris.

Weston, Helen, 1994, 'Representing the Right to Represent: The Portrait of Citizen Belley, ex-representative of the colonies by A.L. Girodet', *Res* 26 (Autumn): 83–109.

# Chapter 3

# Paris and its Foreigners in the Late Eighteenth Century

*Olivier Faron*
*Cyril Grange*

'Comme les étrangers abondent, et arrivent des quatre coins de l'Europe'
Louis-Sébastien Mercier, *Le tableau de Paris*.

The impression is shared by all. Paris attracts foreigners. The statement by Louis-Sébastien Mercier from the late eighteenth century is echoed by Jacques Bertillon's remark of 1895: 'Paris is a city of immigration. Births are rare there, even rarer than in the rest of France. There are not enough adults produced by the population of Paris to meet the ever more strident calls for labour. Their numbers are increased by young men coming from all parts of France and – even more remarkably – from all parts of the world' (Bertillon 1895: 1). The arrival of foreigners is therefore closely linked to the fate of the capital. Nevertheless, this is a historical subject which is not well researched.

## I. Being Foreign in Paris

According to jurists and contemporaries, the situation of foreigners in Paris during the *ancien régime* is relatively favourable. Far from being considered a threat, foreigners benefit from a benevolent attitude. Discriminatory measures remain limited and are quite traditional. A mechanism for the surveillance of foreigners is installed (in a relatively commonplace form) using spies and *mouches*, but it is aimed mainly at powerful foreigners such as the diplomatic representatives of hostile foreign countries (Legat 1995).

The specific control of the majority of foreigners is quite prosaic. From the fifteenth century onwards, royal letters patent prohibit innkeepers from lodging anyone without immediately informing the *Prévôt de Paris*, and burghers of the town from renting out their houses without doing the same. In principle, such declarations are required up to the revolution. Frequently repeated ordinances serve as a reminder.

In the usage of the day, 'foreigner' means 'traveller'. In his *Dictionnaire universel de police*, Des Essarts (1786–90) offers the following definition of 'foreigner': 'Someone who is born under a different sovereignty from that which rules the country where he finds himself. The traveller who goes to a different country from that where he saw the light of day, and who stays there, either for business or for pleasure, is a foreigner'.[1] It is thus the movement over long distances that attracts most attention. A passport is demanded on arriving at and on leaving the city. This state of affairs is even definitively confirmed by the royal decree of 29 June 1745. It must however be emphasised that this rule is not specific to foreigners, as every traveller has to present a passport. In his dissertation, René Rey thus draws the following general conclusion: 'At the outbreak of the Revolution of 1789, foreigners were subject to relatively benign regulations' (Rey 1937: 10).

The revolution at first strives to go even further and to establish the absolute equality of Frenchmen and foreigners. A decree of 30 April 1790 thus declares that 'all those who, born in foreign countries, have established themselves in France, shall be considered French; and, provided they subscribe to the citizens' oath, they shall have the rights of active citizens after five years of uninterrupted residence, if they have purchased real estate, married a French wife, founded a business, or obtained the citizenship of a town; provided that one cannot conclude from the present decree that any of the elections which have taken place have to be repeated'. By another decree of 26 August 1792, the Convention 'grants the title of French citizen' to 'men who by their writings and by their courage have proved themselves so eminently worthy of it'. Famous names form part of this list, such as the Swiss-born Jean-Paul Marat.

However, threats from abroad bring about a complete inversion of this trend. The fear of spies and more generally the deterioration of relations with neighbouring countries led the revolutionaries to backtrack and to break with the dogma of the equality of Frenchmen and foreigners resident in France. This 'defeat of hospitality', to use Sophie Wahnich's expression, can be perceived from 1790–91, when it is still combined with measures indicating openness. After 1793, the rupture is complete. Foreigners now have to be identified, registered, and controlled. This is a clear admission of the failure of an idealised revolutionary humanism, which proved scarcely compatible with the rigid requirements of a *Realpolitik* necessary to preserve the integrity of the nation's territory. 'As long as the humanitarian cosmopolitism remained the law in France, it would be impossible to counter these violent measures with the least act of repression. That is to say that the republic would deprive itself of one of the most effective weapons with which she could hurt her enemies' (Mathiez 1981: 91).

The first measures concern the supervision of hotels (26 April 1790) and the visits to boarding houses (6 December 1791). The inhabitants of Paris now have to declare the names and occupations of foreigners staying with them, on the penalty of criminal charges (1 August 1791). There are also attempts to establish means of supervising foreigners who live in apartments or fashionable houses and are thus not covered by the control of boarding houses (5 February 1792). Some of these dispositions have an impact on long-term developments. One example is the decree of 1 February and 28 March 1792 which prescribes that all people who want to travel in France have to provide themselves with a passport which contains information on their ages, occupations, physical description, domicile, and on whether they are French nationals or foreigners.

Other measures regulate the arrival of foreigners in Paris and define measures which could limit the effects of their migration to the capital (February 1792). Another aim is to get to know the foreign population better. In June 1792, the decision is taken to conduct a survey of the number and types of foreigners. A decree of 19 September 1792 forces foreigners resident in Paris to make a declaration of residence.

Under the Convention, the measures for policing the foreign population become even harsher and are no longer counterbalanced by signs of greater openness. On 26 February 1793, the owners of residential properties are required to inform their municipality of the names of foreigners staying in homes owned by them. In every village and city, a committee is charged with the collection of the owners' declarations of foreigners who reside or plan to reside there; the foreigners themselves had eight days in which to make such a declaration. Foreigners who miss this deadline are removed from their place of residence and have to quit the territory of the Republic within an additional week, on pain of ten years of imprisonment in irons (23 March 1793).

Moreover, under the Convention there are also committees for the surveillance of foreigners organised by the *Comité de Salut Public*. Finally, *cartes de sûreté* are distributed to foreigners living in Paris, from where they can now be expelled (June 1793). A decree of the Convention dated 6 September 1793 contains further security measures relative to foreigners in France. Certain passages of this text demonstrate the radicalisation of control. The first article, for instance, declares that 'Those foreigners born in the territory of powers with which the French Republic is at war, shall be arrested and placed in *maisons de sûreté*, until the National Assembly shall make other arrangements', except for 'artists, labourers, and all those employed in workshops or factories, if they can find two citizens of known patriotism in their community who will vouch for them'. Only Article 6 was milder: 'If their civic spirit is acknowledged, the municipal officers of their district shall inform them that the French Republic admits them to the bounties of her hospitality; their names shall be inscribed on the list of foreigners, which shall be posted in the local sessions room, and they shall receive a certificate of hospitality'. The mechanism of repression is clearly unleashed. It is completed later by certain other texts, for instance the law of 24 Vendémiaire, An II (15 October 1793), which orders that all foreign beggars shall be conducted to the frontier.

## II. Finding the Foreigners through a New Enquiry Regarding the Parisian Population

Who are the foreigners? Where do they come from? How old were they when they arrived? Did they come for political or for economic reasons? A number of particularly interesting questions, which have so far remained practically unanswered. The paucity of sources is often used to explain this. However, there are means of overcoming this difficulty. One possibility is to explore the registers of boarding houses. This is the object of an enquiry undertaken by the *Institut d'Histoire Moderne et Contemporaine* (Juratic 1999: 271–282).

Another option is to use the extraordinary series of *cartes de sûreté*. We are at present converting the entire source base into machine-readable format. At this stage, it is only possible to present results relating to about two-thirds of the surviving material (Faron, Grange 1999). Without dwelling in detail on the research project in its entirety, we should emphasise a few points which concern the situation of foreigners.

The first point is that the introduction of the *cartes de sûreté* took place during the exact period when the attitude towards foreigners changed. The registration is undertaken during the second half of 1792 and all of 1793. It is incidentally very interesting to note that this evolution can be traced in the design of the cards itself. From 19 September 1792 – the date of the decree introducing these cards – until 4 April 1793, the cards were the same for everyone. On 4 April 1793, after a period of unrest and looting and in order to find 'people without occupation, undesirables, and beggars', the cards are exchanged and a differentiation through colour codes is introduced. White cards are issued to citizens over the age of twenty-one residing in Paris, while citizens under twenty-one and foreigners receive red cards. On 27 Nivose An III, a further modification is introduced. Henceforth, the cards will be red for Parisians under the age of fourteen, white for Parisians over fourteen and blue for non-Parisians.

An analysis of the *cartes de sûreté* is thus a means of using one of the rare sources about the foreign population of Paris towards the end of the eighteenth century. Of course, certain people escape this control. Aside from the endless debate about the 'floating population' (Kaplow 1967), it must be emphasised that the bearers of these cards are residents of Paris, not people just passing through. Having a card also presupposes a successful adaptation to an administrative structure which was in a process of construction. One must learn to apply for papers and succeed in obtaining them.

The registers of the *cartes de sûreté* thus gradually reveal the individuals and their identity. It is interesting to note that they mix Parisian, provincials and foreigners. Certain registers of the Panthéon district are particularly valuable as informations on migration conditions are entered in the 'observation' column. A resident of Verviers thus came to Paris 'to receive assistance, having been a victim of the aristocracy'. Next to the names of a number of Belgians, one finds the following remarks: 'refugee from Liège since the Revolution', 'fled from Liège', 'Belgian refugee'. The column for 'occupation' is sometimes also rich in comments of this sort, as the following entry shows: 'Lieutenant-Colonel from the Batavian region, previously refugee'.

For every person, the officials collected the following information:

- the date when the card was issued
- the family name and the given name
- the 'rank' or 'quality', i. e. the occupation
- the age
- the present place of residence
- the previous domicile
- the date of arrival in Paris
- the place of birth
- the signature.

Certain registers are even more complete, because they add supplementary information regarding the physical description to the initial data:

- the height
- the colour of hair and eyebrows
- the shape of the brow
- the colour of the eyes
- the shape of the nose
- the shape of the mouth
- the shape of the chin
- the shape of the face.

How reliable was this registration? One example demonstrates the quality of the operation. We have compared the massive quantitative registration of the *cartes de sûreté* with a qualitative source. This is the journal of an important Italian intellectual, Gorani, who became a French citizen under the provisions of the decree of 26 August 1792.

Born on 15 February 1740 in Milan, Guiseppe Gorani was a member of the Lombard nobility. He was to live a cosmopolitan intellectual life in Austria, Italy, Switzerland, and – France. Let us follow one of his trips to Paris, this time in the course of the year 1793. Departing Strasbourg on 8 January, he passes through Lunéville, Toul.... He indicates in his journal that he is travelling swiftly, in a postal carriage, as his passport is valid only for a short time. On 10 January (?), he arrives at Meaux, where he needs some free time to get his papers in order. He reaches Paris on 14 January. It is worth emphasising that during this first phase of his travels, administrative matters prove extremely important, as they even influence his choice of transport.

Now we can complete his trip thanks to his *carte de sûreté*. It confirms the registration on 14 February (?) 1793 of Joseph

Gorani, 'man of letters', aged fifty. His previous domicile is correctly given as Strasbourg, and he moves to the rue de Seine on arrival. His place of birth also agrees with what we know, as it is stated to be Milan. It is of course understood that he is able to sign. In addition, a previous sojourn at Paris in February 1792 is mentioned, which is also confirmed by Gorani's private journal.

## III. How to Analyse the Foreigners in Paris at the Beginning of the Revolution

In *Le peuple de Paris*, Daniel Roche contrasts two 'quite different realities' for the end of the *ancien régime* (Roche 1981: 25):

(1) 'an immigration of little people': they came primarily from German-speaking Europe, the Netherlands and Switzerland, and were domestic servants, cleaners or low-wage earners;

(2) 'a not negligible contingent of well-qualified professionals': natives of Brussels, Vienna or Switzerland, they were bankers, merchants or master ivory-carvers.

The Swiss are a very good illustration of this: 'The Swiss colony in Paris is numerous and prosperous. It not only includes the porters of the aristocratic mansions of the Faubourg Saint-Germain, almost all of them retired soldiers from the Swiss Guards, but it also counts amongst its members rich bankers from Zurich, Basel or Geneva. It is well known that two of them, Necker and Clavière, are successively in charge of managing the French state's finances' (Mathiez 1918: 9).

This fundamental dichotomy becomes more complex during the Revolution, when the attraction of the new political developments comes into play. It must be called to mind that, traditionally, France attracted both intellectuals inspired by revolutionary ideology like Gorani and different groups of foreigners exiled by their governments. This is true, for example, in the case of the representatives of the democratic opposition banished from Switzerland in 1782, but also of their Dutch (1783) and Flemish (1787) counterparts: 'The refugees from Neuchâtel and Geneva were almost as numerous as the Dutch exiles. The former were democrats who had attempted, in 1781, an ill-fated uprising against the patricians of Fribourg' (Mathiez 1918: 10). Albert Mathiez discovers the overlapping of two major motivations from an example like this: 'Immediately before '89, the number of these foreign immigrants attracted by profit was unusually swelled by political exiles who came to France in search of a refuge rather than a livelihood' (Mathiez 1918: 9). The Geneva revolution of 6 December 1792 had clear consequences.

Many foreigners therefore integrated themselves into the revolutionary movement. Amongst the Swiss exiles, the banker Etienne Clavière, Jacques-Antoine du Rozeray, and the shepherds Etienne Dumont and Etienne Reybaz played major roles, being part of the 'Atelier de Mirabeau'. The most characteristic example is that of Clavière, Mirabeau's principal collaborator on economic questions. He successively became a member of the Jacobin Club, a substitute deputy to the Legislative Assembly and, finally, in March 1792, Minister of Contributions. A surprising figure is Baron Jean-Baptiste de Cloots du Val-de-Grâce, a native of Prussia, who became one of the first members of the Jacobins where he signed as 'Cloots du Val-de-Grâce, Baron in Germany, citizen in France'. He even issued certificates of presence and civic spirit (Lequin 1988: 295–304).

Nevertheless, the undeniable political attraction merely added to traditional economic motives for migration. The central idea, already present in the writings of Mathiez, is that the analysis of such movements must be reconciled with very strong group motivations: 'In sum, the foreign refugees in France, even those most sincerely devoted to the ideas of the Revolutions, were guided in their actions by a more or less clear perception of their personal interests, and, if they belonged to a well-defined group such as the Savoyards, the Fribourgeois, the Liégeois, or the Dutch, their collective interests, which came into play when ambition or necessity forced them to accommodate themselves to the masters of the day'. (Mathiez 1918: 47).

In view of these hypotheses, which new results can a systematic study of the *cartes de sûreté* provide? We will divide this analysis into two parts. Beginning with the specific group of the Italians in Paris, we shall attempt to define the principal questions. We will then proceed to outline the foreign presence in the capital at the end of the eighteenth century.

## IV.  Italians in Paris in the early 1790s

One can estimate that there were roughly 1,000 Italians present in Paris at the end of the eighteenth century. This is simultaneously a lot, or a little, depending on how one relates them to the 600,000 inhabitants of the capital. The interest lies in the logic of these

relationships. The first clear factor is the effect of geographic proximity. Table 1 shows the importance of Piedmont and the slightly
less pronounced one of Lombardy as regions of origin.

Table 3.1: Origins of Italians Resident in Paris According
to the Registers of the *cartes de sûreté* (1792–1793)

| | |
|---|---|
| Piedmont | 32 % |
| Lombardy | 26 % |
| Tuscany | 14 % |
| Rest of the North | 16 % |
| Centre and South | 12 % |

Using Beloch's figures, one can thus conclude that 10 percent of
the population of the peninsula provided 60 percent of migrants to
Paris (Beloch 1994).

A second observation is very striking. It coincides with the existence of firmly established familial migration patterns. In a
paradoxical fashion, certain minor points of departure have a large
impact.

Let us take the village of Craveggia. It is a small mountain village
situated in the province of Novara, with a resident population of
less than 1,000.[2] It is basically as unknown today as it was then,
as its name is spelled in numerous different ways: Cravaigg,
Cravech, Cravege, Craveggie, Cravegio, Cravegia, Graveggia, Grave-
jge... A very minor community, but one which provides one in
twelve of the Italians living in Paris in the late eighteenth century,
even though none of its residents go to Milan, which is a far closer
metropolis. There are a number of striking elements. They
contribute to the perception of very structured migration flows.

The first hypothesis is that we are dealing with a very old migration flow. The years in which immigrants from Craveggia arrive are
evenly spaced out between 1733 and 1792. The political developments do not seem to have affected an influx based on the exchange
of services. The men of Craveggia in effect took on a number of
tasks in the French capital. Two-thirds of these Italians adopt two
complementary crafts, 'fumistes' or 'poêliers' (stove fitters), that is
to say that they build and install stoves and other heating equip-
ment. One can also find 'jewellers', but in much smaller numbers,
and a few 'merchants'.

The other characteristic of such a migration movement is the
degree of interconnectedness. Many of the migrants appear to be

brothers or sons accompanying their fathers. Beyond the familial dimension, one notices a great local concentration. These migrants congregate in streets, or even in neighbouring buildings, rather than in quarters. This is the case in the rue Grenéta, where no fewer than four numbers (28, 43, 52, 60) are mentioned, or in the rue de Bondy.

This type of movement shows in great detail the extreme importance of migration currents over the long term, independently of day-to-day political developments.

Another major result is clear. A metropolis like Paris is at the heart of a veritable urban network which extends throughout Europe. Five cities, in the order of the number of immigrants, Turin, Milan, Genoa, Venice and Lucca, provide no less than 43 percent of Italians resident in Paris during the years 1792–1793. If one argues once more in terms of population reservoirs, then one finds that these 43 percent relate to 3 percent of the Italian peninsula's population during those years (roughly 500,000 of an estimated total of 18,516,000 persons).

A result like this reflects an important reality. At the end of the eighteenth century, the town dwellers, and only the town dwellers, of Europe witness a veritable administrative revolution. The different cities of Europe are putting ever more sophisticated systems of registration into place: of houses, of paupers and finally of all inhabitants. One therefore has to add the divide between town and countryside to that between Frenchmen and foreigners. In the towns, a deep-rooted culture of administrative acculturation develops, which fashions identities (Faron 1997). As Peter Sahlins emphasises in his contribution to this volume, the role of town dweller also involves an introduction to citizenship which increases throughout the course of the eighteenth century.

The departure from home and the integration in a foreign metropolis thus seem to be facilitated by two mechanisms: first, the existence of a long-standing and structured migration flow, as in the case of Craveggia, and second, the ability to practise the administrative techniques required for the successful installation in another city.

## V. The Socio-Demographic Profile of Foreigners Bearing a *Carte de Sûreté*

The total number of foreigners traced by us is 2,651. These are individuals whose place of birth is situated outside the Kingdom of France at the very end of the *ancien régime*. Our only exception from this rule is that we have considered the departments which correspond to Savoy to be part of France. This figure of 2,651 foreigners who held a *carte de sûreté* relates to a total of 90,467 Parisians whose data have been processed so far for whom we have a place of birth.[3] These were registered in 30 of the 48 sections for which the registers survive. As we know the total number of cards issued in each section,[4] we have calculated the total number of foreigners who held a *carte de sûreté* in these sections.

The calculated total of foreigners amounts to 5,712 among an estimated total of 205,275 holders of a *carte de sûreté*. The proportion of foreigners among the bearers of a *carte de sûreté*, that is to say among men aged fifteen or over, is thus 2.8 percent. It is likely that this proportion is somewhat lower for the total population of Paris, as the immigration of men was higher than that of women.

## Geographical Origins of Foreigners in Paris

The majority of immigrants came from the surrounding continental monarchies, among which Belgium ranked first, supplying almost one foreigner in three. In descending order of importance came the German territories and Austria-Hungary, Italy and Switzerland. The percentages recorded for other regions of origin did not exceed 4 percent: 3.4 percent for the Netherlands, 3.1 percent for the United Kingdom and Ireland, 2.7 percent for Luxembourg. The Iberian peninsula is hardly represented at all, with only 0.75 percent.

Table 3.2: Geographical Origins of Foreign Immigrants

| Place of Birth | % |
|---|---|
| Germany, Austria-Hungary | 20.74 |
| Eastern Europe, Scandinavia, Russia | 1.52 |
| Italy, Malta, Monaco | 19.93 |
| Belgium | 31.70 |
| Britain, Ireland | 3.11 |
| Netherlands | 3.41 |
| Luxembourg | 2.69 |
| Switzerland | 12.67 |
| Portugal, Spain, Gibraltar | 0.75 |
| Rest of the World | 2.42 |
| Unknown | 1.07 |
| Total | 100.00 |
| Number | 5,712 |

## The Journey to Paris

The next problem is to discover whether the immigrant came directly from his native country or whether the arrival was the result of a succession of shorter migrations. The information contained in the section 'domicile precedent' is the only, if approximate, indicator of this, as it describes the journey to Paris. However, the absence of any indication of what the officials considered to be a 'previous domicile' prevents us from drawing any firm conclusions.

Taking the totality of the foreign population into account, without distinguishing the time of arrival, hardly permits any conclusions about the way in which immigrants settled. One can see that in the majority of cases (more than four out of five), the 'previous domicile' is in Paris itself. Those foreigners who remained for a certain indefinite time in another French city before coming to Paris made up 9 percent of migrants while those who came to Paris directly accounted for 8 percent. If one takes into account the countries of origin, and only looks at those countries which supplied most immigrants, no significant difference in itineraries appears. If one thus retains only the figures of 9 percent and 8 percent for direct and indirect arrivals respectively, one can estimate that 53 percent of arrivals migrated in stages while 47 percent came to Paris directly. Nevertheless, this statistic rests on those foreigners present in 1793 and, therefore, for earlier periods it only includes the youngest migrants, those least affected by mortality.

Table 3.3: Itinerary of Migrants by Date of Arrival

Itinerary: Place of Departure (%)

| Date of Arrival in Paris | Paris | Rest of France | Other Countries | Country of Birth | Total |
|---|---|---|---|---|---|
| 1790 – 1795 | 71.16 | 11.62 | 1.86 | 15.35 | 100.00 |
| 1780 – 1789 | 88.62 | 5.17 | 0.88 | 5.16 | 100.00 |
| 1770 – 1779 | 91.09 | 1.88 | 0.00 | 7.03 | 100.00 |
| 1760 –1769 | 93.99 | 2.35 | 0.00 | 3.66 | 100.00 |
| 1750 – 1759 | 86.21 | 4.26 | 0.00 | 9.53 | 100.00 |
| Before 1750 | 87.46 | 3.09 | 0.00 | 9.46 | 100.00 |
| Total | 85.00 | 5.75 | 0.77 | 8.43 | 100.00 |

It is therefore necessary to refer to the most recently arrived immigrants – who consist equally of younger and more aged arrivals – to obtain a better estimate of the itinerary followed. For the most recent arrivals (between 1790 and 1795), the proportion of those who name a Parisian address as 'previous domicile' drops. The figures for areas outside Paris must be noted – more than 10 percent of arrivals during that period give an address in a region of France other than Paris. Likewise, more than 2 percent name a country other than their country of birth. Finally, in 15 percent of cases the migration is accomplished 'directly'. Thus, leaving aside the 'Paris cases', the division of the rest of France, other countries, and the native country can be reformulated like this: 46.8 percent of arrivals use an indirect route, whereas 53.2 percent arrive by a direct route. It must be emphasised, however, that by a direct route we mean a place of departure within the migrants' native countries, even though it is impossible to establish whether the migrants have moved within the countries of their birth before setting out for France.

In order to achieve more precision, we have examined the individuals who moved to Paris less than 24 months before the *cartes de sûreté* were introduced and during the first year during which such cards were issued.

Table 3.4: Itinerary of Migrants Who Arrived Less than 24 Months before the Introduction of the *cartes de sûreté*

Itinerary: Coming from (%)

| Paris | Rest of France | Other Countries | Native Country | Total |
|-------|----------------|-----------------|----------------|-------|
| 61.23 | 16.07 | 2.29 | 20.41 | 100.00 |
| (No of cases: 286) | | | | |

Table 3.5: Itinerary of Migrants Who Arrived in the Course of the Year when *cartes de sûreté* Were First Issued

Itinerary: Coming from (%)

| Paris | Rest of France | Other Countries | Country of Birth | Total |
|-------|----------------|-----------------|------------------|-------|
| 51.08 | 22.26 | 3.32 | 23.33 | 100.00 |
| (No of cases: 132) | | | | |

We again leave aside the column 'Paris', the importance of which is in any case reduced for reasons of logic. In the first case the proportion of direct arrivals amounts to 52.6 percent and in the second, to 47.7 percent. We thus find figures close to those observed for the period 1790–95 and 1780–89.[5] We have finally tested the influence of age on the itinerary chosen. It is different if one distinguishes between younger immigrants (those between fifteen and thirty) and older ones (over forty years old). For those who arrived between 1790 and 1795, it appears that 56.1 percent of younger immigrants arrived directly from their native country, whereas only 37.6 percent of the older ones did.

The migrants thus divide into two equal sub-groups: those who came direct to Paris and those who had already spent an extended period of time elsewhere, because the variable of the age at arrival is relatively important.

The analysis of the situation of foreigners in Paris at the end of the eighteenth century produces a contradictory impression. On the one hand, it is comforting to see how the demographic approach to some extent expands the results of previous historical enquiries. At the heart of the registration process one thus finds a citizen who is, as Peter Sahlins put it, seen in the spirit of Enlightenment neither as a woman, nor a child. A citizen who is further classified by age or nationality. On the other hand, the demographic approach can seem disappointing. It comes across insurmountable difficulties or risks simply confirming entrenched ideas. One must nevertheless withstand the temptation to do no more than reconstruct itineraries. Whereas the global shape of the migration process has been described quite well by scholars from Mathiez to Roche, the obstacle of numbers remains to be conquered. It is a matter of understanding how migration flows were structured and, above all, of posing pose a crucial question: how can one construct a hierarchy of the functions of a capital? Our migrating ancestors, French and foreigners, were they adherents of Robespierre or impoverished labourers in search of a livelihood?

More generally, the socio-demographic approach makes it possible to enrich the analysis of migration control. Three dimensions deserve particular emphasis. The first is geography. Under the *ancien régime* or during the Revolution, the notion of a 'frontier' remains fragile. Towns, and above all great cities, constitute particular spaces, subject to autonomous legislative frameworks. The second is the profound motivation of migration. Politics and economics are often much more closely linked than they might appear. Investigating the occupations and tracing the origins and destinations of migrating employees makes it possible to reconstruct a migration network for this purpose. Finally, there is the decisive significance of the Revolution. Before it, the system remains open. After it, 'bureaucratisation' is definitely in the ascendant. The construction of norms, the application of regulations, begin to be inscribed into the politics of population or populations in the widest sense of the term, politics which begin to be theoretically formulated and to take shape in practice at the time.

## Notes

1. 'On donne ce nom à celui qui est né sous une autre domination que celle qui régit le pays où il se trouve. Le voyageur qui passe dans un autre pays que celui où il a reçu le jour, qui y séjourne, soit pour ses affaires, soit pour son plaisir, est étranger'.
2. The population was 834 in 1824. We should like to thank Mauro Reginato for the information with which he provided us.
3. At present, 134,042 individual entries have been processed, of which 90,467 state a place of birth. For several years, the Bibliothèque Généalogique de Paris has entered data into a computer on all registries of security cards issued and preserved in the National Archives. We extend our sincere thanks to Philippe de Chastellux, Director of the Library, who made this still-developing database available to us.
4. In fact, this is the total number of all cards issued, as documented in the Archives Nationales. In some cases, the boxes contain the registers of two or even three sections. The genealogists who first worked with these documents have unfortunately failed to distinguish the different sections in these cases.
5. We should call to mind that we prefer not to use figures for earlier periods, as in those cases the migrants present in 1793 represent only the survivals from those who actually arrived during these periods. As the variable 'age on arrival' influences the choice of itinerary – a direct route is more common for younger migrants – it is preferable not to argue with the older periods, as they contain too many unknowns.

## References

Beloch, Karl Julius, 1994, *Storia della popolazione d'Italia*, Florence.
Bertillon, Jacques, 1895, *Origine des habitants de Paris. Lieu de naissance des habitants de Paris en 1833 et en 1891. Les étrangers à Paris. Leur origine et leurs professions*, Paris.
Blum, Alain, Houdaille, Jacques, 1986, '12 000 parisiens en 1793, Sondage dans les cartes de civisme', *Population*, no 2 (March-April): 259–302.
Des Essarts, Nicolas-Toussaint le Moyne dit, 1786–1790, *Dictionnaire universel de police*, 8 vols, Paris.
Faron, Olivier, 1997, *La ville des destins croisés. Recherches sur la société milanaise du XIX<sup>e</sup> siècle (1811–1860)*, Rome.
Faron, Olivier, Grange, Cyril, 1999, 'Un recensement parisien sous la Révolution: l'exemple des cartes de sûreté de 1793', *Mélanges de l'Ecole Française de Rome*, 111/2: 796–826.
Gorani, Giuseppe, 1998, *Dalla Rivoluzione al volontario esilio (1792–1811)*, édité par Elena Puccinelli, Milan.

Juratic, Sabine, 1999, 'Réseau hôtelier et accueil des étrangers à Paris. XVIIIᵉ–XIXᵉ siècle', in *Les étrangers dans la ville*, eds Jacques Bottin, Donatella Calabi, Paris, pp. 271–282.

Kaplow, Jeffry, 1967, 'Sur la population flottante de Paris à la fin de l'Ancien Régime', *Annales historiques de la Révolution française*: 1–14.

Legat, F., 1995, *La surveillance des étrangers en France dans la seconde moitié du XVIIIᵉᵐᵉ siècle*, Mémoire de DEA, Université Paris IV Sorbonne.

Lequin, Yves, (sous la direction de), 1988, *La mosaïque France. Histoire des étrangers et de l'immigration en France*, Paris.

Albert Mathiez, 1918, *La Révolution et les étrangers. Cosmopolitisme & défense nationale*, Paris.

Rey, René, 1937, *La police des étrangers en France*, thèse de droit, Université de Paris.

Roche, Daniel, 1979, 'Nouveaux Parisiens au XVIIIᵉ siècle', *Cahiers d'histoire*, vol. 24:3: 3–20.

Roche, Daniel, 1981, *Le peuple de Paris*, Paris.

Sapey, C. A., 1843, *Les étrangers en France sous l'ancien et le nouveau droit*, Paris.

Wahnich, Sophie, 1997, *L'impossible citoyen. L'étranger dans le discours de la Révolution française*, Paris.

# Chapter 4

# British Nationality Policy as a Counter-Revolutionary Strategy During the Napoleonic Wars
## *The Emergence of Modern Naturalization Regulations*

*Margrit Schulte Beerbühl*

The French Revolution marked a turning point in the history of nationality. It created a new notion of nationality in the world at large. In France (as well as in the United States of America) members of the state were no longer defined as subjects but as citizens (Brubaker 1992: 49). In Britain, however, there was no sharp break in the history of nationality: nationals continued to be defined as subjects until 1948.[1] Nevertheless, the period of the French Wars brought about important changes in Britain as well. The first immigration laws were passed and although the British government introduced no comprehensive naturalization law during this period, naturalization policy changed in important ways.

This paper focuses on the development of British naturalization policy between the outbreak of the French Revolution and 1818, when a new naturalization law was passed declaring naturalizations undesirable. Anne Dummett and Clive Parry have already pinpointed the French Wars as a watershed in the history of naturalization in Britain. New requirements and new restrictions developed which paved the way for the naturalization law of 1844 (Dummett and Nicol 1990: 85f.; Parry 1954: 84). Nonetheless no detailed historical research into the nature of these changes has been conducted to date.

These changes were closely linked with political and social developments in Britain and abroad during the French Revolutionary Wars. Therefore I will begin with the 1793 Aliens Act before discussing the changes in British naturalization policy. The war years can be divided into two periods: a liberal period up to about 1806-7, which witnessed the removal of religious barriers, and a repressive one from 1807-18, during which new limitations to naturalization emerged.

## I. The 1793 Alien Act

Until 1793 Britain did not have any immigration controls. Neither anti-foreigner riots (Endelman 1979: 200ff.), nor petitions in favour of immigration restrictions could induce the British government to change its mind – not even the outbreak of the French Revolution. It is well known that Britain initially welcomed the Revolution. However, at the end of December 1792 the British government's attitude changed. Within a few weeks Parliament passed the first Aliens Act (33 Geo III, c. 4).

The British Government under William Pitt pressed for an immigration law in December 1792 for various reasons. At home, social unrest had spread throughout the country, demands for a parliamentary reform had become vociferous, and the first political workingmen's clubs were being founded. Domestic developments alone would not, however, have induced the government to change its attitude. Developments in France were the main cause for the British Government's change of heart. From the summer of 1792 Pitt had tried to avoid a war between Britain and France. After the September Massacres, and above all after the declarations of the Convention in November, the chances of Britain remaining neutral declined (*Annual Register*, 1792). The first declaration of the Convention was the unilateral denunciation of the Barrier Treaty that had kept the French out of the Scheldt. This threatened to bring into effect the Treaties of 1713 and 1788, in which Britain had guaranteed the security of Holland. The second was the Decree of Fraternity which promised 'assistance to all people who wish to recover liberty'. This posed a threat to the inner security of Britain. In November and December rumours spread that French spies and saboteurs were preparing an insurrection (Emsley 1977/8: 74–81; Mori 1996: 284–305; Mori 1997: 121–130). In view of these developments, Pitt finally decided to call for measures to maintain internal tranquility. The first immigration law was rushed through Parliament during the last two weeks of December and became law on 8 January. On 1 February 1793 Britain went to war with France.

Although the 1793 Alien Act was merely a temporary measure, it already contained the main elements of modern British immigration legislation. It authorized the ejection of undesirable aliens from the country. Foreigners were allowed to arrive only at certain ports and their movements from the port of arrival to their destination as well as in the country were subject to controls and restrictions. Only foreign overseas merchants were exempt from them: they were allowed to travel freely within the country. However, in the face of the mutinies at the Nore and Spithead, the Irish insurrection and the threat of a French invasion, Parliament decided to toughen the Aliens Act in 1798. Henceforth, foreign merchants came under the same restrictions as other immigrants and foreign travellers.

The immigration law did not derive from racial or economic motives, nor were the numbers of immigrants a primary cause for concern. During the debates on the new immigration law members of Parliament were unanimous in their opinion that the law was only intended as a precautionary measure. Lord Grenville, who had introduced the Alien Bill, stated that the bill was not directed against those refugees who had fled from the terror of the Revolution. He stressed that Britain should remain an asylum for the oppressed. Only those 'who would pull down church and state, religion and God, morale and happiness' should be debarred from entering the realm (*The Parliamentary History of England, from the Earliest Period to the Year 1803*, vol. 30: 188).

By the time the first Alien Act was passed the majority of the refugees had already arrived, but some still came after 1793. We have no exact information on their numbers prior to 1793. Contemporaries spoke of an 'extraordinary influx of foreigners into this country' (ibid.: 174, 197). There are guesses that a total of 30,000 to 40,000 refugees arrived in 1792, among them more than 4,000 Catholic priests.[2] Even after that date it is hardly possible to say anything more precise about their numbers as the surviving documents are very incomplete. According to Ghislain de Diesbach Britain became 'la protectrice la plus sûre des émigrés' during the twenty-five years after the outbreak of the French Revolution (de Diesbach 1975: 246). Of all European countries, Britain took in the largest number of refugees. A large part of the French nobility and of the French clergy, as well as royalist army officers fled to Britain. Between 1794 and 1810 the

British government spent more than 2.9 million pounds from public funds in support of the refugees, in addition to private support (Weiner 1960: 223–5).

## II. The Emergence of New Procedures of Naturalization and Denization

The traditional policy of naturalization was not altered until 1798. In that year, when the Alien Act was tightened, the House of Lords decided that petitioners for naturalization should be subject to stricter control (*Journal of the House of Lords*, vol. 41: 543). To understand the changes, it is necessary to look into the traditional procedure of naturalizing foreigners.

Until 1870 two ways of becoming a British subject existed: denization or naturalization. Denization conferred restricted nationality rights, while naturalization originally conferred full nationality rights. After the accession of the Hanoverian King George I in 1714, all naturalized British subjects were excluded from political rights. Denization was a royal prerogative and was conferred by letters patent, while naturalization was acquired through a private act of Parliament. All children born in Great Britain – no matter from which country their parents came – were considered British subjects. Therefore only first-generation immigrants sought to acquire British nationality. Only Protestants could be naturalized by private act.

The cost of naturalization and denization was high. Around the turn of the century it amounted to between £100 and £120. Denization was the cheaper option, as several petitioners could be included in a single letter of patent. This was not possible in the case of naturalization where every petitioner had to pay the full amount (*British Parliamentary Papers*, 1843, vol. 5: 307f. (henceforth: BPP, 1843)). The number of those who acquired British nationality in the eighteenth century was therefore never high. Only a small wealthy minority of immigrants applied for naturalization.

Before 1798 immigrants simply had to petition Parliament for a private act in order to become naturalized. The respective bill could be brought either before the House of Commons or the House of Lords, where it had to pass three readings and a committee stage. After the bill had passed the first House, it had to go through the same stages in the other House before it became law. In April 1798, the House of Lords decided that in future every petitioner would have to produce a certificate from the Home Office that he had not violated the provisions of the Alien Acts (*Journal of the House of Lords*, vol. 41: 543). No second reading of the bill could take place unless such a certificate had been produced. This decision gave birth to a system of certification, which continued after the reform of naturalization procedures in 1844. The decision the Lords made in 1798 marked an important turning point in the history of naturalization. The Home Secretary was given the power to grant or refuse certificates. The applications for denization also came under the supervision of the Home Office.[3]

## III. The Removal of Religious Barriers: The Denization of Catholics

To what extent did the change in immigration law and the system of certification affect the number of naturalizations and denizations?

Table 4.1: Number of Naturalizations and Denizations, 1771–1818

| Year | Naturalizations | Denizations |
|------|-----------------|-------------|
| 1771–75 | 82 | 35 |
| 1776–80 | 58 | 17 |
| 1781–85 | 48 | 2 |
| 1786–90 | 51 | 15 |
| 1791–95 | 80 | 58 |
| 1796–1800 | 105 | 37 |
| 1801–05 | 106 | 138 |
| 1806–10 | 51 | 74 |
| 1811–15 | 9 | 35 |
| 1816–18[a] | 12 | 20 |

Notes: [a] 3 years only.
*Sources:* Shaw 1923; Naturalization Records for the years 1800–1844, House of Lords Record Office and List of Denizations 1800–1844 in PRO, HO 1.

Until around 1807–09 these changes did not have a negative effect on numbers. Compared to the number of naturalizations and denizations prior to 1790, naturalizations as well as denizations increased in the last decade of the century and continued to do so until about 1806.

The most striking feature is the change in the relationship between naturalizations and denizations. During the entire century there were more naturalizations than denizations. After the turn of the century this ratio changed and the number of denizations now surpassed that of naturalizations. The change becomes even more evident if we compare the totals. Between 1715 and 1800 only 434 persons became denizens, while 1257 were naturalized. From 1801 to 1844, only 377 naturalizations were granted as opposed to 635 denizations.

The increase in the number of denizations was mainly due to the French *emigrés*. The majority of the French refugees were Catholics. As naturalization was only open to Protestants, it was not an option. In the past it had been a more flexible instrument of granting British nationality, especially in times of mass immigration. The Huguenots were made denizens when they fled to Britain in the sixteenth and seventeenth centuries. In the first half of the eighteenth century the overwhelming majority of denizens were Sephardic Jews of Spanish or Portuguese origin. They were not eligible for naturalization due to their religion.[4] Two other groups also sought denization: those who could not afford naturalization and those who did not require the economic privileges which only naturalization conveyed.[5] Denization did not have any religious requirements and, as the majority of letters patent do not mention religion, it cannot definitely be ruled out that there were no Catholics among them. This is unlikely, however, given the strong anti-Catholic feeling in Britain.[6] Between 1715 and 1790 very few French nationals became denizens.[7] The first person to state openly that he was a Roman Catholic was Jean Louis Castera, a merchant born in Bayonne. He became denizen in 1793.[8]

In the last decade before 1806 the number of denizens of French origin rose visibly and peaked in 1803 and 1806. In 1803, 41 foreigners became denizens, 16 of whom came from France. In 1806, 28 of the 46 foreigners made denizens were of French origin. The majority of them belonged to the French nobility and it seems very likely that many were Catholics. Therefore we can conclude that Protestant intolerance towards naturalizing Catholics had begun to crumble.

The new liberal attitude towards Catholics was not only due to the conception of Britain as an asylum for the oppressed, but must be seen within the broader context of the 'Catholic question'. The demand for Catholic emancipation was one of the major domestic political issues during the French Wars. The movement had started in the 1780s. William Pitt had supported Catholic emancipation during his premiership. In 1791 an act was passed which permitted Catholics to build churches in England, and in 1793 another law granted similar relief to Catholics in Ireland (Machan 1964: 10ff.; Hexter 1936: 297–319).

However, Catholics could not obtain naturalization before 1829 (Dummett and Nicol 1990: 79).

## IV. The New Discretionary Power: The Rejection of Naturalization

The increase in naturalizations overall, as well as the denization of Catholics, suggests that the system of certification had not led to stricter controls. A select committee of the House of Commons confirmed this impression in 1843 (BPP, 1843, vol. 5: 2f.). The surviving documents from the age of the French wars, however, convey a different impression. The Home Office used every available means to enquire into the circumstances of applicants. It employed the resources of the Alien Office and the local police, as well as members of the town councils to obtain information about applicants before issuing a certificate. The slightest doubtful circumstances, i.e. any remote or likely relationship with a person who was suspected of sympathies towards the French Revolution, or even denunciations in anonymous letters, resulted in a refusal of a certificate.[9]

Up to about 1807 few applications for naturalization were rejected. In 1798, 19 applicants were naturalized and 3 were turned down. Between February 1801 and June 1802, 38 foreigners petitioned for naturalization, of whom only five did not become British subjects.[10] However, the interval between the application and the royal assent had increased. In the eighteenth century, it usually varied between a minimum of few weeks and a maximum of two months. In 1801 some applicants had to wait for over a year to obtain naturalization.[11]

Table 4.2. Naturalizations and Denizations, 1811–1818.

|      | Naturalizations | Denizations |
|------|-----------------|-------------|
| 1811 | –               | 6/21[a]     |
| 1812 | 7               | 4/11        |
| 1813 | –               | 1           |
| 1814 | 1               | –           |
| 1815 | 1               | 2           |
| 1816 | 1               | 3/13        |
| 1817 | 2               | 2           |
| 1818 | 7               | 2/5         |

Notes: [a] The first figure states the number of letters patent, the second the number of persons included. *Sources: see Table I*

After 1806 the annual number of naturalizations dropped to the pre-war level and reached its lowest point between 1812 and early 1818. Only 5 foreigners were naturalized between 1811 and 1818. The number of foreigners who became denizens was somewhat higher, because several could be included in a letter of patent. The actual number of denization letters, however, was never more than 9 in any one year.

Various domestic and external factors contributed to this change. Napoleon's conquests on the continent and the blockade made relations with the other continental countries more difficult. The preservation of law and order at home became one of the main concerns of the Home Office. After 1806 political radicalism gathered momentum and became intertwined with labourers' demands for minimum wages. According to Edward P. Thompson, 'sheer insurrectionary fury has rarely been more widespread in English history' than in 1811–12, when Luddism broke out (Thompson 1968: 624). From then on, hardly any naturalizations or denizations were granted. In June 1812, a new government was formed under Lord Liverpool, whose cabinet was known for its opposition to reform (Cookson 1975: 395–576; Derry 1990: 151–97; Emsley 1996: 147–82). Viscount Sidmouth, the Home Secretary, was not only vehemently opposed to parliamentary reform and Catholic emancipation, but also suppressed social unrest with great severity. Moreover, he considered all foreigners to be potential revolutionaries, who had to be kept out of the country. Therefore he not only advocated the prolongation of the Alien Act after the end of the Napoleonic Wars, but also refused to naturalize foreigners.[12]

An examination of the entry books preserved in the Home Office reveals that the number of immigrants remained high after the turn of the century and began to rise again towards the end of the Napoleonic Wars. The refugees who arrived after 1810 were, however, not the same as those of the 1790s. At the beginning of the Revolution French royalists, priests, and other loyalists had fled to Britain. When the wars came to an end and the old monarchies on the Continent were being restored, those who had supported the ideas of the Revolution were forced to look for a place of asylum. In face of the reactionary policies of Continental states, public opinion in Britain began to sympathize with democrats there. The number of aliens deported under the immigration laws dropped sharply towards the end of the wars. According to Dinwiddy, the Alien Acts were mainly used against the Bonapartists after 1814, as some of them were deported (Dinwiddy 1968: 208). The debates on the renewal of the Alien

Act after 1814, however, show that Sidmouth and Castlereagh were not so much concerned with the activities of the Bonapartists as those of the potential revolutionaries.[13]

After 1814 opposition in Parliament to the Alien Act increased. Sidmouth was reproached for refusing asylum to continental democrats. He was charged with an insufficient regard for liberty and constitutional government, and for having 'a desire to please too much the arbitrary governments of Europe'.[14] A storm of protest arose in Parliament in 1815, when members found out that Sidmouth had taken steps in 1813–14 to circumvent the law. On his recommendation, the Foreign Office had issued circulars to all British representatives in foreign countries that no foreigner should be allowed to embark on a ship for Britain unless he had been supplied with a proper passport by one of his Majesty's ministers or consuls abroad. To prevent the immigration of suspicious characters, ministers and consuls were also vested with the power to enquire into the motives and objects of those applying for passports.[15]

While the Alien Acts caused considerable debate in Parliament, the naturalization policy was hardly noticed by the public or by MPs. Between 1806 and 1809 steps had been taken to restrict the naturalization of foreigners. The new power acquired by the Home Office became visible around 1810. The sequence of the naturalization procedure had changed. At the beginning of the century the majority of foreigners petitioned Parliament before they applied for a certificate. By 1810 the procedure had been reversed. The number of petitions to Parliament dropped dramatically. The surviving register of applications reveals that the majority of applicants first turned to the Home Office to verify their chances of naturalization or denization before petitioning Parliament. According to the register of applications, 224 foreigners applied for naturalization or denization between 1810 and 1819. Only 85 foreigners received the certificate, 119 were rejected and in 20 cases the application was not pursued.[16]

The reasons for this restrictive naturalization policy did not lie with the applicants themselves. Most of them belonged to the very respectable community of foreign overseas merchants resident in London. Among those who were refused British nationality between 1806 and 1818 were well-known merchants such as John Henry Schröder, George Oppenheimer, and the Swiss banker Francis Maubert.

The drop in naturalizations and denizations between 1806 and 1818 was mainly due to a new Home Office policy. Sometime before 1810, the Home Office introduced new qualifications, which turned naturalization into an uncertain affair. With Viscount Sidmouth as Home Secretary, British naturalization policy became highly arbitrary.

Before 1870 the naturalization laws did not contain any residential qualifications. In the eighteenth century many foreigners had stayed in England for a very short time, sometimes less than a year, before acquiring British nationality. John Frederick Schröder applied for naturalization within a year of his arrival in England (Roberts 1992: 26f; see also Barreau 1954: 1). Others left for the colonies or other countries shortly after naturalization.[17] From 1806, however, only long-term residents in Britain had a chance of becoming British subjects. Even temporary absence from the country for commercial or other reasons became a ground for denying naturalization applications.[18] Disregard of the Alien Laws was another possible reason. George Oppenheimer was not made a denizen because he had neglected to prolong his licence of residence.[19] Even then 'good conduct and long residence' was not a sufficient reason for granting naturalization or denization.[20]

Commercial disadvantages arising from the lack of British nationality had been the main reason for acquiring British nationality in the eighteenth century. Under Sidmouth, commercial or professional reasons were no longer accepted as sufficient qualifications for naturalization.[21]

Those applicants who wished to purchase real estate, or either inherited or wished to bequeath property, had the best chances. Foreigners were forbidden to buy, and could not inherit or bequeath freeholds. Although the wish to buy a freehold was one of the main conditions for the acquisition of British nationality, the declaration of one's intent or desire to purchase real estate was not sufficient in Sidmouth's eyes. Again and again he refused naturalization to foreigners who had only declared an intention; in his view it was essential that they had at least made a contract to purchase. But reaching agreements about the purchase of real estate prior to naturalization involved financial and above all legal risks. At the very least it meant moving on the fringes of legality, if not actually infringing the law. Many foreigners therefore shrank from contracting for a freehold.[22] The value of the estate in question as well as the marital status of applicants were also a matter of concern for the Home Office.[23] Foreigners who had signed contracts for the acquisition of real estate were refused British nationality, if they were not married and had no children. Celibacy was taken to indicate a lack of genuine will to remain in England.[24]

The inheritance of real estate or the desire of a foreigner to bequeath his property was another important reason for naturalization or denization. Foreigners did not always know that it was illegal for them to buy real estate and bought freeholds. Others acquired real estate in the name of an English-born subject who acted as their trustee. Many of them applied for naturalization when they were old or in ill health and wanted to bequeath their property to their children. According to English law the property of foreigners passed to the Crown after their death. But in contrast to France, where the property of aliens was frequently seized after their death, the British Crown was not generally interested in it (Dubost and Sahlins 1998: 95, 301ff.; Dubost 1997: 147). The Home Secretary generally granted naturalization in these cases if the applicant pleaded ill health and old age.[25] He also naturalized foreigners if they or their children were about to inherit real estate. Foreigners could not even act as guardians to children unless they were British subjects.[26]

Although these reasons were among those most likely to ensure the success of an application, there was no legal right to naturalization. Even where such conditions were met, some foreigners were not naturalized or granted denizenship.[27] Between 1714 and 1798 no applications for naturalization or denization were refused. Clive Parry therefore concluded that access to British nationality was thought of as a right (Parry 1954: 97). Since the introduction of the certificate, naturalization and denization had become a matter of discretion. The high number of refusals, especially between 1810 and 1818, and the frequently arbitrary way in which nationality was refused reveal that it was an act of grace, which the Home Secretary could refuse at any time and without explanation.[28]

Sidmouth's repressive naturalization policy caused much discontent among the wealthy foreign merchant community and they began to search for other possibilities of changing their status as aliens. In the spring of 1818 some of these merchants found a loophole in the law. They discovered a forgotten clause in the Charter of the Bank of Scotland that declared that anybody buying shares of the Bank worth £80 became a Scottish subject. Since the union with Scotland in 1707 all Scots had become British subjects. The charter of the Bank of Scotland had been confirmed several times by the Westminster Parliament, most recently in 1802. This clause did not contain any of the restrictions of private naturalization acts. It conveyed full political rights, had no residential or religious requirements, did not require any oath of allegiance or supremacy and was much cheaper.[29] This forgotten clause undermined all the Home Office's efforts.

By the time Sidmouth learned of this clause, 49 merchants had already become British subjects under the terms of the bank's charter. In order to close this loophole, on Saturday 6 June he introduced a new naturalization bill 'to prevent Aliens [...] from becoming naturalized, or being made or becoming denizens'. As it was close to the end of the parliamentary session and the royal assent was due on the 10 June, he had the standing orders suspended in order to allow the new bill to be passed within four days.[30] Protests from the Bank of Scotland, as well as from George Oppenheimer and some other foreign merchants had been submitted in spite of the limited time available, but there was no determined opposition. Sidmouth's success, however, was only partial. The MPs did not follow him unconditionally. As they were unwilling to enter into a general discussion on a possible reform of the naturalization laws, they merely agreed to suspend the Bank of Scotland's privileges for one year. Sidmouth also failed to insert a clause making the bill retrospective. 114 foreigners had bought a sufficient amount of Bank of Scotland stock to become naturalized before Sidmouth's naturalization bill passed into law. Most of them were part of London's merchant community, for example George Oppenheimer, Francis Maubert, and John Henry Schröder. Some members of the French and Italian nobility also made use of this option.[31]

Sidmouth's naturalization act can be seen as the climax of the Home Office's repressive and arbitary naturalization policy. After 1818 the number of naturalizations and denizations gradually began to rise again. However, the pre-war level of naturalizations was reached only shortly before the reform of naturalization procedures in 1844. The proportion of applications which were refused and granted also changed. Between 1818 and 1830, 111 applications were granted and 75 were either refused or not proceeded with.[32]

The Catholic Relief Act of 1829 finally opened naturalization to Catholics. After the resignation of Lord Liverpool's government, commercial or professional grounds were again recognized as sufficient reasons for naturalization or denization. The immigration controls were considerably relaxed in 1826 and soon fell into disuse after a further amendment of the law in 1836 (Bevan 1986: 62f.).

Though the number of naturalizations and denizations increased, discontent with the old naturalization law and procedure grew. The political demands of the French Revolution had created a new political consciousness not only among the lower orders, but also among the middle and upper classes. In 1832 the franchise had been conceded to £10 householders, but wealthy naturalized British subjects were still denied political rights. They were frequently nominated to local school boards, charity boards, or as councillors, only to find that they could not be elected because naturalized subjects were barred from holding political office. John Lewis Greffuhle of the famous French banking family was naturalized in 1803. He left England after he discovered that he could not stand for a seat in Parliament. Others, like Maubert, threatened to leave the country for the same reason (BPP, 1843, vol. 5: 75; Antonetti 1973). However, when Parliament reformed the naturalization law in 1844 it could not bring itself to concede political rights without conditions. Naturalized foreigners were not generally given full political rights until the second reform in 1870.

To sum up, the main elements of the 1844 Naturalization Act were developed during the Napoleonic wars to counteract revolutionary tendencies and to preserve the social order. The arrival, residence, and naturalization of foreigners came under the control of the Home Office and naturalization was granted at the Home Secretary's discretion. The 1844 Naturalization Act officially conferred the executive power in these questions on the Principal Secretary of State for the Home Department. After this reform the Home Office charged no fees for naturalizations, but continued to restrict naturalization to respectable applicants and usually denied it to persons without property. The desire to purchase real estate and commercial or professional disadvantages that could be removed by naturalization remained the best preconditions for a successful application (Fahrmeir 2000). In many respects the naturalization legislation of 1844 merely recognized and confirmed the changes which had occurred during the war years.

## Notes

I should like to thank Professor Wolfgang J. Mommsen, Professor em. Hans Georg Kirchhoff, and Dr. Susanne Brandt for their helpful comments on an earlier version of this paper.

1. In the nationality act of 1948 the term 'subject' was replaced with 'citizen' for this first time, but the term 'subject' was not dropped altogether, not even in the most recent nationality act of 1983 (on the act of 1948 see Fransman 1989: 134, 138; see also J. Mervin Jones 1956: 83ff.).

2. Wilson 1959: 82; Wagner 1994: 59, note 17. For a more detailed analysis of the numbers see Wilkinson 1952: 109ff.
3. PRO, HO1/6–12, and especially PRO, HO 5/24 (2 vols. arranged alphabethically).
4. Samuel 1970: 111–144 counted 203 Jewish names between 1703 and 1800. His list must, however, be treated with caution, as it includes some Protestants and Catholics without Jewish background.
5. Denizens were excluded from membership in the large trading companies and could not own a British vessel or become licensed brokers. They were not exempt from alien duties.
6. J.M. Ross figures on Catholic denizens are implausible. He simply deducted the number of Jews from the total numbers of denizens without considering that many Protestant foreigners preferred denization out of various financial or economic reasons: Ross 1974: 4.
7. Only biographical research can reveal their religion.
8. PRO, HO 44/41 No 209, 4 September 1793; he received his Letters Patent on 9 December 1793. (Shaw 1923: 201).
9. See case of Dirk Vander Hoeven, PRO, HO 1/13.
10. Numbers compiled from the *Journals of the House of Lords and House of Commons* for these years. The number of naturalizations refused during the years 1798 and 1799 differs slightly from Julian Hoppits data. For 1800, he counted three petitions for naturalization as failed, but they were in fact granted in 1801 (Hoppit 1997: 568–576).
11. Alexandre Comte de Vandes had petitioned Parliament on 9 March 1801. He did not receive his certificate before 18 May 1802. His naturalization bill became law on 3 June 1802 (*Journal of the House of Lords*, vol. 43: 40, 611, 657).
12. See his speeches during the debates on the renewal of the immigration laws between 1814 and 1818; also DNB, vol.1 under *Addington*, p.120; Ziegler 1985.
13. See *The Parliamentary Debates: Forming a Continuation of the Work Entitled "The Parliamentary History of England from the Earliest period to the Year 1803" Published under the Superintendence of T. C. Hansard* on the Alien Bills of 1814, 1816, and 1818; esp. vol. 28 (1814): 712ff. and Lord Castlereagh's speech in vol. 34 (1816): 451ff., vol. 38 (1818): 1018.
14. Ibid., vol. 30 (1815): 659, 800f., vol. 38 (1818): 820.
15. Ibid., vol. 30 (1815): 319ff.
16. Numbers compiled from PRO, HO 5/24.
17. Gottlieb Lebrecht Sultzbergen told the Lords' Committee that he had stayed in England about a year and that he intended to go to Surinam as a British subject to run his estates there (*Lords Comittee Books* vol. 44: 366, 21 July 1800). George Bong, a native of Sweden, embarked for East India before his bill reached the final stage (ibid, vol. 43: 15, 6 March 1799).
18. See case of Charles Winckelman, (PRO, HO 5/24).
19. PRO, HO 5/24.
20. See Sidmouth's reply to Walther Seyzinger's application (PRO, HO 1/13, 31 May 1817).
21. See cases of Charles Winckelman and Francis Maubert (PRO, HO 5/24; PRO, HO1/13, Maubert's letter to Lord Sidmouth, 15 May 1818).
22. See case of Emanuel Brandt, the founder of the famous London banking house (PRO, HO 5/24).
23. PRO, HO 5/25 under Bergaresch; see also the application of J. B. A. Girardo (PRO, HO 5/25).

24. See cases of Aaron Worms in 1811 and Nicholas Henry Binder in 1810 (PRO, HO 5/24). Their applications were refused because they were single.
25. See case of Walther Seyzinger (PRO, HO 1/13, his memorial dated 12 April 1817).
26. See applications of Fred. Wm Hoffman in 1812 and 1823. His daughter, a baby, had inherited a freehold estate (PRO, HO 1/13).
27. See the cases of Joseph Schaller, a shoemaker from Bavaria and of Joachim Antonio Fructuoso, a native of Spain (PRO, HO 5/24 and PRO, HO 1/13).
28. The applications often carry the remark 'refused' without any further comment.
29. Bank of Scotland Archive, Edinburgh, List of Proprietors 1818; *The Parliamentary Debates* vol. 38 (1818): 1018f., 1266ff.
30. 58 Geo III, c.96 and c.97; *Journal of the House of Lords*, vol.51: 760f.; *The Parliamentary Debates, vol.38* (1818): 1290–4, 1296–1313.
31. Bank of Scotland Archive, BS 20/5/3.
32. See vol. 2 of the Register of Applications (PRO, HO 5/24).

# References

Antonetti, Guy, 1973, *Greffuhle Montz et Cie. Une banque à Paris au XVIII<sup>e</sup> siècle (1789–1793)*, Paris.
Barreau, Paul, 1954, Draft of a Biography on John Henry Schröder, unpublished manuscript, Schröder Archive, London.
Bevan, Vaughan, 1986, *The Development of British Immigration Law*, London.
*British Parliamentary Papers (BPP) 1843: Report from the Select Committee on Laws Affecting Aliens*, vol. 5.
Brubaker, Rogers, 1992, *Citizenship and Nationhood in France and Germany*, Cambridge Mass.
Cookson, J. E., 1975, *Lord Liverpool's Administration. The Crucial Years 1815–1822*, Edinburgh.
De Diesbach, Ghislain, 1975, *Histoire de l'émigration 1789–1814*, Paris.
Derry, John W., 1990, *Politics in the Age of Fox, Pitt and Liverpool. Continuity and Transformation*, Basingstoke.
Dinwiddy, J. R., 1968, 'The Use of the Crowns's Power of Deportation Under the Aliens Act, 1793–1826', *Bulletin of the Institute of Historical Research*, 41: 193–207.
Dubost, Jean-François, and Peter Sahlins, 1998, 'Et si on faisait payer les étrangers?' Louis XIV, les immigrés et quelques autres*, Paris.
Dubost, Jean François, 1997, *La France italienne XVI<sup>e</sup> –XVII<sup>e</sup> siècle*, Paris.
Dummett, Anne, and Andrew Nicol, 1990, *Subjects, Citizens, Aliens and Others. Nationality and Immigration Law*, London.
Emsley, Clive, 1996, *British Society and the French Wars 1793–1815*, Basingstoke.
Emsley, Clive, 1977/8, 'The London "insurrection" of Dec. 1792: Fact, Fiction or Fantasy?' *Journal of British Studies*, 17: 74–81.
Endelman, Todd M, 1979, *The Jews of Georgian England 1714–1830. Tradition and Change in a Liberal Society*, Philadelphia.
Fahrmeir, Andreas, 2000, *Citizens and Aliens: Foreigners and the Law in Britain and the German States, 1789–1870*, New York.
Fransman, Laurie, 1989, *Fransman's British Nationality Law*, London.
Hexter, J.H., 1936, 'The Protestant Revival and the Catholic Question in England 1778–1829', *Journal of Modern History*, 7: 297–319.
Hoppit, Julian, 1997, *Failed Legislation*, London.
Jones, J. Mervin, 1956, *British Nationality Law*, Oxford.

Journals of the House of Lords, vol. 41 (1798), vol. 51 (1818).

Lords Committee Books, House of Lords Archive.

Machan, G. I. T., 1964, *The Catholic Question in English Politics*, Oxford.

Mori, Jennifer, 1996, 'Reponses to Revolution: The November Crisis of 1792', *Historical Research*, 69:284–305.

Mori, Jennifer, 1997, *William Pitt and the French Revolution 1785–1795*, Edinburgh. *The Parliamentary Debates. Forming a Continuation of "The Parliamentary History of England, from the earliest period to the year 1803", Published under the Superintendence of T.C. Hansard, reprint New York 1970. The Parliamentary History of England, From the Earliest Period to the Year 1803, reprint New York 1966.*

Parry, Clive, 1954, *British Nationality Law and the History of Naturalization*, Milan.

Roberts, Richard, 1992, *Schroders, Merchants & Bankers*, London.

Ross, J. M., 1974, 'Naturalization of Catholics 1603–1844', *The London Recusant*, 4: 1–9.

Samuel, W. S., 1970, 'A List of Jewish Persons Endenizened and Naturalised 1609–1799', *Transactions of the Jewish Historical Society of England*, 22: 111–44.

Shaw, W. A., 1923, *Letters of Denization and Acts of Naturalization for Aliens in England and Ireland 1603–1700*, Manchester.

Thompson, Edward P., 1968, *The Making of The English Working-Class*, Harmondsworth.

Wagner, Michael, 1994, *England und die Französische Gegenrevolution 1789–1802*, Munich.

Weiner, Margery, 1960, *The French Exiles 1789–1815*, London.

Wilkinson, E.M., 1952, 'French Emigres in England 1789–1802. Their Reception and Impact on English Life', PhD thesis, Oxford.

Wilson, Francesca M., 1959, *They Came as Strangers. The Story of Refugees to Great Britain*, London.

Ziegler, Philip, 1985, *Addington. The Life of Henry Addington, First Viscount Sidmouth*, New York.

# Part II

---

# An Age of Experimentation

*Controlling Movement in the Nineteenth Century*

# Chapter 5

# Passports and the Development of Immigration Controls in the North Atlantic World During the Long Nineteenth Century

*John Torpey*

In 1926, B. Traven, the German-speaking radical best known as the author of the *Treasure of the Sierra Madre*, penned a novel-length screed against passports and other documentary requirements for ordinary travellers, which he regarded as one of the chief outcomes of the First World War. In his story of adventure on the high seas titled *The Death Ship*, Traven wrote: 'It seems to me the sailor's card, and not the sun, is the centre of the universe. I am positive that the great war was fought, not for democracy and justice, but for no other reason than that a cop, or an immigration officer, may have the legal right to ask you, and be well paid for asking you, to show him your sailor's card, or what have you. Before the war nobody asked you for a passport' (Traven 1991: 40f.).

Traven's remarks concerning the official preoccupation with identity documents designed to regulate human movement marked the culmination of an era that had witnessed an extraordinary expansion of the capacity of states to control the migration of populations using documentary (and of course other) means. The growth of this capacity was, in fact, one of the central features of their development *as* states. Following a century of stagnation resulting from an unprecedented period of relative peace among European countries, the burst of state growth in Europe after the First World War derived from and bore witness to the marked expansion of the role of states in

everyday social life.¹ The bureaucratic means they employed to
regulate population movements and to identify those eligible for
the social goods that states had to offer played a central part in
the creation of the more expansive 'protectionist state'² that
emerged from the Great War.

In order to exist as nation-states – territorial and membership
organisations '"of" and "for" a particular, distinctive, bounded
nation' (Brubaker 1992: chapters 1 and 2, esp. pp. 43–49) – states
must be in a position to 'embrace' or 'grasp' their members and
to distinguish them from non-member others, an aim that has
typically come to be achieved through identification documents
of various kinds.³ Prior to the French Revolution, individuals in
continental Europe were subjects of their sovereign, as well as
members of various estates and sub-national bodies, rather than
citizens of a country. Under these circumstances, descriptions of
a person's social standing – residence, occupation, family status,
etc. – were generally regarded as adequate indicators of a
person's identity for purposes of passport controls in France
(Nordman 1996). Yet the Revolution had ushered in a putative
legal equality and homogeneity among those residing within
France that simultaneously set them off more sharply from the
inhabitants of other states. As the French example ramified
through the continental state system, states sought to embrace
their nationals more firmly than was possible with the lax
methods of the *ancien régime*, and to demarcate them more
clearly from non-nationals. The fulfilment of these aims necessitated greater precision in distinguishing between 'us' and 'them';
the legal stabilization of persons' names played an important role
in the process.⁴ By the time of the First World War the emergence of a protectionist state and the corollary expansion of state
capacities went far toward realizing states' ability to distinguish
between 'who is in' and 'who is out'. Passport controls were a
central element of this broader development.


## The French Revolution and Controls on Movement

The promulgation of a unitary concept of citizenship and the
abolition of feudal privileges in the French Revolution betokened
an end to status-based distinctions in the freedom of movement
and a gradual democratisation of the practices associated with
identifying French citizens and distinguishing them from others.
In the process, the freedom of co-nationals to move *within*
national territorial spaces and to depart from them advanced

decisively. But these changes first required considerable struggle and conflict among proponents and detractors of documentary controls on movement.

Passport controls had been a vital mechanism of domination under the Old Regime in France, and were clearly regarded as such by many who made the revolution there in the late eighteenth century. Among the various restrictions to which the French revolutionaries objected was Louis XIV's edict of 1669 that had forbidden his subjects to leave the territory of France, and related requirements that those quitting the kingdom be in possession of a passport authorizing them to do so (Nordman 1996: 1123; Grossi 1905: 145; and Burguière and Revel 1989: 66). In addition, commoners on the move *within* eighteenth-century France were technically required to have one of two documents: a passport issued by the town hall in one's native village or the so-called *aveu*, an attestation of upright character from local religious authorities. The principal purpose of these documentary requirements was to forestall any 'untoward' migration to the cities, especially Paris. They were at least occasionally effective in achieving their aims, but administrative lassitude and the well-meaning assistance of a variety of benefactors frequently rendered impotent the state's use of documentary controls as a means of regulating movement.[5]

Despite the relative ease with which passport requirements could often be skirted, these controls on movement appeared among the many complaints regarding royal government and aristocratic privilege that were presented in the *cahiers de doléances* during the meeting of the Estates General convened at Versailles in early 1789. Thus the *cahiers* of the parish of Neuilly-sur-Marne pleaded 'that each must be free to go or come, within and outside the kingdom, without permissions, passports, or other formalities that tend to hamper the liberty of its citizens ...'[6]

Soon after the uproar sparked by the King's flight to Varennes in mid-1791 and the attendant renewal of restrictions on the movements of Frenchmen, the National Assembly finally completed its task of writing a new constitution for France. The matter of controls on movement occupied a central place in its deliberations. Indeed, the very first 'natural and civil right' guaranteed by the Constitution of September 3–14, 1791 was that of the freedom 'to go, to remain, [and] to depart'.[7]

The parliament became more specific in its defense of the freedom of movement on September 13th. During that day's deliberations, the Marquis de Lafayette proposed the abolition of all controls on the movements of Frenchmen. The proposal stated that 'there will no longer be any obstacles impeding the right of every French citizen to travel freely within the realm, and to leave it at will', and specifically eliminated passports.[8] The National Assembly did not, however, eliminate the *livret*, an identification certificate required of workers – but not of self-employed artisans or peasants – that often functioned much like a passport. Though enforcement of this requirement during the nineteenth century was uneven, documentary controls on the movements of industrial labourers persisted as a result of the perception of such persons as emanating from the 'dangerous classes' (Zeldin 1973: 198f.). Still, judging from the celebratory cries reported in the *Archives parlementaires*, it would appear that the members of the Assembly believed they were making a major contribution to the cause of human freedom when they abolished passport controls on the French people, constraints they viewed as symptomatic of the arbitrary power of the *ancien régime*.

Yet the demands of revolutionary struggle and international conflict led to a reversal of this liberal move fairly soon thereafter, and passport controls on Frenchmen and foreigners came and went in subsequent years in response to those exigencies. With the *coup d'état* of 18 Fructidor, An V (September 4, 1797), anti-foreign and revolutionary sentiments welled up afresh as the Directory attempted to clean the house of its opponents and enemies. For Frenchmen, this meant a wave of terror – 'a reversion to the spirit of '93', as Donald Greer put it – against refractory clergy, emigrés, and many who were confused with them in the ensuing fracas. The 'Fructidorian Terror' thus spurred a new stream of emigration, not least of those members of the Council of 500 purged and condemned to deportation by the law of 19 Fructidor with which those who carried out the *coup* asserted their predominance (Greer 1951: 102f.; Lefebvre 1964: 197–201). By the end of September 1797, the Directory moved to consideration of a new passport law intended to give them the upper hand in the midst of all the confusion. After a false start[9], the government adopted a statute that has been described as 'the starting-point for modern aliens legislation'.[10]

Non-resident foreigners then in France were obliged to present their passports to the administration of the *département* in which they happened to find themselves, and to have the destination of their travels and their current residence inscribed as in the case of Frenchmen. Copies of these passports were to be sent to the Ministry of Foreign Relations as well as to that of the General Police. In a move presumably directed at the English, the surveillance measures already enjoined in law against those arriving in

French ports were reaffirmed. Finally, Article 7 brought the *coup de grâce*: all foreigners travelling within France, or resident there in any capacity other than that of an accredited official mission on behalf of a neutral or friendly power, and who had not acquired French citizenship, were 'placed under the special surveillance of the executive Directory, which may withdraw their passports and compel their departure from French territory if it judges their presence susceptible to disturbing the public order and peace'.[11] The optimistic cosmopolitanism of the early days of the Revolution had been obliterated in the flames of revolutionary war, and the high-flown ambiguities of the Declaration of the Rights of Man and Citizen had been resolved in favour of the nation-state.[12] Although it would still take some time to shift from a schema that identified the foreigner in terms of 'familiar vs. unfamiliar' to one distinguishing between 'nationals and non-nationals', foreigners – increasingly identifiable by the papers they carried – were more and more likely to be routinely regarded as suspects (Noiriel 1998).

The French Revolution thus ushered in three important developments with respect to the state regulation of migration. First, with the democratisation of law and the introduction of a putatively unitary concept of citizenship, passport controls on movement theoretically applied to all Frenchmen, from the privileged to the lowliest peasant, although the persistence of the *livret* until the end of the nineteenth century surely discriminated against the movements of many a humble work-seeker. Second, the distinction between nationals and foreigners became more sharply defined, codified, and implemented in practice. Finally, controls on the movements of French nationals within the country gradually began to fall by the wayside. Under the growing pressure of forces unleashed by the French Revolution, other countries began to introduce similar changes in their practices regarding controls over movement (Geselle 2001 and forthcoming). These processes would take hold across Western Europe during the course of the nineteenth century. The shift toward greater freedom of movement was particularly apparent in the German lands as they moved toward the construction of a unified nation-state.

## Germany's Elimination of Passport Controls in 1867

The century-long period of relative peace that followed the Congress of Vienna comprised the framework for the advancing dissolution of feudal ties where they still held sway, a process that in Prussia began during the Napoleonic wars and was in part a form of compensation to those elements of the male population drafted into military service during those conflicts (Sheehan 1989, 232f.). Liberation from traditional constraints and obligations also gained impetus from the example set by the abolition of feudalism in France in August 1789. In short, keeping the peasants bound to the land grew increasingly untenable in western Europe, though the European East remained as yet little affected by this trend.

This newly won freedom among the lower classes was a matter of deep concern to the guardians of social order. In early nineteenth-century Germany (but surely not only there), the nervous view spread that 'nothing has appeared... to replace the previous patronage [of the lord] over the peasant' (Lüdtke 1989: 46). The heightened possibility that large numbers of 'masterless men' might be found travelling the country's roads unhindered profoundly disturbed those responsible for superintending the 'dangerous classes'. Yet the decline of serfdom combined with the labour needs of an industrial capitalist economy *in statu nascendi* to promote a dramatic slackening of restrictions on movement in the course of the nineteenth century.

The Peace of Prague (1866) that concluded Prussian hostilities with Austria mandated that Prussia form a new confederacy in the German lands to replace the moribund German Confederation. In May 1867, the Prussian *Landtag* assented to a new constitution, and the North German Confederation was born.[13] Though largely comprised of and certainly dominated by landed nobles, the *Reichstag* of the Confederation soon turned its attention to the concerns pressed upon it by liberals and industrialists. Not least among these were the matters of freedom of movement and travel, which preoccupied the *Reichstag* because of their connection to the economic well being of the fledgling German confederation.

As part of the effort to deal with these concerns, Bismarck had a new passport law for the North German Confederation introduced into the *Reichstag* on 18 September 1867.[14] In most respects the law followed the terms of the Passport Treaty of 1865 between Saxony, Bavaria, Hanover, and Würtemberg. The bill thus proposed to abolish passport and visa requirements for subjects of the states of the Confederation as well as for foreigners, irrespective of whether they were entering, leaving, or moving about within the territory comprised by the Confederation's member-states. The law also forbade the continued use or introduction of so-called 'residency cards' (*Aufenthaltskarten*) throughout the territory of the Confederation. The law intended to abolish only those documents designed purely to regulate residency; those necessary for the continued practice of a trade – even though they might be referred to as 'residency cards' – were permitted to remain. The legislators' purpose here was clearly to eliminate restrictions on *residency* rather than on access to occupations, which they understood would persist in certain areas.

At the same time, the proposed law re-affirmed the right of the authorities to demand that travelers 'legitimate themselves' in some reliable fashion. In furtherance of this objective, the bill provided a legal right to a passport for any subject of the Confederation who wished to request one, as long as no legal grounds stood in the way. This provision sought to facilitate movement by guaranteeing subjects of the Confederation access to travel documents they might have felt would be useful, even if they were not legally required. Moreover, the proposed law mandated that the costs associated with the issuance of a passport should not exceed the modest sum of one *Thaler*, and could indeed be distributed *gratis* at the discretion of the issuing state. The bill also envisioned a standardization of the passport documents used by the various states. Finally, the bill reserved to the presiding authority of the Confederation (*Bundespräsidium*) the right to re-institute passport controls temporarily in the event that 'the security of the Confederation or of an individual member state, or the public order, appears threatened by war, internal unrest, or other developments'.

It is also worth noting that the right to a passport was granted exclusively to subjects of the Confederation. The failure to mention any terms upon which foreigners might gain access to German passports – though in fact they continued to do so – suggests that the interstate system of documentary controls was taking more coherent shape as a framework regulating the movements and identities of strictly demarcated bodies of citizens defined by their legal nationality. Less and less frequently would persons travel in alien territories with papers issued by another state than that of which they were nationals.

The perception clearly had taken hold among important elements of the German political elite that the expansion of opportunities for physical mobility had made it increasingly impossible to enforce passport controls successfully. Nonetheless, the elimination of passport controls was not to undermine the capacity of the police to embrace the population and track criminals, for all persons would still be required to produce valid identification on demand. Indeed, it was precisely because many other states required passports, and because states typically could compel persons to identify themselves, that the proposed law sought to institute the right of all subjects of the Confederation to request a passport if they wished to have one.

In addition, the authors of the new law observed that, because some of the signatories of the 1865 Passport Treaty were now members of the North German Confederation, the Confederation needed to develop a passport policy that met with their assent. Here the most likely source of potential friction was the North German law's rejection of special passport obligations for the 'dangerous classes' as had been provided for in the 1865 treaty. Despite the bill's broad similarities with that agreement, in this respect the proposed law went much further toward liberalizing passport policy than had the earlier treaty. 'It would seem completely unjustified', wrote the bill's authors, 'given the general abolition of passport requirements, if one were to make exceptions that would disadvantage precisely those classes of travellers who have previously been most harassed by the constant police control of their travel documents, leaving entirely aside for the moment the effort in time and resources demanded of the authorities them-selves in the face of the very large number of itinerant journeymen and other work-seekers, and which effort is out of all proportion to the usefulness of those efforts in the individual cases'.

Aside from expanding the area in which freedom from passport requirements held sway, therefore, the most important feature of the bill lay in what it did *not* do: no groups of the population were singled out as liable to comply with special passport or visa oblig-ations. This absence of particular restrictions on the lower orders marked the most significant departure of the 1867 law from the provisions of the earlier treaty, and was a sign of the advancing democratisation that had been propelled forward by the French Revolution. The North German law of 1867, which was soon taken over as Imperial law, remained the fundamental statute regarding passport controls until after the Second World War.

Already in 1879, however, the Imperial government invoked the law's emergency clauses and imposed passport restrictions on those coming from Russia in order, it said, to forestall the impor-tation of a plague that had broken out there. Travellers returning to Germany from Russia were now required to have in their possession a passport that had been visaed within three days of their departure by the German embassy in Saint Petersburg or by a German consular official, and visaed again upon their arrival at the German border. These restrictions went through various permutations until, in 1894, yet another update of the law abol-ished visa requirements on those returning from Russia, but left the passport requirement intact.[15]

The various revisions of the original February 1879 ordinance suggest that the German restrictions on entrants from Russia were not entirely related to the plague. The influx of Polish labour probably played a role as well. Despite the insistence of agricultural (and some industrial) employers that they needed labour, Bismarck – citing the "threat to the state potentially posed by a Polonization of a large segment of the Prussian population" – ordered the expulsion from Germany of some 40,000 Polish workers in 1885, and Poles were excluded from Germany for the next five years (Herbert 1990: 9–37; esp. 12f.). The demand for labour continued unabated, however, and after Bismarck's fall in 1890 the importation of Polish workers was resumed under strict conditions (Brubaker 1992: 133).

The sustained controversy over the importation of Polish workers ultimately led to the imposition in 1908 of a *Legitimationszwang* mandating that all foreign workers carry an identification card. These documents were an essential part of the creation of 'a system of surveillance of foreigners as complete and total as feasible, as well as [of] an extensive bureaucracy for their supervision and control' in the form of the German Farm Workers Agency (*Deutsche Feldarbeiterzentrale*), first established in 1905. Still, the degree of effectiveness of these restrictions should not be overestimated (Herbert 1990: 34–44, quote 43).

Alternatively, the continued existence of passport requirements for travellers from Russia may have been a way of punishing that country for its continued insistence upon passport controls as a requirement of entry into its territories, in contradiction to the more open-handed practice then established in most of western and central Europe.[16] Indeed, on the very eve of the First World War, a German student of the passport system wrote, 'Because in recent times the position of foreigners has grown much different from before... most modern states have, with but a few exceptions, abolished their passport laws or at least neutralised them through non-enforcement... [Foreigners] are no longer viewed by states with suspicion and mistrust but rather, in recognition of the tremendous value that can be derived from trade and exchange, welcomed with open arms and, for this reason, hindrances are removed from their path to the greatest extent possible'.[17] Whatever the truth content of this picture of the situation of 'foreigners', these remarks suggest the enormous influence that economic liberalism still held in the minds of many Europeans. It was this set of ideas, shaken but not destroyed by the Great Depression of the 1870s, that undergirded the unprecedented movement toward the relaxation (and, as in

Germany, the elimination) of passport controls in late nineteenth-century Europe.

The German passport law of 1867 was indicative of a broader
European shift toward greater freedom of entry and exit, even
for foreigners. In England, for example, the passport provisions
of the 1836 Aliens Restriction Act went largely unregarded until
the Aliens Act of 1905 revived them in response to the threat of
massive immigration by East European Jews (Zolberg 1997:
311-3). Indeed, Lord Granville wrote in 1872 that 'by the existing law of Great Britain all foreigners have the unrestricted right
of entrance into and residence in this country' (Plender 1988: 67).
Similarly, in France, with the exception of the period of the Paris
Commune, the once-severe passport controls on internal movement had become 'entombed in desuetude'. The enforcement of
passport controls on those entering and exiting the country was
widely ignored in the late nineteenth century, not to be rejuvenated until the Great War.[18] Under the influence of an
'overwhelming consensus' during the 1860s and early 1870s that
economic liberalism was the surest recipe for prosperity, as
Hobsbawm has put it, 'the remaining institutional barriers to the
free movement of the factors of production, to free enterprise
and to anything which could conceivably hamper its profitable
operation, fell before a world-wide onslaught' (Hobsbawm 1975:
35-39, quote 35f.).

The second half of the nineteenth century thus bore witness to
an increasing freedom of movement for the lower orders of
society, who were liberated from the feudal shackles and documentary restrictions that had once bound them to their
birthplaces. The period also saw a democratization of legal
standing, such that the 'internal foreign nation' comprised of the
lower classes had to be elevated to at least a legal par with their
social 'betters'. These developments came together under the
ideological aegis of economic liberalism, which however held no
strong brief for the sanctity of national borders. The result of this
extraordinary conjuncture was that passport restrictions on
movement generally subsided throughout Western Europe.

## The Great War and the Emergence of the Modern
## Passport System

Yet a trend away from free international movement and toward
greater restriction had also been underway for some time, the
intensity of which depended on the country concerned. This was

part of a larger trend toward the 'nationalisation' of European states: that is, their stricter attention to distributing positions and benefits to their own nationals rather than others.[19] Toward the end of the century, this tendency found explicit expression in a Prussian decree strictly prohibiting the relevant authorities from issuing passports to foreigners other than in exceptional cases, a departure from a practice still common at that point. 'Close examination [of the applicant's nationality] is necessary', the order insisted, 'because unpleasant negotiations must take place that often result in Germany having to take the passport-holder in simply because of his possessing a German passport'.[20] In part as a result of the nationalisation of welfare provisions and the increasing assumption by political leaders of responsibility for economic well being, the distinction between 'national' and 'foreigner' – a distinction implemented and made knowable by documents – was growing sharper.[21] An international system of states comprised of mutually exclusive bodies of citizens was taking firmer shape, not least because governments increasingly had the capacity to get documents into people's hands identifying them as belonging to one country or another.

Just as there were often external determinants of citizenship laws that might be thought to be at the very heart of state sovereignty (Brubaker 1992: 69f.), passport controls on movement might be imposed in one state as a result of the restrictions laid down by another. Such was the case with the Italian passport law of 1901. The law, which remained the major legislation on passports until 1967, appeared to be a departure from the widespread warm feelings toward the freedom of movement in Europe. Certainly its detractors regarded its requirement that transoceanic travellers be in possession of a passport before purchasing their steamer tickets as the re-introduction of a noxious constraint on exit. In fact, however, the legislation aimed not to choke off exit, but rather to ensure that Italian emigrants – too many of whom, according to the law's backers, had been rebuffed in recent years – would not be denied *entry* into American ports. This intention could not have been made clearer than by the decree's requirement that passports be delivered within twenty-four hours of a legitimate request, a provision reiterated in the law on emigration adopted the same day.[22]

The 1901 law thus reflected not so much the re-awakening of slumbering authoritarian habits as it did the ruling elite's acceptance of Italy's peripheral position in the Atlantic economy. The law's antagonists were nonetheless correct in claiming that, even if the law was not presently intended to restrict departures, it could be used to that end at some later time. The coming of the Great War would prove to be that later time.

The booming of the guns of August 1914 brought to a sudden close the era during which foreigners were relatively free to traverse borders. In response to the outbreak of the conflict, passport controls that had been 'entombed in desuetude' were re-introduced across the continent. For example, in France, passport restrictions from the revolutionary period that had been 'allowed to lapse' were restored in the face of the crisis (Plender 1988: 90, n.132; Burguière and Revel 1989: 67). Similarly, in Britain, the Aliens Restriction Act, 1914 sharply enhanced the power of the government, 'when a state of war exists', to prohibit or impose restrictions on the landing or embarkation of aliens in the United Kingdom. The law made no explicit mention of pass-port requirements, which in any event had already been rejuvenated in 1905. Still, the law put the onus of proving that a person was not an alien on that person, making documentary evidence of one's nationality largely unavoidable, particularly if one did not look or sound 'British', whatever that might mean. It also provided for the possibility of requiring aliens to live – or of prohibiting them from living – in certain areas, and of regis-tering with the authorities their place of domicile, change of abode, or movements within the UK. Finally, the Act made provi-sion for the appointment of immigration officers to carry out the order, which helped strengthen the bureaucratic momentum for keeping passport controls in place after the war.[23]

The German government, too, adopted new controls under the emergency clauses of the liberal 1867 law. Already on July 31, 1914, Germany implemented 'temporary' passport restrictions on anyone – not just aliens – entering the Empire from abroad. In the interest of permitting the return of eager or otherwise mobi-lized soldiers, the requirement was relaxed for those who could produce papers demonstrating that they were German subjects, stateless former Germans, or permanent residents of the Empire who had only been abroad temporarily. This provision presum-ably was implemented for the good reason that these people might very well not have had passports when they originally left Germany. Meanwhile, in order to avoid the flight of unwilling cannon fodder, those owing military service were to be eligible for passports for exit from Germany only with the approval of their commanding officers. At the same time, foreigners in any area of the Empire declared to be in a state of war were required to have a passport giving a proper account of their person. In the absence of a passport, other satisfactory documents were to be accepted, again presumably because the new regulations might have left them with their papers.[24]

The Italians' first move concerning documentary controls on movement after the outbreak of hostilities was to recall those passports already in circulation among their citizens. A decree of August 6, 1914 suspended the right of emigration of those obliged to do military service, annulling all passports in their possession. Like the German passport regulations, this order indicated the close connection between passport controls and efforts to insure that military recruits for the defence of the *patrie* would not be wanting.[25] Immediately on the heels of the Treaty of London that brought Italy into the war, the government in May 1915 further tightened the passport requirements for Italians going abroad to work. Now, those bound *anywhere*, not just across the Atlantic, had to have a passport in order to leave, and in order to get one they had to present a work contract to the officials of the Royal Commissariat of Emigration.[26] On the same day, the Italian government imposed passport requirements on foreigners wishing to enter the Kingdom, reversing many years of an open-door policy.[27]

At first, reflecting the persistence of the view that such controls were acceptable only during time of war, the newly re-instituted passport requirements were typically thought of as provisional measures, responses to a state of emergency. Leo Lucassen has noted that few contemporaries would then have predicted the end of the laissez-faire era in international migration (Lucassen 1997). Yet the generalized anxiety about borders that existed during the war did not subside with its end. Instead, the 'temporary' measures implemented to control access to and departure from the territories of European states persisted into the inter-war period. Although based on the liberal 1867 law of the North German Confederation abolishing passport requirements, for example, an order of June 1919 reiterated and rendered permanent the wartime requirement that anyone crossing the borders of Germany in either direction be in possession of a passport with visa, as well as the paragraph insisting that all foreigners in the territory of the Empire carry a passport.[28]

In Britain, similarly, the wartime restrictions on aliens won greater permanence with the Aliens Order, 1920, which extended the validity of previous restrictions beyond the war's end. These restrictions, according to the Order, 'should continue in force... not only in the [wartime] circumstances aforesaid, but at any time'. Henceforward, *anyone* entering or leaving the UK was required to have 'either a valid passport furnished with a photograph of himself or some other document satisfactorily establishing his national status and identity'. The passport became the backbone of the system of documentary substantiation of identity used to register and watch the movements of aliens in the U. K. The Order also mandated the maintenance of a 'central register of aliens' under the direction of the Secretary of State.[29]

The persistence of strictures on movement across national borders derived in considerable part from economic policies that dramatically reversed the economic liberalism that had characterized the late nineteenth-century period of relatively unrestricted movement. Free trade gave way to protectionism, the constraints of which helped bring on the Great Depression of the 1930s. Eric Hobsbawm has noted succinctly the dramatic consequences of these shifts for migratory movements: 'the rivers of international migration dried to trickles' (Hobsbawm 1990: 132).

Now, the rapidly improving technological possibilities for movement were met by intensified controls on ingress into the territories of European states. Egidio Reale, the leading contemporary analyst of the new passport regime that emerged from the war, described its impact with a variant of the Rip Van Winkle story: a man awakes during the interwar period from a slumber of some years to find that he can talk on the telephone to friends in London, Paris, Tokyo, or New York, hear stock market quotations or concerts from around the globe, fly across the oceans – but not traverse earthly borders without unprecedented bureaucratic formalities in the course of which his nationality would be closely scrutinized (Reale 1930: 1f.).

As a result of the new documentary restrictions on international movement, 'the laissez-faire era in international labor migration had come to a close' by the mid–1920s (Dowty 1987: 83). An important cause of this caesura was the erection of rigid barriers against the entry of many Europeans into the United States, which had long since closed off virtually all immigration from Asia.[30] Although a passport would not become a permanent legal requirement for the departure of United States citizens from American territory until the Second World War, the United States, too, allowed initially temporary, wartime passport restrictions on the entry of aliens to persist beyond the First World War.[31] Along with refurbished visa procedures that determined at the point of departure whether would-be European emigrants would gain access to the United States, these requirements facilitated the administrative implementation of the well-known restrictive laws of the 1920s that followed soon thereafter (Higham 1988: 300–30). These documents were essential to the administration of immigration restriction, facilitating the task of immigration officers at Ellis Island and elsewhere of determining whether a would-be immigrant belonged to one of the nationalities whose immigration was to be curtailed under that legislation.

## Conclusion

In his autobiographical recollections, Stefan Zweig reported that 'before 1914 [he] travelled from Europe to India and to America without passport and without ever having seen one', whereas after the war passports and any number of documents became absolutely essential to international movement (Zweig 1953: 410f.). Passports and related documents such as visas have, indeed, come to play a role in immigration control that was unthinkable before the First World War. The ubiquity of 'the passport nuisance' (Fussell 1980: 24) evidences the extent to which bureaucratic administration has come to rely upon identification documents in its efforts to constrain immigration, and thus to defend the boundaries of the nation-state. The International Labour Office of the League of Nations was thus quite correct to state that the passport is an 'institution which Governments are not very willing to suppress, since it enables them to control, by purely administrative means and without having recourse to any special legislation, both the departure of their own nationals and the entry of foreigners' (International Labour Office 1928: 79). Passports and other identification documents, which facilitate modern states' 'grasp' of individuals and whole populations by constructing an intelligible and durable relationship between state agencies and particular persons, have considerably enhanced states' ability to regulate human movement.

## Notes

I would like to thank Leo Lucassen and Caroline Ford for their helpful comments on earlier drafts of this paper.

1. See Mann 1993: Chapter 11. On 'The Hundred Years' Peace', see Polanyi 1944: Chapter 1.
2. I borrow this term from Carl Strikwerda (1997: 65), who argues – correctly in my view – that the 'welfare state' should be seen simply as one aspect of a more broadly active and paternalistic state in the twentieth century.
3. I explicate this argument in greater detail in Torpey 1998 and 2000.
4. Jane Caplan (2001) discusses the legal stabilization of personal names as a central aspect of the emergence of a 'culture of identification' in the nineteenth century.

5.  On the relatively lax enforcement of passport controls in pre-revolutionary France, see Hufton 1974: 229 and Schwartz 1988: 193f.
6.  *Cahiers des États Généraux*, Vol. 4 (Paris: Librairie Administrative de Paul Dupont, 1868), p. 759. See also the *cahiers* of the bourg d'Ecouen, Paris hors les murs, ibid., p. 509.
7.  Constitution française, *Collection Complète des Lois, Décrets, Ordonnances, Réglements, etc.* [hereafter *Collection Complète*], ed. J. B. Duvergier, Vol. 3 (Paris: A. Guyot, 1834), p. 241.
8.  *Archives Parlementaires*, 1. Serie, vol. 30, pp. 621, 632.
9.  For the run-up to the law, see *Le Moniteur*, vol. 29, pp. 22, 29, 33, 39, and 43.
10. Plender 1988: 65, quoting the scholar of international law Atle Grahl-Madsen.
11. *Collection Complète*, vol. 10, pp. 79–80.
12. For a recent discussion, see Wahnich 1997.
13. Gordon Craig (1978: 11–12, 18–19) tells us that 'a Prussian agent in Württemberg reported to Berlin [in 1866] that people were saying that the constitution of the [North German] Bund contained "only three articles: 1. pay, 2. be a soldier, 3. keep your mouth shut."'
14. *Stenographische Berichte über die Verhandlungen des Reichstages des Norddeutschen Bundes* [hereafter *Verhandlungen*], 2. Band, Anlagen, Berlin, 1867, p. 23.
15. For this series of decrees, see 'Verordnung, betreffend die Paßpflichtigkeit der aus Rußland kommenden Reisenden', 2 February 1879, in *Reichsgesetzblatt 1879*, p. 9; 'Verordnung, betreffend die Paßpflichtigkeit der aus Rußland kommenden Reisenden, 14 June 1879', *Reichsgesetzblatt 1879*, p. 155; 'Verordnung, betreffend die Paßpflichtigkeit der aus Rußland kommenden Reisenden', 29 December 1880, *Reichsgesetzblatt 1881*, p. 1; and 'Verordnung, betreffend die Paßpflichtigkeit der aus Rußland kommenden Reisenden', 30 June 1894, *Reichsgesetzblatt 1894*, p. 501.
16. On the anomalous stringency of passport requirements for entry into Russia during this period, see Bertelsmann 1914: Einleitung, and Brunialti 1915: 679.
17. Bertelsmann 1914: 18–19. In his survey of the international legal opinion available in his time (pp. 13–17), Bertelsmann was unable to muster any consensus for the view that states had an unequivocal right to bar foreigners from entry into their territory.
18. The quotation is from *La Grande Encyclopédie* (multiple volumes published around 1900), vol. 26, p. 57; see also Burguière and Revel 1989: 67; Brunialti 1915: 676; de Vattel 1863: 514 n. 1; d'Hartoy 1937: 69–71; and Plender 1988: 90 n.132.
19. Noiriel and Offerlé (1997: 79) note the 'precociousness' of France in this respect.
20. Preussische Verordnung of 1 December 1892, quoted in Bertelsmann 1914: 20–21.
21. See Noiriel and Offerlé 1997: 79–83. See also Noiriel 1991, esp. part III.
22. See the law no. 23 on emigration and the Royal Decree no. 36 on passports, both of 31 January 1901, in *Raccolta Ufficiale delle Leggi e dei Decreti del Regno d'Italia* [hereafter *Raccolta Ufficiale*], *1901*, vol. 1 (Roma: Stamperia Reale), pp. 50–78 and 218–239. On the uses of passports for the purpose of facilitating rather than constraining movement, see Lucassen 2001.

23. 4 & 5 Geo. 5, c. 12, 5th August 1914, *The Public and General Acts, 1914*, pp. 26–28. In a pattern that would recur in British history after World War II, the nearly simultaneous British Nationality and Status of Aliens Act, 1914 (7th August 1914, 4 & 5 Geo. 5 c. 17), further described as an 'Act to consolidate and amend the Enactments relating to British Nationality and the Status of Aliens', was motivated by the need to determine who exactly was an alien for purposes of alien restriction.

24. 'Verordnung, betreffend die vorübergehende Einführung der Paßpflicht', 31 July 1914, *Reichsgesetzblatt 1914*, pp. 264–5.

25. 'R. decreto del 6 agosto 1914, n. 803, che sospende la facoltà di emigrare ai militari del R. esercito e della R. Marina', *Raccolta Ufficiale, 1914*, vol. 3, pp. 2804–5.

26. 'R. decreto 2 maggio 1915, n. 635, concernente l'espatrio per ragioni di lavoro', *Raccolta Ufficiale, 1915*, vol. 2, pp. 1723–7. According to the 'Decreto Luogotenenziale 23 dicembre 1915, n. 1825, che proroga sino alla fine della guerra il termine di validita' stabilito nell'art. 12 del R. decreto 2 maggio 1915, n. 635, circa l'espatrio per ragioni di lavoro' (*Raccolta Ufficiale, 1915*, vol. 5, pp. 4623–4), the requirement that those going abroad to work had to present a labour contract before doing so was to be abolished with the end of the war.

27. 'Decreto-legge del 2 maggio 1915 [n. 634], concernente il soggiorno degli stranieri in Italia', *Raccolta Ufficiale, 1915*, vol. 2, pp. 1708–22.

28. 'Verordnung, über die Abänderung der Verordnung vom 21. Juni 1916, betreffend anderweite Regelung der Paßpflicht', 10 June 1919, *Reichsgesetzblatt, 1919*, pp. 516–7. Three weeks earlier, the German government had announced stiffened penalties for transgression of the passport laws and for various transgressions of proper procedure with respect to border controls. See 'Verordnung, betreffend Strafbestimmungen für Zuwiderhandlungen gegen die Paßvorschriften', 21 May 1919, *Reichsgesetzblatt, 1919*, pp. 470–1.

29. Aliens Order, 1920, March 25, 1920, *The Statutory Rules and Orders and Statutory Instruments Revised to December 31, 1948*, vol. II (London: His Majesty's Stationery Office, 1950), pp. 1–48.

30. See Zolberg 1997. The Chinese had been welcomed in previous years and many held American citizenship; identification documents were thus critical to their ability to establish that they had a right to enter the United States after the adoption of measures to exclude them after 1875.

31. See 'An Act to prevent in time of war departure from or entry into the United States contrary to the public safety', May 22, 1918, *U.S. Statutes at Large*, vol. 40, part I, p. 559; and Public Law #79, 'An Act To regulate further the entry of aliens into the United States', November 10, 1919, *U.S. Statutes at Large*, vol. 41, part I, p. 353.

# References

Bertelsmann, Werner, 1914, *Das Passwesen: Eine völkerrechtliche Studie*, Strassburg.

Brubaker, Rogers, 1992, *Citizenship and Nationhood in France and Germany*, Cambridge, MA.

Brunialti, Attilio, 1915, 'Passaporti', in *Enciclopedia Giuridica Italiana*, ed. Pasquale Stanislao Mancini, vol. 13, part I, Milano.

Burguière, André and Jacques Revel, eds, 1989, *Histoire de la France, vol. 1: L'Espace français*, Paris.

Caplan, Jane, 2001, '"This or That Particular Person": Protocols of Identification in 19th-Century Europe', in *Documenting Individual Identity: The Development of State Practices in the Modern World*, eds Jane Caplan and John Torpey, Princeton, pp. 49–66.

Craig, Gordon, 1978, Germany, 1866–1945, Oxford.

Dowty, Alan, 1987, *Closed Borders: The Contemporary Assault on Freedom of Movement*, New Haven.

Fussell, Paul, 1980, *Abroad: British Literary Traveling Between the Wars*, Oxford.

Geselle, Andrea, 2001, 'Domenica Saba Takes to the Road: The Origins and Development of a Modern Passport Regime in Austrian Lombardy and the Veneto', in *Documenting Individual Identity: The Development of State Practices in the Modern World*, eds Caplan and Torpey, Princeton, pp. 199–217.

Geselle, Andrea, forthcoming, 'Passaporti ed altri documenti di viaggio. Modalità e controllo del movimento in territorio veneto', in *Dopo la Serenissima: Società, Amministrazione e Cultura nell'Ottocento Veneto*, ed. M. Berengo, Venezia.

Greer, Donald, 1951, *The Incidence of Emigration During the French Revolution*, Cambridge, MA.

Grossi, Vincenzo, 1905, 'Emigrazione', in *Diritto Amministrativo Italiano*, ed. V.E. Orlando, Milano.

d'Hartoy, Maurice, 1937, *Histoire du passeport français*, Paris.

Herbert, Ulrich, 1990, *A History of Foreign Labor in Germany, 1880–1980: Seasonal Workers/Forced Laborers/Guest Workers*, translated by William Templer, Ann Arbor.

Higham, John, 1988 [1955], *Strangers in the Land: Patterns of American Nativism, 1860–1925*, 2nd edn New Brunswick.

Hobsbawm, E. J., 1975, *The Age of Capital, 1848–1875*, London.

Hobsbawm, E. J., 1990, *Nations and Nationalism Since 1780*, Cambridge.

Hufton, Olwen, 1974, *The Poor of Eighteenth-Century France, 1750–1789*, Oxford.

International Labour Office, 1928, *Migration Laws and Treaties, vol. 1: Emigration Laws and Regulations*, Geneva.

Lefebvre, Georges, 1964, *The French Revolution, vol. 2: From 1793 to 1799*, translated by John Hall Stewart and James Friguglietti, New York.

Lucassen, Leo, 1997, 'The Invention of the Alien: Immigration Controls in an Emerging Welfare State and the Implementation at the Local Level in the Netherlands (1918–1940)'. Paper presented at the annual meeting of the Social Science History Assocation, Washington, D. C., October 1997.

Lucassen, Leo, 2001, 'A Many-Headed Monster: The Evolution of the Passport System in the Netherlands and Germany in the Long Nineteenth Century', in *Documenting Individual Identity: The Development of State Practices in the Modern World*, eds Caplan and Torpey, Princeton, pp. 235–55.

Lüdtke, Alf, 1989, *Police and State in Prussia, 1815–1850*, translated by Pete Burges, Cambridge.

Mann, Michael, 1993, *The Sources of Social Power, vol. 2: The Rise of Classes and Nation-States, 1760–1914*, Cambridge.

Noiriel, Gérard, 1991, *La Tyrannie du national: Le droit d'asile en Europe, 1793–1993*, Paris.

Noiriel, Gérard, 1998, 'Surveiller les déplacements ou identifier les personnes?: Contribution à l'histoire du passeport en France de la I[ère] à la III[è] république', *Genèses: Sciences sociales et histoire* 30 (March): 77–100.

Noiriel, Gérard, and Michel Offerlé, 1997, 'Citizenship and Nationality in Nineteenth-Century France', in *European Integration in Social and Historical Perspective*, eds Jytte Klausen and Loise A. Tilly, New York.

Nordman, Daniel, 1996, 'Sauf-Conduits et Passeports', in *Dictionnaire de l'Ancien Régime*, ed. Lucien Bely, Paris: 1123–4.

Plender, Richard, 1988 [1972], *International Migration Law*, 2nd edn, Dordrecht.

Polanyi, Karl, 1944, *The Great Transformation: The Political and Economic Origins of Our Time*, Boston.

Reale, Egidio, 1930, *Le Régime des passeports et la société des nations*, Paris.

Schwartz, Robert, 1988, *Policing the Poor in Eighteenth-Century France*, Chapel Hill.

Sheehan, James J., 1989, *German History, 1770–1866*, Oxford.

Strikwerda, Carl, 1997, 'Reinterpreting the History of European Integration: Business, Labor, and Social Citizenship in Twentieth-Century Europe', in *European Integration in Social and Historical Perspective*, eds Jytte Klausen and Louise A. Tilly, New York.

Torpey, John, 1998, 'Coming and Going: On the State Monopolization of the Legitimate "Means of Movement"', *Sociological Theory* 16:3 (November): 239–259.

Torpey, John, 2000, *The Invention of the Passport: Surveillance, Citizenship, and the State*, Cambridge.

Traven, B., 1991 [1926], *The Death Ship: The Story of an American Sailor*, 2nd edn, Brooklyn.

de Vattel, Emmerich, 1863 [?], *Le Droit du Gens: ou Principes de la loi naturelle*, revised edition by P. Pradier-Fodéré, Paris.

Wahnich, Sophie, 1997, *L'impossible citoyen: L'étranger dans le discours de la Révolution française*, Paris.

Zeldin, Theodore, 1973, *France, 1848–1945, vol. 1: Ambition, Love and Politics*, Oxford.

Zolberg, Aristide, 1997, 'The Great Wall Against China: Responses to the First Immigration Crisis, 1885–1925' in *Migration, Migration History, History: Old Paradigms and New Perspectives*, eds Jan Lucassen and Leo Lucassen, New York, 291–315.

Zweig, Stefan, 1953, *The World of Yesterday*, London.

# Chapter 6

# 'Beggars appear everywhere!'
## *Changing Approaches to Migration Control in Mid-Nineteenth Century Munich*

*K.M.N. Carpenter*

In 1843, Munich's Police Direction suggested that the bourgeoisie post guard dogs and affix bells in their homes so that they could alert neighbours in cases of emergency. Middle-class residents were also advised to station one person at home constantly and to lock all doors. As far as police officials were concerned, these measures had become critical for preserving the city's 'public safety'. Authorities further noted that they hoped such defensive policies would encourage only 'hard-working men' to reside in Munich.[1]

This last remark is perhaps the most revealing part of the Police Direction's recommendation, for it indicates the city government's real motivation. Lower-class men hardly represented a significant threat to Munich's middle classes and their property; they were, however, becoming an uncontrollable segment of the population. Since 1810, the number of residents had more than doubled to '100,000 souls'.[2] By the middle of the nineteenth century, journeymen comprised roughly half the adult male population. Only 19 percent of these men had been born in Munich. The rest were considered 'foreign', even though the majority came from the surrounding Bavarian countryside. (By the 1840s, 69 percent of journeymen listed their birthplaces as elsewhere in Bavaria, while only 12 percent came from outside the country entirely.[3]) So rapid was the influx of migrant workers into the Bavarian capital that the Police Director commented: 'The Munich of 1800...no longer exists'.[4]

Concern with migrant workers who might swell the ranks of the urban poor was nothing new in Bavaria. As early as the late 1700s, journeymen wandered regularly to find sustaining employment. By the beginning of the nineteenth century, *Landflucht* ('fleeing the countryside') for work in larger towns and cities had become common. Although scholars have generally believed that German men did not move frequently until the middle of the century, recent studies on German migration patterns suggest that high mobility rates existed well before the onset of industrialisation (Jackson 1997).

As early as 1818, Munich citizens already complained about the growing numbers of unemployed journeymen, who flocked to the nation's capital from nearby towns. Officials observed that 'beggars appear everywhere', and middle-class residents claimed it was 'almost impossible' to fend off unemployed journeymen and day labourers asking for money (Doege 1990: 112, 122). Despite this disdain for migrant workers, they were nonetheless tolerated for most of the first half of the nineteenth century. While laws against vagrancy had a long history in Bavaria, their strict enforcement was widely disregarded. Residents and authorities may have considered the journeymen and day labourers who accounted for the majority of vagrants and beggars as bothersome, but neither actually regarded these men as criminals.

This tolerance was in part due to Bavaria's 'tradition of almsgiving'. The predominantly Catholic population viewed beggars charitably, and giving them money functioned as an active demonstration of their faith (Baumann 1983: 151–79). As late as the 1840s, Munich's Police Director had difficulty dissuading residents from 'opening their doors' to 'every vagabond' (Hummel 1987: 295). Moreover, the artisan culture involved wandering in search of work, lodging, and food, and journeymen often relied on handouts from strangers for their survival during times of unemployment. For these reasons, vagrancy and begging carried few stigmas, and migrant workers wandered with few, if any, legal repercussions (Küther 1983: 31).

Even reforms during the 1820s did not discourage men from leaving their rural Bavarian hometowns for Munich. As the state brought guilds under its control, the government sought to monitor all aspects of artisans' lives, including residency, marriage, and employment (Birnbaum 1984: 144). To avoid arrest for vagrancy, authorities demanded that journeymen produce identification and employment documentation. The latter was usually the 'worker book', which detailed the places and dates of previous positions. Migrant workers also needed to apply for *Wanderschaft* licenses, which allowed them to wander for specified time periods. After expiration, journeymen were required to return to their hometowns before embarking on their next *Wanderschaft* (Küther 1983: 41). Despite these tighter regulations, many men disregarded restrictions limiting their mobility and worked in the black market. For the most part, Munich's authorities ignored and even encouraged this practice.

This encouragement, however, did not last. By the late 1830s, city and state officials began viewing unemployed journeymen as representing an urgent social problem (Reulecke 1990: 71f). In an address to the Bavarian *Landtag*, Interior Minister Öttingen-Wallerstein warned representatives about the 'growing demoralization' among migrant workers, which placed Bavaria's 'peace and order' at risk (Zorn 1962: 121). Conservatives agreed, noting that the number of journeymen arriving from the surrounding countryside 'seemed to grow larger and more threatening every day' (Zorn 1962: 136). This perception persisted into the 1840s when the king himself noted that workers who had not been born in Munich represented a particular threat to the city's public order.[5] By this time, 'nothing' appeared 'more dangerous to officials' than the 'raw classes' of journeymen, who had 'no right to residency' in the Bavarian capital.[6]

This growing intolerance toward unemployed men not originally from Munich represented a policy shift toward migrant workers. What accounted for this change among Bavarian officials and how they attempted to control migrating artisans serves as a useful case study for illustrating how German authorities in general sought to bring greater social control over itinerant populations. More specifically, the tactics police officials employed reveal how this issue shaped urban governance in mid-nineteenth century Munich.

When Elector Maximilian Joseph became King Maximilian Joseph I on 1 January 1806, he ceremoniously cut his hair short to symbolise Bavaria's transformation from a small dukedom into a modern country (Schlaich 1965: 463). Traditional *Altbayern* ceased to exist, and Munich became the fast growing capital of the *Königreich Bayern*.

This change in Munich's status had wide-ranging effects on the city's construction trades that lasted for four decades. The *Haupt- und Residenzstadt* needed buildings, ranging from the *Landtag* to police headquarters, to accommodate the rapidly expanding bureaucracy and administration (Birnbaum 1984: 22, 32). When Bavaria's second king, Ludwig I, ascended the throne in 1825, he was determined to give his kingdom an historical soul. To this end, he transformed the capital's streets and public squares, such as the Ludwigsstrasse and the Königsplatz, into his personal showplaces. Munich's cityscape changed so dramatically that Ludwig's subjects derisively referred to him as a *Baukönig* ('building monarch').

Criticism aside, the bourgeoisie quickly followed the king's lead. Entrepreneurs opened new businesses, and established businessmen expanded theirs. Taverns, restaurants, and shops proliferated. In 1801, Munich had only 1,790 buildings. In 1824, this number had risen to 2,780. By the 1840s, the city boasted almost 3,500 buildings (Birnbaum 1984: 86f.).

This construction boom attracted thousands of artisans throughout Bavaria, with smaller numbers of journeymen also arriving from other parts of Germany, Switzerland, and Austria. The plenitude of available work often influenced the majority to make Munich their permanent base (Puschner 1985: 384f.). Reasons for relocating to the capital were numerous. Changes in Bavaria's military compulsion coupled with laws allowing for greater freedom of movement throughout the countryside encouraged journeymen by the scores to leave their Bavarian hometowns (Birnbaum 1984: 86f.) These men frequently believed that construction work was easier to find in Munich, and they perceived the standard of living as higher (Blessing 1971: 772). The *Residenzstadt* was also close to towns where construction work was similarly booming.[7]

Travelling to other locations, however, was often unnecessary. During the 1820s and 1830s, construction grew more rapidly than any other Munich trade. Every summer, between four and six thousand journeymen arrived from nearby towns such as Augsburg and Ingolstadt seeking employment on public construction sites as carpenters, masons, and joiners (Zwehl 1985: 87). These positions were so attractive that by the 1830s, every second artisan in Munich worked in the construction trade (Birnbaum 1984: 86f.).

Initially, the government encouraged this influx. State and city officials needed plentiful, cheap labour for building projects, and they frequently ignored their own policies regulating migration. A hiring dispute in 1840 illustrates how willing authorities were to overlook ordinances. Despite laws requiring journeymen to have set employment before arriving in Munich, city officials circumvented construction guilds and hired over one thousand journeymen from neighbouring towns for work on administrative buildings. Guild masters protested to the Interior Ministry that these men arrived without legal paperwork and remained free from guild supervision and restrictions. Although the magistrate assured that this contracting had occurred only as 'an exception', masters claimed that such hiring practices were not unusual (Birnbaum 1984: 168). Even masters were not innocent of hiring journeymen 'under the table'. Beginning in the 1830s, masters often employed many journeymen simultaneously or engaged workers for limited piecework at low wages (Birnbaum 1984: 60).

By the middle of the 1840s, the city's need for workers had contributed to a *Gesellenstau* ('abundance of journeymen'), which coincided with the decline of extensive building projects (Birnbaum 1984: 58). Munich's most intensive period of expansion was nearing completion, and no new large-scale projects were planned. Authorities no longer needed so many journeymen in the capital, but decreasing construction did little to discourage men from migrating from the Bavarian countryside. Indeed, journeymen continued to arrive in greater numbers, and Munich residents complained about the high numbers of migrant construction workers, who refused to leave after completing their work (Küther1983: 50).

The growing population of migrant workers struck officials as particularly threatening, because rising unemployment meant growing poverty (Matz 1980: 53). During the early 1840s, wages in the building industry decreased dramatically just as Munich's cost of living began to rise.[8] Poor harvests coupled with grain speculation led to dramatic increases in staple food prices.[9] As in the rest of Germany, Bavaria had entered the 'hungry forties', and Munich's *Bürgermeister* feared that many unemployed journeymen would 'go without bread'.[10]

Ironically, the monarchy's push to modernise Bavaria exacerbated lower-class poverty. The 1825 Freedom of Trade Law transferred guild regulation to the state, which controlled training, production, and membership. New guidelines decreased aid available to journeymen by limiting the number of recipients. Only the 'regularly employed' and those who paid monthly membership dues were eligible for unemployment assistance. Decreasing daily wages made it impossible for most artisans to afford these dues (Birnbaum 1984: 168).

Not surprisingly, unrest among journeymen had become widespread by the early 1840s. In 1843, minor skirmishes over food prices occurred in several lower-class establishments.[11] While authorities preferred to dismiss the incident as a drunken brawl, the following year they had no choice but to take the discontent among journeymen seriously. On 1 May 1844, a three-day food riot occurred when men protested against the government-sanctioned increase in the beer price and destroyed thirty-three breweries throughout the city.[12]

Even though the participants had acted out of hunger, the Interior Ministry labelled 'the practised rioting' as 'the worst type', because protesters had exhibited 'no respect for the law and for government'.[13] Most alarmingly, journeymen employed in the construction industry constituted the bulk of protesters. Almost 70 percent of these men had not been born in Munich, with 63 percent coming from small towns in Bavaria and the rest citing their birthplaces as elsewhere in Germany, Austria, or Switzerland.[14] Since city residents were traditionally 'obedient and law-abiding', authorities were convinced that unemployed journeymen both 'in and outside Munich' had attempted to establish their own 'public authority'.[15] Bringing migrant workers under control therefore seemed the only means for re-establishing official order.[16] How officials proceeded to do this represented a change in how they treated migrants living in the Bavarian capital.

Following the riots, it became clear that 'the officers and servants of the Royal Police Direction were not even *slightly* prepared for this critical moment'.[17] The Interior Minister reluctantly conceded that Munich's police forces were too weak to handle the larger population.[18] Such observations heightened official anxieties about the rising legions of urban poor. Although the number of residents had grown considerably since 1800, the police force had not. Established in 1812, the Gendarme Corps Commando was under the Police Direction, whose primary responsibility was to protect Munich's 'peace, order, and safety' (Wirsing 1992: 88). It also provided community services such as registering newcomers and monitoring trade, with the military intervening in cases of civil unrest (Bauschinger 1968: 47). For this reason, the Police Direction had not been significantly augmented since its creation. In the middle of the 1840s, it still employed only 115 men.[19]

Despite unrest, state and city budgets could not provide sufficiently for increasing the police force, and officials continued to rely on the military during crises.[20] This contingency alone, however, was not enough to re-establish government authority. Although the police had previously been lax about enforcing *Fremden-Controlle* ('foreigner controls'), officials now planned to do so with greater rigidity and regularity (Bauschinger 1968: 62).

The Police Direction's authority included regulating passports and residence permits, stationing watches at city entry points, and arresting and removing vagrants and beggars who could not cite Munich as their birthplace from the city (Wirsing 1992: 66f.). The central government therefore ordered the police to focus on these measures for removing 'all unemployed foreign workers' from the capital as quickly as possible.[21] Officials hoped this would 'clean the city' of all 'unemployed [migrant] workers'.[22]

The Police Director accordingly informed gendarmes responsible for registering migrant workers that it had become 'more than necessary' to conduct 'thorough research' into journeymen's backgrounds before granting residence permits. New arrivals were no longer allowed to establish even temporary residency unless they could first prove that they had steady and sufficient incomes.[23] Police authorities also increased efforts to monitor the wandering licenses of 'travelling artisans, actors, and wandering foreigners', who were to adhere strictly to their routes (Doege 1990: 15).

The government recognised that migrating workers would not always register with the authorities, and the Police Direction deployed additional patrols targeting vagrant workers and illegal residents. Gendarmes patrolled Munich's lower-class sections with greater frequency, using the pretext that too many journeymen were 'on the streets' until all hours of the night. Police arrested men who were out after breweries and taverns closed for the evening and brought them to police headquarters for background checks.[24] Vagrants who had not been born in Munich and illegal residents were expelled immediately (Doege 1990: 115).

During the 1840s, gendarmes also escorted vagrant workers to the city's employment offices where the magistrate ordered them either to find immediate work or report at railroad construction sites outside Munich.[25] Unemployed workers arrested for begging were transported back to their Bavarian hometowns or countries of origin without delay (Doege 1990: 115). The Police Direction justified these actions, noting that vagrant workers 'frequently practise[d] petty theft' (Zwehl 1985: 121).

These measures met with limited success. In four years, vagrancy arrests increased 20 percent, and those for 'failing to register' rose by an astonishing 53 percent. Not surprisingly, journeymen, the majority of whom came from nearby towns, accounted for most of the arrests. Despite such increases, these statistics do not indicate that the number of migrant workers in Munich substantially decreased. The Police Direction still employed too few gendarmes to have any real impact on illegal migration. Unemployed journeymen maintained low profiles by avoiding heavily patrolled areas. Moreover, many vagrants and illegal residents returned to Munich only a short time after being expelled, an action easily taken given the proximity of their hometowns to the Bavarian capital.[26]

The financial expenses involved in removing illegal residents proved even more problematic. Expelling migrants entailed higher transport costs than either the state or city government was willing to bear (Hummel 1987: 298). For all its efforts, Munich's police authorities lacked the ability, both in terms of gendarme numbers and finances, to enact a stricter migration policy. Even the Police Director himself confessed that he lacked the 'slightest [financial] means' to implement an 'effective *Fremden-Controlle*' with respect to migrant workers.[27]

Both the Interior Ministry and the Police Direction therefore agreed that it had become necessary to restructure policing to handle the city's new social order (Hardtwig 1990: 61f.). This re-organisation corresponded with how other nineteenth-century German states modernised their police authorities to represent the 'modern' incarnation of the state.[28] In southern Germany in particular 'the suspicion of mobile people resulted in policies of intensive *Überwachung* ['surveillance'] and *Beobachtung* ['obser-vation']'. Since lower-class migrants posed potential threats to government authority, they became frequent targets of concen-trated surveillance (Wirsing 1992: 118–20).

This focus on observing the lower classes was not limited to Germany. Recent studies have shown that throughout Europe, 'the state was becoming more intrusive into the lives of its citi-zens during the nineteenth century'.(Cohen 1998: xi). 'Notions of social control' began 'to dominate the thinking of police reform-ers', who sought to 'extend control over the dangerous classes' (Taylor 1997: 3). This meant that 'the people, and particularly the working classes, were being subjected to an unprecedented degree of scrutiny and control over a wide range of activities' (Taylor 1997: 90). By the middle of the nineteenth century, the police worked to maintain 'a constant, unceasing pressure of surveillance upon all facets of life in working-class communities' (Storch quoted in Taylor 1997: 90).

Munich was no exception with regard to this development. Despite protests from the Finance Ministry, high-ranking offi-cials believed that monitoring journeymen's 'public and private lives' was the only means the government possessed for estab-lishing 'the strictest controls' over migrant workers.[29] In 1845, the Interior Ministry thus granted the police authorities 'excep-tional funding' to monitor journeymen.[30] This financial support enabled 'police officers or inspectors to carry out a thorough research and observation service'.[31] A royal proclamation re-emphasised that the king himself considered this surveillance to be critically important.[32]

By the second half of the 1840s, city and state officials therefore began 'casting a deep look' at migrant workers living in Munich.[33] Gendarmes were ordered to be 'especially watchful' in their revised roles as information gatherers, and they observed 'those who did not have Munich as their hometown' both during employment and recreation.[34] For example, officers placed shifts at Munich's largest construction sites under surveillance, hoping that an official presence would deter inappropriate behaviour among journeymen.[35] The government also instructed masters to limit journeymen's free time and 'to hire only responsible men'.[36] Masters would be held liable for their journeymen's conduct, and the threat of heavy fines encouraged masters to report suspicious behaviour immediately.[37]

Lower-class centres of sociability, however, became the most important sites for surveillance. In Bavaria, breweries and taverns provided lower-class men with 'consumption, communication, and recreation', and journeymen frequented these places almost exclusively during their free time (Blessing 1981: 109f.; Roberts 1981: 81f.; Sandgruber 1986: 21). Here, they vented frustrations and engaged in political discussions. Free from workplace constrictions, men felt they could complain about their poor living and working conditions, high food prices, and the lifestyles of the nobility with relative impunity (Wiegelmann 1976: 14).

For this reason, 'police spies' targeted breweries and taverns for 'the closer monitoring' of the 'journeymen class'.[38] Parisian police authorities had been using such surveillance techniques in lower-class gathering places since the late eighteenth century. Spies disguised themselves as customers and eavesdropped on conversations, methods that proved more successful for maintaining control over these public places than did 'overt, official repression' (Haine 1996: 24). In Munich, this strategy was carried out in a similar manner. Undercover officers blended with clientele in lower-class drinking establishments and monitored conversations.[39] Regular interrogations of barkeepers and beer maids provided additional information that supplemented official gendarme reports.[40]

Authorities learned how well surveillance techniques worked within two years. In 1846 'undercover means' enabled the police to learn that journeymen were complaining with greater frequency about their low wages and rising unemployment.[41]

When migrant plasterers and carpenters threatened to repeat the 1844 riots, the Police Direction placed 'this class in particular under increased observation'.[42] Additional surveillance confirmed that another food riot was to take place that spring, and the Interior Minister co-ordinated police and military forces to deter journeymen. Using surveillance as a means of controlling the migrant population had therefore allowed police authorities to prevent civil disorder even before it had begun (Carpenter 1998: 170–235).

The 1840s proved to be a turning point for how Bavarian officials handled migrants to Munich. Until this decade, the Police Direction was somewhat lax in enforcing migration controls, and journeymen had been arriving in the Bavarian capital at high rates since the beginning of the century. To a large degree, state and city authorities condoned this practice, because they needed plentiful and cheap labour for work on the city's construction sites.

By the late 1830s, the government began viewing the legions of migrant workers as a threat to Munich's peace and order. During the 1840s, civil unrest by rioters who had not been born in Munich seemed to confirm these fears. The migrant population needed to be brought under control, and authorities responded by attempting to enforce existing migration laws with greater intensity. Unfortunately for authorities, the more rigorous application of these policies proved both ineffective and too expensive. The numbers of journeymen relocating to Munich did not decline appreciably, and the costs for clearing the city of vagrants, beggars, and illegal residents were higher than officials had anticipated.

Rethinking traditional approaches to migration controls had thus become necessary if officials hoped to re-establish their authority. The Interior Minister and Police Director worked together and determined that restructuring police duties would enable them to overcome current limitations. Surveillance represented the most significant component of this reorganisation by allowing officials to observe migrant workers in environments to which the former ordinarily had little access.

Authorities recognised that intense observation would not necessarily reduce the number of migrant workers residing in Munich. They nevertheless hoped that this measure would better address the city's changing social and economic order. Beginning in the mid 1840s, gendarmes targeted journeymen for 'precise surveillance'. Once it became clear how effective observing 'this class of resident' had become, the Police Direction adopted it as a regular measure for managing a population that had become difficult to control.[43]

Even the Revolution of 1848 did not vitiate the efficacy of surveillance. Although authorities believed that they had brought the lower classes under control, they were unprepared for how the bourgeoisie reacted to Lola Montez, the king's new mistress. A 'Spanish dancer', Montez infuriated the nobility by being made a countess, and she mocked the middle classes at every opportunity. By early 1848, the king's relationship with this woman went beyond criticism and triggered demonstrations throughout the capital. These protests influenced Ludwig I to abdicate in favour of his son Maximilian (Seymour 1995: 222f.).

This transfer of power did not mean the end of unrest in Munich. Members of the middle classes and university students followed revolutionary leads in Berlin and Vienna and staged protests in front of city hall. Maximilian II relied on surveillance to learn what the most moderate demands of the middle classes were, and he responded by granting minor concessions. To a large degree, the new king kept the revolution in check by adapting the security measures that his father had taken just a few years earlier against migrant workers (Reiter 1983: 201–5).

Although the lower classes had not played a significant role in the revolution, Maximilian continued a strict campaign against the unemployed, beggars, and vagrants by calling for the 'rigid deployment of the *Fremdenpolizei*'. He considered this policy crucial for maintaining civil discipline, and the 'suspicious surveillance of the poor and outsiders' became a significant component of his domestic policy (Krauss 1997: 320).

By the end of the 1840s, the desire to curb the 'mean-spirited class of journeymen' had forced Munich's authorities to formulate a new tactic for handling migrant workers.[44] Surveillance represented an important facet of the state's control, with undercover gendarmes providing officials with crucial intelligence concerning the behaviour of migrants. Surveying 'this class of resident' ultimately proved more effective than traditional means for re-establishing what officials perceived as social and political order in the Bavarian capital.

## Notes

1. Hauptstaatsarchiv München. Ministerium des Innern (henceforth: Minn) 46233. Royal Proclamation. Munich, 27 October 1843.
2. Minn 46128. Police Direction to King Ludwig I. Munich, 23 May 1844. By contrast, the Bavarian population had grown only twenty-two percent during the same period. Hummel 1987: 261.

3. Ibid., Praesidium to Ludwig . Government Statistics. Munich, 21 January 1845.
4. Ibid., Police Direction to Ludwig. Munich, 23 May 1844.
5. Minn 46233. Royal Proclamation. Munich, 27 October 1843.
6. Minn 46128. Memo to Interior Ministry. Munich, 6 November 1845.
7. Minn 46128. Police Direction to Ludwig. Munich, 10 June 1844.
8. Journeymen earned daily wages in Kreuzer. In 1840, public construction workers earned forty-eight Kreuzer. In 1844, this wage decreased to between forty-four and forty-two Kreuzer. By 1845, unskilled journeymen earned as little as thirty Kreuzer per day. See Schmeller 1956: 370; Minn 46128. Report Concerning Decrease in Public Building, 1844. Munich, 29 September 1844; Regierungsakt (henceforth: RA) 15830. Police Direction to Praesidium. Munich, 18 April 1846.
9. Minn 46128. Police Direction to Interior Ministry. Munich, 14 June 1844; *Königlicher Polizey-Anzeiger von München*. Food Price Summary, 1840–1843.
10. For a discussion of the "hungry forties," see Sperber 1994; Hummel 1987: 289.
11. *Münchner Tagblatt*. Munich, 7 May 1843.
12. For a thorough discussion, see Carpenter 1998.
13. Minn 46128. Interior Minister to Ludwig. Munich, 8 May 1844.
14. RA 15894. Arrest Records. May 1–3, 1844.
15. Minn 46128. Praesidium to Police Direction. Munich, 22 October 1844; Praesidium to Ludwig. Munich, 30 May 1844.
16. Ibid., Police Direction to Interior Ministry. Munich, 10 June 1844.
17. Minn 46128. Interior Ministry Memo. Munich, Circa June 1844.
18. Ibid., Interior Minister to Ludwig. Munich, 8 May 1844.
19. Minn 46128. Memo to Gendarme Corps Commando. Munich, 6 May 1844. See also Döllinger 1939.
20. RA 15831. Memo to Munich authorities. Munich, 7 March 1846.
21. Minn 46128. Praesidium to Police Direction. Munich, 22 October 1844.
22. RA 15894. Report to Interior Ministry. Munich, 30 May 1844.
23. RA 15921. Police Direction to Praesidium. Munich, 4 December 1845; RA 15830. Interior Ministry to Police Direction and Praesidum. Munich, 24 April 1846.
24. RA 15921. Police Direction to Praesidium. Munich, 18 May 1845.
25. RA 15921. Police Direction to Praesidium. Munich, 4 December 1845.
26. RA 15894. Landgericht Au to Praesidium. Au, 11 May 1844.
27. Minn 46128. Police Direction to Interior Minister. Munich, 6 November 1845.
28. Siemann 1983: 69. For discussions on the restructuring of European police forces during the nineteenth century, see: Taylor 1997; Cohen 1998; Crossman 1996.
29. RA 15921. Police Direction to Praesidium. Munich, 14 October 1844.
30. Minn 46128. Police Direction Report. Munich, 18 April 1845.
31. Ibid., Police Direction to Interior Minister. Munich, 6 November 1845.
32. Ibid., Royal Proclamation. April 1845.
33. Ibid., Interior Minister to Ludwig. Munich, 6 November 1845.
34. Ibid., Police Direction to Interior Minister. Munich, 6 November 1845; RA 15921. Government Memo. 18 May 1845.
35. RA 15830. Interior Ministry to Police Direction and Praesidium. Munich, 24 April 1846.
36. Minn 46128. Royal Proclamation. April 1845.

37.  Ibid., Praesidum to Police Direction. Munich, 22 October 1844. The Police Direction observed that this policy would be difficult to implement, since 'masters no longer [had] any moral influence over journeymen'. These men no longer 'shared the same table', and  masters no longer had the 'opportunity to observe their journeymen's behavior'. Ibid., Police Direction Report. Munich, 24 February 1846.
38.  RA 15921. Police Direction Report. Munich, 15 March 1845.
39.  See, for example, RA 21921/1. Gendarme Report. Munich, 6 July 1844.
40.  Minn 46128. Praesidum Memo. Munich, 18 March 1845.
41.  RA 15831. Gendarme Company Commando to Praesidium. Munich, 7 February 1846.
42.  Ibid., Gendarme report. Munich, 11 February 1846; Police Direction Report. Munich, 24 February 1846.
43.  Minn 46128. Interior Minister to Ludwig. Munich, 5 May 1846; Police Direction Report. Munich, 18 April 1845.
44.  RA 15831. Gendarme Report. Munich, 12 February 1846.

# References

Baumann, Angela, 1983, ‚Armut muß verächtlich bleiben', in *Kultur der einfachen Leute*, ed. R. van Dülmen, Munich.
Bauschinger, G., 1968, *Das Verhältnis von städt. Selbstverwaltung und königl. Polizei in München im 19. Jahrhundert*, Dissertation, Munich.
Birnbaum, Michael, 1984, *Das Münchner Handwerk im 19. Jahrhundert (1799–1868)*, Munich.
Blessing, Werner K., 1981, 'Konsumentenprotest und Arbeitskampf: Vom Bierkrawall zum Bierboycott', in *Streik*, eds K. Tenfelde and H. Volkmann, Munich.
Blessing, Werner K., 1971, 'Zur Analyse politischer Mentalität und Ideologie der Unterschichten im 19. Jahrhundert', *Zeitschrift für Bayerische Landesgeschichte*, 34.
Carpenter, Kim N., 1998, *"Sechs Kreuzer sind genug für ein Bier!" The Munich Beer Riot of 1844: Social Protest and Public Disorder in Mid 19th-Century Bavaria*. Dissertation. Georgetown University.
Cohen, William B., 1998, *Urban Government and the Rise of the French City: Five Municipalities in the Nineteenth Century*, New York.
Crossman, Virginia, 1996, *Politics, Law and Order in Nineteenth-Century Ireland*. New York.
Doege, Michael, 1990, *Armut in Preußen und Bayern, 1770–1840*. Munich.
Döllinger, G., 1939, *Sammlung der im Gebiete der inneren Staats-Verwaltung des Königreichs Bayern bestehenden Verordnungen*, Munich.
Haine, W. Scott, 1996, *The World of the Paris Café: Sociability among the French Working Class, 1789–1914*, Maryland.
Hardtwig, Wolfgang, 1990, 'Soziale Räume und politische Herrschaft. Leistungsverwaltung, Stadterweiterung und Architektur in München 1870 bis 1914', in *Soziale Räume in der Urbanisierung. Studien zur Geschichte Münchens im Vergleich 1850 bis 1933*, eds Wolfgang Hardtwig and Klaus Tenfelde, Munich.
Hummel, Karl-Joseph, 1987, *München in der Revolution von 1848/49*, Göttingen.
Jackson, James H., 1997, *Migration and Urbanization in the Ruhr Valley, 1821–1914*, Atlantic Highlands.
Krauss, Marita, 1997 *Herrschaftspraxis in Bayern und Preussen im 19. Jahrhundert. Ein historischer Vergleich*, Frankfurt.

Küther, Carsten, 1983, *Menschen auf der Straße. Vagierende Unterschichten in Bayern, Franken und Schwaben, 1750–1800*, Göttingen.

Matz, Klaus-Jürgen, 1980, *Pauperismus und Bevölkerung. Die gesetzlichen Ehebeschränkungen in den süddeutschen Staaten im 19. Jahrhundert*, Stuttgart.

Puschner, Uwe, 1985, 'Lohn und Lebensstandard. Arbeiter-und Handwerker-löhne in München und Augsburg in vor-und frühindustrieller Zeit', in *Aufbruch ins Industriezeitalter, vol. 2, Aufsätze zur Wirtschafts-und Sozialgeschichte Bayerns, 1750–1850*, ed. Rainer A. Müller, Munich.

Reiter, Hermann, 1983, *Die Revolution von 1848/49 in Altbayern*, Munich.

Reulecke, Jürgen, 1990, 'Die Armenfürsorge als Teil der Kommunalen Leistungsverwaltung und Daseinsvorsorge im 19. Jahrhundert', in *Kommunale Leistungsverwaltung und Stadtentwicklung vom Vormärz bis zur Weimarer Republik*, ed. Hans Heinrich Blotevogel, Cologne.

Roberts, James S., 1981, 'Drink and Working-Class Living Standards in Late 19th-Century Germany', in *Arbeiterexistenz im 19. Jahrhundert*, eds Werner Conze and U. Engelhardt, Stuttgart.

Sandgruber, Roman, 1986, *Bittersüße Genüsse. Kulturgeschichte der Genußmittel*. Vienna.

Schlaich, Heinz W., 1965, 'Der bayerische Staatsrat. Beiträge zu seiner Entwicklung von 1808/09 bis 1918', *Zeitschrift für Bayerische Landesgeschichte*, 28.

Schmeller, Johann Andreas, 1956, *Tagebücher, Vol. II: 1801–1852*, Munich.

Seymour, Bruce, 1995, *Lola Montez: A Life*, New Haven.

Siemann, Wolfram, 1983, 'Polizei in Deutschland im 19. Jahrhundert', in *Literatur und Kriminalität. Die gesellschaftliche Erfahrung von Verbrechen und Strafverfolgung als Gegenstand des Erzählens. Deutschland, England und Frankreich, 1850–80*, ed. J. Schönert, Tübingen.

Sperber, Jonathan, 1994, *The European Revolutions, 1848–1851*, Cambridge.

Storch, R.D., 1975, 'The Plague of Blue Locusts: Police Reform and Popular Resistance in Northern England, 1840–1857', *International Review of Social History*, 20.

Taylor, David, 1997, *The New Police: Crime, Conflict and Control in Nineteenth-Century England*, Manchester.

Wiegelmann, Günter, 1976, 'Tendenzen kulturellen Wandels in der Volksernährung des 19. Jahrhunderts', in *Ernährung und Ernährungslehre im 19. Jahrhundert*, ed. Edith Heishkel-Artelt, Göttingen.

Wirsing, Bernd, 1992, '"Gleichsam mit Soldatenstrenge:" Neue Polizei in süddeutschen Städten. Zu Polizeiverhalten und Bürger-Widersetzlichkeit im Vormärz', in *"Sicherheit und Wohlfahrt:" Polizei, Gesellschaft und Herrschaft im 19 und 20. Jahrhundert*, ed. Alf Lüdtke, Frankfurt.

Zorn, Wolfgang, 1962, 'Gesellschaft und Staat im Bayern des Vormärz', in *Staat und Gesellschaft im deutschen Vormärz, 1815–1848*, ed. Werner Conze, Stuttgart.

Zwehl, Konrad von, 1985, *Aufbruch ins Industriezeitalter, vol 3, Quellen zur Wirtschafts-und Sozialgeschichte Bayerns vom ausgehenden 18. Jahrhundert bis zur Mitte des 19. Jahrhunderts*, Munich.

# Chapter 7

# Qualitative Migration Controls in the Antebellum United States

*Gerald L. Neuman*

It is well known that the United States imposed no *quantitative* limitations on immigration until the 1920s. It is too often forgotten that the federal government and many of the states sought to impose a variety of *qualitative* controls on migration, even before 1875, the year from which federal immigration law is conventionally dated. These laws emerged from a fragmented policymaking structure, including the laws of the several states, congressional legislation, and international treaties. In some instances, federal law supported state policies; in other instances they may have conflicted. Substantively, the migration controls of the antebellum period (i.e., preceding the Civil War of 1861–1865) may be grouped under five general headings: regulation of the movement of alien criminals; regulation of movement of the poor; regulation connected with labour regimes, including slavery; quarantine; and regulation of the movement of free blacks.

Implementation of these policies was also institutionally complex. State laws were enforced, with varying degrees of efficiency, by state executive officials, sometimes with the assistance of state courts. Federal laws authorized enforcement by federal officials and federal courts, and sometimes by state courts as well. Federal officials also cooperated in the enforcement of some state laws, including diplomatic intervention with foreign governments that supported emigration inconsistent with state policies.

The intertwining of federal and state migration policies was also visible in the constitutional law background. The antebellum period witnessed recurrent legal and political disputes over the scope of the federal commerce power and the complementary or overlapping scope of the state police power in the field of migration. In the late nineteenth century, after the vindication of the Union and the abolition of slavery, these disputes were resolved in favor of federal power, and the actual exercise of that power by Congress led to the extinction of state immigration law. In the antebellum period, greater doubts were expressed about federal power, and judicial opinions appeared to validate the exercise of the state police power for the purpose of protecting the people of the state against perceived harms from undesirable immigrants, at least within categories sanctioned by tradition.[1]

## A. Migration of Criminals

### 1. Exclusion of Convicts

State statutory policies limiting the migration of persons convicted of crime arose from the British practice of transporting convicts to the colonies. Once the United States achieved independence, Great Britain could no longer openly require it to receive convicts, but the risk remained that Britain and other European nations would deport their criminals to the United States disguised as ordinary immigrants. The Congress of the Confederation (the predecessor of the Congress created by the U.S. Constitution of 1787) adopted a resolution in September 1788, recommending that the states 'pass laws for preventing the transportation of convicted malefactors from foreign countries into the United States'.[2] Within a year, Connecticut, Massachusetts, Pennsylvania, South Carolina, and Virginia enacted such legislation; Georgia had already done so in 1787. After the adoption of the Constitution, other states enacted similar legislation.

Despite all this legislative activity, incidents continued to occur in which foreign governments commuted the sentences of prisoners on condition of their emigration, and facilitated their passage to the United States (Jones 1992: 94, 120; Moltmann 1976). Although opposition to such practices was a rather uncontroversial aspect of antebellum proposals for immigration restriction, the general hesitancy of Congress to regulate immigration prevented the enactment of federal legislation on the subject before the Civil War. The federal executive branch, however, sometimes cooperated in the implementation of state policies opposing this practice. U.S. consuls transmitted information that came to their attention about foreign governments' policies and plans, and the United States lodged diplomatic protests against such policies. Indeed, Günter Moltmann's study of German-American interactions over this issue reached the conclusion that the German states that engaged in these practices halted them because they endangered good commercial relations with the United States (Moltmann 1976: 188–9).

In the course of collecting information from its diplomats concerning the policies of foreign governments, the federal government received valuable advice from its consul in Leipzig. The consul was Friedrich List, the German political economist, who had emigrated to the United States as a political exile from Würtemberg in 1825, and then returned to Germany as a naturalized U.S. citizen in 1832 (Focke 1976: 74–7). List devoted much attention in the course of his career to the emigration from the German states, its costs and benefits and the manner in which government policies could influence it (Focke 1976; Moltmann 1978: 33–43). List proposed that persons intending to emigrate to the United States be required to obtain an official testimonial regarding their criminal records, which would be subject to certification by the U.S. consul in the seaport; carriers transporting passengers without such testimonials would be subject to substantial fines.[3] This recommendation reflected existing visa regimes in some continental countries (see Fahrmeir 2000: 109, 133f.), and prefigures the modern U.S. visa process, adopted after the federal government had taken over responsibility for immigration control from the states.

Under antebellum conditions, List's proposal would have required a greater degree of systematic coordination than U.S. federalism was able to provide. For example, it would have required specification of the type of criminal record that should bar migration; List's suggested standard was 'that they have not been punished for a crime (political punishments excepted) for the last three years [and] that they have not been in a jail or workhouse during that period'. This reliance on events within the most recent three years would have created a more stringent limit than the legislation of some states, which addressed only convicts who had been compelled to emigrate, and less stringent than the legislation of others, which forbade the landing of persons who had been convicted at any time in the past. The antebellum politics of states' rights would have made it difficult for Congress to overcome these divergences by adopting a uniform federal standard. Moreover, individual states could not adopt List's proposal themselves. They lacked the power to impose on federal consuls the duty to provide certifications needed for the implementation of state law; states welcomed the arrival of immigrants whom they considered desirable, and would not have wanted to cut off immigration from ports in which consuls failed to cooperate with their laws.

## 2. *Extradition*

Extradition of accused criminals differs from exclusion or deportation in that extradition involves the delivery of an accused criminal to a foreign government at its request. Although the United States has not objected in principle to extradition of its own citizens, U.S. extradition treaties have often applied only to alien defendants, because the treaty partners objected to extraditing their own nationals (Moore 1891: 159-67).

The first U.S. provision for international extradition was contained in the Jay Treaty of 1794 with Great Britain, and the first case to arise under the treaty produced a major scandal, in part because there was no legal specification of the procedures to be employed in carrying out extradition, including the respective roles of the federal executive and judiciary (Moore 1891: 89-90; Cress 1975). The provision was allowed to expire, and the United States did not enter into another extradition treaty until 1842, also with Great Britain. Throughout those years, the federal government maintained its position that it could not grant extradition due to the absence of an authorizing statute or treaty (Moore 1891: 21, 30-3, 92f.).

Given the absence of federal extradition, some states attempted to fill the gap by exercising a power to grant international extradition under state law (Moore 1891: 55, 59-69). The Supreme Court put an end to this practice, however, through its 1840 decision in *Holmes v. Jennison*.[4] Although a majority of the Justices agreed that a state's police power included the power to exclude or expel an alien criminal for the protection of its own population, the Court asserted that a state's compliance with a foreign government's extradition request would amount to the conduct of foreign relations reserved exclusively to the federal government by the Constitution.

From 1842 onward, the federal government increasingly entered into extradition agreements with foreign governments. After a brief period in which federal extraditions rested directly on treaty provisions without statutory procedures, in 1848

Congress enacted a general statute granting jurisdiction to federal and state judges and federal commissioners (a form of subordinate federal magistrate) to conduct extradition hearings.[5] If the judge or commissioner deemed the evidence sufficient to sustain the charge of an offence extraditable under the treaty, he was to certify this fact and submit the evidence to the Secretary of State, who then had discretion to issue a warrant for surrender of the accused to the foreign government.

State courts played a perhaps surprising additional role in the antebellum period: they sometimes used their habeas corpus powers to review extradition decisions of federal judges and commissioners, directing the release of prisoners whose extradition they deemed unjustified.[6] This conflict between state and federal courts for final authority over the return of fugitive foreign criminals paralleled the more politically explosive struggle for authority over the return of fugitive slaves. The latter conflict produced a decision of the Supreme Court in 1858, unanimously denying the power of the states to release federal prisoners.[7]


## B. Barriers to Migration of the Poor

The states inherited from the colonial period the tradition of the English poor laws, which made the relief of the poor the responsibility of the local community where they were legally 'settled' (Rothman 1971: 20–5, 46–8; Riesenfeld 1955: 223f.). These laws gave localities various powers to prevent the settlement of persons who might later require support, and to 'remove' them to the place where they were legally settled. Accordingly, some of the most important provisions of state immigration law are sprinkled through the state poor laws. Meanwhile, the poor laws evolved considerably between 1776 and the Civil War. States moved at an uneven pace from the traditional system of local fiscal responsibility for transfer payments to a more centrally financed system that relied more heavily on institutionalization.

State and local efforts to avoid the burden of immigrants who could not support themselves had very limited results. The states were more successful in raising money to defray the expense of support than in preventing their landing, although at some periods financial disincentives may have led carriers to screen their passengers.

The poor laws typically imposed penalties on persons who intentionally brought a pauper or indigent person into the state and left him there. Other techniques including reporting requirements, designed to inform officials about the characteristics of the passengers being landed, and bonding requirements, authorizing officials to demand that carriers post security to indemnify the state or town if the passenger should later become a public charge.[8] Security requirements depended on an efficient, solvent bonding system, which was not necessarily present, and the incentives would shift where the laws gave the carrier the option of making a fixed 'commutation payment' in lieu of bond. The size of the commutation payment for passengers identified as presenting a significant risk of future indigence could be quite substantial in relation to the price of the ticket.[9] International removal of paupers to the place from which they had come was sometimes legally authorized, and occasionally actually enforced (e.g., Commissioners of Alien Passengers 1855, 15–16, 36 [reporting removals to Canada and Ireland]).

Recognizing the ineffectiveness of state legislation to prevent the arrival of paupers, and concerned that European countries were deliberately exporting their poor, some states called upon Congress to adopt federal legislation. But even in 1855, at the height of the antebellum nativist movement, efforts to enact a bill to prevent the immigration of criminals and paupers triggered states' rights objections in the Senate and rejection by the House of Representatives (Hutchinson 1981: 40f.). As in the case of convicts, the more significant role was played by the federal Executive branch, which responded with diplomatic protests to some incidents of reported dumping of paupers (House of Representatives 1838: 47; Klebaner 1961: 304f.).

Also in a manner similar to the case of convicts, Friedrich List's proposal for consular screening of emigrants could not be adopted by individual states. In some respects, List's proposal was particularly salient to the poor law policies, which were fundamentally economic (although 'pauperism' was also thought to involve moral harms, possibly contagious). Screening before embarkation would have avoided the economic expense of reshipping emigrants who were rejected on arrival, as well as the human cost, which was particularly high given the lengthy transatlantic crossings of the antebellum period. The economic cost could have been shifted to the carriers through a more stringent application of carrier responsibility, which could have induced more rigorous screening of passengers by the carriers, as occurred after the federal public charge exclusion took effect in 1882. So long as the laws of the port states varied in their requirements, however, stricter state laws would probably have shifted the landing of poorer passengers to other states. (Those states in turn might have tightened their own requirements if the immigrants remained and became burdensome, or they might have encouraged the immigrants to pass on by land to other states. Some immigrants in the antebellum period did in fact choose routes through states with less stringent laws on their way to states with more stringent laws; and the poor laws attempted to address these loopholes as well (Klebaner 1958: 273).) Ultimately, a uniform federal policy was adopted to achieve effective enforcement.

## C. Labour Regimes

Prior to the Civil War, labour relations were often structured as status relations with far reaching consequences. Three particular examples of subordinated status resulted in specific migration controls: slavery, indentured servitude, and the binding of seamen to their vessels. Control of the international slave trade shifted from the states to the federal government in 1808 as a result of a specific constitutional provision. Indentured servitude (and the trade in indentured servants) was regulated exclusively by the states until its decline as a vehicle for immigration. The return of deserting seamen to their vessels or to their countries was regulated by the federal government, within a framework of bilateral treaties.

### 1. Slaves

The most extreme form of involuntary migration of unfree labour was the slave trade. The 'Migration or Importation' Clause of the U.S. Constitution barred Congress until 1808 from prohibiting the importation of slaves into any of the original states that were willing to receive them. By the time that period had expired, nearly every state where slavery had not been abolished enacted its own prohibition against importation of slaves from abroad.[10] Congress added a federal prohibition of the international slave trade effective from 1808 onwards.

As the nineteenth century progressed, federal enforcement of the ban on the international slave trade increasingly occurred within the context of international cooperation toward that end. The United States was hardly a leader in that international movement, and its devotion to enforcement activities varied over time, but it eventually joined in international enforcement measures such as patrolling the West African coast to intercept slave ships (Du Bois 1969: 131–50; Howard 1963; Jones 1977: 69–78, 142–5).

State regulation of the movement of slaves took a variety of forms. Some slave states sought at various times to exclude the interstate slave trade, or to keep out individual slaves whose characteristics were considered objectionable.

While some free states prohibited the bringing in of slaves because of moral opposition to slavery (and therefore sought to free them), other free states opposed the entry of all blacks, whether slave or free. Illinois, for example, banned all black immigration, and sought to expel fugitive slaves rather than to protect them. The Supreme Court upheld this prohibition in *Moore v. Illinois*, on the grounds that the state could rightfully prevent the immigration of persons 'unacceptable' to it.[11]

## 2. Indentured Servants

Mary Sarah Bilder has emphasized the conceptual importance of indentured servitude as a regulated form of immigration in the colonial and early post-Independence periods (Bilder 1996). Indentured servitude was a form of bound labour for a definite period of years under contract, and it provided a method by which European emigrants who lacked other assets could finance their passage to North America. White indentured servants provided the primary source of the labour supply in British North America in the mid-seventeenth century; their economic importance was later overtaken by the lifetime enslavement of Africans and their descendants (Galenson 1981; Steinfeld 1991). Indentured servants were imported; they were sold; during the period of their service the law recognized property rights in them that could be sold, assigned, and inherited. Although the institution rested on contract, it was highly regulated by law in the colonies and later in the states.

As a vehicle for immigration, the indentured servant trade largely disappeared by 1819. Historians dispute the reasons; Bilder cites 'the combination of a series of economic depressions, interruptions of transatlantic shipping, and a cultural discomfort about white bound labor [as] the most persuasive explanation' (Bilder 1996: 760).

Bilder observes that colonies that generally encouraged importation of indentured servants nonetheless 'sought to discourage the importation of certain categories of indentured servants based on ethnicity, religion, age, health, and past behavior', by imposing duties (i.e., taxes) or other liabilities on the importers (Bilder 1996: 773). She interprets these laws as treating the indentured servants as commodities, or, in her phrase, as articles of commerce.

In the later colonial period, Bilder notes the development of protective regulation to safeguard indentured servants against their importers. Such regulation increased after Independence. Bilder interprets the later regulation as expressing concern for the emigrants themselves as persons whose interests required protection rather than as articles of commerce whose importation was to be encouraged or discouraged. This shift in perspective might have contributed to the states' ability to defend their protective legislation against the charge that they were engaged in direct regulation of foreign commerce. As it happened, the indentured servant trade essentially died out before the legal confrontations over the scope and effect of the federal commerce power began to reach the courts in the 1820s, and the influence of the indentured servant trade on those disputes was at most indirect.[12]

## 3. Deserters from Foreign Ships

Under maritime law, seamen who unjustifiably leave their ships before the completion of the voyage have been viewed as committing desertion. Prior to the twentieth century, U.S. law provided physical enforcement against desertion (Moore 1891: 611–20). The United States was party to numerous bilateral treaties providing that if a seaman deserted in a foreign port, a consular officer could initiate proceedings for his arrest and return to his home country. The United States's first treaty of that kind, with France, predated the ratification of the Constitution.

Congress enacted general legislation specifying procedures for the implementation of these treaties in 1829. The statute authorized a foreign consul to apply for a judicial order that the alleged deserter be arrested and, after hearing, delivered to the consul 'to be sent back to the dominions of any such government'.[13] Without an applicable treaty, arrest for desertion was not legally authorized.

The early federal action in this field reflected the close connection between enforcement of seamen's obligations and the conduct of foreign commerce. Presumably federal enforcement was not seen as threatening state prerogatives, because seamen were returned for the benefit of the foreign vessel (either directly or as a deterrent to desertion), and not for the protection of the state in which they deserted.

## D. Quarantine

The principal vehicle for addressing the impact of migration on public health concerns in the antebellum period was quarantine (Cumming 1921). As practiced in that period, quarantine involved the temporary isolation of travelers who were suspected of carrying dangerous contagious diseases, either on individual grounds or because of their route of travel. From 1796 until after the Civil War, state authority over quarantine legislation enjoyed the unequivocal endorsement of the federal government. The issue first arose in 1796, when a Congressman proposed that the President be authorized to regulate the quarantine of foreign vessels arriving in United States ports. The proposal failed by a large majority, and Congress instead authorized the President to direct federal customs officials to aid in the execution of state quarantine and health laws.[14]

Quarantine practices should be distinguished in two respects from the modern federal immigration exclusions that began in 1891. First, quarantine usually targeted acute diseases with high mortality rates, such as smallpox and cholera; later federal immigration exclusions extended to chronic diseases, whose victims were not likely to recover or die after a limited period of isolation. Second, quarantine laws applied to a state's own citizens as well as to aliens and citizens of other states.

In most cases, quarantine laws operated by delay and not by permanent exclusion. In times of perceived peril, quarantine was more likely to be strictly enforced. Maritime quarantine might lead to the death of the would-be immigrant who was stopped at the port, rather than deportation to another country, or to admittance of the immigrant after he or she had survived the disease. But as a barrier to free migration it had serious practical significance.

## E. Racial Exclusion: Restrictions on Migration of Free Blacks

I have left for last one of the most peculiar, but politically one of the most important, categories of migration control in the antebellum United States: control of the movement of free blacks. Slave states insisted that such regulation was essential to the preservation of their institutions, some free states objected to it, and other free states adopted similar legislation themselves. The slave states' insistence on maintaining state rather than federal control over the movement of free blacks was probably a primary cause of the federal government's failure to adopt qualitative restrictions on immigration before the Civil War.

Slave state legislation restricting free blacks was voluminous (Berlin 1974; Fields 1985; Franklin 1971).[15] The mere visibility of black people living in freedom was regarded as a grave threat to the operation of the system of slavery, and slaveholders also feared that free blacks would encourage escape, or provoke slave revolts. Slave state legislation usually barred the entry of free blacks who were not already residents of the state. Penalties were often imposed on persons bringing in free blacks.

To the extent that these laws were directed at immigration from abroad, they had some congressional support. Several of the state prohibitions on entry of free blacks had been enacted in the wake of the successful slave revolt in Haiti. In 1803, the Southern states succeeded in obtaining the enactment of a federal statute prohibiting the importation of foreign blacks into states whose laws forbade their entry.[16] Thus, the states secured a federal endorsement, and at least some cooperation in the enforcement of these laws.

One particular aspect of slave states' policies regarding the entry of foreign blacks created special difficulties in the antebellum period, the regulation of free black seamen arriving in Southern ports (Hamer 1935a, Hamer 1935b; Neuman 1993: 1873–7). Several states, led by South Carolina, adopted requirements that any black seamen arriving on a vessel be held in jail at its master's expense until the vessel left, or 'quarantine' regulations requiring black crew members to remain on the ship and forbidding local blacks to communicate with them. Enforcement of such laws produced diplomatic protests from both Britain and France. Supreme Court Justice William Johnson concluded that the South Carolina statute infringed both the federal power over foreign commerce and a commercial treaty with Britain.[17] Johnson's opinion was violently denounced in South Carolina, and neither Johnson nor the federal government was able to prevent enforcement of the statute. In 1844, Massachusetts sent agents to South Carolina and Louisiana to institute judicial proceedings to test the constitutionality of the laws as applied to African-American sailors on U.S. vessels, but the agents were forced to flee under threat of mob violence. Ultimately the British found it necessary to bypass Washington and to undertake diplomacy directly with the Southern states. The consuls achieved some success in Louisiana and Georgia, and eventually even in South Carolina, which agreed to permit black sailors to remain on their ships in port.

The controversy concerning the exclusion of free black sailors illustrates how state immigration law could create a persistent diplomatic embarrassment for the United States that the federal government proved powerless to solve. It also demonstrates how exclusive federal control of immigration was threatening to perceived Southern interests, and how Southern states were willing to resort to defiance or even violence to protect those interests.

## Conclusion

The antebellum regimes hardly provide a model of the smooth functioning of federalism in the context of migration control. The friction and conflict that they exhibited is not a necessary feature of federalism in the migration context, but a contingent feature of U.S. federalism in the antebellum period. To a significant degree, it resulted from the slave states' distrust of federal power over migration of free blacks and slaves, which would potentially threaten the security of the slavery system. The removal of these issues by the Civil War made possible a uniform federal migration policy and a coordinated system of implementation.

## Notes

1. The constitutional jurisprudence is discussed in Neuman 1993 and Neuman 1996. Fuller treatment of several categories of migration control discussed in this chapter, including extensive citations of state statutes, which cannot be included here for reasons of space, may be found in those works.
2. Journal of Congress 13 (1788): 105–106.
3. House of Representatives 1838, 54–55. List's proposal also extended to the problem of pauper exclusions discussed infra; he suggested that the local magistrate should attest that the emigrants were 'able to maintain themselves by their labor or capital', and that the consul have the power to refuse certification to emigrants 'who, in his opinion, would become a burden to the community on their arrival in the United States'.
4. 39 U.S. (14 Pet.) 540 (1840).
5. Act of 12 August 1848, ch. 167, 9 Stat. 302.
6. See In re Heilbronn, 11 F.Cas. 1025 (S.D.N.Y. 1854) (No. 6323); In re Heilb[r]onn, 1 Parker's Crim. Rep. 429 (N.Y. Sup. Ct. 1853); 6 Op. Att'y Gen. 227, 237, 270, 290 (1853–54) (executive opinions re conflict in Heilbronn case); Swisher 1974: 179–80 (discussing N.Y. state court release and subsequent disappearance of Metzger).
7. Ableman v. Booth, 62 U.S. (21 How.) 503 (1858).
8. State and local bonding and communtation requirements are described in Klebaner 1958.
9. In 1854, for example, Massachusetts officials reported commutation payments varying between $5 and $25, and averaging $21, for 114 alien passengers identified as presenting an intermediate risk of becoming a public charge (Commissioners of Alien Passengers 1855, 36.) According to

one author, the price of an adult's ticket from Liverpool to New York in 1850 averaged in the $17-$20 range (Page 1911: 738). Even a few dollars could have had a significant marginal effect on the poor.

10. Du Bois 1969: 71–4. States received federal support in the enforcement of their statutes prior to 1808 by means of the 1803 federal act discussed infra.
11. 55 U.S. (14 How.) 13, 18 (1853).
12. This is my characterization. Professor Bilder concludes that contention over whether indentures servants were articles of commerce had a much more significant influence on the course of the later debates.
13. Act of 2 March 1829, ch. 41, 4 Stat. 359.
14. See Annals of Congress, 5 (1796): 1227, 1347–59. Even in 1866, Congress rejected a proposal to substitute uniform federal regulation of quarantine (Benedict 1970, 184–93).
15. Given the greater national importance of the slave states' laws, I omit here discussion of restrictions on free blacks in some 'free' states. See Neuman 1996: 35 & nn. 47–8.
16. Act of 28 February 1803, ch. 10, 2 Stat. 205. The prohibition applied to importing or bringing in 'any negro, mulatto, or other person of colour, not being a native, a citizen, or registered seaman, of the United States, or seamen, natives of countries beyond the Cape of Good Hope ... provided always, that nothing contained in this act shall be construed to prohibit the admission of Indians'. The arrival of free blacks expelled from Guadeloupe provided the immediate impetus for the statute (DuBois 1969: 84f.).
17. Elkison v. Deliesseline, 8 F. Cas. 493 (C.C.D.S.C. 1823) (No, 4,366).

# References

Benedict, Michael Les, 1970, 'Contagion and the Constitution: Quarantine Agitation from 1859 to 1866', *Journal of the History of Medicine* 25: 177.
Berlin, Ira, 1974, *Slaves Without Masters: The Free Negro in the Antebellum South*, New York.
Bilder, Mary Sarah, 1996, 'The Struggle over Immigration: Indentured Servants, Slaves, and Articles of Commerce', *Missouri Law Review* 61: 743.
Commissioners of Alien Passengers and Foreign Paupers (Massachusetts), 1855, *Report of the Commissioners of Alien Passengers and Foreign Paupers: 1854, Massachusetts House Documents No. 123*, Boston.
Cress, Larry D., 1975, 'The Jonathan Robbins Incident: Extradition and the Separation of Powers in the Adams Administration', *Essex Institute Historical Collections* 111: 99.
Cumming, Hugh S., 1921, 'The United States Quarantine System During the Past Fifty Years', in *A Half Century of Public Health*, ed. Mazÿck P. Ravenel, New York.
Du Bois, W.E.B., 1969, *The Suppression of the African Slave Trade*, Baton Rouge, 1969.
Fahrmeir, Andreas, 2000, *Citizens and Aliens: Foreigners and the Law in Britain and the German States, 1789–1870*, New York.
Fields, Barbara J., 1985, *Slavery and Freedom on the Middle Ground: Maryland during the Nineteenth Century*, New Haven.
Focke, Harald, 1976, 'Friedrich List und die südwestdeutsche Amerikaauswanderung 1817–1846', in *Deutsche Amerikaauswanderung im 19. Jahrhundert*, ed. Günter Moltmann, Stuttgart.
Franklin, John Hope, 1971, *The Free Negro in North Carolina 1790–1860*, New York.

Galenson, David W., 1981, *White Servitude in Colonial America: An Economic Analysis*, Cambridge.

Hamer, Philip M., 1935a, 'Great Britain, the United States, and the Negro Seamen Acts, 1822–1848', *Journal of Southern History*, 1: 1.

Hamer, Philip M., 1935b, 'British Consuls and the Negro Seamen Acts, 1850–1860', *Journal of Southern History*, 1: 138.

House of Representatives (United States), *H.R. Report No. 1040, 25th Congress, 2d Session*, Washington, D.C. 1838.

Howard, Warren S., 1963, *American Slavers and the Federal Law 1837–1862*, Westport.

Hutchinson, E.P., 1981, *Legislative History of American Immigration Policy 1798–1965*, Philadelphia.

Jones, Howard, 1977, *To the Webster-Ashburton Treaty: A Study in Anglo-American Relations, 1783–1843*, Chapel Hill.

Jones, Maldwyn Allen, 1992, *American Immigration*, 2nd edn, Chicago.

Klebaner, Benjamin J., 1958, 'State and Local Immigration Regulation in the United States Before 1882', *International Review of Social History*, 3: 269–95.

Klebaner, Benjamin J., 1961, 'The Myth of Foreign Pauper Dumping in the United States', *Social Service Review*, 35: 302.

Moltmann, Günter, 1976, 'Die Transportation von Sträflingen im Rahmen der deutschen Amerikaauswanderung des 19. Jahrhunderts', in *Deutsche Amerikaauswanderung im 19. Jahrhundert*, ed. Günter Moltmann, Stuttgart.

Moltmann, Günter, 1978, *Aufbruch nach Amerika: Friedrich List und die Auswanderung aus Baden und Württemberg 1816/17*, Tübingen.

Moore, John Bassett, 1891, *A Treatise on Extradition and Interstate Rendition*, 2 vols, Boston.

Neuman, Gerald L., 1993, 'The Lost Century of American Immigration Law (1776–1875)', *Columbia Law Review*, 93: 1833–1901.

Neuman, Gerald L., 1996, *Strangers to the Constitution: Immigrants, Borders, and Fundamental Law*, Princeton.

Page, Thomas W., 1911, 'The Transportation of Immigrants and the Reception Arrangements in the Nineteenth Century', *Journal of Political Economy*, 19: 732–49.

Riesenfeld, Stefan A., 1955, 'The Formative Era of American Public Assistance Law', *California Law Review*, 43: 175.

Rothman, David J., 1971, *The Discovery of the Asylum: Social Order and Disorder in the New Republic*, Boston.

Steinfeld, Robert J., 1991, *The Invention of Free Labor: The Employment Relation in English and American Law and Culture, 1350–1870*, Chapel Hill.

Swisher, Carl B., 1974, *The Taney Period, 1836–64*, New York.

# Chapter 8

# The Transformation of Nineteenth-Century West European Expulsion Policy, 1880–1914

*Frank Caestecker*

Alien policy took its contemporary shape in the first half of the twentieth century. By 1940 the distinction between tolerated and unwanted immigration, which is still valid today, was set throughout Western Europe. By the end of the nineteenth century, the transformation of alien policy had begun. This chapter is an outline of the logic of nineteenth-century alien policy which focuses on one aspect of alien policy, expulsion policy.

While, over the last two decades, the origins of twentieth-century alien policy have been well-researched by historians, they have paid little attention to nineteenth-century regulation of migration. One of the reasons for this lack of interest can be explained by a deficit of historical research on twentieth-century alien policy. Although historians have unravelled the intentions of twentieth-century policy makers, few have analysed to what extent these intentions materialised. This is a much more complex topic. While research on the officially proclaimed alien policy focuses on the central authorities, assessing the implementation of this legislation demands research on a local basis of a myriad of enforcement agencies, including the courts. It also has to take into account migrants' responsive strategies.

Nineteenth-century regulation of migration and even alien policy was not the sole jurisdiction of the central authorities. Local authorities had significant input in defining the stranger, who was not entitled to access their territory or their welfare community. Even the concept of alien was nebulous in this age of limited political centralisation.

The deficit of historical research becomes particularly apparent in the lack of research on expulsion policy. Expulsion has received only scant attention even in the, by now, vast literature on twentieth-century alien policy.[1] Analysis of expulsion procedure and practice is, however, key to the understanding of the changing logic of alien policy. Expulsion policy can also indicate how far alien policy extended beyond mere rhetoric and what resources were put at the disposal of the authorities to enforce their policy. In the nineteenth century, expulsion policy is also a key to understanding the aims of regulation of international migration. Who were the undesirable immigrants? What were the criteria for exclusion? First, I will provide an overview of the nineteenth-century alien policy and then a closer look at expulsion policy.

## 1. Alien policy of the nineteenth century, focusing on aliens as criminal and political actors

The nineteenth-century state withheld from intervening in the social sphere, so migration regulation was not considered a political matter. The limits of nineteenth-century state action in migration were strictly defined. The central aim of alien policy was to prevent aliens from disturbing public order. Disturbing public order had a political connotation; subversive aliens had to be expelled. What subversion implied was, of course, subject to change. In Prussia, taking part in a strike was sufficient provocation to be brought to the border (Kulczycki, 1994: 62; Peters-Schildgen 1997: 52–53). The German obsession with subversion caused immigrants to be closely supervised during their stay. In Imperial Germany all aliens were required, by state law, to register with the local police authorities. They were compelled to obtain an official residence permit which could greatly vary in duration. Once the residence permits had lapsed, the authorities could refuse a renewal of this permit and thus order them to leave the country. In 1885, this was done on a large scale. About forty thousand immigrants, mostly Poles of Austrian-Hungarian and Russian nationality, some of whom were long-time residents, were expelled from Prussia. This radical decision can be attributed to the Prussian political strategy to create the German people. This mass expulsion did not aim at the regulation of the labour market, but at protecting a Nation which was (perceived as being) threatened by Polish nationalism. Poles (and Jews) were considered subversive immigrants and therefore security risks (Neubach 1967; Bade 1987, 1980; Wertheimer, 1987).

Besides subversive aliens, aliens who had committed a crime could be expelled after serving their prison sentence. Destitute immigrants were in many cases considered criminals, since begging and vagrancy were criminal offences. Foreign vagrants and beggars were, in most cases, not sentenced for this offence, but taken to the border.[2] European expulsion policy throughout the nineteenth century limited itself largely to those aliens who were not able to secure themselves a livelihood in the host country.

Subversive aliens were a minority within the total number of expellees. This group of political expellees has received the most attention in historical writings, and also the only ones to have been a topic in contemporary public discussion. Destitute aliens were, by and large, the largest group to be expelled. It was not the state which prevented them from earning a living, but the market. Throughout the whole of the nineteenth century the authorities did not concern themselves with industries calling upon foreign labour to supplement their labour force or even to supplant strikers. The authorities did not intervene when an immigrant did the work an unemployed national was willing to do, or if an entrepreneur of foreign nationality residing in the country successfully competed against a local producer. As long as the immigrant had sufficient means of support, he had no cause for concern (Noiriel, 1988: 74; Caestecker, 2000: 11f). Destitute immigrants were expelled to prevent their applying for social assistance.[3] The harshness of expulsion policy was mitigated by facilities for resident aliens. The liberal ideology of the nineteenth century wanted to protect the individual against arbitrary state powers. Inhabitants without citizenship were also considered worthy of protection. In this way resident aliens in liberal regimes were protected against administrative decisions in favour of expulsions. Based on the Alien Law of 1839, resident aliens in Belgium could only be expelled by a decision of the King (by Royal Decree), while in the Netherlands the expulsion of resident aliens, based of the Alien Law of 1849, depended on the Judiciary in the case of destitution, or on the King in the case of disturbing public order; in addition, those aliens in the Netherlands had the right to appeal. In France and Belgium, aliens could even acquire the status of *domicilié* which put them on a par with nationals, apart from the acquisition of political rights, which implied that they could not be expelled at all. In authoritarian Prussia (and later the German Reich) no facilities at all were provided for settled immigrants.

Liberalism even had its influence on the manner in which aliens were deported. From 1850 onwards, Belgium systematically granted a choice of border to their expellees. The Netherlands and

France offered this possibility to some expellees only.[4] These liberal regimes accorded this facility to undesirable aliens in order to respect the procedure of extradition which stipulated that an alien could only be extradited if the crime he had committed was also considered a crime by the extraditing state. Deporting unwanted aliens, even if the expelling state ignored the fact that the alien was fleeing persecution in his or her country, could be equated with extradition. This provision was the result of a liberal ideology which acknowledged the very different regimes in Europe and the resulting different conceptions of what a crime was. Providing expellees with a choice of border also respected the principle of individual liberty which was the core of liberal ideology. The choice of border also demonstrates the lack of importance attached to nationality in the nineteenth century. Until the end of the nineteenth century, the direct relationship between state and citizen had hardly any importance for the majority of the population as the state was hardly present in daily life (Caestecker 1997: 328ff.; Noiriel 1991: 63–100). The concept of being returned to one's country was, therefore, not self-evident.

In order to convince undesirable aliens to leave permanently, legislation was enacted which punished non-compliance with an expulsion order. In France, Belgium and the Netherlands, mid-century legislation, largely instigated by the social fears of 1848, provided prison terms up to 6 months for *rupture de ban d'expulsion*. In Belgium and the Netherlands only resident expellees who had been expelled by Royal Decree (in the Netherlands also by a decision of the Judiciary) were criminally triable. Unwanted aliens who had been perfunctorily expelled ran no risk of a prison sentence upon return. In France, however, all returnees were liable to prison terms (Leenders 1993:265, Caestecker 2000:10, De Boeck 1929: 597, Barthelemy 1936:21).

## 2. The Transformation of Expulsion Policy at the End of the Nineteenth Century

Figure 8.1 illustrates the expulsion policy in Belgium and the Netherlands. It refers to all aliens removed from Belgium, either at the border, or from within. For the Netherlands, it only refers to those removed from within the country. The number of expellees jumped steeply in the last quarter of the nineteenth century. This was the result of the recession during which the number of wandering poor rose considerably while occupational opportunities diminished. The spectacular rise in expulsions was, however, not merely a reflection of social and economic change; politics was its main determinant.

After 1860 no more aliens were stopped from entering Belgium which illustrates the spectacular change in the manner in which immigration was being controlled. Before 1860, immigration control within Europe had taken place at the border or in the border regions; after 1875, immigration control, or rather alien control, was taking place within the country.[5] At the same time, visa regulations were abolished (Wennemann 1997: 94; Leenders 1993: 86 and 104). Notwithstanding these spectacular changes at the borders, immigration control throughout the nineteenth century hardly changed. The period 1860–1875 can not be considered a watershed in immigration control, as the logic behind immigration control had not changed.

The figures used for Figure 8.1 have to be looked at critically.[6] The way in which the statistics were put together reflects specific interests behind them, as well as influencing our perception of reality. The statistics on expulsion expressed the diligence of the administration charged with executing alien policy, rather than reflecting the reality of the immigration of undesirable aliens. This is already clear by the way in which the counting was carried out. The number of expelled persons were not counted, but the number of expulsions. Thus a given person could be expelled numerous times in the course of a year, and each expulsion was counted separately in these figures. Therefore, these figures are rather a function of a specific state policy targeting undesirable aliens, and the rise in the number of expulsions is also a function of the more general increase of state presence in society. Throughout the nineteenth century state control increases. In particular, at the end of the nineteenth century, there was an increase in the number of policemen (Leenders 1993: 136, Van Outrive et al.1992: 64ff.) This implied that unwanted aliens were increasingly confronted with the state. Not only did the number of aliens expelled, or rather the number of expulsions, rise considerably at the end of the nineteenth century, the manner in which aliens were expelled also underwent a crucial change.

## *Free border choice or deportation to the country of origin*

Throughout the nineteenth century, Belgium, the Netherlands, and France granted a choice of border to their expellees. In Prussia (later the German *Reich*), however, unwanted expellees had no input into the direction in which they were deported.

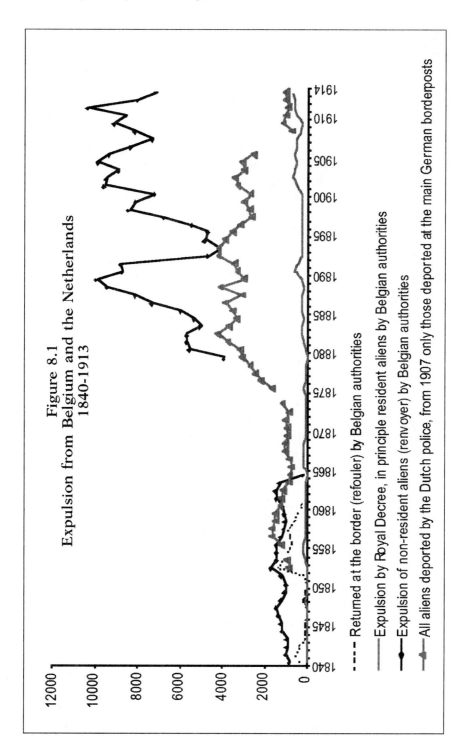

Figure 8.1
Expulsion from Belgium and the Netherlands
1840-1913

- - - Returned at the border (refouler) by Belgian authorities
—— Expulsion by Royal Decree, in principle resident aliens by Belgian authorities
······ Expulsion of non-resident aliens (renvoyer) by Belgian authorities
—▲— All aliens deported by the Dutch police, from 1907 only those deported at the main German borderposts

Expulsion in Prussia, certainly from the middle of the century onwards, seems to imply the return of the expellees to their so-called country of origin.[7] The Prussian authorities repatriated the expellees, or at least expelled them in the direction of their country of nationality. That the Prussian authorities (later German *Reich*) did not grant border choice to expellees was due to the authoritarianism of this regime.[8] In these regimes, there were no claims about the unwilling extradition of aliens.[9] There was also much less ideological commitment to individual liberty. In addition, in Prussia, and later in the German *Reich*, nationality was considered to be an important element in the identification of a person earlier than in any other country.[10]

The national logic in deportation procedure was imposed by Prussia even beyond the German *Reich*. Since 1849, the Prussian (later German) authorities had been asking the authorities of the neighbouring countries to select their undesirable aliens whom they expelled to Prussia (the German Reich) on the basis of state membership.[11] These requests were not taken into consideration, the border choice for expellees was a cherished tradition of liberal regimes. In 1884, the German authorities decided unilaterally to stop the "chaos" at their Western border. All vagrants, except for the German nationals who were expelled to the German Reich by the police force of the neighbouring countries were sent back. Only those third-country nationals, among the vagrants, who could document that they had to pass through the German Empire to return to their country and who had funding for the transit fare, would not be returned. The Belgian (and Dutch) authorities indignantly refused to pay for the repatriation of able-bodied aliens. All the third-country expellees whom the German authorities could catch at the border were returned. The Dutch authorities, given their geographical position, were seriously afflicted by the Germany's decision to close its border. Their first reaction was to deport any Spanish, French, or Italian vagrants, whom the Belgian authorities had deported to the Netherlands, back to Belgium, as pushing them over the German border was no longer feasible. Finally, the Netherlands concluded a bilateral agreement with the German *Reich* – the German-Dutch Settlement Treaty (*vestigingsverdrag*) of 1906 – which included provisions for deportation procedures. It stipulated that the signing parties accepted their nationals, and gave free passage to the destitute among them who had to pass through their territory to return to their country of nationality, if the transit fare were paid for. This Dutch-German agreement of 1906 implied that the Dutch authorities handed over the expellees and their documents to the German authorities (and *vice versa*) at agreed times and places.[12] Liberal claims about unwilling extradition of aliens were refuted by asserting that unwanted aliens could still voluntarily depart in the direction of the country of preference before being deported. In addition those aliens who were to be deported but were sought in Germany could still claim special treatment in order to prevent extradition. The Dutch authorities claimed this provision was even an improvement for the latter category because previously they had to leave the country, while now they could claim asylum (Krabbe 1912: 68ff., Seppen and Walraven 1950: 254ff.).

Although Belgium and France did not conclude agreements with Germany which stipulated the expulsion procedure in detail, both countries changed their expulsion procedure fundamentally. The free border choice was abolished. The French and Belgian authorities realised it was senseless to let foreign vagrants decide for themselves whether or not to be brought to the Dutch (or German) border. In this way, they would never get rid of them. This new expulsion procedure was not only due to German insistence, but at least in the Belgian case to technocrats in the administration, who were far more committed to the efficiency of their expulsion policy than to the liberal values cherished by the Belgian political authorities. These technocrats played an important role in outlining the new expulsion policy. They considered the free choice of border for the expellees to be a nuisance, which even promoted international vagrancy. They advocated a national solution to the plague of vagrants; every state had to discipline its own vagrants.

The effort to rationalise the removal of undesirable aliens on a national basis was sealed with diplomatic agreements. The already mentioned Dutch-German agreement (1906) had been preceded by a German-Swiss agreement (1890), a Belgian-Dutch agreement (1888), a French-German agreement (1891), a French-Belgian agreement (1896), a German-Belgian agreement (1896), a British-Belgian agreement (1897).... These treaties stipulated that every country had to accept its own nationals who had emigrated or give free passage to those who had to pass through their territory. The issue of the transit fare for third-country nationals, in most cases, was not mentioned in these agreements and continued to pose problems. The agreements made it impossible for the expelling state to force third-country nationals onto the territory of neighbouring states without the consent of that state. Expulsions were no longer a unilateral affair. Constraints were imposed by the neighbouring countries. Expellees could only "voluntarily" be made to cross the border of the neighbouring country of which they were not a citizen. Afterwards they could still be returned to the expelling state, but seen that their intrusion into the territory of the neighbouring state was voluntary the expelling state could no longer be accused of breaching the bilateral agreement (Barthelemy 1936:107, Caestecker 2000:39, De Boeck 1927: 580f, Martini 1909: 135).

The radical rupture of most European states with the traditional practice of free choice was the result of a new, national, logic in all practices of the states of Western Europe. At the end of the nineteenth century, nationality became an all pervasive point of identification. This process is closely intertwined with the increasing state regulation of society. The active presence of the state in social life meant that membership of a state affected everyday activities. Through military service, the expansion of social policy, and democratic franchise, the state became much more present in daily life. State membership entailed more and more rights and obligations. In order to delineate nationals clearly, the criteria for state membership were rationalised and codified all over Europe at the end of the nineteenth and beginning of the twentieth centuries (Brubaker 1992, Caestecker 1997, 2000, Heijs 1995). Being a member of a state, which nationality one had, became a fundamental point for personal identification and also for deportation procedures.

The main difficulty in implementing these new deportation procedures was that the nationality of the expellee had to be clearly established in order to determine where they had to be expelled to. The mere attribution of nationality turned out to be extremely troublesome. During the sometimes long diplomatic negotiations to determine the nationality of undesirable aliens, they remained in the charge of the state which wanted to expel them (Martini 1909: 135, Darut 1902: 180, Schläpfer 1969: 160, Hehemann 1987: 262, 324ff., 343ff.).

This important change in the manner in which undesirable aliens were expelled also caused refugee policy to become a distinct area within immigration policy. Throughout most of the nineteenth century, refugees, when expelled from their first country of asylum, could try their luck in a country other than their country of origin. From the 1880s onwards, when unwanted aliens were deported to their country of origin, which was for most refugees their country of persecution, this possibility was excluded. Liberal regimes such as Belgium and France, and, to a lesser extent, the Netherlands immediately and explicitly forbade the expulsion of refugees in order not to violate human rights. Special facilities were provided for the (politically) persecuted. All aliens who were to be expelled had to be questioned about whether they were pursued for political reasons. If so, the central authorities had to be informed about those who claimed to be refugees. Their allegations had to be verified and genuine refugees were not to be deported (Caestecker 2000: 40f, Martini 1909: 137, Krabbe 1912: 110).

## The Repression of Returnees

Regulation of expulsion on the basis of state membership was an expression of the willingness to make state intervention more efficient. At the same time, a repressive strategy to combat unwanted immigration was pursued. More resources were put at the disposal of the authorities to convince undesirable aliens to leave the country. At the end of the nineteenth century, the authorities considered that it was only by making unauthorised stays much more perilous that unwanted aliens would be dissuaded from staying put. In Belgium and France no legislative changes were introduced, but extensive use was made of the freedom which the existing legislation offered. In Belgium from 1881 onwards an increasing number of foreign vagrants, who were not residents, were expelled by Royal Decree. This enabled the authorities to bring those aliens to court, should they make a subsequent return (Caestecker 2000: 32ff).

At the end of the century increasing numbers of foreigners in France who had been sentenced for even minor offences were expelled. Executing an expulsion order no longer depended on the undesirable alien's willingness to leave the country. When an alien's presence on French territory was not considered beneficial to the country, the authorities increasingly resorted to deportation. For those whose nationality remained ambiguous, or where deportation could be unlawful extradition, the French Minister of Interiors ordered that they should be brought close to the border and given a short time to leave the country. If they did not do so, they were brought before the court for *rupture de ban d'expulsion*. In France, the creation of the undocumented alien in 1888, also gave an impetus to repression. From that year onwards, foreigners were obliged to declare their presence with the local authorities and, from 1893 onwards, to pay a residence tax if they were engaged in any kind of labour. This implied that the stay of foreigners was much more strictly regulated, with a much higher likelihood that a foreigner would break the law.[13]

Figure 8.2 illustrates the increased repression of unwanted aliens in Belgium and France. In the Netherlands, until the end of the 1880s, the central authorities did not consider it worthwhile to obtain more resources to combat unwanted immigration. In the 1890s, a change in mood occurred. Deportation policy after 1906 was perhaps an answer to this newly felt need.[14] During the sometimes long negotiations between the Dutch and German authorities (and for third-country nationals also authorities of other countries), the aliens to be deported were held in custody in the Netherlands. The local police authorities were responsible for these prisons. They could be held for a long time, as sometimes it took considerable time to have documentary proof of somebody's nationality and to get the necessary authorization for their deportation to Germany. This implied considerable cost for the Dutch authorities (Seppen en Walraven 1950: 256, Krabbe 1912). It is possible that the Dutch authorities believed this investment would yield a return by diverting foreign vagrants away from the Netherlands.

## Conclusion

For most of the nineteenth century the destitute aliens were just a nuisance, but the determination to get rid of them clearly grew by the end of the century. This does not mean that most of the nineteenth century can be characterized as tolerant and cosmopolitan, rather that the state was indifferent to the fate of most people residing on its territory, of whatever nationality. At the end of that century, the distinction between national and alien acquired a relevance which it had not had during most of the nineteenth century. This is expressed in the intensified repression of unwanted aliens at the end of the nineteenth century. A dividing line between foreigners and nationals expressed the strong expansion of the socio-political intervening capacity of the state. This expansion of its sphere of action transformed the state into a nation-state. While, for most of the nineteenth century, the state was principally something that took (taxes and conscripts), by the end of the century it also gave. The transformed state - the nation-state - increasingly catered to the needs of its citizens, while at the same time excluding persons of foreign nationality on its territory from the benefits of its expanded tasks. This political change coincided with increasing international migration which amplified the effect of the change in alien policy.

   With hindsight, the intensified repression of undesirable aliens (including the abolishment of free border choice) at the end of the nineteenth century was part of a process which ended in the restrictive alien legislation of the interwar period. The harsh treatment of unwanted aliens is the negative side of a dialectical process, a process of inclusion (the creation of the citizen,

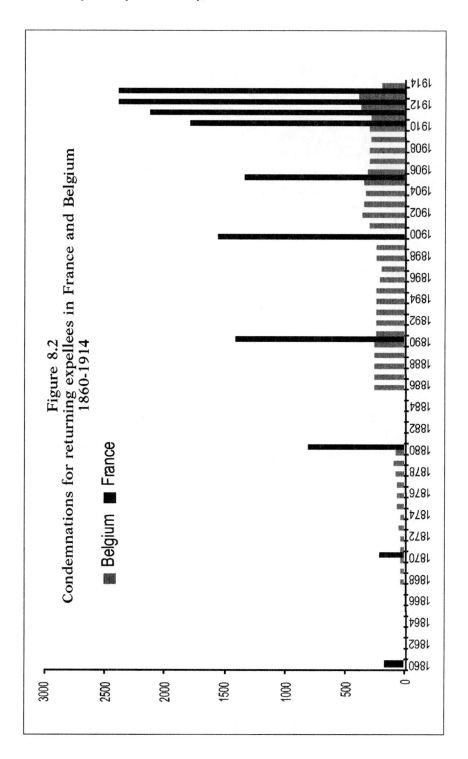

Figure 8.2
Condemnations for returning expellees in France and Belgium
1860-1914

member of the nation-state) and exclusion (the creation of the foreigner and in its most accentuated form, the illegal alien). A process that simultaneously created a welfare state and a new form of police state.

## Notes

1. For example in the vast literature on refugee policy in the 1930s, the central authorities' decision-making process is carefully scrutinised, but the extent in which the decision to expel Jewish or political refugees was executed is largely taken for granted and has hardly been investigated. This lack of research on expulsion policy is partly due to the difficulty to investigate this part of policy as it requires analysis based on the personal files of (would-be) expellees. For an overview of the refugee policy in the 1930s (Caestecker and Moore 1999).

2. Circular letter of Goblet, 16.3.1887. Journal de droit international privé (Clunet) 1887: 383. Circular letter of the Dutch Minister of Justice, 5.4.1851. Algemeen Politieblad, 1851, bijlagen. Report on the Laws of Foreign countries respecting the Debarkating or Entry of Political convicts, Paupers or others into such countries. House of Commons, 1873. ARA (Algemeen Rijksarchief Brussel), MJ (Ministerie van Justitie), 348. (Sachße and Tennstedt 1980: 245, Caestecker 2000: 7, De Boeck 1927: 539).

3. The codification of membership of the welfare community was meant to shield it against strangers. By the end of the nineteenth century the stranger mostly coincided with the foreign poor. This issue of membership of the welfare community was dependent on the transformation of social policy throughout the nineteenth century from an undifferentiated caritas, in which public welfare was less important than private welfare to a social policy with a dominant input of public welfare which aimed at the regulation of the labour market. How the authorities distinguished between deserving and undeserving poor within their modern social policy and to what extent membership in the local community or in the national community (citizenship) was necessary in order to be catalogued under the deserving poor is important for the understanding of alien policy and expulsion policy, but will not be addressed here in detail.

   Since the middle of the fifteenth century public relief had been organised locally. The local authorities limited their expenses by refusing assistance to immigrants. If people born elsewhere became needy they were to be expelled to their *Heimat* or their *Heimat* had to reimburse the expenses. For aliens applying for public relief implied expulsion from the country. In the nineteenth century this *Heimatprinzip* was to give way to the principle of relief residence (*Unterstützungswohnsitz/Domicile de secours*) whereby one could apply for welfare in the place where one resided. This was introduced in France during the French Revolution and in Prussia in the middle of the nineteenth century. By the end of the long nineteenth century Belgium and all states in the German Reich (Bavaria only in 1916) also abstained from forcing nationals to leave the place of residence for their place of birth in the case of destitution. By the beginning of the twentieth century all countries had also designed criteria to exclude immigrants of foreign nationality from the welfare community. The welfare community was transformed from a local to a national community (Van Damme 1990a and b, Olshausen 1907, Guttmann 1992, Steinmetz 1993, Wagniart 1999: 173ff.).

4. In Belgium border choice for expellees was introduced in the alien law of 1835 which was prolonged every three years until it became a statute law in 1897. Although the law only explicitly granted border choice to resident aliens (those expelled by Royal Decree), it became applicable to all aliens from 1850/1852 onwards (Caestecker 2000: 7).

   In the Netherlands, article 12 of the alien law of 1849 provided border choice for those resident aliens who were unwanted due to disturbing public order and expelled on order of the King. This implied that aliens expelled for destitution (vagrants) could not claim this provision, but quite often this facility was also granted to this group of unwanted aliens (Leenders 1993: 106 and 112). However, it does not seem that the free border choice was systematically offered to all expellees in the Netherlands as was the case in Belgium. The *Procureur-generaal* of 's Hertogenbosch wrote to the *Administrateur* of the (Belgian) *Sûreté Publique* (SP) on 4.8.1881 that he himself would prefer that the border choice would be abolished altogether. According to him: "The expellee had to be brought to the border closest to his Fatherland, because, at least in most cases, one has the most chances in one's own country to find a job or some help by kinship. This policy was not only the best out of a humanitarian point of view but also out of a police point of view for the expelling as well as the receiving state. But also here exceptions have to be tolerated. If an alien can find a job in a certain region or city which is not directly situated in the direction of his region of birth I am not opposed to make an exception to the general rule." Procureur-generaal de Jans van Becken Dank, 's Hertogenbosch to the Administrateur of the Sûreté Publique (further SP), 4.8.1881. ARA, MJ, 367.

   In France free border choice was not mentioned in the law, but in practice refugees and deserters were granted free border choice. Interior Department to Department of Foreign Affairs, 14.6.1882. Archives nationales, Ministère de l'Intérieur (F7-further AN F7), 12586. Note SP, 27.4.1876. ARA, MJ, 158. (Alphand 1910: 41ff., De Boeck 1927: 580).

5. From the mid-1880s onwards European authorities tried again to exercise a greater control at their borders over the migrants who passed through their country on their way to the New World as an increasing number of migrants were turned down at the American shore. After being repatriated to their European embarkation port (Antwerp, Hamburg, Bremen, Rotterdam, Calais) these migrants were stuck there penniless and became a burden on public welfare. The shipping companies agreed to reimburse all expenses for the upkeep of these stranded migrants, in exchange border control of transit-migrants was subcontracted to this private sector. For example at the Russian-Prussian border agents of the shipping companies decided which people were liable to be refused by American authorities and those would-be emigrants were refused access to the territory of the German Reich. For example in 1903 8827 Eastern European migrants were stopped at the border in this way (Just 1988: 98ff., Caestecker 2000: 38).

6. The Dutch figures for the 1910s refer to the number of persons deported to the German border (Riding 1913: 210ff.) Hauptstaatsarchiv Düsseldorf, Regierung Aachen, 23.423. France also knew an increase in the number of expulsions: an average of 2,888 in the period 1876–1880 and 4,275 in 1885. Rapport du Garde des Sceaux sur l'administration de la Justice quoted in Barthelemy (1936:43). Expulsion from the German Reich (*Reichsverweisung)* was only applicable to criminals (in fact mainly beggars and vagrants) as it could only take place after a decision by the court. *Reichsverweisung* was only a very small number of the total expulsions from the

German states. The individual member-states of the German Empire
decided about most of the expulsions. For example in 1911 the Hansestadt
Bremen expelled 140 aliens (*Landesverweisung*), while in the same town in
the period 1881–1913 only twenty aliens were ordered to leave the Reich
(*Reichsverweisung*). In 1908 4,798 persons were expelled from Prussia,
2,669 in 1909 and 3,480 in 1912 (Elsner 1985: 43, Herder 1913: 17, Barfuss
1986: 174ff., Lucassen 1990: 367, Caestecker 2000: 32).

7.  Laws of foreign countries regarding the admission and continued residence
    of destitute aliens. Presented to both the Houses of Parliament by
    Command of her Majesty, September 1887. ARA, MJ, 347 (De Boeck 1927).

8.  The extent in which the liberal German states had liberal provisions in their
    expulsion policy is still to be investigated.

9.  For example, deserters and draft evaders, even if they were French nation-
    als could not count on any compassion when they fled to Prussia. They
    were mercilessly deported to the country they had fled (Alphand 1910).

10. Military service is a good case in point, the principle all over Europe in the
    nineteenth century was that all male residents, whether they were of foreign
    nationality or not had to fulfil their military obligations. Males of foreign
    nationality had to do this either in their country of nationality or in the
    country of immigration. The stateless had to fulfil their military obligations
    in the country of immigration. In France and Belgium, male immigrants
    were able to retain their foreign nationality, not only if they were enlisted
    on the lottery list (*list de tirage*), but even when they served in the French
    or Belgian army. In Germany those immigrants who fulfilled their military
    obligations in Germany were first compelled to entreat the German nation-
    ality. At the end of the nineteenth century, aliens residing in Prussia
    between 20 and 22 years of age who had not yet fulfilled their military
    obligations either in their own country or in Prussia had to choose either
    to leave Prussia or to entreat for Prussian nationality. This regulation is
    highly likely linked to the military build-up in Germany at the time (Förster
    1996: 470ff., Caestecker 1997: 33, 1999: 252). ARA, MJ, 661.

    Administrative documents were also an expression of the importance of
    nationality in the German Reich. The document needed for the declaration
    of arrival in a municipality in the German Empire, the *Heimatschein*
    mentioned the nationality of the bearer while in neighbouring countries
    there was no mention of nationality in similar documents (Caestecker 1999:
    251).

11. By the 1880s Switzerland, Italy, Bavaria and Spain also refused access to
    their territory to third countries nationals who were deported by the neigh-
    bouring countries (De Boeck, 1927: 582).

12. The Dutch compliance was also due to the wish to protect Dutch citizens
    working in the German Reich. The large Dutch community in Germany was
    treated harshly by the German authorities because most men refused to do
    their military service in Germany. Dutch emigrants who had settled in
    Germany generations earlier preferred to fulfil their military obligations in
    the Netherlands because the militia law of 1860 exempted the Dutch living
    abroad from serving in the army. A change of law in 1901 which increased
    the military obligations for Dutchmen abroad changed little as those living
    abroad who were born before 1883 were exempt. The issue was settled by
    the agreement of 1906 according to which only those Dutch emigrants in
    Germany who bragged about this privilege to locals and stirred up dissat-
    isfaction could still be expelled (Bundesarchiv Berlin, R1501, 8291; Krabbe
    1912: 95ff., Förster 1994). It is surprising that neither Leenders nor

Lucassen mention this Dutch-German agreement as it revolutionised Dutch deportation policy and had an important impact on respectively refugee policy and the deportation of gypsies.
13. Wagniart 1999:128 and 272. Martini 1919: 55ff. AN F7, 112548 and 12586.
14. In 1886 the Minister of Justice Modderman did not consider that returnees posed any problem: "vagrancy has only a temporary character, foreign vagrants can within a short time span start an industrious life and it would be unjust to punish them if they returned...Anyway when vagrants are time and again expelled when they return, they will stop returning" In the second half of the 1890s some Ministers advocated a tougher policy to stop unwanted aliens from returning. ARA, MJ, 367 (Krabbe 1912: 58ff., Stokvis 1931: 19

# References

Alphand, 1910, 'L'expulsion des déserteurs et l'extradition déguisée', *Revue de droit international privé Darras et de Lapradelle*: 35–56.
Bade, Klaus J., 1980, 'Massenwanderung und Arbeitsmarkt im deutschen Nordosten von 1880 bis zum Ersten Weltkrieg', *Archiv für Sozialgeschichte*, 20: 265–323.
Bade, Klaus J., 1987, 'Labour, Migration and the State: Germany from the Late 19th Century to the Onset of the Great Depression', in *Population. Labour and Migration in 19th- and 20th-Century Germany*, ed Klaus J. Bade. Leamington Spa, pp. 59–86.
Barfuss, Karl Marten, 1986, *Gastarbeiter in Nordwestdeutschland, 1884–1918*, Bremen.
Barthelemy, X., 1936, *Des infractions aux arrêtés d'expulsion et d'interdicton de séjour*, Paris.
Brubaker, Rogers, 1992, *Citizenship and nationhood in France and Germany*. Cambridge, Mass.
Caestecker, Frank, 1998, 'The Changing Modalities of Regulation within Continental Europe 1870–1940', in *Regulation of Migration. International Experiences*, eds A. Böcker et al., Amsterdam, pp. 73–98.
Caestecker, Frank and Bob Moore, 1998, 'Refugee Policies in Western European States in the 1930s. A Comparative Analysis', *IMIS-Beiträge*, 7: 55–103.
Caestecker, Frank, 1997, 'In het Kielzog van de Natie-Staat. De Politiek van nationaliteitsverwerving, -toekenning en-verlies in België, 1830–1909', *Belgisch Tijdschrift voor Nieuwste Geschiedenis*, XXVIII/3-4: 323–49.
Caestecker, Frank, 1999, 'Migratiecontrole in Europa gedurende de 19de eeuw: een schets', in *Docendo discimus. Liber americorum Romain Van Eenoo*, eds J. Art et al., Gent, pp. 241–55.
Caestecker, Frank, 2000, *Alien Policy in Belgium, 1840–1940. The Creation of Guest Workers, Refugees and Illegal Aliens*, Oxford.
Darut, J.A., 1902, *L'expulsion des étrangers. Principe Général. Application en France*, Aix.
De Boeck, Ch., 1927, 'L'expulsion et les difficultés internationales qu'en soulève la pratique', *Recueil des cours de l'Académie de droit internaitional*.
Elsner, L. and Lehmann, J., 1988, *Ausländische Arbeiter unter dem deutschen Imperialismus, 1900 bis 1985*, Berlin.
Förster, Stig, 1994, 'Militär und staatsbürgerliche Partizipation. Die allgemeine Wehrpflicht im Deutschen Kaiserreich 1871–1914', in *Die Wehrpflicht. Entstehung, Erscheinungsformen und politisch-militärische Wirkung*, ed. Roland Förster. Munich, pp.55–70.

Förster, Stig, 1996, 'The Armed Forces and Military Planning', in *Imperial Germany*, ed. R. Chickering, Westport, pp. 455–510.

Guttmann, Thomas, 1992, *Armut in der Großstadt: eine politische und sozialgeschichtliche Untersuchung ihrer Ursachen und Strukturen in München vom 1868 bis zum Ausbruch des Ersten Weltkriegs*, Munich.

Hehemann, R., 1987, *Die "Bekämpfung des Zigeunerunwesens" im Wilhelminischen Deutschland und in der Weimarer Republik, 1871–1933*, Frankfurt.

Herder, 1913, ,Wanderarmenwesen an der deutsch-belgischen und an der deutsch-holländischen Landesgrenze', *Caritas*, XIX/13–14: 13–17, 79–83.

Heijs, Eric, 1995, *Van Vreemdeling tot Nederlander. De verlening van het Nederlandschap aan vreemdelingen 1813–1992*, Amsterdam.

Just, Michael, 1988, *Ost-und südosteuropäische Amerikawanderung 1881–1914: Transitprobleme in Deutschland und Aufnahme in den Vereinigten Staaten*, Stuttgart.

Krabbe, J., 1912, *Toelating en uitzetting van vreemdelingen*, Leiden.

Kulczycki, John J., 1994, *The Foreign Worker and the German Labor Movement. Xenophobia and Solidarity in the Coal Fields of the Ruhr, 1871–1914*, Oxford.

Leenders, Marleen, 1993, *Ongenode gasten. Het vluchtelingenbeleid in Nederland, 1815–1938*, Hilversum.

Lucassen, Leo, 1990, *En men noemde hen zigeuners. De Geschiedenis van Kaldarasch, Ursari, Lowara en Sinti in Nederland, 1750–1944*, Amsterdam.

Lucassen, Leo, 1995, ,"Het paspoort als edelste deel van de mens" Een aanzet tot een sociale geschiedenis van het Nederlandse vreemdelingenbeleid', *Holland*, XXVII/4–5: 263–283.

Martini, A., 1909, *L'expulsion des étrangers*, Paris.

Noiriel, Gérard, 1988, *Le creuset français. Histoire de l'immigration XIX^e–XX^e siècles*, Paris.

Noiriel, Gérard, 1991, *La Tyrannie du National. Le droit d'asile en Europe 1793–1993*, Paris.

Neubach, H., 1967, *Die Ausweisungen von Polen und Juden aus Preußen, 1885–86*, Wiesbaden.

Olshausen, 1907, *Die Fürsorge für Ausländer in Deutschland*, Leipzig.

Peters-Schildgen, Susanne, 1997, *"Schmelztiegel" Ruhrgebiet. Die Geschichte der Zuwanderung am Beispiel Herne bis 1945*, Essen.

Riding, E., 1913, 'Wanderarmenwesen an der deutsch-holländischen Landesgrenze', *Caritas*, XIX: 210–13.

Sachße and Tennstedt, 1980, *Geschichte der Armenfüsorge in Deutschland. Vom Spätmittelalter bis zum Ersten Weltkrieg*, Stuttgart.

Schläpfer, Rudolf, 1969, *Die Ausländerfrage in der Schweiz vor dem Ersten Weltkrieg*, Zürich.

Seppen, G., en W. Walraven, 1951, *Handleiding tot de kennis van Vreemdelingen en grensbewaking*, Alphen aan de Rhijn.

Steinmetz, George, 1993, *Regulating the Social. The Welfare State and Local Politics in Imperial Germany*, Princeton.

Stokvis, Benno, 1931, 'De wet van 13.8.1949, stbl. 39 en strafbepalingen tegen vreemdelingen', *Tijdschrift voor Strafrecht*, XLI: 167–214.

Van Damme, D., 1990a, 'Onderstandswoonst, sedentarisering en stad-plattelandtegenstellingen. Evolutie en betekenis van de wetgeving op de onderstandswoonst in België (einde achttiende tot einde negentiende eeuw)', *Belgisch Tijdschrift voor Nieuwste Geschiedenis*, XXI/1–2: 483–534.

Van Damme, Dirk, 1990b, *Armenzorg en de staat*, Gent.

Van Outrive, Lode, Ponsaers Paul en Cartuyvels Yves, 1992, *Sire, ik ben ongerust 1794–1991*. Leuven.

Wennemann, Adolf, 1997, *Arbeit im Norden. Italiener im Rheinland und Westfalen des späten 19. und frühen 20.Jahrhunderts,* Osnabrück.

Wertheimer, J., 1987, *Unwelcome Strangers. East European Jews in Imperial Germay,* New York.

Wagniart, J., 1999, *Le vagabond à la fin du XIX^e siècle,* Paris.

# Chapter 9

## Foreigners and the Law in Nineteenth-Century Austria
### *Juridical Concepts and Legal Rights in the Light of the Development of Citizenship*

*Birgitta Bader-Zaar*

Concepts of citizenship emerged in the Western half of the Habsburg lands – here referred to as Austria – from the end of the eighteenth century onwards, gradually leading to the loss of the original meaning of *Bürger* which had referred to the rights of municipal burghers (*Stadtbürger*). As in other European countries, the homogeneity of the state was to be emphasised. Thus, the question arose what impact this was to have on aliens residing on Austrian territory. The introductory survey of the development of the legal status of foreigners presented here shows the solutions adopted in Austria. Interest in the analysis of the development of citizenship and foreignness in the Habsburg Empire is fairly recent in Austria (cf. Heindl and Saurer 2000). As I will argue here, the legal discourse on aliens – traced in commentaries of the law, legal textbooks and manuals – as well as legislation concerning legal rights of aliens essentially points towards a gradual widening of the gap between citizens and foreigners. Only in the 'constitutional' period of the 1860s did the definition of citizen rights as political rights attempt to clearly mark foreigners as outsiders. In other respects their status varied, depending on economic and political interests and their implementation within the system of migration control. No comprehensive legislation ever reviewed the status of foreigners

– or, for that matter, that of citizens – in the long nineteenth century. Even a consistent legal definition of aliens was absent from the law. While the German term *Ausländer* clearly referred to nationals of other countries, the term *Fremde* (in the sense of 'stranger') could refer to aliens but also to Austrian nationals travelling into other lands on Austrian territory or residing in a locality or municipality in which they had not been formally accepted as a member. The status as stranger was especially relevant for poor relief for which only citizens were eligible, and which was provided only by the commune or municipality to which a person officially belonged, even if he or she did not reside there. (This right was termed *Heimatrecht* from 1849.)

## Juridical concepts of foreigners

In legal discourse citizenship was the foil against which concepts of foreigners were placed. As Hannelore Burger has shown, the term *Staatsbürger*, i.e. citizen, first appeared in Austrian legal texts in 1797, in the Westgalizisches Gesetzbuch, the forerunner of the general codification of civil law in 1811 (*Allgemeines Bürgerliches Gesetzbuch*; ABGB) (Burger 1999a: 214–21). In his 1811 commentary to the ABGB Franz von Zeiller defined citizens as members of the state (*Mitglieder des Staates*) (Zeiller 1811, vol. 1: 133), thus emphasizing the homogeneity of the state in contrast to the hierarchical structures of the estates in the several lands. However, a legal definition of the term did not exist in Austrian legislation. The ABGB only determined how citizenship was to be acquired, basically by birth from Austrian parents. Furthermore, *ius sanguinis* was complemented by several possibilities of naturalization. Considering the lack of a legal statement on the contents of the term citizenship, commentators in the first half of the nineteenth century were inclined to equate *Staatsbürger* with II, § 3 of the code of 1786 (*Josephinisches Gesetzbuch*) which declared that 'all those living in the Austrian hereditary lands under the power of the sovereign are to be viewed as nationals [*Inländer*] and subjects [*Untertanen*]'. This idea of citizenship was essentially determined by territory and – in an era of absolutism – did not include any schemes for political rights.[1]

Turning to foreigners, we find that the territorial component was the determining factor in the perception of their status. Predating the introduction of the concept of citizenship, the Codex Theresianus of 1766, a draft compilation of legislation concerning civil law, defined foreigners as 'subjected to foreign rule [*auswärtige Botmäßigkeit*]' (I, 2, § 21) and the *Josephinisches*

*Gesetzbuch* declared in the previously cited II, § 3 that foreigners 'enjoyed common protection by the lands during their passage through or their stay in the hereditary lands, but were not to be considered as subjects' (Krasnopolski 1907: 16).

Nevertheless, commentaries on the law were inclined to bind foreigners closer to the state in the context of state security. In Carl Anton von Martini's *Lehrbegriff des allgemeinen Staatsrechts* of 1783 we find foreigners referred to as *zeitliche Untertanen* – temporary subjects, who fell under the power of the sovereign by entering the territory and were thus obliged 'to refrain from all that upsets the security of the state' (Martini 1783/1969, 3: § 269, p. 138). The status of foreigners did not quite equal that of native-born subjects. The basic principle that foreigners were responsible for their actions under the same laws as Austrian born subjects could – according to Martini – be altered by treaties or special legislation on foreigners (ibid., § 272, p. 139f.). Such specific legislation included, for instance, tariffs preventing foreigners from offering their merchandise cheaper than natives and depriving the latter of their "honourable livelihood' (ibid., § 275, p. 141).[2] In addition to the perception of foreigners as economic competitors Martini touched upon the problem that they were not participants in the 'civic contract' (*bürgerlicher Vertrag*) and could thus not be expected to act in the public interest, i.e. to assume guardianships, enter military service, or accept other public offices against their will (Ibid., § 278, p. 142).

In Franz von Zeiller's commentary on the ABGB the idea of foreigners as 'temporary subjects' recurs (Zeiller 1811, vol. 1: 133). This category was still active in 1840 when Franz von Egger published his revision of Martini (Egger 1840, vol. 1: § 269, p. 168). Zeiller, however, also uses the term 'temporary inhabitants' (*zeitliche Einwohner*), which suggests the promotion of immigration as a motive for this usage. He notes the positive aspects of the concession of civil rights (*bürgerliche Rechte*) to foreigners: 'Thus [the state] promotes communication advantageous for its own citizens, it induces foreign subjects to take up at least a temporary stay in the territory, and it induces fair-thinking foreign regents in other countries to concede civil rights to resident citizens of such enlightened states also in their territory' (Zeiller 1811, vol. 1: 141). So, besides promoting immigration, the ideas of enlightenment were to be dispersed.

Nevertheless, for Zeiller such a 'liberal' government attitude required some measures of restraint (ibid., 135): First, foreigners enjoyed the protection of civil law, but could not be admitted to the same advantages as citizens as they did not carry an equal portion of the public burden; second, the concession of rights was dependent on reciprocity with foreign states;[3] and, third, exceptions to this had to be made when conditions demanded it. Full enjoyment of rights could only be granted with citizenship.

The absence of a comprehensive alien law was to some extent compensated by Johann Vesque von Püttlingen's overview of the legal status of foreigners in civil, criminal, commercial, military, and police law, published in 1842. Vesque von Püttlingen brought to attention the different terms which were used for citizens and foreigners in Austrian legislation, of which I will only mention those for foreigners: *Fremde* or *Ausländer, Einwohner fremder Staaten* (residents of foreign states), *Staatsbürger eines fremden Landes* (citizens of a foreign country), *fremde Landeskinder* (foreign nationals), or *fremde Untertanen* (foreign subjects) (Vesque von Püttlingen 1842: § 1, p.1, note 2). In contrast to Austrian citizens – or 'subjects', as Vesque von Püttlingen preferred to put it – foreigners were subjected to a foreign supreme power (*oberste Gewalt*), although they had accepted some duties or acquired some rights owing to their contingent stay on Austrian territory, acquisition of land, or the settlement of valid legal transactions (ibid., § 1, p. 1f.).

Vesque von Püttlingen, incidentally, pointed out the complications of alien and citizen status in Austria in some special cases: the Hungarian case the protection issued by the Habsburg Monarchy to certain persons in the Ottoman Empire (*Schutzgenossen*) and the issue of dual or plural citizenship (ibid., § 2, p. 2; Burger 2000: 103–105). *Sujets mixtes*, originally individuals with two or more nationalities, referred in Austria mainly to Polish nobles who owned property in Galicia as well as other parts of the former kingdom of Poland (Pacholkiv 2000: 555–558). An attempt to end this privilege of dual nationality through the Convention of 3 March 1815 between Austria, Prussia, and Russia failed. Many nobles refused to declare their permanent residence and thus become subjects of the sovereign in whose territory their residence lay. A further special legal existence of foreigners, the *Indigenat* or *Incolat*, conceded equal citizens' rights to foreigners. This legal status survived in Bohemia, Moravia, Silesia, Galicia, Hungary, and Croatia after 1848, as a condition for foreigners to own real estate listed in the registers of noble property (*landtäfliche Güter*) (Vesque 1842: § 2, p. 3; Burger 1999a: 220).

In the second half of the nineteenth century the territorial aspect of the definition of foreigners prevailed, but possible exclusions were emphasized. Joseph Unger, for example, defined foreigners as persons who were not members of a certain state (*Staatsgenossenschaft*), and – in the case of Austria – had not been accepted tacitly by, or been born to, a member of the Austrian state (Unger 1876, vol. 1: § 40, p. 299). Here, the reference to *ius sanguinis* is made explicit for the first time in legal commentaries. The most exclusionary definition of foreigners is to be found at the beginning of the twentieth century in the *Österreichisches Staatswörterbuch* where Jiří Pražák describes a foreigner as 'a person who is not entitled to citizenship in the considered territory' (Pražák 1905: 365). Pražák understands *Staatsbürgerschaft* primarily in the sense of citizen rights and not nationality.

The juridical literature cited here pictured foreigners essentially as a homogeneous group. However, laws did differentiate. For example Jews were a group with a special status. Foreign Jews were treated as foreigners but also subject to the special regulations in force for Jews in the Habsburg lands (Vesque von Püttlingen 1842: § 27, p. 29, § 252, p. 352; Scherer 1905: 946–971; Stoklásková 2000: 665–669). Additional regulations dealt with Jews who were Turkish nationals and enjoyed the privileges of the treaties between the Habsburg and Ottoman Empires facilitating trade (Vesque 1842: § 200, pp. 231–241; Stoklásková 2000: 669–674). The special status and legal discrimination of Jews regarding freedom of religion and civil rights finally ended in the period from 1859 to 1868.

Laws also indicated who was welcome on Austrian territory and who was not. 'Gypsies' were considered as especially undesirable in the Habsburg Monarchy. After having been expelled in 1744 and 1749, the state aspired to settle and assimilate them in the following years. Vagrancy was not to be condoned and decrees in several lands in the late eighteenth and first half of the nineteenth centuries provided for the deportation of newly arrived 'gypsy' families (Reiter 1996: 185ff.). Those caught wandering about without an apparent destination or without a permit for the trade they exercised were generally to be treated as foreigners if they could not prove that they were members of a certain commune or municipality (Pace 1896, vol. 3: 660). By prohibiting peddling for foreigners, an economic lure to Austria was to be curtailed.

## Control and legal rights

J.L.E. von Barth-Barthenheim, in his detailed book on the tasks of the Austrian administrative police published in 1829, gives us a comprehensive account of the classes of people who were not to travel into or through the lands of the Habsburgs, often not differentiating between foreigners and Austrian subjects, a further example for the junction of the term *Fremde* for foreigners and nationals travelling outside their place of domicile. The poor, especially beggars and vagrants who would only burden the state – e.g. Italians described in detail in 1781 with their monkeys, dogs, dancing bears, and other animals or foreigners with show cases, organs and similar musical boxes (Kropatschek 1785, vol. 1: 271f.) – were denied entry. Security and public order became the central concern of the administration when dealing with foreigners at the end of the eighteenth century, given that the war with France and French emigration brought unwelcome prospects of Jacobin unrest. A special division of the police (*Fremdenpolizei*) was established in 1794 to prevent the entry of 'dangerous people' and to register all foreigners. It was the 'ambiguous, ill-disposed and businessless' foreigner who was to be kept away from Austria (Barth-Barthenheim 1829, vol. 1: 28). Secret agents, persons deported from other countries, deserters, foreign priests, and peddlers were viewed with suspicion (Vesque von Püttlingen 1842: § 249, p. 349f.; Stokláskova 2000: 648–660). If unwelcome persons nevertheless succeeded in entering the country and were found travelling through Austria, deportation occurred (Vesque von Püttlingen 1842: §§ 254–265, pp. 352–365; Wendelin 2000).[4] In addition, foreigners not adhering to government expectations regarding moral conduct or political ideas were likely to be deported. Deportation was also the fate of impoverished foreigners, as public welfare was limited to Austrian subjects (cf. also § 2, Heimatgesetz, 1863, RGBl. 105). Control of foreign travellers was ensured through unified passports in the whole of Austria from 1801 on (Burger 2000: 76–79, 82f.; Geselle 2000; Stokláskova 2000: 632–47). Besides identifying its carrier the passport indicated the route the traveller took to his or her destination, which required special permission. However, travellers do not seem to have been troubled by police checks on their journey through Austria if their papers were in order (Burger 2000: 83f.). At their destination foreigners were to be registered with the police until they departed. Compulsory registration remained an obligation even after freedom of movement inside the Habsburg Monarchy was introduced in 1857, but passports lost their significance once controls were lifted at the outer borders of the Monarchy in 1865.

Security and public order were legally balanced by ensuring foreigners had largely equal treatment in civil law. At first, the French constitution of 1791 was reflected in § 55 of the *Westgalizisches Gesetzbuch* of 1797, which granted equal rights only 'as long as they [i.e. foreigners] did not become unworthy of the protection of the laws'. This reservation of unworthiness was dropped in the ABGB of 1811, which was and is the most important piece of legislation concerning the status of foreigners in relation to civil law. Although the ABGB also dealt with the foreigner's legal capacity and general capacity to act and enter into liabilities (Articles 34 to 37), which were defined by domicile or citizenship (if no domicile existed), these were issues open to interpretation and entailed debates up to the end of the monarchy, especially regarding freedom of marriage (Krasnopolski 1907; Steinlechner 1911: 65f.). Legal regulations of the state of origin clearly were not authoritative for the legal capacity of a foreigner in the case of slavery or serfdom which was prohibited in the Habsburg lands (Vesque von Püttlingen 1842: § 47f., p. 47f., § 56, p. 53).

Apart from the ABGB several decrees and treaties touched on the question of freedom of fortune and inheritance (Vesque von Püttlingen 1842: §§ 72–94, pp. 64–100). The famous *droit d'aubaine* or *ius albinagii* which decreed that the properties of dead foreigners should fall to the state and which had been part of the French Code civil from 1804 to 1819, did not exist in Austrian law. The fate of legacies depended on reciprocity (Vesque von Püttlingen 1842: § 73f., pp. 65–70; Unger 1876, vol. 1: § 40, p. 302 and note 18). Foreigners also had the basic right to own landed property – with the exception of farmsteads –,[5] but this again depended on reciprocity. On the other hand, trade and commercial activities varied regionally and depended on the existence of freedom of trade and commerce, on guilds and systems of concessions (Vesque von Püttlingen 1842: §§ 180–193, pp. 212–226). According to the commercial codes (*Gewerbeordnung*) of 20 December 1859 (*RGBl.* 227), however, only Austrian citizens could enter a trade, the admittance of foreigners depending on treaties or decisions of the Minister of the Interior (Milner 1880: 79, note 3). The right to exercise a trade was to be opened up in 1883 (*RGBl.* 39), again reciprocity could be asked for.

With the introduction of citizens' rights in the 1860s, especially the 'Staatsgrundgesetz über die allgemeinen Rechte der Staatsbürger' of 21 December 1867 (*RGBl.* 142), the scope of exclusion from, and respectively inclusion in, these rights was clearly defined. While the 'individual sphere' (Pražák 1905: 365) was to be protected, political rights especially were seen as a prerogative of specially defined groups of citizens. One exception to the protection of the 'individual sphere' was deportation, which could be ordered if no penal legal proceedings had been instigated. Abbé Sièyes' dictum of 1789 that women, children, and foreigners, did not contribute anything to the public effort and therefore must not actively influence public matters prevailed in Austria, too (Sewell 1988: 107). Foreigners were neither entitled to suffrage nor to membership in political associations (§ 30 of the law on association, 15 November 1867, *RGBl.* 134), nor to the management of meetings in which public matters were to be discussed (§ 8 of the law on assemblies, 15 November 1867, *RGBl.* 135). Nevertheless, there were some instances in which foreigners did exercise political rights in Austria: They were permitted to claim suffrage in the provincial diets and were admitted to membership in the Upper House (*Herrenhaus*) of Austrian parliament (*Reichsrat*) if they headed a domestic noble family which entailed these rights (*Indigenat*), but these were only a tiny minority. The seaport of Trieste was a special case, with the strong economic interests of the foreigners residing in the city. After a five-year-residency, foreigners could vote for the city council (patent of 12 April 1850, RGBl. 139, § 34). Foreigners were also eligible to the Chamber of Commerce in Trieste in which they could fill one third of the seats (§ 7, 9 June 1868, *RGBl.* 85).

Constitutionalism of the 1860s conceived the public sphere essentially as a political sphere and therefore tended to exclude foreigners from all its domains. Public positions were now to be closed to foreigners. Any office related to legal proceedings, to editorship of periodical publications, and to teaching positions in public and private education required Austrian citizenship (for a detailed list cf. Pace 1896, vol. 2: 974, note 1). Leading ecclesiastical functions had already been restricted to Austrian citizens since the eighteenth century (Vesque von Püttlingen 1842: § 12f., pp. 11–13). Temporary enlistment in military service – long open to foreigners with the exception of the frontier guards – was now admitted only in exceptional cases subject to approval by the country of origin (*RGBl.* 1868/151).

## Naturalization

The authors of the ABGB maintained that full civil rights could not be conceded to foreigners as these did not carry the burdens of citizenship, especially personal taxation and services for the state (Ofner 1889, 2: 608). Accordingly, the acquisition of citizenship, basically a status attained by birth, as a legitimate child of Austrian parents, is dealt with at length in the ABGB for the first time for the whole of Austria, having previously been handled by the several lands. This was to remain the basic legal text for naturalization until 1918. A general law on citizenship announced in 1867 was never passed.

As Burger (2000: 108–127, 141–161) has dealt with most aspects of naturalization extensively, I will only summarize its central conditions here. According to § 29 ABGB, foreigners were automatically naturalized if they:

(1) held a position in public administration on certain levels – as mentioned above, possible until 1867;

(2) led a certain business necessitating permanent residence in Austria,[6] e.g., as clarified in various decrees, manufactures in which the master craftsmanship of a guild was awarded, and commerce, with the exceptions of wholesale business and the lithographic trade (Milner 1880: 42–44). While this measure aimed at promoting immigration, it ultimately lost its relevance around the middle of the nineteenth century and was abolished by the new trade regulations of the emperor's ordinance of 27 April 1860 (RGBl. 108);

(3) resided permanently for at least ten years in one of the provinces – with the exception of free ports – on the condition that they had not received any punishments for a crime. The length of ten years had been criticized in the discussions around the birth of the ABGB and a shorter period had been proposed, but the ten years-clause remained (Ofner 1889, vol. 2: 609).

Foreign women, as well as any illegitimate minor children legitimised by their father, automatically received Austrian citizenship through marriage with an Austrian. If a male foreigner acquired Austrian citizenship, his wife and legitimate minor children did so as well.

The fundamental form of naturalization, however, was the voluntary action of the state (§ 30). Citizenship could be conferred upon application, after property, earning capacity, and the moral conduct of the applicant had been inspected. Incidentally, there were cases in which women applied for citizenship in their own right (Burger 1999b: 38–44; Burger 2000: 154–161). A decree of 1813 interpreted naturalization as an act of grace by the state which was reserved to the highest-ranking authority of the court (*Hofkanzlei*). Personal residency – irrespective of the length of stay – was now a strict requirement, and the abolition of the property requirement in 1816 and 1824 soon shifted the interest of the state to moral conduct. In the following years authority over naturalization moved to the provinces (1829), then to the Ministry of Interior (1853), and finally returned to the provinces in 1859. In the meantime, the regulations concerning naturalization were restricted: in 1833 automatic naturalization after a permanent residence of ten years was abolished, as foreigners who did not wish it had also been transformed into Austrian citizens. Now, individuals had to explicitly apply for citizenship. Following the introduction of *Heimatrecht* in 1849, it was necessary to receive assurance of admission into a rural commune or municipality as a prerequisite for citizenship, while a formal discharge from the original state was not necessary and depended on the regulations of that state (Pace 1896, vol. 2: 926f., Burger 2000: 164–167).

## The absence of an alien law

The numerous decrees and ordinances dealing with the rights and naturalization of foreigners lead us to the question of failure regarding the codification of an alien law in Austria. Of course Austria did not stand alone in this regard. The immigration laws of Britain and the United States, as countries attracting large numbers of immigrants, remained exceptions in Europe and North America. In Austria, the state did not view immigration as a problem of national dimensions. The lands of the Habsburgs generally did not attract large numbers of foreign immigrants in the eighteenth and nineteenth centuries. Internal migration, especially into less populated areas in the eastern and south-eastern parts of the Habsburg monarchy, and seasonal migration were more typical, besides the immigration of political, cultural, and commercial elites (Fassmann and Münz 1995: 13). The mercantilist population policy of the second half of the eighteenth century nevertheless encouraged immigration as a means to strengthen the economic and military power of the state, and later to improve agriculture. Financial support, exemption from military service, and the right of remigration (Vesque von Püttlingen 1842: § 32, p. 33f.) were to attract settlers not only to Hungary but also to Galicia (cf. Pacholkiv 2000: 598–601) and the Bukowina. However, the war with France meant that the interest of the state decreased (Stokláskova 2000: 696–711), financial support ceased in 1810, and only private enterprises continued to encourage migration until the middle of the nineteenth century.

In the second half of the nineteenth century, Austria became a destination for migrants from eastern and southeastern Europe, but in 1910 only about 632,000 foreigners (approximately 2.2 percent of the Austrian population) lived in the Austrian half of the Habsburg Monarchy, and 277,000 (approximately 1.3 percent of the Hungarian population) in the Hungarian half (Fassmann 1991: 53–56). These figures, of course, give no information on the proportion of naturalized immigrants. The largest proportion of immigrants to Austria – more than 50 percent – arrived from Hungary, which appeared in these statistics because of the independent status conferred in the compromise of 1867 (*Ausgleich*) and the military's interest in the number of conscripts, approximately 20 percent of whom came from Germany, 14 percent from Italy, and 7 percent from Russia. Over half of the immigrants were blue-collar workers, the rest mainly white-collar workers or day labourers and domestic servants. In Hungary, the share of migration from Austria, especially from Galicia, Bohemia, and Moravia was even larger: nearly 85 per cent. As these figures show, de facto internal migration between Austria and Hungary was of primary significance. The main destination of migrants was Vienna – one third of all immigrants moved there – followed by the border region between Austria and Hungary and between Austria and its other surrounding states, especially Russia, where most of the settlers were Jews, and Italy.

The lack of immigration accounts for immigrants, or foreigners in general, being a minor issue in the Austrian parliamentary debates from 1861 onwards. They appear mainly in three instances:

(1) Calls to promote tourism and to attract foreign guests, especially to the Alpine regions;

(2) protests against deportation of foreigners who, for example, had been active in strikes or had breached the press law and therefore were viewed as a danger for the public order;

(3) antisemitic motions by radical German nationalists, such as Georg von Schönerer, for the prohibition of immigration and residency by foreign Jews.

The problem that loomed large in the parliamentary debates and public discussion from the turn of the nineteenth century onwards, however, was emigration, which experienced a sharp rise after freedom of movement had been enacted in 1867. In contrast to many other European countries, such as France (1860),

Switzerland (1888), Germany (1897), Italy (1901), and even Hungary (1909), efforts to handle administrative problems connected with mass emigration through comprehensive legislation failed, owing to conflicts of interest between various branches of government, especially commerce and the military, as well as parliamentary chaos resulting from nationalistic strife (Chmelar 1974).

## Conclusion

Rogers Brubaker has pointed out how the development of a 'legally homogeneous national citizenry' after the revolution in France, led to a nation-state which was 'sharply bounded externally' and thus marked foreigners 'clearly and axiomatically as outsiders' (Brubaker 1992: 46). It took until the middle of the nineteenth century for juridical authors in Austria to absorb the French view, and to turn away from an immigration-friendly range of vision and a concept of 'temporary subjects/inhabitants'. The widening of the gap between the two categories of citizen and foreigner can be observed in legislation. Although restrictions such as the closure of certain positions and trades, and of the poor law, existed at the turn of the eighteenth century, the ABGB of 1811 basically conferred equal rights to foreigners, although always under the condition of reciprocity. A gradual change is to be observed from the 1830s owards, when naturalization came to be viewed as a voluntary act of the state and automatic accession to citizenship, after ten years of permanent residency, ended. From the end of the 1850s onwards, economic possibilities were further limited. The most distinct rejection occurred in the period of constitutionalism in 1867/68, when foreigners were generally excluded from rights and positions in the public sphere.

This widening gap between citizens and foreigners in juridical concepts and legislation, however, reaches its limits in Austria, not only semantically, owing to the use of the term *Fremde* for foreigners and citizens moving outside of their place of domicile, or economically in the opening of commerce to foreigners in 1883. The idea of a homogeneous nation-state could have been enhanced by a law on citizenship and an alien law. However, this was never an issue in Austria. Of course the influx of migrants from abroad was so low that no actual need existed to further specify foreigners in the legal sense. But it also seemed inopportune to meddle too much with terms and to initiate public debates. Hungary had provided for a law on citizenship (1879) and on emigration (1909), thus underlining its independent position within the Dual Monarchy. While the Habsburg Monarchy maintained the concept of 'nationality of the Empire' (*Reichsangehörigkeit*) for Austrian and Hungarian citizens alike in relations to foreign countries, an Austrian law on citizenship and foreigners would have had to reflect on the actual status of Hungarian citizens within Austria, and would have entailed a debate on the question of citizenship for all the national minorities in Austria. This might ultimately have promoted the disintegration of the Empire in the face of claims for autonomy, especially by the Czech-speaking population. Given the multinational fabric of Austria, where eight officially recognized languages were spoken, a large variety of social structures and cultures was to be found, and the protection of rights of minorities was the central problem of daily politics, any overemphasis on homogeneity of citizenship, or sharp distinction of foreigners, might backfire. The government's interest – also considering experiences with the problems encountered in materializing a codification of laws on emigration – was to leave space for adjustments and a path to manoeuvre if necessary. Constitutional legislation of 1867, which entrenched civil rights and above all political rights – a contested field throughout the nineteenth century – had to suffice to safeguard the state's cohesion.

## Notes

I would like to thank Dr. Hannelore Burger and Prof.emer. Dr.DDr.h.c. Gerald Stourzh for their valuable comments on various versions of this paper. This paper is part of a larger research project on legal rights of foreigners in Austria during the long nineteenth century in an international comparative perspective.
1. Hannelore Burger has thus convincingly refuted the prevalent idea in constitutional studies that Austrian citizenship was traditionally only based on ius sanguinis (Burger 1999a: 218 note 39, also Burger 2000: 103, note 332).
2. In the early nineteenth century the question of economic competition was softened. In his revision of Martini Franz von Egger mentions monopolies as an interference to the benefit of citizens. Insofar as no rights were encroached upon, low-priced offers as such, were not prohibited (Egger [2]1840, 1: § 275, p. 169).
3. The terms used to describe this principle in juridical literature in general are *Reziprozität* (reciprocity) and *Retorsion* (retaliation). In the following I will use the term "reciprocity". For decrees regarding reciprocity cf. Winiwarter [3]1844, 1: 114–119; also Unger [4]1876, 1: § 40, p. 306f.
4. Legislation on deportation was to be condensed in the *Reichsschubgesetz* of 27 July 1871 (RGBl. 88).
5. Subjects of the German confederation were exempt from this rule if they wished to acquire farmsteads in the Austrian provinces belonging to the *Deutsche Bund* (Hofkanzleidekret 14 April 1825).
6. With the exception of Venice (Austrian territory until 1866) and Trieste (Vesque 1842: § 11, p. 11).

# References

Barth-Barthenheim, J.L.E. v., 1829, *System der österreichischen administrativen Polizey, mit vorzüglicher Rücksicht auf das Erzherzogthum Oesterreich unter der Enns. Ein Versuch*, vol. 1, Vienna.

Brubaker, Rogers, 1992, *Citizenship and Nationhood in France and Germany*, Cambridge, Mass./London.

Burger, H., 1999a, 'Zum Begriff der österreichischen Staatsbürgerschaft. Vom Josephinischen Gesetzbuch zum Staatsgrundgesetz über die allgemeinen Rechte der Staatsbürger', in *Geschichte und Recht. Festschrift für Gerald Stourzh zum 70. Geburtstag*, eds T. Angerer, B.Bader-Zaar and M. Grandner, Vienna 207–23.

Burger, H., 1999b, 'Zur Geschichte der Staatsbürgerschaft der Frauen in Österreich. Ausgewählte Fallstudien aus der ersten Hälfte des 19. Jahrhunderts', *L'Homme. Z.F.G.* 10, no.1: 38–44.

Burger, H., 2000, 'Paßwesen und Staatsbürgerschaft', in *Grenze und Staat*, eds W. Heindl and E. Saurer, Vienna: 1–172.

Chmelar, H., 1974, *Höhepunkte der österreichischen Auswanderung. Die Auswanderung aus dem im Reichsrat vertetenen Königreichen und Ländern in den Jahren 1905 –1914*, Vienna.

Egger, F. Ritter v., 1840, *Das natürliche öffentliche Recht, nach den Lehrsätzen des seligen Freiherrn C.A. von Martini, vom Staatsrechte, mit beständiger Rücksicht auf das natürliche Privat-Recht des k.k. Hofrathes Franz Edlen von Zeiller*, 2nd edn, 2 vols, Vienna.

Fassmann, H., 1991, 'Einwanderung, Auswanderung und Binnenwanderung in Österreich-Ungarn. Eine Analyse der Volkszählung 1910', *Österreichische Osthefte* 33: 51–66.

Fassmann, H., and R. Münz, 1995, *Einwanderungsland Österreich? Historische Migrationsmuster, aktuelle Trends und politische Maßnahmen*, Vienna.

Geselle, A., 2000, 'Bewegung und ihre Kontrolle in Lombardo-Venetien' in *Grenze und Staat*, eds Heindl and Saurer, Vienna: 345–515.

Heindl, W., and E. Saurer, eds, 2000, *Grenze und Staat. Paßwesen, Staatsbürgerschaft, Heimatrecht und Fremdengesetzgebung in der österreichischen Monarchie 1750–1867*, Vienna.

Komlosy, A., 1995, 'Ein Land – viele Grenzen. Waren- und Reiseverkehr zwischen den österreichischen und den böhmischen Ländern (1740–1918)', in *Kulturen an der Grenze. Waldviertel, Weinviertel, Südböhmen, Südmähren*, eds A. Komlosy, V. Buzek and F. Svátek, Vienna, 1995, 59–72

Komlosy, A., 1996, '"Zur Belassung am hiesigen Platze nicht geeignet..." Selektion und Kontrolle der Zuwanderung ins Kernland der Habsburgermonarchie', *Jahrbuch für Landeskunde von Niederösterreich*, N.F. 2, no. 2: 569–576.

Krasnopolski, H., 1907, *Staatsangehörigkeit oder Domizil? Ein Beitrag zur Auslegung des § 34 BGB*, Vienna.

Kropatschek, J., ed, 1785–1790, *Handbuch aller unter der Regierung des Kaisers Joseph des II. für die K.K. Erbländer ergangenen Verordnungen und Gesetze in einer Sistematischen Verbindung*, 18 vols, Vienna.

[Martini, C. A. v.,] 1969, *Des Freyherrn von Martini Lehrbegriff des allgemeinen Staatsrechts*, 4 vols, Vienna, 1783–1784, reprint 1 vol., Aalen.

Milner, E., 1880, *Die österreichische Staatsbürgerschaft und der Gesetzesartikel L:1879 über den Erwerb und Verlust der ungarischen Staatsbürgerschaft*, Tübingen.

Ofner, J., ed, 1889, *Der Ur-Entwurf und die Berathungs-Protokolle des Oesterreichischen Allgemeinen bürgerlichen Gesetzbuches*, 2 vols, Vienna.

Pace, A., ed, 1895–1913, *Ernst Mayerhofer's Handbuch für den politischen Verwaltungsdienst in den im Reichsrathe vertetenen Königreichen und Ländern*, 5th edn, 7 vols, Vienna.

Pacholkiv, S., 2000, 'Das Werden einer Grenze: Galizien 1772–1867', in *Grenze und Staat*, eds Heindl and Saurer, Vienna: 517–618.

Prazák, J., 1905, 'Ausländer', in *Österreichisches Staatswörterbuch. Handbuch des gesamten öffentlichen Rechtes*, eds E. Mischler and J. Ulbrich, 2nd edn, vol. 1, Vienna: 365–67.

Reiter, I., 1996, 'Ausgewiesen, abgeschoben. Eine Geschichte des Ausweisungsrechts in Österreich vom ausgehenden 18. bis ins 20. Jahrhundert', unpublished manuscript, Vienna.

Riedel, M., 1972, 'Bürger, Staatsbürger, Bürgertum', in *Geschichtliche Grundbegriffe. Historisches Lexikon zur politisch-sozialen Sprache in Deutschland*, eds O. Brunner, W.Conze and R. Koselleck, vol. 1, Stuttgart: 672–725.

Scherer, J., 1905, 'Juden: A. Geschichtlich', in *Österreichisches Staatswörterbuch. Handbuch des gesamten öffentlichen Rechtes*, eds E. Mischler and J. Ulbrich, 2nd edn, vol. 2, Vienna: 946–71.

Sewell, W.H., 1988, 'Le citoyen/la citoyenne: Activity, Passivity, and the Revolutionary Concept of Citizenship', in *The French Revolution and the Creation of Modern Political Culture, vol. 2: The Political Culture of the French Revolution*, ed. C. Lucas, Oxford: 105–23.

Steinlechner, P., 1911, 'Zur Würdigung der Bestimmungen des österr. allg. bürg. Gesetzbuches über die örtliche Geltung der Gesetze', in *Festschrift zur Jahrhundertfeier des allgemeinen bürgerlichen Gesetzbuches. 1. Juni 1911*, part 2, Vienna: 53–93.

*Stenographische Protokolle über die Sitzungen des Hauses der Abgeordneten des österreichischen Reichsrathes.*

Stokláskóva, Z., 2000, 'Fremdsein in Böhmen und Mähren', in *Grenze und Staat*, eds Heindl and Saurer, Vienna 2000: 619–718.

Unger, J., 1876, *System des österreichischen allgemeinen Privatrechts*, 4th edn, vol. 1, Leipzig.

Vesque von Püttlingen, J., 1842, *Die gesetzliche Behandlung der Ausländer in Oesterreich nach den daselbst gültigen Civilrechts-, Straf-, Commerzial-, Militär- und Polizei-Normen, nebst einer einleitenden Abhandlung*, Vienna.

Wendelin, H., 2000, 'Schub und Heimatrecht', in *Grenze und Staat*, eds Heindl and Saurer, Vienna: 173–343.

Winiwarter, J., 1844–1859, *Handbuch der Gesetze und Verordnungen, welche sich auf das Oesterreichische allgemeine bürgerliche Gesetzbuch beziehen*, 3rd edn, 4 parts, Vienna.

Zeiller, F. v., 1811–1813, *Commentar über das allgemeine bürgerliche Gesetzbuch für die gesammten Deutschen Erbländer der Oesterreichischen Monarchie*, 4 vols, Vienna.

# Chapter 10

# Empowerment and Control
## *Conflicting Central and Regional Interests in Migration Within the Habsburg Monarchy*

*Andrea Komlosy*

At the end of the eighteenth century, the Habsburg Monarchy was characterized by strong regional disparities. Before the State Constitution was passed in 1867, emigration was severely restricted by various laws. Immigration was limited to master craftsmen and journeymen who were travelling within the networks of their professional guilds, to economic elites (entrepreneurs, merchants, skilled labourers) who were encouraged by special incentives, and refugees, provided they were not considered a threat to state security. Many investors, engineers and skilled labourers from Western Europe came from countries that had at one time belonged to the monarchy, e. g. the southern Netherlands, Swabia etc. Even after the liberalization of emigration, internal migration was far more important than in- and out-migration across state-boundaries. In 1910, 62 percent of the Cisleithanians (inhabitants of the *Österreichische Reichshälfte*, i. e. the part of the Dual Monarchy governed from Vienna) were living within the boundaries of their community of birth. 31 percent were considered internal migrants who had crossed boundaries of districts (*Bezirke*) or lands (*Länder*). The share of emigrants was 6.5 percent or 1,845.000 persons, thus clearly exceeding the number of immigrants from abroad (632,000), almost 80 percent of whom were citizens of the Hungarian part of the monarchy (Transleithania was the part of the Dual

Monarchy governed from Budapest). In Transleithania the mobile part of the population was somewhat smaller (31 percent), with the percentage of those leaving the country at the turn of the century increasingly overtaking internal migrants (Faßmann 1990/91: 93f.). This paper will concentrate on migration within the boundaries of the Habsburg Monarchy. The empirical evidence relates to the Austrian and Bohemian Lands, mainly to Lower and Upper Austria, and to Bohemia and Moravia.[1] Representing the industrially most advanced part of the monarchy, they contained the regions that were most affected by migration processes, including regions of internal emigration as well as centres of demographic growth.

## Internal Migration

Migration is a general social phenomenon and not one restricted to the period of urbanisation and industrialisation. Internal migration includes: short-distance migration within a given region; migration from rural regions to the expanding towns and industrial centres; seasonal migration (e.g. to work in agriculture or construction); itinerant migration (to carry on journeymen's work, trade or peddling); migration of tramps and paupers.

The lack of reliable statistics prior to the mid-nineteenth century leaves us without a general perspective of the long-term quantitative development of migration. Given the fact that migration had also been a pre-industrial mass-phenomenon, it is possible that the number of cases and persons did not increase during industrialisation. However, the nineteenth century did experience substantial qualitative changes. Internal migration movements showed:

(1) a tendency towards increasing distances (often leading first to a regional and then to a transregional destination);

(2) a change of push – pull factors resulting in different occupations, itineraries and biographies of migrants;

(3) a shift from temporary migration to permanent exodus from rural and peripheral areas. Lack of job stability and social security at the places of destination nevertheless caused continuing movements from one place to another, including return migration to the native region, especially as the growing urban and industrial communities were refusing to take social responsibility for their new residents.

**(4)** the increasing significance of the Lands of the Bohemian Crown (Bohemia, Moravia, Silesia), which became the main regions supplying Vienna and the metropolitan region around the capital with labour. They replaced southern Germany, the main origin of people migrating to Vienna until the beginning of the nineteenth century (Weigl 2000: 134). The shift to Bohemia was linked with the rise of internal migration at the expense of migration from abroad.

Migration, even if it takes place within a single country, links a region of outmigration to a new destination. If we investigate the reasons for migration as well as the origins, the routes and the destinations of the migrants, we have to take push – pull factors into account.[2] Push factors explain which changes in the region of origin were responsible for the decision to migrate; pull factors consist of economic, social and psychological attractions which encourage potential migrants to choose a specific (and not just any) destination. One of the main forces encouraging migration was the break-up of the local/regional orientation of economic life that became relevant in the Habsburg Monarchy in the eighteenth century. As a consequence, many people lost their traditional sources of income in agriculture and the crafts and were ready to accept new jobs. In some regions, proto-industrial manufacture offered new earnings within the rural surroundings, at least for a while. The notorious shortage of labour even encouraged marriages and the founding of new families involved in proto-industry. Where the putting-out system was transforming the local population into a proto-industrial labour-force, considerable internal emigration was postponed. Only in some cases, however, did decentralised proto-industrial production give rise to an industrial core region; in many others mechanization and centralisation of manufacture were linked with the spatial concentration of the factory industry in urban and industrial centres. In most cases rural industrial producers, whether organized in guilds or as part of the proto-industrial putting-out system, lost their competitiveness as soon as factories concentrated in industrial centres. The closure of their workshops forced them to look for a job in the growing urban and industrial areas. The same happened with peasants, who could not compete with the rising productivity of big estate agriculture. On the other side, the growing towns and industrial regions had enormous demand for labour and relied on migrants to engage in industrial and construction work.

Our approach to migration is based on evaluating the functional role of a region or country within the transregional

division of labour, which emerged from market integration on a
state- as well as an inter-state level. Along with the integration of
regions in a transregional framework of a national economy or
into the world economy respectively, existing differences between
the regions gave way to growing regional disparities polarizing
the national as well as the international space into core regions
and peripheries linked by a relationship of "structural dependency".[3] Under these circumstances, values generated in the
periphery were converted into profits for the core. Migration has
to be embedded into the context of this complex relationship of
centres and peripheries. Core regions became poles of attraction
for labour, while peripheries became suppliers of migrants. Cores
and peripheries offered different job opportunities, different
wage levels and standards of living. It was not this difference that
engendered migration, however. The extent to which people were
severed from their traditional livelihoods was decisive for their
departure. It corresponded to the degree of peripheralisation of
their home region. Only the existence of economic interaction
between a given periphery and a core region established the lines
of communication on which push – pull factors effectively met
(Parnreiter 1994: 27f).

   In the Habsburg Monarchy, these lines were most developed
between cores and peripheries within the industrializing regions
of the Empire, the Austrian and the Bohemian Lands. The Vienna
region attracted migrants more than any other urban centre of
the Empire. The gap in economic development and in living standards was much higher between the western industrializing part
of the monarchy, including Austria and Bohemia, and the
predominantly agrarian eastern and south-eastern provinces.
These provinces did not, however, represent a major source of
migration to the central industrial areas in the Austrian west
because of the absence of links. Lower and Upper Austria, Styria,
Bohemia and Moravia-Silesia, representing the industrially
developed part of the Empire, were interconnected by a network
of dependency relationships between poles of industrialization
that attracted additional population and regions of rural exodus.
Although the Hungarian part of the Empire was predominantly
agrarian itself, the picture there is similar. Links with the
Austrian and the Bohemian regions were negligible compared to
the lines of communication that connected the fertile plains in
the centre of the country with the mountainous or remote
provinces supplying the big estates with seasonal farm hands.
The Carpathian and southern countries of the monarchy
belonged to the poorest areas of the Empire. The long distance

from central Cisleithania, ethnic and cultural differences, and the paucity of economic transactions, did not permit a considerable migration to the central regions of the monarchy, although people could hardly make a living at home. German and Jewish settlement was encouraged by the government in Bukovina after the conquest by Austria at the end of the eighteenth century. As soon as emigration became legal, the agrarian provinces in the east and south-east of the monarchy turned into centres of mass-migration of the non-German population to America as well as – on a seasonal basis as farm-labourers – to Germany (Faßmann 1996: 34).

Internal migration under the Habsburg Monarchy appears as a slow, hesitating process, involving only a part of the members of a family while leaving others at home, including return-migrations, often lasting more than one generation until a definitive move to a new place had occurred (Komlosy 1996: 566–69; Koralka 1995: 275–88). For young adults migration may have offered better living without the social restraints of a rural neighbourhood. On the other hand, families were mobilized much energy in order to avoid migration and to find ways to make a living in their home region, for instance by combining the production of cash crops with different types of wage-work, as well as a high degree of self-sufficiency (Komlosy 1993b: 116f.). According to age, gender, professional capabilities and to persons' roles in the familial configuration at a specific moment of his or her life, lower-class rural people fulfilled various types of paid or unpaid activities, thus contributing to the whole family's livelihood.

A main distinction can be made between artisans, whether masters, journeymen or apprentices, who migrated within the exigencies and possibilities offered by their respective trade networks, and the agrarian rural population of peasants, cottagers, servants and farm labourers. The following considerations will concentrate on the latter. Their attitude towards migration was influenced strongly by the social and economic position of the rural household as well as the migrant's position within the household economy. Descendants of peasants who were set to take over the holding usually did not consider leaving their home. Their brothers and sisters were open towards migration, however. Leaving the home village offered chances to overcome the status of servant and farm-labourer. Because of their low social status, the unhoused rural poor were most ready to cut the family ties with their more affluent relatives. On the other hand, cottagers and smallholders who owned a house and a small plot of land were hardly interested in giving up their independent economic existence voluntarily; many of them had only achieved their new legal and social status by the increase of income generated by the manufacturing system. Familiar with combining various sources of income such as the cottage-industry, agriculture and wage-work, temporary migration was nothing new for them. Sending the father, a son, or a daughter, to take up a job in a distant area was seen as a contribution to the strategy of income pooling that allowed the family to maintain the household in the home region. Migration was considered a possible way to obtain an income supplement, the aim of migration being the maintenance of traditional ways of living in the countryside. Conditions in the region of origin may have changed only gradually in a way that made maintaining the rural home impossible. In the meantime, the migrating members linked the different pillars of the household economy, on the one hand sending home earnings, on the other being supplied with food and care by the family back home in case of illness or joblessness. This sometimes lasted for more than one generation.[4] From the perspective of an entrepreneur employing a migrant labourer, this family connection offered advantages: temporary employment was voluntarily accepted. In the case of full-time employment, wages did not have to include social costs: these were taken over by the family back home. Employers of migrant labourers could thus benefit from the work carried out by rural family members in support of their migrating relative. By paying migrants lower wages than permanent residents, employers were able to increase their profits. Migrant labour therefore represents an important link between peripheral areas depending upon job opportunities in growing towns, and the core regions which were not only supplied with labour, but with a specific labour-force.

## Laws Regulating Migration

Until the middle of the eighteenth century, when a major state reform was initiated, dependent persons were subjected to the power of their feudal lord (*Herrschaft*). A special permit was required to leave the manorial estate. Nobles, clergymen and government officials were allowed to move freely; craftsmen and merchants were travelling under the protection of their guilds. Numerous documents served as passports. By reforming the administration in 1749, Maria Theresia aimed to strengthen state power vis-à-vis feudal lords and their political representation, the

Estates (*Stände*), and to place feudal subjects under the state bureaucracy's control.[5] As a consequence, manorial administration was subordinated to state authorities. New administrative bodies on the level of districts (*Kreise*), lands (*Länder*) and the central state were entitled to restrict the feudal lords' power over their subjects and to empower them to travel and migrate. At the same time, they selected and controlled travellers and migrants. Issuing and restricting passports became an important means of regulating the movement of citizens within the monarchy (Komlosy 1995: 63–68; Burger 2000: 9–32). A flood of passport regulations was passed in order to define the rights of migration and residence for single regions and groups of the population. Although the travel regulations of the late eighteenth century appear very confusing and enforcing them effectively was difficult, they furnish evidence of the central state's claim to supervise and control the movement of all subjects. By this means, subjects were transformed into state citizens under direct control of the sovereign.

There were various conditions of subjection to feudal lord in the different lands and regions of the monarchy. The Austrian Lands showed a very moderate form of dependence, which obliged the subjects to provide services and tributes to the feudal lord. These duties were usually converted into monetary payments during the second half of the eighteenth century. In the Bohemian Lands – as a result of the defeat and the expulsion of the domestic Protestant aristocracy during the Thirty Years' War – the wealth and power of the landed aristocracy who had gained their possessions as reward for their loyalty to the Catholic Emperor was much greater (Hroch and Petrán 1981: 138–40). There, serfdom was only abolished in 1781, when passport regulations first became applicable to large parts of the subjugated population.

After 1781, the passport legislation of the Austrian Lands was more or less applied to the Lands of the Bohemian Crown. The following lines of development can be shown (Komlosy 1995: 63–68; Burger 2000: 9–32). As soon as subjects had achieved the right to leave the seignorial soil, travelling and migration had become possible for them. Emigration laws did not foresee departure from the state. But in order to migrate to the territory of a different manorial estate within the monarchy, Austrian subjects from 1749 onwards, and Bohemian subjects from 1781 onwards, only had to pay a parting fee; their feudal lord was no longer entitled to prevent their departure. A passport was necessary as soon as somebody wanted to cross the border of the home district. Depending on the person and the destination, different authorities had to agree in order for a passport to be issued: in general the local manorial or municipal office (*Herrschaftsamt, Magistrat*), the district authority (*Kreisamt*) and – in case of male persons liable to conscription – a military authority. A passport for a journey to another land (*Land*) of the monarchy – especially to one where military conscription was still exercised by the local lords – or across the monarchy's frontiers had to be issued by a superior public authority. While nobility and clergy and government officials did not need a passport for travelling within the limits of the monarchy (Hungary was considered to be a foreign country in this context for various reasons), they were subject to special regulations for travelling abroad (especially during the wars with Napoleon), which were more rigid than in the case of persons who were travelling for of economic reasons (Burger 2000: 32f). Students and professors were also subject to special travel restrictions. One of the reasons why imperial authorities were restricting noblemen's tours and other noble traditions of transnational exchange after 1750 was the aspiration to distinguish useful from useless journeys. Merchants' and craftsmen's trips were considered to belong to the former, young aristocrats' tours to the latter.

A first attempt towards summing up the various laws regulating travel and migration was achieved by the Emigration Law of 1784 (*Auswanderungspatent*) (Handbuch 1786, vol. 6: 279–99). Arguing that "journeys are often taken as a pretext to migrate abroad", it aimed to prevent Austrian citizens from leaving the country. Detailed regulation of travel was considered a means of hindering international emigration. Another complete collection of migration laws can be found in the laws of military conscription and recruitment (*Konskriptionspatent*) (Handbuch 1785, vol. 3: 37–95). The first half of the nineteenth century showed tendencies towards generalization, but no substantial reform was passed until the abolition of the manorial system in 1848 (Burger 2000: 20). From this year on the remaining administrative and legislative competences of the manorial authorities were taken over by district authorities and district courts. In cooperation with the central state authorities they were responsible for issuing passports, still required for every journey across the boundaries of the home district. Passports for travelling within the Monarchy were abolished only in 1857. The Constitution of 1867 finally entitled every citizen of the Austrian part of the Monarchy (*Cisleithania*) to choose a residence at any place in the state's territory. It also authorized the citizens to migrate abroad according to the migration laws.

Another legislative context for the regulation of internal migration was the right of domicile. Since the middle of the eighteenth century, domicile laws had been passed in order to define the authority that was responsible to take care of paupers (Mayrhofer/Pace 1896, vol. 2: 974–1054; compare also Herzog 1837 and Wendelin 2000: 195–199). The domicile law assigned each person to a certain locality. On the one hand, this assignment represented the beginning of public social care, when no private safety net was available, on the other hand, domicile laws made it possible to get rid of paupers who were not eligible for domicile in the community where they lived. There was no general domicile law in the Habsburg Monarchy until 1863. In the course of the eighteenth and the first half of the nineteenth century guiding principles defined the right of domicile as the right of residence in a community linked to the legal claim to emergency social care. If somebody was not born in his community of residence, he or she usually acquired the right of domicile after ten years of continuing stay. Before then, persons who became impoverished risked compulsory deportation to the community where they were domiciled. For migrants, this was a crucial point: before having obtained the right of domicile at their destination, loss of income or relatives who could support them resulted in compulsory return to the place of origin. A migrant who did not yet dispose of the right of domicile was therefore considered a foreigner at his or her place of residence, and risked deportation as an 'undesirable person' under certain conditions. This legal discrimination vis-à-vis residents with full rights made migrants extremely vulnerable: the risk of compulsory removal to the community of legal domicile put pressure on them to accept lower wages and worse conditions of labour and living, thus turning them into second class residents. It was not only the relationship of mutual support with their families elsewhere that classified migrants as cheap labourers. A second disadvantage was the legal definition of migrants as foreigners, even if their home communities were located nearby.

## Conflicting Interests

Between 1749 and 1900, travel and migration regulations can be seen as a major political concern, reflecting the conflict between central and regional interests within the Habsburg Monarchy (Komlosy 2000: 839–844). General state interests are here considered to be interests representing the ambition of the sovereign to establish a direct relationship with the inhabitants by restricting the competence of intermediary powers such as local feudal lords, urban municipalities, guilds or Estates (*Stände*), which were acting on a local, regional, or land (*Länder*) level. Establishing a complete central administration, which gradually deprived the traditional local and regional authorities of their power, opened the sovereign's way towards building a modern state and national economy. In the Habsburg lands with their federal tradition, central state power had to be shared with various regional and local bodies. Instead of replacing them, they were integrated into the system of public administration, where they served as state authorities on the lowest level while still pursuing particularistic interests opposed to the general state idea. In general, but not in every case, the interests of the state bureaucracy corresponded with those of the *bourgeoisie*, living in the core regions. But we can observe a dispute between military, state security and political economy circles pursuing different aims concerning travel and migration. In the first half of the nineteenth century the central government's harmony was disturbed by the representatives of state security who feared that the migration of labourers would destabilize law and order in the towns, especially in Vienna. For a while, they were successful in passing a law forbidding the building of factories in Vienna as well as within a circle of thirty kilometres around the capital (1802–1811) (Slokar 1914: 29–50; Komlosy 2000: 844). Commercial and industrial groups, by contrast, supported the primacy of economic development against other considerations.

The antagonistic interests were embedded into the economic competition among regions, which was fuelled by the abolition of customs-barriers between the different lands (*Länder*) of the monarchy and the formation of a single market from 1775 (Beer 1893). Rights protecting local and regional markets were undermined by measures to build a national market. Thus interests linked with traditional regional economies – representations on the level of the lands (*Länder*), towns, guilds and corporations – lost their influence. Protectionist policies were becoming a state affair exercised through the collection of customs, which increasingly moved from inner-state to state borders, as well as by conferring monopolies and state subsidies upon certain regions or producers entitling them to ignore the economic regulations traditionally exercised by municipal councils and guilds (e. g. the right of towns to collect duties and taxes, to oblige merchants to stop and offer their products, the guilds' rights to limit the number of practitioners of a certain trade, to watch over the quantity and quality of production and to control vocational education within their territorial limits).

The state bureaucracy was considered to represent the trans-regional interests of the central state. In consequence, it favoured the needs of central regions over those of peripheral and rural ones. From the point of view of central state interests, migration was considered to be a means of supplying urban and industrial centres with labour, except for migration that was opposed for security reasons. Traditional regional powers viewed their inhabitants from a local and or, regional perspective considering them to be a source of wealth and labour, unwilling to dismiss them as long as they were needed within the regions. Between 1749, when manorial authorities were put under the control of the state's district authorities, and 1848, when the manorial system was abolished, both types of authorities were involved in issuing passports: the manorial or the municipal office served as the immediate authority handling the passport application, the district office (or the *Gubernium* on the level of the lands) as the state authority responsible for supervision and appeals. If the feudal lords declined to issue a passport, e. g. with the argument that there was a lack of domestic servants in the home district, the applicant could appeal to the district authority, which could decide in his favour (Komlosy 1995: 63). The intervention of state bureaucracy in the relationship between subject and landlord represented an act of empowerment emancipating the rural population from the immediate interest of the feudal lord. The district authorities representing the central state, as well as the core regions' interests, had to guarantee that passports were issued according to the demands of urban and industrial regions, thus encouraging migration to the destinations of high demand. They informed the issuing offices, at the lowest level, of projects such as road building and construction which had a high demand for labour. The construction of canals and railways, for instance, required thousands of persons whose mobility was not to be hindered by refusing passports. When more and more railway lines opened in the middle of the nineteenth century, district authorities were advised to issue passports valid for unlimited journeys on a specific railway line for a whole year.

The migration of people who were unlikely to serve as good labourers at their new residence, was to be prevented. In this context, district authorities were agents of control who made sure that lower authorities did not issue passports to people who might turn into a burden for urban centres. Local authorities were therefore advised to be strict in their selection of migrants. In August 1847, for example, the Government of Lower Austria informed the Prague *Gubernium*, that "people from the Budweis district had been arrested in Lower Austria for begging, lack of identity and joblessness". In consequence, the Budweis district office was advised to prevent the local authorities from issuing passports to Austria to these kinds of people. They were instructed not to issue any passports at all to the elderly, or to migrants with children, people who seemed incapable of earning their living or who had already been deported from Austria as 'undesirable'; passports should be reserved for those who 'really have the capacity to earn their living by manual work and can furnish evidence not to be unwilling to work' (22 August 1847) (Komlosy 1996: 572). One can find thousands of instructions of this kind in the archives. Both in the case of empowerment, and in the case of restriction, district authorities were serving as the main bodies that communicated the interests and needs of the core regions, whether concerning the labour market or state security, to local offices responsible for the administration of passports. Local functionaries had difficulty in understanding the frequently conflicting messages, which led to a number of misunderstandings and misinterpretations that produced a gap between the normative intentions of the rules and the policies that were effectively applied. This is why, on the one hand, urban centres were constantly lacking labour, while on the other, rural paupers who were not supposed to migrate were reaching the large towns. There they risked deportation to their home communities. This was also a permanent risk for migrants who lost work or family support, if they did not yet have the right of domicile at their new residence.

The acquisition of a new domicile became markedly more difficult in the Habsburg Monarchy during the second half of the nineteenth century. Before 1863, four to ten years of permanent residence entitled a migrant to apply for a certificate of domicile. The Domicile Law of 1863 no longer foresaw the possibility of achieving the right of domicile within a prescribed period (Komlosy 1996: 566; compare also Mayrhofer and Pace 1896, vol. 2: 980 and Wendelin 2000: 226–228). While more and more migrants were moving to the towns and industrial centres of the monarchy, the number of residents with the right of domicile was frozen. As a consequence, the number of migrants who risked being returned to their home community kept increasing. Between 1869 and 1900, the percentage of people who were not eligible for domicile in their community of residence grew from an average of 21 to 40 percent in Cisleithania. For example, in 1900 in Vienna only 38 percent of residents were domiciled, and in Prague not more than 20 percent (*Österreichische Statistik*, vol 44, Volkszählung 1900: XXVII–XXIX).

As passports were no longer required for domestic travel from 1857, and the constitution of 1867 guaranteed free choice of residence all over the Austrian Monarchy, domicile restrictions denied the realization of these rights to all citizens who needed public social support outside the community where they were domiciled. The restrictions placed on conferring the right of domicile contributed to separating the population of the centres of immigration into first and second class citizens. Deportations of migrants to their communities of domicile became the daily duty of authorities, occupying thousands and thousands of officials, until a reform of the law was passed in 1896 and became valid in 1901. As domicile was a right that women obtained by marriage, and children through their father, the deportation transports did not necessarily lead a person into his or her community of origin. But the limits on eligibility during these crucial years guaranteed that the centres of migration did not have to carry the social costs of unemployment or pauperisation within their borders (Klabouch 1968: 71). By conveying paupers to their community of domicile, urban centres got rid of the social problems caused by urbanization and industrialization. Here, the interests of the urban *bourgeoisie* and state security coincided: at the expense of the workers who were migrating between their regions of origin (to which they might be transferred against their will) and the industrial centres which were relying on their labour, but refusing to accept social responsibility for them as residents.

## Notes

1. For empirical details see Komlosy 1993a, 1995, 1996, 2000.
2. For a discussion of the changes in the appreciation and the definition of push and pull factors in the analysis of migrations see Ehmer 1998.
3. The theoretical concept is presented in Komlosy 2000.
4. Tamara Hareven provides rich empirical evidence of the role of family networks in migration processes; for the theoretical concept see Hareven 1993: chapter 1, 1–8.
5. For a summary of the administrative reforms of the eighteenth-century Habsburg Monachy compare Komlosy 2000.

## References

Beer, Adolf, 1893, 'Die Zollpolitik und die Schaffung eines einheitlichen Zollgebietes unter Maria Theresia', *Mittheilungen des Instituts für oesterreichische Geschichtsforschung*, 14: 237–326.

Burger, Hannelore, 2000, 'Paßwesen und Staatsbürgerschaft', in *Grenze und Staat. Paßwesen, Staatsbürgerschaft, Heimatrecht und Fremdengesetzgebung in der österreichischen Monarchie 1750–1856*, eds Waltraud Heindl and Edith Saurer, Vienna-Köln-Weimar: 3–172.

Ehmer, Josef, 1998, 'Migration und Bevölkerung. Zur Kritik eines Erklärungsansatzes', *Tel Aviver Jahrbuch für deutsche Geschichte*, 27: 1–25.

Faßmann, Heinz, 1990/1, 'Einwanderung, Auswanderung und Binnenwanderung in Österreich-Ungarn um 1910', *Demographische Informationen*: 92–101.

Faßmann, Heinz, 1996, 'Auswanderung aus der österreichisch-ungarischen Monarchie', in *Auswanderungen aus Österreich von der Mitte des 19. Jahrhunderts bis zur Gegenwart*, eds Traude Horvath and Gerda Neyer, Vienna-Köln-Weimar: 33–56.

*Handbuch aller unter der Regierung des Kaisers Joseph des II. für die k. k. Erbländer ergangenen Verordnungen und Gesetze in einer systematischen Verbindung*, vol. 3, Vienna, 1785; vol. 6, Vienna, 1786.

Hareven, Tamara K., 1993, *Family Time and Industrial Time. The Relationship between the Family and Work in a New England Industrial Community*, 2nd edn, Lanham.

Herzog, Franz Tobias, 1837, *Sammlung der Gesetze über das politische Domizil im Kaiserthume Österreich*, Vienna.

Hroch, Miroslav, and Josef Petrán, 1981, *Das 17. Jahrhundert – Krise der Feudalgesellschaft?* Hamburg.

Klabouch, Jiri, 1968, *Die Gemeindeselbstverwaltung in Österreich 1848–1918*, Vienna.

Komlosy, Andrea, 1993a, 'Wo die österreichischen an die böhmischen Länder grenzen: Kleinraum – Zwischenraum – Peripherie', in *Kontakte und Konflikte. Böhmen, Mähren und Österreich: Aspekte eines Jahrtausends gemeinsamer Geschichte*, ed. Thomas Winkelbauer, Horn pp. 491–520.

Komlosy, Andrea, 1993b, '"Wo der Webwaaren-Industrie so viele fleißige und geübte Hände zu Gebote stehen". Landfrauen zwischen bezahlter und unbezahlter Arbeit', in *Frauen-Arbeitswelten*, eds Birgit Bolognese-Leuchtenmüller and Michael Mitterauer, Vienna pp. 105–132.

Komlosy, Andrea, 1995, ‚Ein Land – viele Grenzen. Waren- und Reiseverkehr zwischen den österreichischen und den böhmischen Ländern (1740 – 1918)', in *Kulturen an der Grenze – Kultury na hranici. Waldviertel-Weinviertel-Südböhmen-Südmähren*, eds Komlosy Andrea/Buzek Václav/Svátek Frantisek, Vienna: 59–72.

Komlosy, Andrea, 1996, '"Zur Belassung am hiesigen Platze nicht geeignet ... " Selektion und Kontrolle der Zuwanderung ins Kernland der Habsburgermonarchie', *Jahrbuch für Landeskunde von Niederösterreich*, 62:2: 555–584.

Komlosy, Andrea, 2000, 'Ökonomische Grenzen', in *Grenze und Staat. Paßwesen, Staatsbürgerschaft, Heimatrecht und Fremdengesetzgebung in der österreichischen Monarchie 1750–1856*, eds Waltraud Heindl and Edith Saurer, Vienna-Köln-Weimar pp. 807–876.

Koralka, Jirí, 1995, 'Stände, Klassen und Nationalitäten. Soziale Schichtung und politische Macht im 19. Jahrhundert', in *Kulturen an der Grenze – Kultury na hranici. Waldviertel-Weinviertel-Südböhmen-Südmähren*, eds Komlosy Andrea/Buzek Václav/Svátek Frantisek, Vienna: 263–268.

Mayrhofer, Ernst, and Anton Pace, 1896, *Handbuch für den politischen Verwaltungsdienst in den im Reichrathe vertretenen Königreichen und Ländern*, 5th edn, vol. 2, Vienna.

Parnreiter, Christof, 1994, *Migration und Arbeitsteilung. AusländerInnenbeschäftigung in der Weltwirtschaftskrise*, Vienna.

Slokar, Johann, 1914, *Geschichte der österreichischen Industrie und ihrer Förderung unter Kaiser Franz I.*, Vienna.

Weigl, Andreas, 2000, *Demographischer Wandel und Modernisiernug in Wien* (= Kommentare zum Historischen Atlas von Wien 5), Vienna.

Wendelin, Harald, 2000, 'Der Schub', in *Grenze und Staat. Paßwesen, Staatsbürgerschaft, Heimatrecht und Fremdengesetzgebung in der österreichischen Monarchie 1750–1856*, eds Waltraud Heindl and Edith Saurer, Vienna-Köln-Weimar pp. 174–343.

# Chapter 11

# Was the Nineteenth Century a Golden Age for Immigrants?
## *The Changing Articulation of National, Local and Voluntary Controls*

*David Feldman*

## I

The history of Britain in the twentieth century has been punctuated by a series of legal and administrative devices designed to limit, deter and regulate immigration. At its close, aspiring immigrants and asylum seekers have to confront a series of legal and bureaucratic obstacles as they attempt to establish their claim to settle. Yet, at the beginning of the century, the ports of Britain were open to all and the right to asylum was unqualified.

The modern regulation of immigration to Britain can be traced to the Aliens Act of 1905. Legislation introduced in 1793 and 1803 to deal with the circumstances of war with France was finally repealed in 1826. Between that date, however, and 1905, immigration to Britain was free from state control. For most of the nineteenth century, information gathered at British ports was of such poor quality that, apart from the snapshot provided by the census, ministers and civil servants had no reliable guide to the dimensions of immigration. As a result, in the late nineteenth century, when the influx of East European Jews to Britain began to excite the concern of social reformers, politicians and journalists, no-one was able to provide an accurate estimate of their number (Gainer 1971: 6–14).

It was the agitation against Jewish immigration which gave rise to the 1905 Aliens Act. The Act introduced a new species of official – the immigration officer – to operate the apparatus of exclusion. Immigrants now had to demonstrate that they were able to support themselves and their dependents in a state of 'decency'. Although the Aliens Act made special allowances for victims of religious and political persecution, with the exception of the pogrom year of 1906 this clause was interpreted narrowly, so that the annual number of refugees fell dramatically; just five were allowed into the country in 1910 (Feldman 1994: 355f.).

It is not surprising, then, that the Aliens Act of 1905 has been presented both by contemporaries and by historians as a decisive break from preceding practice. Among contemporaries, this view was shared both by opponents and supporters of the legislation. The Acts's advocates aligned their cause with other modernising reforms, which, they argued, would help Britain adjust to a world in which its industrial, commercial and naval pre-eminence was increasingly open to question. The practice of allowing the unrestricted immigration of enfeebled foreigners accustomed to lives of immiseration was compared unfavourably with the restrictive laws enforced by competitors such as Germany and the United States. The supporters of immigration restriction saw themselves as in tune with the demands of a new age. At the same time, Liberal opponents of restrictive legislation were portrayed as sentimentalists, attached to outdated shibboleths and at odds with new realities (Feldman 1994: 268–90).

Opponents of the Aliens Act were no less certain of the legislation's novelty. They claimed that the government's attempt to limit immigration was nothing less than a mutilation of national tradition. One Liberal MP, speaking in the House of Commons, appealed

> To all who are anxious to preserve the right of asylum, and all who are devoted to that traditional great policy of this country, to vote against a measure which renders it possible that mere officialdom shall be able to exclude the political refugee from this country. ... I have inherited traditions which compel me to vote against a measure which I think would tend to impair the world-wide and historical reputation which this country has enjoyed for centuries as being a sanctuary for the politically distressed. (*Parliamentary Debates*, fourth series, vol. 145: 793)

Less emotively, the jurist A.V. Dicey perceived 'a marked reaction against England's traditional policy of favouring or inviting the immigration of foreigners' (cited in Gainer 1971: 150).

Historians too have added their agreement to these voices from the past. In the nineteenth century, they argued, freedom of movement for individuals chimed well with the ascendant economic doctrine of free trade. Open borders, they pointed out, also drew on the commonplace assumption that both British institutions and the British people prized liberty and toleration. The 1905 Act has been presented as a new form of state inter-vention, introducing a regime of regulation where previously there had been none, as a break from nineteenth-century policies which had favoured both free trade and the right of asylum, and as the foundation on which a more rigorous regime of exclusion and regulation was erected during and after the First World War (Porter 1979; Feldman 1989; Dummett and Nicol 1990: 103–7).

But to what extent was the nineteenth century a golden age of freedom for immigrants to Britain? It is certainly the case that between 1823 and 1905 no-one was refused entry to the country. Furthermore, a rising, although relatively small, number of immigrants took advantage of this freedom to enter Britain. The census of 1851 enumerated only 50,289 foreigners in England and Wales; just 0.28 percent of a population of more than 18 million. The number of foreigners doubled over the next twenty years and the upward trend moved forward still more quickly with the large influx of Jewish immigrants from the early 1880s. In these years the country was open to entry by rich and poor alike, monarchists and republicans, conservatives and revolu-tionaries. At the level of national policy, then, the 1905 Aliens Act was indeed a turning point.

Yet if we are to see the Act in its full significance we need to place it in the broad context of those tasks that the central state in nineteenth-century Britain aspired to perform. For the ambi-tion and endeavour of central government in the nineteenth century was constrained. These limitations were both fiscal and ideological. First, the tasks of central government were defined and carried out within limits set by the declining level of taxa-tion and of state expenditure as a portion of Gross National Product. Second, it was also confined and shaped by the strong ideological preference of politicians and voters for delegating functions to local or voluntary agencies (Daunton 1999; Thane 1990: 1f.). Acknowledging the importance of this broad context for immigration policy in the nineteenth century should lead us to examine not only at the action (or inaction) of ministers and civil servants in the capital but also to take account of the activ-ity of a host of local authorities and voluntary agencies.

## II

The most numerous immigrants in nineteenth-century Britain were the Irish. The number of Irish in Britain totalled over 400,000 in 1841 and rose to 806,000 in 1861. Although Ireland was joined by the Act of Union with rest of the United Kingdom in 1801, the Irish in Britain are best seen as 'internal immigrants'. In part this is on account of their distinct religious, cultural, and political background. The Irish were largely a Catholic population, some were Gaelic-speaking, and many detested the Act of Union. Still more important, not all of the laws of England and Wales extended to Ireland. Particular laws applied to Ireland and to the Irish in England.

A law of 1819 allowed poor law officials to remove Irish men, women and children from England and Wales as soon as they applied to the poor law for assistance. This was a significant deterioration in their legal situation; hitherto the Irish had been repatriated only if they were found committing acts of vagrancy.[1] Armed with this new power, between 1824 and 1831, English and Welsh parishes expelled 51,556 Irish poor, returning them to Ireland through the ports of Liverpool and Bristol.[2]

The legal basis for expelling Irish paupers changed in 1845. Parish officers and Poor Law Guardians now needed the authority of two justices of the peace who were able to choose not to issue a warrant for removal. Nevertheless, in the face of the massive migration resulting from the Irish famine, this improvement in law did not lead to a reduction in the number of Irish sent home: between 1845 and 1849 29,079 Irish persons were removed from parishes in England and between 1849 and 1854, more than 50,000 Irish were sent back to Ireland from Liverpool and London alone.[3]

If this was the position of the Irish, what of the treatment of those who were unambiguously foreign? Parish officers, poor law guardians and justices of the peace had no authority to expel even foreign vagrants. As one magistrate complained: 'we cannot dispose of them in any way; all we are empowered to do is confine them in a house of correction, or to find them labour which we cannot do'.[4] Nevertheless, immigrants were expelled from the country but it was voluntary organisations who did this work, rather than the state.

The best documented case is that of Jewish immigrants. The Jewish communal authorities had always repatriated a number of the foreign Jewish poor who migrated to England (Endelman 1979: 167; Pollins 1982: 43). But in the face of the unprecedented immigration of Jews from eastern Europe from the 1880s this policy assumed new dimensions. Roughly 120,000 Jewish immigrants settled in Britain between 1880 and 1914. Between 1881 and the implementation of the Aliens Act in 1906, two Jewish organisations in London, the Jewish Board of Guardians and the

Russo-Jewish Committee, between them repatriated to Eastern Europe roughly 31,000 Jews (Feldman 1994: 303).

But Jews were not the only immigrants repatriated in the nineteenth century. By the late 1880s there were separate societies in London for destitute Frenchmen, Belgians, Italians and Germans as well as a Society of Friends of Foreigners in Distress, and in each case repatriation of immigrants was a significant part of their activity. The Société Française de Bienfaisance à Londres provided relief in a number of ways; it contributed money, bread, and rent but it also sent back to France a large portion of those who came to it for help. Repatriation accounted for 29 percent of the 7,662 individuals helped by the society between 1881 and 1888, and for 16 percent of its expenditure in the same period.[5] The activity of the Société Belge de Bienfaisance over the same period had a broadly similar shape; 22 percent of its applicants were repatriated, which in this case accounted for 30 percent of all expenditure.[6] In the cases of the German Society of Benevolence and the Society of Friends of Foreigners in Distress, another charity with strong connections to the German immigrant population, repatriation was a significant but less prominent activity. In the former case, only 6 percent of applicants were repatriated and 10 percent of funds were spent on this activity, in the latter the respective figures were 3 percent and 5 percent.[7] These variations between the societies, in part, reflect their different counting practices. For instance, in the case of the Society of Friends of Foreigners in Distress the percentage that the society reported it repatriated was considerably reduced by its practice of counting each application for relief as a new 'case', even when the applicant was being helped three or four times in the year. The Chairman suggested that this inflated the number of cases by between 50 and 60 percent.[8] More significant than these differences between the charities, perhaps, is the fact that all of them left the immigrants vulnerable to repatriation.

From this point of view, we can see that the debate over the Aliens Act was not between a policy of restriction and one of free immigration, but over whether this should be the responsibility of the state or of voluntary organisations, and whether regulation should be at the port of entry or once immigrants had entered the country. In 1887, the annual report of the Jewish Board of Guardians argued explicitly that its own efforts at repatriation and emigration rendered legislation unnecessary (Jewish Board of Guardians, *29th Annual Report*: 13). In 1902, the President of the Board conceded there should be legislation to prohibit the immigration of criminals, people involved in 'immoral trades' and those with a 'physical incapacity'. But, he argued, the state should not be the only agency regulating immigration and settlement; not all immigrants would succeed in their new lives and it would be the task of the Jewish Board of Guardians to repatriate these 'failures'.[9]

## III

It is clear, therefore, that immigration control in the nineteenth century arose in the context of the practice of poor relief and philanthropy. In order to understand the operation of repatriation in these years, therefore, we must move beyond a narrow consideration of immigration law to examine the interaction of immigrants with both official and voluntary poor relief.

The poor law in England in the early nineteenth century was national in scope but intensely local in its fiscal and daily operation. The system was supported by compulsory taxation raised locally in more than 8,000 parishes and its functions were carried out by individuals elected from the inhabitants of a district, not by centrally appointed officials (Oxley 1974). Within this structure the question of which parish or township should take responsibility for which poor person was a matter of great importance. For so long as welfare was financed and administered locally, migration – even over short distances – that led individuals to cross the boundaries of one poor law district to enter another, created a population of 'strangers' who were entitled to nothing more than emergency poor relief in the place to which they had moved.

The entitlements of migrants under the poor law were determined by the Law of Settlement. This set out the various routes through which a 'stranger' could acquire an entitlement to poor relief – a 'settlement' – in the parish to which he or she had migrated (Taylor 1976; Rose 1976). But changes to the law in the early-nineteenth century made it increasingly difficult for migrants to gain a new 'settlement' (Pashley 1852: 269).

Migrants who could not establish their entitlement to support in the parish in which they lived and who also stood in need of poor relief could be expelled. They were sent to the parish in which they were entitled to poor relief. Poor law authorities, anxious to restrict the burden on the poor rates, regarded this power of removal as an essential bulwark against a flood of applications for relief. In part, this was because the threat of removal inhibited applications for relief. One poor law inspector pointed out how the threat of removal 'is hung up, as it has been expressed, *in terrorem* over the heads of the poor', to deter them from applying for relief.[10] But in many cases the poor were sent away. Between 25 March 1827 and the same date the following year 43,677 individuals were removed in this fashion from parishes in England and Wales.[11]

Within this wider system of expulsion the Irish were a special case. Irish immigrants arrived without a legal settlement and, on account of their disproportionate poverty, the great majority of them did not acquire one. Poor law officials shared the conventional opinion that the Irish were improvident and likely to prey on the poor law if given the chance to do so.[12] In several towns the additional burden the Irish placed on the poor rate, particularly after the famine immigration of the late 1840s and early 1850s, appeared to confirm this conventional image. In Bradford, for example, in March 1855 38 percent of all paupers were Irish-born.[13] In Liverpool, the largest centre of Irish settlement in England, in April 1854, the Irish amounted to 31.2 percent of all those in receipt of poor relief, and 38.4 percent of those in receipt of poor relief in Manchester.[14] Figures such as these led Poor Law Guardians to believe that the threat of removal to Ireland was a vital deterrent without which they would be inundated.[15]

The Irish were also a special case, however, because in the first half of the century the poor law system treated them with particular severity. In one important respect the Law of Settlement did provide security for English paupers. For everyone born in England and Wales, or who had acquired a legal settlement somewhere in England or Wales, there was a parish or township that was obliged to look after them. They might be ejected from a particular place but they remained within the welfare system. But this was a system which extended only to England and Wales; the Scots and, more significant numerically, the Irish had no place within it. Scotland had its own poor law but before 1838 Ireland did not have any poor law at all. Even once a Poor Law was introduced in Ireland it did not impose a similar inclusive obligation on local authorities to support all paupers. Whereas English paupers were delivered into the hands of a parish that was obliged to relieve them, destitute Irish immigrants were merely deposited on Irish soil (Rose 1976: 39).

The position of the Irish under the poor law improved after 1846, as Parliament and the civil service imposed uniform standards and practices on the local poor law authorities. Beginning with the Poor Removal Act of 1846, the power of removal was greatly reduced. The most important provision of this law was that anyone who had been in a parish for five years and who in that time had not gained a legal settlement, could not be ejected. A further Act in 1861 reduced the residence requirement before irremovability took effect from five years to three, and the unit for residence was no longer restricted to a single parish but to the considerably larger unit of the poor law union. In 1865 the residency requirement was further reduced to just one year (Rose 1976: 30f.). As a result, the number of removals fell considerably: by 1868 the figure was just 8,351.[16] At first there was controversy and confusion over whether the 1846 Act extended to the Irish and whether they too could be protected from removal. But once the scope of the law had been established the number of Irish removals also fell dramatically; there were just 5,125 Irish removals in 1855 and a mere 508 in 1865.[17]

The relationship of foreign subjects to the poor law in England resembled neither that of the English nor the Irish. On one side, the Law of Settlement did not empower poor law officials or magistrates to expel foreigners. On the other side, before the start of the nineteenth century it was unclear whether local poor law authorities were obliged to relieve needy foreigners. A judgement of 1803, however, banished this element of doubt; henceforth it was clear that poor law authorities were obliged to offer foreigners at least casual relief.[18]

But the position of needy foreigners remained precarious. In part this was because the obligation placed on parishes by this judgment was minimal. It did not require them to give anything more than relief to overcome a crisis.[19] As a result, it seems that immigrants only applied to the poor law as a last resort. The Society of Friends of Foreigners in Distress was established in 1806, three years after the landmark ruling in 1803, with the explicit intention of helping 'especially those who are not entitled to parochial aid' (Panayi 1995: 27). The tendency to exclude immigrants from the poor law left them heavily dependent on charities designed to support particular immigrant, ethnic or religious minorities. In the early twentieth century – the first point for which we have data collected at a national level – the British born were twice as likely as aliens to be in receipt of poor relief. In 1907, 4.9 percent of the population of England and Wales were supported by the poor law and in 1911 the figure for the alien population was just 2.5 percent.[20]

Dependence on voluntary charity rather than official poor relief did not release immigrants from a logic that left them vulnerable to repatriation. Charities which ministered to immigrants, like the poor law authorities, drew on a narrowly defined pool of funds. In one case this was defined by the parish or the

poor law union, in the other case it was centred on the philan-
thropically active minority within a particular immigrant, ethnic
or religious population. In both cases, new immigrants placed an
additional demand on a limited pool of funds. New immigrants,
in this way, threatened the welfare of the population already
included within the embrace of welfare. The logic of the situation drove both the poor law bodies and the immigrant charities
to limit their obligations and to expel a minority of applicants.

In some cases, perhaps, repatriation – a free passage home –
was what an immigrant desired. But if we judge from the best
documented case – that of the Jews – the overwhelming majority
did not choose to go freely. In the case of the Jewish Board of
Guardians – which after its creation in 1859 was responsible for
the greatest part of Jewish charity in London – we have a clear
picture of the framework of privation and powerlessness in which
the 'choice' to return home was made. In 1903 the President of
the Board explained how, typically, repatriation was instigated.

> He [the applicant] tells us he cannot succeed without charity. He has
> been here, say nine months. We say, if you cannot succeed here, and as
> you had nothing to bring you here you had better go back. He rather
> demurs the first time, but the second time he agrees and goes.[21]

One leading advocate of this policy argued that 'all those whose
physical, mental or trade incapacity...all the indolent loafers and
parasites, must be promptly, very promptly returned to their
native lands' (*Jewish Chronicle*, 3 February 1893: 15).

## IV

The passage of the Aliens Act is a landmark in the history of
immigration control in Britain. But the Act does not signify the
transition from a nineteenth-century regime characterised by an
absence of immigration controls to the appearance and elaboration of controls in the twentieth century. Rather, it marked a
departure from a practice of ejection operated by local authorities and voluntary agencies. This set of disbursed arrangements
was now replaced by a policy of rejection, operated at the port
of entry by central government. The Aliens Act signified a radical
rearticulation of the ways in which governmental and voluntary
agencies strove to regulate immigration. The history of immigration control was thus at the very front of a process of state
formation during which both the boundaries of the state and the
roles of agencies both within the state and civil society were
transformed (Daunton 1996).

## Notes

1. P[arliamentary] P[apers] 1821 IV, *Report from the Select Committee on the Existing Laws Relating to Vagrancy*: 4f.
2. PP 1831–2 XLIV, *Number of Irish Poor shipped from Bristol and Expense thereof*, 1823–31: 461; PP 1833 XXXII, *Number of Irish Poor shipped under passes from Liverpool to Ireland in each year since 1823*: 352f. We should bear in mind, however, that not all of those expelled were unwilling to go: a portion were Irish migrant labourers who took advantage of the law to engineer a free passage home.
3. PP 1850 L, *Orders of Removal*: 13; PP 1854 LV, *Poor Removals*: 321–3.
4. PP 1821 IV, *Report on the Existing Laws Relating to Vagrancy*: 68.
5. PP 1889 X, *Report from the Select Committee on Emigration and Immigration (Foreigners)*, q[uestion] 206.
6. Ibid., q. 228.
7. Ibid., qq. 246, 269.
8. Ibid., qq. 251f.
9. PP 1903 IX, *Royal Commission on Alien Immigration*, qq.15,319, 15,661, 15,720–3.
10. PP 1853–4 XIII, *Report from the Select Committee on Poor Removal*, q.2369.
11. PP 1829 XXI, *Poor Rates. Abstract of Returns*, 102–3.
12. See for instance PP 1860 XVII, *Report from the Select Committee on Irremoveable Poor*, qq. 2180, 3676.
13. PP 1854–5 XIII, *Report from the Select Committee on Poor Removal*, qq.1171–3.
14. PP 1853–4, *Report on Poor Removal*, qq. 3057, 3076.
15. For example, ibid., qq. 458, 2360.
16. PP 1867–8 LX, *Orders of Removal*: 2–3.
17. PP 1856 XLIX, *Orders of Removal*: 2–3; PP 1867/8 LX, *Orders of Removal*: 2–3.
18. *English Reports*, vol. 102, 1910: 770; PP 1843 XXI, *Ninth Annual Report of the Poor Law Commissioners*: 29f.
19. PP 1821 IV, *Report on the Existing Laws Relating to Vagrancy*: 24.
20. The figure of 4.9 per cent is given in PP 1908 XCII, *Poor Law Relief (Paupers Relieved in a Year and Periods of Relief)*: 358; PP 1913 XVI, *Aliens Act 1905. Seventh Annual Report of His Majesty's Inspector under the Act*: 77 gives the number of aliens in receipt of poor relief. The census of 1911 enumerated 373,516 aliens in England and Wales. The real difference between the percentages of British-born subjects and aliens in receipt of poor relief was higher than the one given here. This is because the figure for the British-born in receipt of poor relief excludes lunatics and casual paupers, while the figure for aliens includes not only these categories but also the British-born children of aliens.
21. PP 1903 IX, *Royal Commission on Alien Immigration*, q. 15,691.

## References

Daunton, M., 1996, 'Payment and Participation: Welfare and State Formation in Britain 1900–1951', *Past and Present*, February: 169–211.
Daunton, M., 1999, 'Trusting Leviathan: British Fiscal Administration since 1842', in *Trust and Governance*, eds V. Braithwaite and M. Levi, New York.
Dummett, A, and D. Nicol, 1990, *Subjects, Citizens, Aliens and Others. Nationality and Immigration Law*, London.

Endelman, T., 1979, *The Jews of Georgian England 1714–1830*, Philadelphia.

Feldman, D., 1989, 'The Importance of Being English: The Aliens Act and the Decline of Liberal England', in *Metropolis London. Histories and Representations since 1800*, eds D. Feldman and G. Stedman Jones, London: 56–84.

Feldman, D., 1994, *Englishmen and Jews. Social Relations and Political Culture, 1840–1914*, New Haven.

Gainer, B., 1971, *The Alien Invasion*, London.

Oxley, G.W., 1974, *Poor Relief in England and Wales 1601–1834*, Newton Abbott.

Panayi, P, 1995, *German Immigrants in Britain during the Nineteenth Century, 1815–1914*, Oxford.

Pashley, R., 1852, *Pauperism and Poor Laws*, London.

Pollins, H., 1982, *Economic History of the Jews in England*, London.

Porter, B., 1979, *The Refugee Question in Mid-Victorian Politics*, Cambridge.

Rose, M.E., 1976, 'Settlement, Removal and the New Poor Law', in *The New Poor Law in the Nineteenth Century*, ed. D. Fraser, London: 25–43.

Taylor, J.S., 1976, 'The Impact of Pauper Settlement, 1691–1834', *Past and Present*: 42–74.

Thane, P., 1990, 'Government and Society in England and Wales, 1750–1914', in *Cambridge Social History of Britain*, ed F.M.L. Thompson, Cambridge.

# Chapter 12

# Revolutionaries into Beggars
## *Alien Policies in the Netherlands 1814–1914*

*Leo Lucassen*

## Introduction

An important invention of the French Revolution was the passport system, devised to control the movement of both internal
and external migrants (Torpey 2000).[1] One of the consequences
of this new monitoring device, which is closely linked to the shift
from indirect to direct rule, was that aliens were defined at a
national level, as citizens of another state (Noiriel 1988: 71).
Notwithstanding the importance of this redefinition of the aliens
concept, several scholars have argued that this did not automatically imply that from then on the state was able to control
migration. Not unlike its neighbours during the nineteenth
century, the French state was rather weak and not able to live up
to its totalitarian image. The aspirations and claims of the
national state that replaced the old corporate order were often
much broader than what could be achieved in practice. The
bureaucracy of the national state was still very small and the
implementation of national laws and regulations at the local level
was far from successful.

In the course of the nineteenth century the power of the state
to regulate and monitor society, in order to make it 'legible', to
use the imagery of James Scott (Scott 1998), increased. Albeit
slowly, partially and not always straightforwardly, the awareness
that the state had to take some responsibility for social issues,
gained ground. One of the consequences was that immigrants
from other countries were increasingly regarded as potential

dependants on poor relief and as a threat to the financial interests of the receiving state. The framing of immigration in more
socio-economic terms, that would become dominant in the twentieth century, coincided with the abolishment of the passport
system in most European countries around 1860, heralding a
liberal period of free migration until the outbreak of the Great
War in 1914.

The relation between the business cycle of the passport system
and the changing role of the state in society leaves us with a
paradox. How can one explain that passports and migration
controls flourished in a period when national states were weak,
whereas when the state extended its powers and began to
consider immigrants as a potential socio-economic threat, it
lifted all restrictions? In this chapter I will address this question
by looking into the aliens policy of the Netherlands in the nineteenth century. By focussing on aliens as a national category, I
shall first of all try to reconstruct how the embryonic national
state tried to implement a national aliens policy at the local level
during the first half of the nineteenth century. Finally, by briefly
describing the aliens policy after 1860, I shall show that it may
be somewhat deceptive to interpret the abolishment of passports
as a lack of state interest in migration control.

## The supervision of aliens in the Netherlands (1814–1860)

As in most European countries, the Dutch passport system was
based on the French example, whereas the supervision and registration of aliens had partly indigenous roots. Under French
influence, the divergent local measures were in part replaced by
the general obligation to register travellers who spent the night
in a boardinghouse. Before going into the implementation of the
national aliens policy at the local level, I shall first sketch out the
most important developments in both passport legislation and
aliens registration from the unification of the Netherlands under
King William I in November 1813.

At the end of November 1813, William I, who in 1795 had fled
to England with his father, the last hereditary *stadhouder* of the
Dutch Republic, returned to the Netherlands. He accepted the
title of Prince, and, soon thereafter, King, of the Netherlands,
enlarged in 1815 by the addition of the southern Netherlands.
Within two weeks of his accession the first regulations on passports were issued. The most important Royal Decree dated from

12 December 1813. It stipulated that Dutch citizens who wanted to go abroad needed a passport (issued by the Ministry of Foreign Affairs) and that aliens who wanted to visit the Netherlands had to have their passports initialled by the Dutch central authorities.[2]

It has to be stressed that the legal concept of aliens did not yet have the same meaning as in the twentieth century. It had changed from a local into a national category, but a clear distinction was made between those who resided in the country (alien residents) and those who lived abroad and visited the Netherlands. The former were exempted from the passport regulations and were – in other domains – treated as Dutch citizens.[3] Aliens who resided in the kingdom could travel freely, but were advised to procure an internal passport, to prevent their being mistaken for 'real' foreigners. Aliens from abroad could easily be recognized 'by their speech and other external signs'. Moreover, they were not supposed to have Dutch internal passports or other papers proving that they were Dutch residents.[4] In terms of rights and obligations, the position of aliens resident in the Netherlands changed only very slowly, without ever reaching the outsider status of aliens who did not reside in the Netherlands. In this chapter I shall therefore restrict myself to aliens in the latter sense.

The adoption of the French passport system was first of all motivated by (political) reasons of public safety (aliens as spies or sources of political unrest). However, there were other motives as well, which applied not so much to incoming aliens, as to departing citizens. Thus, Dutch citizens who wanted an internal or external passport had to prove that they were not of conscription age.[5] Furthermore, it is indicative for the new relationship between the national state and its citizens that the passport system was also used to prevent citizens with debts, or who were being sought by the authorities, to leave the country.[6] The state was, of course, dependent on the local authorities for information about applicants for passports. Therefore their advice played an important role in the decisions of the Ministry of Foreign Affairs to grant external passports (as a favour, not as a right).

Considerations about the national labour market, on the other hand, were virtually absent. Excluding aliens because they could pose a threat to Dutch workers did not (yet) enter the mind of Dutch bureaucrats. Due to the overriding political concern with aliens, the varying in passport regulations followed the political tide. Throughout the nineteenth century, the French in particular were considered to be a revolutionary danger. Only after the turn of the century was this role taken over by Russians (after 1917) and Germans (especially after 1918). English travellers, on the other hand, were treated with much more leniency, and could also enter without passports.

In March 1814, a few months after his accession, William I decided that, as the uniform nation-state was taking shape, it was time to set rules in order to supervise more strictly the presence of aliens, especially in the big cities.[7] This brings us to the second element of the aliens policy. Foreigners were to report to the local police, who in turn had to check their passports, register them and send monthly lists to the Ministry of Justice. Moreover, the police could make use of the lists of aliens brought in every morning by the owners of boarding houses and hotels. Similar to the passport regulations, seasonal workers, such as raft builders and mowers, were exempted from registration.[8]

An innovation in local supervision was the introduction of the 'safety card' in March 1815.[9] This card was issued as a sort of receipt – and at the same time functioned as a residence permit – for the passports that alien travellers who wanted to stay longer than twelve hours in a given municipality had to hand in to the police. When they decided to leave, they could pick up their passports and return the safety card. The passport was given a visa mentioning the next destination, where the procedure was repeated. Thus, in theory, a watertight surveillance system was created, which would enable the police to know at any given moment the whereabouts of any alien. As with other measures issued under the pressure of political turmoil, the safety card was not abolished when things settled down. It remained latent, to be revived when necessary.

## *The Belgian Separation (1830–1839)*

In August 1830, an insurgent movement started in Brussels with the aim of establishing an independent Belgian state. As the king did not succeed in suppressing Belgian insurgents by military force, and as England was in favour of separation, within months Belgium had declared its independence and produced its own Constitution. Only in 1839 did the Dutch king give up his stubborn resistance against partition. This crisis gave rise to a strict watch on the borders and to surveillance of aliens, especially in border towns and big cities in the west of the country.

First of all, the existing regulations on passports and surveillance were sharpened. Furthermore, the safety card was revived and finally all suspect persons coming from the 'southern insurgent provinces' had to be arrested. Additional decrees followed, which put the border area under military rule with severe controls on migration and commercial traffic. The aim was to isolate Belgium and to prevent imports and exports. The 1830s thus created a sort of curfew situation for aliens (as well as for the Dutch), especially for those who wanted to travel north to south, and this led to a heightened awareness of aliens by local and military authorities. The dispute with Belgium ended in June 1839, when King William I finally recognized the new state at his southern border after signing the Treaty of London a few months earlier. As a result, most special regulations concerning aliens, including most visa requirements, were cancelled.[10] Until the end of the 1840s, when revolutions swept Europe and the Netherlands drafted its first Aliens Act (1849), the central government took a much more passive stand than in the decade earlier.

This tranquillity is somewhat deceptive, however, because at the local level the legacy of the extraordinary surveillance of aliens in the 1830s was clearly visible. Important cities, such as Rotterdam, but also important fortified border towns that had been put under military rule, during the conflict with Belgium, such as Nijmegen in the east, did not suddenly give up their surveillance practices. This brings us to the important question of how the central aliens policies were implemented at the local level, and how this new policy affected the development of these local practices.

## From national to local: the cases of Nijmegen and Rotterdam (1830–1860)

Our knowledge about the local aliens policy in nineteenth-century Netherlands is even more patchy than our knowledge of the actions and motives of the central authorities, as described above. The only substantive study is by Marij Leenders (1993), who concluded that, especially in the first half of the nineteenth century, there were big differences in implementation between cities. Leenders's picture is a mix of local autonomy, incompetence and ignorance, to a certain extent comparable with the analysis of Noiriel (1998) of the French aliens policy in the nineteenth century. Local officials did not read or understand (or simply forgot) circulars from the central level, and, even when they did, they often ignored them, because it did not suit their (local) interests.

Although I agree with many of Leenders's and Noiriels's conclusions, it seems to me that their analysis is at times too one-sided and underrates the influence of the central initiatives on the development of the local aliens policy, as well as the inter-action between the central and local levels. In the following section I shall elucidate this by elaborating upon the local prac-tices in Nijmegen and Rotterdam. Before doing so, however, it is important to realize that these two cases are *not* representa-tive for the local level in the Netherlands. First of all, our knowledge of local practices is simply too patchy to allow such assessments. Furthermore, there were big differences between the countryside and big(ger) cities. Throughout the nineteenth century, complaints can be heard that mayors in villages and small towns lacked the most basic knowledge about the regula-tions issued by the central level, and – moreover – were not in the least interested in upholding such a policy. But it is doubt-ful that Rotterdam and Nijmegen set the tone among cities. As border towns, they were much more exposed to foreign trav-ellers, whose passports had to be checked. This section therefore deals not so much with the aliens policy at local level, but with the aliens policy in important border towns, a category which includes places like Maastricht and Roosendaal in the south, Vlissingen and Amsterdam in the west, and Arnhem and Venlo in the east. The fact that relatively considerable information is available about these cities in the archives of the central author-ities (especially these of the Ministries of Justice and Foreign Affairs) is, in itself, already an indication that they occupied a special position.

## Nijmegen

Nijmegen, situated in the east of the Netherlands near the Pruss-ian border on the banks of the river Waal (an important branch of the Rhine), was a small city. Due to its location on one of the main waterways, however, it was an important border town, through which many immigrants from the east entered the kingdom. As far as we can deduce from the information avail-able at the central level, it seems that the military regime in Nijmegen, which lasted from 1830 until 1839, was quite severe. All foreigners who entered or passed the town had to show their passports and explain where they wanted to go and with what purpose. In cases where identification was lacking or untrust-worthy, persons could be detained or sent back.

A good illustration of the problems that arose was shown when an English traveller, Sir William Mac-Beau, arrived in a steamer from Cologne. From a letter of the military commander to the

Justice department we get a clear picture of the way the local police operated, and the bureaucratic stumbling-blocks that foreign travellers had to face. In the beginning of September 1834, the chief of police went to the quay where the steamers from Germany were moored, in order to check the passports of travellers before they left the boat:

> Among the passengers was an old man, who was very angry and reacted in an extremely uncivilized manner, about the impertinence of the Dutch authorities to ask him, Sir William Mac-Beau, general-major in service of His Majesty the King of Great Britain, for his passport. Something, which neither the Prussian, nor the Belgian authorities had ever done, out of consideration 'pour la glorieuse Angleterre'.

The chief of police observed that Mac-Beau had a passport, issued by the English agent in Frankfurt, but that it did not have a visa for the Netherlands. He then sent him to his boarding-house to cool off. The following morning Mac-Beau had composed himself and was given permission to continue his travel through Rotterdam to England.[11]

The correspondence between the Justice Department and Foreign Affairs shows that this was not an isolated incident. Local authorities in Nijmegen and Rotterdam often had great trouble, especially with English travellers, who refused to show their passports and often insulted the Dutch police. Not all of them were as lucky as Mac-Beau, who probably intimidated the Nijmegen police by his upper-class appearance. There are other reports, which make clear that some English travellers were sent back, or – when they misbehaved – locked up.[12] Notwithstanding the complaints of the diplomatic representative of Great Britain in the Netherlands about the treatment of British subjects, the severe stance of the Nijmegen military commander in a number of cases was fully backed by the Ministry of Justice.

When the conflict with Belgium ended in 1839, the military authorities were discharged and the chief of police again became solely responsible for the local aliens policy. Interestingly, he had great trouble to adjust to the new, more relaxed situation. He wanted to continue the strict control of aliens, because he was afraid that otherwise all kinds of 'riff-raff' would pour into the country. This soon led to a conflict with the civilian authorities, who favoured a much more liberal aliens policy and who were glad that life had resumed its normal course. The mayor and the city council wanted the chief of police to restrict himself to checking only those aliens who came directly from abroad and leave others in peace. The correspondence on this matter with the Justice Department makes clear that the chief of police, who disagreed with such a lukewarm approach, had the approval of the ministry. All aliens who spent the night in Nijmegen, irrespective of from where they came from, had to be checked: only those passing through were to be left in peace.[13] Since the correspondence on this matter ends abruptly in July 1839, it is not clear from this case whether the central authorities remained so strict. We shall therefore shift our attention to Rotterdam where a few years later a very similar conflict arose between the police and the civil authorities.

## Rotterdam

Rotterdam was much bigger than Nijmegen and not only an important hub for travellers (and emigrants heading for the United States) coming from German and other European states by water, but also a major seaport. Moreover, it was a central node in the overland traffic between the south (France and Belgium) and the rest of the country, especially Amsterdam. To give an impression of this traffic, there were, in 1839, three boats each week to England; two boats each week from England (Hull and Newcastle); every five days a boat from Le Havre, and one from Dunkirk; every day boats arrived from the Rhine, with a daily boat from Antwerp and a twice-weekly boat from Ghent.[14] In November 1830, the Justice Department decided that the Rotterdam police had to be reinforced with a special chief of police, by the name of Klinkhamer, for the control of aliens.[15] As is apparent from the files in the Rotterdam archives, this official took his task very seriously and sent lists of foreigners (names, birth places, address, destination etc.) to the provincial governor every week.[16] In the summer of 1831 some thirty aliens per day had their passports registered in Klinkhamer's office. As in Nijmegen, in 1839 the civilian authorities wanted to get rid of the strict controls. In a letter to the director of the municipal police force they explained their motives:

> We feel that, especially in a nation characterized by commerce, the coming and going of foreigners should be made as easy and pleasant as possible. They should not be bothered by formalities and lose time, when there are no sound reasons to do so. Only when the conduct of travellers arouses severe suspicion, the police has to act, and even then with prudence and an exception to the rule. Civilization and politeness, but also our commercial interests demand, that we attract as many proper aliens as possible.[17]

They therefore assumed that the special bureau of Klinkhamer would be closed. His colleague, the director of the Rotterdam police, protested in Nijmegen. He stressed that the control on aliens was a matter for the higher police authority, and therefore not to be decided by local civilian authorities in Rotterdam. Furthermore, he underlined that the Royal Decree of 31 October 1830, the basis for the strict aliens policy during the Belgian crisis, had not been withdrawn. If Klinkhamer were to be dismissed, the work of checking some seven thousand passports per year would continue and burden the other three chiefs of police.[18]

The Ministry of Justice agreed with the director of police and argued that only the measures in relation to the relationship with Belgium were abolished in 1839, not the aliens controls in general. The ministry therefore deemed it necessary that the police continued the practice that had developed in the 1830s.[19] It is unclear what happened in the end, but what is striking, is that we see the same development as in Nijmegen. The police, supported by the Ministry of Justice, had got used to a certain bureaucratic procedure and were not willing to give up their 'infrastructural power' (Mann 1988: 26), although circumstances had changed dramatically. Local civil authorities, on the other hand, and possibly also central authorities with diverging interests, like the Ministry of Foreign Affairs (which was anxious not to be bothered by complaints of foreign travellers, because it could hinder diplomatic relations with other states) tried to curb the power of the police and supported a more liberal policy.

Although we do not know enough of the practice of the aliens policy in Rotterdam, there is evidence that to a certain extent the police won the battle. In 1845, a new director of police was appointed, who reorganized and thereby centralized the force. Among other things, he wanted to improve the surveillance of aliens. In politically turbulent times the police had to be ready to tighten procedures. In a letter to the provincial governor, he stressed that in the preceding years the surveillance of aliens had been defective, especially as only those who stayed in Rotterdam were registered and checked. He therefore proposed to check all aliens, most of whom who arrived by boat (railways that connected Rotterdam were only built in the 1850s), and withhold their passports. In the meantime they were given a safety card. For those who wanted to continue their travels immediately to another Dutch municipality, the same procedure had to be followed. The Rotterdam police director anticipated two major advantages: all aliens were checked, and by issuing safety cards to aliens who only passed through, they did not have to wait to have their passports checked, but could continue their travels almost immediately. Their passports were then sent after them to their final destination in the Netherlands.[20]

Although the Ministry of Justice foresaw difficulties, they agreed to a test. After a few months the Rotterdam police proudly presented the first results of the new policy and underlined that they wrote down the details of each alien and his passport in extensive registers. Another report, half a year later, reveals that almost all travellers had proper passports. Only some 3% were unable to show such an identity card. Half of this 3% could prove who they were and what the purpose of their visit was, the other half was sent back and expelled.[21] There were only a few complaints and no passes had been lost. From the fact that the registers, which are kept in the municipal archive of Rotterdam, were up-to-date for the first fifteen years, we can deduce that this practice lasted until at least 1860. From that year onwards the number of aliens registered decreases dramatically (by a factor of 10). As the same sudden break can also be observed in the aliens registers of Amsterdam, we may deduce that in that year the decision was made to abandon the very strict registration procedure.

## The limits of free migration after 1860

The sudden break in the local aliens policy can be explained by the political and economic liberalization in Western Europe, which coincided with the transport revolution and an increase in geographical mobility (Hochstadt 1999). One of the side effects was the abolition of passport requirements around 1860 and the start of a much more liberal migration regime (Strikwerda 1999; Torpey 2000; Lucassen 2001).

It would be wrong, however, to assume that states were no longer interested in the identity of immigrants. As the state became more involved in socio-economic issues, concerns over immigrants as potential receivers of poor relief emerged around the middle of the nineteenth century. This is illustrated by the first Dutch Aliens Act of 1849, characterized by contemporaries as a 'beggars act'. Although it was meant to make migration easy, it enabled authorities to refuse entrance to destitute immigrants (as well as to those of whom it could be expected that they would become dependent on poor relief) and gave them the power to expel aliens (Van Eijl 2000). Thus from 1850 onwards, thousands of foreigners were expelled each year. As expellees were only accepted by the state of origin when their citizenship could be established, some sort of identification was needed. Therefore the class of immigrant workers who wanted to work abroad had an interest in carrying identification papers (be it work booklets or birth certificates).

From the 1870s onwards, German authorities went even further by making it obligatory for Dutch migrant workers to carry nationality certificates (Lucassen 2001). Afraid that the German state would become responsible for poor relief when a foreign worker became unemployed or ill, state officials were very keen on establishing the state and parish of origin. That Germany was so 'progressive' in this area may be explained by the strong involvement of the Bismarckian state in social arrangements for its working population (Steinmetz 1993). As I argued elsewhere (Lucassen 1998) it seems not too far-fetched to assume a causal relationship between the emergence of the (albeit embryonic) welfare state and legislation to control the entrance of immigrant workers on to the national labour market.

## Conclusion

Returning to the paradox put forward in the introduction, this chapter has tried to make it clear that the aliens policy during the nineteenth century was multi-layered and more complicated than is often assumed. In this conclusion I will deal with two sets of assumptions that need revision: first, that after 1860 a regime of free migration was established in Europe, and, second, that aliens policy essentially worked from the top down.

As I have argued, after 1860 the state's interest in migrants remained. What changed were the underlying motivations, as well as the methods of control and monitoring. Thus in the Netherlands, as well as in most other Western European countries, we see a transformation from a political to a socio-economic regime. During the first half of the nineteenth century, authorities were mainly worried by aliens who might disturb public order by spreading revolutionary or insurrectionary ideas and activities. In France, this fear also informed the regulating of internal migration streams. Departments were ordered not to issue too many internal passports to Paris and other big cities, because this could endanger the fragile political equilibrium. Noiriel therefore argues that the constant monitoring of migrants by the French police shows the weakness of the state and should not be regarded as a sign of strength or of modernization (Noiriel 1998: 51–58).

As the revolutionary era waned in the second half of the nineteenth century, concerns about the political danger that
foreigners might pose decreased. At the same time, state officials became more interested in what was in the foreigner's
wallet than in what was going on in his or her head. Means of
subsistence were by no means a new focal point. From the
Middle Ages onwards, local authorities had tried to keep out
migrants whom they thought might cost them money. What was
new, was that with the emergence of direct rule the national
state became involved. At first it was mainly interested in internal migrants, most of them workers, as studies of on both
Germany and Great Britain have shown (Lucassen 1996;
Feldman 1999), but, increasingly, foreign workers were targeted
as well. In this sense, the police surveillance of internal migrants
foreshadowed the aliens policy of the late nineteenth and twentieth centuries.

The implementation of this central policy at the local level was
the second theme of this chapter. It is tempting to create, as
Noiriel has done, an image of an amorphous heap of abortive
and failed top-down attempts to create uniformity. Tempting,
because one can find enough validations to back up such a
conjecture. There was no lack of incompetent, ignorant, and
obstructing local officials in the nineteenth century. But as true
Popperians, we must look the other way, and search for refuta-
tions. The cases of Nijmegen and Rotterdam fulfil this condition
and show that a general image of a failed implementation is false.
These two examples may not be representative of Dutch cities in
general, but at least we can say that the situation was different
in important border towns. Here the legal opportunities offered
by the central level to uphold controls were much more
welcomed.

The semi-autonomous position of the local authorities is in
itself already an indication that we should not regard the aliens
policy as a simple top-down process, just as it would be misleading to see the central aliens policy as a linear one. Both cases
show that the local police in Nijmegen and Rotterdam – against
the will of the civil authorities – were, once given the opportunity, eager to follow the instructions offered by the central level,
in this case the Ministry of Justice. Moreover, they often went
further, as the initiative of the Rotterdam police in 1845 shows,
thus making the development of the aliens policy an interactive
process that generated its own momentum, which therefore must
be placed in a broader context of bureaucratisation and specialization of the police force.

For a better understanding of the development of the aliens policy we therefore need an open mind and must avoid preconceived ideas. Instead, it proved very rewarding to analyse case studies in detail. Only then can we see what really went on, and see how local officials were able to exert influence and follow their own agenda. Finally, we have noticed that the police often had different aims and interests than those of their civilian counterparts. Especially when it came to the policy towards aliens, the aims of the police (surveillance) and of the mayor (freedom of movement) often conflicted. To broaden our insight into the way aliens policies worked in the nineteenth century, it is essential not only to focus on top-bottom relations, but also on opposing interests at the local level.

## Notes

All translations into English are by the author. I thank Corie van Eijl for her remarks on an earlier version. The sources I consulted were the archives of the ministries of Foreign Affairs (FA) and Justice (JUS) in the General State Archive in The Hague (ARA), the Municipal Archive in Rotterdam (GAR) and the Appendix to the Law Gazette (Bijlagen tot het Staatsblad, BSB).

1.  It is important to stress that passports had various functions, both for the holder (right to move freely, proof of one's identity and nationality, right to assistance and protection against expulsion) and the state (preventing the departure of one's citizens, to stimulate emigration, to control immigration and to monitor the population). Moreover the relevance of these functions differed over time (Lucassen 2001).
2.  *Nederlandsche Staats Courant* (NSC), 1814, no. 42.
3.  Aliens who lived more than six years in the Netherlands, even when they were not explicitly admitted, could not easily be expelled, had a right to appeal for poor relief (RD, 15-1-1825 no. 100, published in *BSB* 1826: p. 14), and could obtain Dutch Foreign passports (at least when they had fulfilled military service) (Minister of Foreign Affairs to the king, dd 20-5-1826, no. 15, *ARA*, FA, 2.05.01, 3209).
4.  Royal Decree (RD), dd 20-12-1813 (*ARA*, JUS, 2.09.01, 4788).
5.  All men had therefore to produce their certificate of baptism, issued by the local administration. The only way for young men to obtain a passport was to prove that they were exempted from military service (RD 16-1-1814, no. 19, *Staatsblad*, 1813-1814, no. 12). This also concerned aliens who resided in the Netherlands. Until about 1850, they also fell under the Conscription Act (RD 25-6-1817, *ARA*, FA, 2.05.01, 3209). See also the instruction of 24-11-1817 (*BSB* 1817: p. 870).
6.  Letter of Foreign Affairs to the provincial gouvernor of Overijssel, dd 5-6-1839, no. 11 (*ARA*, FA, 2.05.01, 1774).
7.  Resolution of the general secretary of state to the attorney-generals, dd 7-3-1814 no. 326 (*ARA*, JUS, 2.09.01, 4788).
8.  Circular of the attorney general to the police, dd 22-3-1814 (idem).
9.  RD dd 24-3-1815 no. 21 (*BSB* 1848: p. 225) and RD dd. 29-3-1815 no. 170 (*BSB* 1815: p. 18).
10. RD, dd 12-6-1839, no. 21 (*Staatsblad*, no. 2, 1839).

11. Letter from the military commander of Nijmegen dd 4-9-1834 no. 469 (*ARA*, JUS, 2.09.01, 5198).
12. Correspondence in 1836 (idem).
13. Letter from the attorney general in Gelderland to the Justice Department, dd 26-7-1839 no.20 (*ARA*, JUS, 2.09.01, 4788).
14. Letter from the director of police, dd 12-8-1839 no. 123/82 (idem).
15. Also in Den Bosch and some other (unnamed) cities similar special police directors were appointed in 1830.
16. *GAR*, NS, 3509, no. 865. See also 1519, no. 1095.
17. Letter from the mayor & aldermen of Rotterdam, dd 27-7-1839 no. 1665/1026 to the director of police in Rotterdam (*ARA*, JUS, 2.09.01, 4788).
18. Letter from the director of police in Rotterdam, dd 12-8-1839 no. 123/82 (idem).
19. Letter, dd 27-6-1840, no. 48 to the provincial gouvernor of South-Holland (idem).
20. Letter of the director of police in Rotterdam, dd 3-4-1845 no. 9 to the attorney-general of South Holland (idem).
21. Letter dd 30-4-1846 no. 103 (*ARA*, JUS, 2.09.01, 4789).

## References

Feldman, David, 1999, 'Immigration, les immigrés et l'État en Grande Brétangne aux XIX$^e$ et XX$^e$ siècles', *Le Mouvement Social* 188: 43–60.
Hochstadt, Steve, 1999, *Mobility and Modernity. Migration in Germany 1820–1989*, Ann Arbor.
Leenders, Marij, 1993, *Ongenode gasten. Van traditioneel asielrecht naar immigratiebeleid, 1815–1938*, Hilversum.
Lucassen, Leo, 1996, *"Zigeuner". Die Geschichte eines polizeilichen Ordnungsbegriffes in Deutschland (1700–1945)*, Cologne.
Lucassen, Leo, 1998, 'The Great War and the Origins of Migration Control in Western Europe and the United States (1880–1920)', in *Regulation of migration. International experiences*, eds A. Böcker et al., Amsterdam, pp. 45–72.
Lucassen, Leo, 2001, 'A Many-Headed Monster: The Evolution of the Passport System in the Netherlands and Germany in the Long Nineteenth Century', in: *Documenting Individual Identity: the Development of State Practices in the Modern World*, eds John Torpey and Jane Caplan, Princeton, pp. 235–255.
Mann, Michael, 1988, *States, War and Capitalism. Studies in Political Sociology*, Oxford.
Noiriel, Gérard, 1988, *Le creuset français. Histoire de l'immigration XIX$^e$–XX$^e$ siècles*, Paris.
Noiriel, Gérard, 1998, *Réfugiés et sans-papiers. La République face au droit d'asile XIX$^e$–XX$^e$ siècle*, Paris.
Scott, James C., 1998, *Seeing like a State. How Certain Schemes to Improve the Human Condition Have Failed*, New Haven.
Steinmetz, George, 1993, *Regulating the Social. The Welfare State and Local Politics in Imperial Germany*, Princeton.
Strikwerda, Carl, 1999, 'Tides of Migration, Currents of History: The State, Economy, and the Transatlantic Movement of Labor in the Nineteenth and Twentieth Centuries', *International Review of Social History* 44: 367–394.
Torpey, John, 2000, *The Invention of the Passport. Surveillance, Citizenship and the State*, Cambridge.
Van Eijl, Corrie, 2000, 'Immigration Policy in the Netherlands, 1849–1914', paper presented at the *European Social Science History Conference* (Amsterdam 12–15 April 2000).

# Part III

---

# New Determinants of Migration Control

*Commercial Interests, Unions and Politicians*

# Chapter 13

# The Archaeology of 'Remote Control'

*Aristide R. Zolberg*

Gerald Neuman has persuasively demonstrated that, 'Contrary to popular myth, the borders of the United States were not legally open prior to the federalization of immigration law in the late nineteenth century' (Neuman 1996: viii).

But when and how did the 'myth' become into being? And how widely was it believed? Referring to the state and local enactments that form the basis of his analysis, Neuman himself concedes at the outset that historians 'have not been wholly unaware of the existence of these laws'. Many of these, as well as enactments to prevent the immigration of convicts, felons, lunatics, and others deemed undesirable, were prominently featured in two comprehensive collections of historical and contemporary immigration materials edited by Edith Abbott in 1924 and 1926, at a time when the protracted struggle to reduce immigration culminated in a series of unprecedented restrictionist victories (Abbott 1924; Abbott 1926). As is often the case, each of the opposing camps in the struggle over contemporary issues sought to demonstrate that 'history' was on its side. In short, defenders of the 'liberal' status quo – as of 1920, with regard to Europe, this meant immigration limited by 'qualitative' requirements alone – argued that the American tradition, as established by the Founders, was clearly 'immigrationist'.[1] A major response was elaborated by Roy Garis (1927). With regard to the 'lost century', Garis included not only state and local enactments, but also national legislation, notably the more demanding naturalization laws adopted by the Federalists in the 1790s and a lengthy series of 'passenger' acts that limited the number of persons that could be carried on incoming ships. Beyond this, he also surveyed numerous *unsuccessful* attempts to enact restrictive national laws. There is no gainsaying that, despite their ultimate failure, these provide evidence of widespread opposition to 'open' immigration on the part of important segments of the national political class at various points in the course of the 'lost century'.

Why does all this matter? Whereas Neuman is primarily concerned with contemporary policy debates, my own objective is to envision projects and policies pertaining to immigration as broadly understood in relation to the development of American society and politics. From this perspective the 'myth of open borders' severely obfuscates understanding if it is taken as representing historical reality.

A more appropriate conceptual baseline is the notion that, at any given time, the American stance was complex and hence variegated. Prospective immigration was envisioned not as an undifferentiated mass, but rather as an aggregate of distinct components, of special concern to different elements of American society. Overall, these several components were evaluated in the light of two very different sets of concerns, making for shifting stances along two axes ranging from pro- to anti-immigration. The first was economic, the other pertained to diffuse considerations related to the character of the American republic, most of which would be captured today by the concept 'identity' (Zolberg 1999: 82–90). Whereas the first has been widely recognised and appropriately theorized, the second has been dubbed 'nativism' and dealt with only as an aberration (Higham 1994). However, this can be envisioned more analytically in the perspective of 'nation-formation' as reflecting responses to the prospect of deviation from established cultural 'boundaries'.[2] From the perspective of various American actors, the two axes sometimes operated to reinforce each other in support of immigration or against it, but often operated in contradiction with each other: immigrants who were economically valuable might be undesirable as prospective members of the national community.

One of the key arguments in this chapter is that from the 1830s onwards until about 1855, there was growing opposition to immigration, fully comparable in its determination to the period 1890–1925. Historians of 'nativism', which ultimately contributed to the destruction of the 'second' party system, have suggested that the mid-nineteenth-century movement did not actually seek to reduce immigration (Anbinder 1992; Knobel 1996: 134). Their conclusion is based on the absence of restrictive federal enactments comparable to those of the early twentieth century. However, this chapter will demonstrate that the nativist movement did secure the enactment of a number of state and local laws explicitly designed to reduce immigration, as well as of federal measures designed to do so indirectly by regulating ships. The absence of federal legislation limiting immigration directly, as would be done from 1875 on, is attributable to two specific factors. One is the connection of immigration with the struggle over slavery by way of the issue of federal control over 'persons' – i.e. states' rights. The other is the eagerness of the emerging elements of American industrial capitalism to block attempts to limit immigration, including exploiting the states' rights issue through the courts.

Nevertheless, during this period the various successful and unsuccessful attempts to regulate immigration amounted to a 'rehearsal' for 'remote control'.

Half a century after independence, if immigration were a familiar feature of their mindscape Americans hardly thought of themselves as 'a nation of immigrants'. From 1820 to 1830 the white population increased by nearly 2.7 million, of which recorded immigration contributed about 5 percent; and even if official numbers were augmented by half to allow for unchecked arrivals, immigration would amount to only one-twelfth of decennial white population growth. White residents of the United States consisted overwhelmingly of native-born citizens of several generations' standing, mostly English-speaking Protestants of British stock, imbued with the distinct collective identity that Tocqueville labelled somewhat inaccurately 'Anglo-American'.

A spectacular increase in immigration occurred in the 1830s. In the course of the sailing season that began in the spring of 1832, recorded arrivals escalated to 60,482, nearly three times the ongoing level and twice the historical maximum to date. Of the 34,193 whose country of origin was recorded, only 5,331 came from Great Britain; 12,436 were Irish – their religion unspecified but probably mostly southern Catholics – and 10,194 German. New annual records were set in 1834, 1836, 1837, and again – after a brief respite attributable to the financial panic of the latter year – in 1840, when the number reached 84,066. For the decade as a whole, recorded immigration amounted to approximately 15 per cent of total white population growth, a proportion three times higher than in the 1820s. In the ten-year period beginning in 1832, the U.S. enumerated over 650,000 immigrants, of whom only one fourth were of British stock. To these should be added the unknown number landed surreptitiously to evade regulations or entering by way of British North America, the bulk of whom were Irish.

Most of the new arrivals remained in the seaboard cities as 'hands'; there was little subsequent upward mobility. Between 1825 and 1845, while New York City's population grew by half, the proportion of foreign-born increased more than threefold, from 11 to 35 percent. Concurrently, the city's workforce shifted from 'mechanics' to wage workers. As the latter were overwhelmingly foreign-born, the emergence of a proletariat was dramatised in New York, and in the urban segment of American society generally, by the alien character of the new class. Significant as early as 1830, the cultural division of labour between American- and foreign-born workers became steadily sharper in the second quarter of the century. British and German newcomers were somewhat more likely to enter into the ranks of 'mechanics', dominated by the native-born, whereas the Irish remained overwhelmingly proletarian. During this period, for the first time, immigration amounted to the formation of a critical mass, sharply differentiated from native Americans by way of ethnic origins, religion, and class.

Under the impact of these startling changes, the diffuse reservations which had been voiced perennially concerning the moral impact of immigration were given more reasoned form by intellectuals and began to figure as a prominent element of American political discourse. Notwithstanding their fervent nationalism, educated Americans remained largely imbued with the culture of Britain, sharing as a matter of course in its deeply imbedded prejudices toward the Irish. Each eagerly awaited shipment of reviews brought with it reactions to the invasions of the ancestral island by the 'simian race', echoing and reinforcing the dismay provoked by the spectacle of 'Irish hordes' in New York, Boston, or Philadelphia.[3]

As a new unruly working class, the Irish were frightful; but as Roman Catholics, the Irish – to whom were added many of the Germans – were dangerous. Romanism had long stood as the negative pole in relation to which Puritanism defined its own moral disposition. Anti-Catholicism was fuelled as well by the controversies surrounding Catholic emancipation in Britain in the late 1820s. Beyond this, the ideological war launched by the Holy See against political liberalism in the wake of the revolutionary upheavals of 1830, whose manifesto was issued in 1832 as the encyclical *Mirari Vos*, provided realistic grounds for suspicion among even the least paranoid that Catholic immigrants constituted a manipulable mass which might be used to undermine the world's only liberal republic. One may say, without exaggeration, that the Irish, in particular, came to be viewed by

*what about*
*South America?!*

mid-century as an alien race, in the literal sense of that term. Albeit more pronounced among the Whigs, anti-Catholicism was by no means a limited partisan affair (Knobel 1996: 40–87).

What is surprising is that no one advocated the obvious solution advanced by those who shared such concerns in a later age: minimise the danger by restricting immigration. A satisfactory explanation of why those who bewailed the political impact of immigration stopped short of advocating outright restriction must begin with a consideration of contemporaneous evaluations of its economic impact. Whereas the moral appraisal led to a negative conclusion, the economic resulted in a positive balance sheet. The contribution of immigration to economic development was so much taken for granted by American businessmen that the question was seldom argued explicitly; and the validity of the prevailing view has been sustained by recent econometric analyses of the consequences of nineteenth-century trans-Atlantic population movements (Thomas 1973). Under these circumstances, one can reasonably infer that, notwithstanding the emergence of a nativist ideology and a sharpening of the political conflict between natives and aliens at the local level throughout the country, the American business community would resist any attempt to solve the immigration problem by eliminating the culturally deviant segment, a method which would have resulted in an unacceptable reduction of the ongoing flow.

A consideration of the relationship between the two aspects of immigration, moral and economic, also helps to account for the fact that, although the second party system coalesced in part around the ethnic cleavage immigration produced, the system functioned on balance to prevent immigration from becoming a partisan issue at the national level, and thereby to forestall the possibility of wholesale restriction.

The Whigs embodied an outlook akin to Weber's spirit of capitalism, combining a religious sensibility derived from Puritanism, revived by the second Great Awakening, with 'a vision of America as an economically diversified country in which commerce and industry would take their place alongside agriculture' (Howe 1979: 16). Although the Whigs emerged as the party of business, they were also out to enlist support from a recently enlarged electorate; and in this respect, they appealed to Yankee Protestant natives and immigrants of British origin. The Whig rank-and-file was overwhelmingly 'nativist'; but while their leaders undoubtedly shared in this sensibility, the party's commitment to a business-minded economic program dictated stalwart adherence to the established immigrationist policy.

The Democratic Party emerged as, among other things, the party of workers in northern urban areas. This electorate initially still consisted mostly of native Americans, many of them 'mechanics' active in workingmen's organizations, who regarded the large influx of cheap labour as a threat to their income and status. Limiting the damage by restricting immigration presented itself as an obvious solution. However, it was not the only possibility. The other was to secure for American workers an equivalent to the 'exit' available to their European counterparts, by way of cheaper or altogether free public land. Both alternatives surfaced within the New York Democratic camp in the mid-1830s. Providing access for the American common man to life as an independent farmer was a central part of the Democratic programme; and the aspiration was widely shared by an indigenous working class which had gained access to citizenship and was not yet proletarianised. So long as this remained possible, the attention of eastern workingmen was as much focused on getting out of the wage market as on preventing others from getting in (Zahler 1941: 38).

In any case, whatever negative dispositions were manifested toward immigration at the rank-and-file level were overridden by the Democratic Party's organisational interest in recruiting the new arrivals. Although both parties attempted to do so, the Democrats, as defenders of the interest of the common man, were more attractive to poor immigrants in general, and to Catholics in particular. The communal and class conflicts associated with immigration engendered mounting tensions within each of the parties; but so long as the second party system held fast, attempts to preserve the cultural status quo by imposing restrictions that would have the effect of significantly reducing immigration were very unlikely to succeed.

With this outcome foreclosed, nativist efforts were directed toward forestalling the incorporation of newcomers into the body politic, a process that was tantamount to the erection of an internal boundary between indigenous citizens and alien workers. The most common proposal, initially advanced by the Native American Association in 1837 and set forth repeatedly throughout the antebellum period by Whigs as well as nativist organisations, was to lengthen the residency requirement for naturalization from five to twenty-one years: the length of time it took a native American to reach legal majority and, in the case of white males, to exercise voting rights (Abbott 1926: 324f., 744f., 755; Potter 1976: 245). But the use of this solution with respect to European arrivals, which required congressional action, was strenuously opposed by Democrats. The 1802 naturalization law prevailed.

Deterred from achieving the more comprehensive restriction-ist policies to which they aspired, those who opposed immigration fell back on a reinforcement of the fence erected earlier on against Europe's undesirables. However, at this point their voice became indistinguishable from the general outcry against convicts and paupers.

The objective of arresting the flow of convicts and paupers went back to the colonial era and was so widely shared that one can speak of a genuine consensus in the matter, with the singular exception of the American shipping industry, whose narrow inter-ests dictated sheer maximisation of the mass of passengers and opposition to all forms of regulation that might negate achieve-ment of this objective. Destitution was indeed very widespread among self-financed immigrants, even if its incidence did not increase as a proportion of incoming numbers, as the cumulative impact of a flow of unprecedented magnitude resulted in the formation of a critical mass that constituted a genuinely new problem. This was coupled with a widely shared belief, itself based on credible evidence, that European governments intervened so as to effect the transfer to America of undesirables who could not have gone abroad of their own accord. Strengthening the fence against convicts, paupers, and others likely to become public charges, would genuinely reduce the social costs that massive immigration entailed, and hence also render it more acceptable to the port-of-entry taxpayers on whom those costs were imposed. Inextricably intertwined, these considerations provided the foun-dations for a bipartisan consensus on the necessity of more vigorous governmental intervention to counter 'dumping'.

But the achievement of this objective was hampered by the conjunction of two very different obstacles. The first consisted of the inherent administrative problems of operationalising cate-gories such as 'convicts' and especially 'paupers' in relation to a mass consisting overwhelmingly of destitute Europeans, and of enforcing concomitant restrictions upon arriving passengers, since the limited organizational development of the Department of State foreclosed in practice the elimination of undesirables prior to embarkation. It also proved extremely difficult to differ-entiate between voluntary emigrants and those who were being involuntarily removed. The second obstacle arose from a key feature of American political structure. Given the multitude of ports-of-entry – including the Canadian loophole – effectiveness dictated regulation at the national rather than at the state level. However, given the nature of immigration as a social process, the national solution unavoidably raised important constitutional issues, at a time when the problem of states' rights was moving to the centre of the political arena. It will be remembered, in this respect, that the Jacksonians were generally determined to reverse the previous trend toward greater power of the national government, particularly in the sphere pertaining to the exercise of authority over individuals.

At the same time, the future of state regulatory activity in the sphere of immigration was itself becoming increasingly doubtful. Affirmation by the Supreme Court in 1824 of the supremacy of the national government in the sphere of international and interstate commerce, including navigation, provided grounds for challenging the constitutionality of attempts by the states to regulate immigration by way of fiscal measures such as bonding and head taxes. The shipping industry was quick to take advantage of the constitutional penumbra in its efforts to minimise interference (Klebaner 1958: 287). Such a challenge was launched as early as 1826, in response to an action of debt instituted by the State of New York to recover penalties under the bonding act passed two years earlier. Although the defendant was precluded for technical reasons from attacking the act on constitutional grounds and was found liable in 1828, another challenge began to wind its way through the courts the following year, even as pressures for more vigorous state intervention increased (Tuerk 1951: 8f.).

These considerations entered into play in a complex manner. Each of the eastern seaboard states can be thought of as internally divided on the issue of restricting paupers and such, since they encompassed the opposing organisational actors most directly concerned with the issue: on one side, the welfare establishment, which dealt with the mounting costs of relieving destitute aliens, and, on the other, the shippers who thrived on bringing in as many aliens as possible. It was also difficult for the states to act in concert because they competed for shipping and believed that stricter regulations enacted by any one of them would deflect not only undesirables, but also international commerce, towards the others. As problems mounted and the shippers appeared likely to succeed in challenging the constitutionality of state regulations, the eastern states launched a drive to secure a national solution, which would not only be more effective but would also ensure parity among the states with respect to their competitive position; but, at that level, their initiative was countered by what was in effect a coalition of immigrant-hungry Westerners and southern guardians of states' rights.

The shipper-engineered challenge to state regulation of immigration finally reached the U.S. Supreme Court in 1834 on a certificate of division from the Circuit Court of the Southern District of New York. The case, City of New York vs. Miln, again arose out of an action by the state to recover debt. When first argued, with John Marshall still at the helm, it was believed that four out of seven justices considered the law to be unconstitutional as a regulation of international commerce. However, because two of the putative majority were absent from the court, Marshall in effect foreclosed a minority victory, by the unprecedented ruling that the court could not hand down a decision, since its practice was not to deliver judgments in constitutional cases unless four judges concurred in making it a majority opinion (Tuerk 1951: 8f.). Although the case was set for reargument at a later date, the handwriting was clearly on the wall so far as the states were concerned, at the very time that immigration was escalating, bringing in its wake mounting welfare costs and nativist anger. It was even being argued that paupers should be deported altogether, as British counties had done under the old Poor Law (Abbott 1924: 112).

The case was still pending in the spring of 1836, when the Massachusetts legislature took the initiative for congressional action. The House instructed the Commonwealth's representatives and senators to use 'their endeavors to obtain the passage of a law by Congress to prevent the introduction of paupers into this country, or to favor any other measures which congress may be disposed to adopt to effect the object' (Abbott 1924: 112–14). Accordingly, on July 4, 1836, the Senate of the United States resolved to direct the Secretary of the Treasury to collect facts on the 'deportation' of paupers from Europe to the United States. The survey was conducted over the next year by way of reports from U.S. consuls and duly reported to the Senate in 1837.

It should be noted that the term 'deportation' suggests a more explicit use of state coercion than was usually exercised in the course of 'shoveling out' paupers (Abbott 1924: 114–9). Consequently, the investigation produced ambiguous results. With respect to Germany, consular reports states unequivocally that no instances of deportation could be found. Reports from Ireland explained – with unintended irony – that there were no proper paupers in that country because it possessed no poor laws whatsoever. Since the mass of Irish were so poor that they could not possibly leave on their own, but nevertheless emigrated at a much higher rate than the British, one could infer two things: first, most of those who left of their own were slightly above the poverty line; second, a minority were assisted by landlords wishing to consolidate their holdings. With respect to Britain, there were many reports of contracts entered into by parishes with ship owners for wholesale removal of paupers; but they emphasised that even such emigration was overwhelmingly voluntary. Cases of outright deportation were rare, amounting to perhaps 600 out of 16,000 sailings out of Liverpool in 1830.

Organised around a strict construction of 'deportation', the investigation disconfirmed notions that U.S. problems resulted from a European plot. But its conclusions justified urgent action since they indicated that little could be achieved by securing a change of policy on the part of the countries of origin.

While the Congress was contemplating further action on these matters, the U. S. Supreme Court finally issued its decision in City of New York vs. Miln. Contrary to earlier expectations, the court, now headed by Roger Taney, ruled six to one in favour of the constitutionality of the New York statute on the grounds that it was 'not a regulation of commerce, but of police; and that being so considered, it was passed in the exercise of a power which rightfully belonged to the states'. Story was the lone dissenter (Tuerk 1951: 9f.).

The case warrants special attention because the court's pronouncements provided the most comprehensive statement of constitutional doctrine in the sphere of immigration to date, and determined the shape of immigration policy for the remainder of the antebellum period. In particular, analysis of Miln demonstrates that the common historical wisdom, whereby the absence of federal regulation of entry prior to 1882 is taken as an indicator of the persistence of consensual laissez-faire until that date, is based on a profound misunderstanding. Although the case dealt with immigration, the court seized upon it as an opportunity to implement the constitutional doctrine to which it was committed in the sphere of states' rights. Adumbrating the Charles River Bridge case handed down later that year, Miln signalled an end to the court's steadfast support of the growth of national power (*New York v. Miln, 2 Paine 429; 8 Peters 120 [1834]; 11 Peters 102 [1837]*). The Jacksonian justices endorsed the established policy of selective immigrationism and shared in the new consensus with respect to the need for more active governmental intervention to restrict paupers and convicts. But by upholding state regulation and grounding it on the powers reserved to them under the Tenth Amendment, while concomitantly putting Congress on notice that federal action must be limited to passenger legislation, they foreclosed the implementation of a more effective solution to the major problem of immigration in the name of a higher political objective.

The Miln pronouncements pulled the rug from under pending congressional action. They did so at a critical time, when the effects of a sudden immigration crisis might well have assured passage of a national immigration law nearly half a century earlier than in fact occurred. Although the Secretary of the Treasury duly reported to the Senate on 'deportation', no further action was taken by that body. The House had also appointed a Select Committee on Foreign Paupers and Naturalization Laws. Its report, dated July 2, 1838, included a letter from Friedrich List, U.S. Consul at Leipzig, with the suggestion – not implemented until the twentieth century – that consuls be empowered to regulate immigration at the point of departure. On the basis of this, the Committee on the Judiciary was instructed – Miln notwithstanding – to prepare a bill prohibiting the entry of paupers. Although they did so, recommending sanctions of up to $1,000 for masters who took on board, with the intention of transporting them to the United States, aliens in a number of undesirable categories – 'idiots', 'lunatics', persons who were 'incurably diseased' or who had been found guilty of an 'infamous crime' – the proposal fell by the wayside (Abbott 1924: 127f.).

Now that constitutional doubt was removed, state and local authorities acted with deliberate speed. In New York City, Mayor Aaron Clark warned that undesirables, evading New York state regulations by landing on the New Jersey side of the bay, were continuing to pour into the city. Not only did the new arrivals overtax relief facilities, but they were a source of moral and political peril as well. The Mayor therefore proposed confining arrivals on their vessels until arrangements to forward them beyond New York City were completed. Meanwhile, he indicated his intention to require of them the maximum possible commutation fee, i.e. $10 per capita. Further plans included negotiations with New Jersey for relevant action, extension of the term of residence required for naturalization, as well as enlargement of the city's police force 'for both the day and the night time'.

The New Jersey loophole was closed when that state imposed a head tax on all immigrants, ranging from $1.00 to $10.00, depending on the degree to which they appeared likely to constitute a public charge (Klebaner 1958: 314). Massachusetts enacted a new and more comprehensive passenger law shortly after the Miln decision (Tuerk 1951: 11). Combining the two prevailing forms of fiscal regulation, it empowered town officials to appoint officers with the authority to require ten-year bonds of $1,000 for lunatics, idiots, aged and infirm persons, as well as paupers: and to collect a head tax of $2.00 for all other aliens landed. Much as New Jersey did in relation to New York, Maine followed suit a year later. Although the sum of state regulations probably amounted to a less effective policy instrument than a national law, the proliferation of measures did indicate a shifting emphasis toward greater selectivity. This was not incompatible with an immigrationist outlook in the face of evidence that forces in Europe assured a steady enlargement of the emigrant pool.

The great mid-century migration occasioned by social upheavals in Europe – a concatenation of famine, depression, and revolution – and the concomitant triumph of emigrationism among its governments, struck the United States like a tidal wave and transformed it quite suddenly into a nation of immigrants.

On the eve of this event, there was still room for considerable debate over the importance of immigration in relation to endogenous processes governing the development of American society. The annual flow from Europe had begun to rise again after 1839, passing the 100,000 mark for the first time in 1842, and, after a two-year recess, again in 1845. This was sufficient to maintain issues related to immigration on the political agenda of the seaboard states and to fuel nativism. It was after the Polk election that the 'Native Americans' held their first national convention in Philadelphia on July 4, 1845. Theirs was a catastrophic view; they reasoned that whereas immigration presented little danger in the early days of the Republic, because the influx was limited by the prohibitive costs of voyage, slender inducements to come, and a scarcity of population in Europe, changing conditions now fostered an unmanageable 'torrent' (Abbott 1926: 744ff.). As against this, it was possible to argue as late as 1845 that there was less cause for concern than the '"Native" Papers' would have it, because foreigners constituted 'comparatively small and decreasing numbers' (Abbott 1926: 754). This was not quite accurate; but it was the case that the rate of increase of immigration since 1832 was approximately the same as that of population, so that the contribution of immigration to white population growth remained stable at about one-sixth of the total; annual arrivals at the level of the early 1840s amounted to one half of 1 percent of a white population numbering about 17 million.

As it was, the catastrophic prediction was the more accurate. The European wave mounted rapidly from 154,405 in 1846 to 414,933 in 1854, a level not equalled again until 1873. Altogether, it deposited nearly 2.5 million people in the United States within a nine-year period, adding nearly 13 percent to the country's white population.[4]

According to the 1850 census, taken halfway through the wave, the proportion of foreign-born among the white population reached 11.5 percent for the nation as a whole, and 15.5 percent in the Northeast alone. The absolute number of foreign-born nearly doubled in the next decade, so that by 1860 the proportions were 15 and 22 percent respectively (Abbott 1926: 328–37). The dramatic change was particularly visible in the cities. By 1855, when New York City passed the half-million mark, over half the population was foreign-born, a five-fold increase in their proportion in thirty years (Bridges 1984: 96). Nor was the phenomenon any longer limited to the eastern seaboard: in 1860, immigrants amounted to 44 percent of the population in the three cities of Ohio, 50 percent in Chicago and Milwaukee, 48 percent in Detroit, 61 percent in St. Louis, and 50 percent in San Francisco.

Moreover, as the 1860 census report observed, 'The European class would be far more numerous were their descendants also included'. The remark is noteworthy because it presages the formal incorporation of a distinction among 'native-born' between those of 'native' and 'foreign' stock in the census of 1870. Non-British immigrants constituted over 75 percent of arrivals in the 1830s and an even higher proportion later on. The largest groups remained the Irish, who peaked at 221,253 in 1851 (58 percent of the year's total) and the Germans, who attained their maximum of 215,009 in 1854 (50 percent of arrivals). The 1850 census, which already reflected administrative attentiveness to the country's growing ethnic heterogeneity, pointed out that of the foreign-born enumerated in the United States only approximately one-fifth were of British 'founding stock'. By 1860, the proportion had fallen to 14.18 percent, a mere one seventh of the total.

What has just been sketched out is an outcome: the result in the first instance of processes whose locus was in Europe, but also of an absence of barriers to entry into the United States. The question remains, still, how was it that no such obstacles were erected? It is a puzzle because all historians of the period concur in their assessment that, under the impact of the tidal wave, hostility towards immigrants reached unprecedented intensity, to the point, according to some, of contributing at least as much to the breakdown of the second American party system as did the sectional conflict over slavery. If, as was argued earlier, it was the party system which had kept nativists from achieving their objective of preserving the cultural status quo by reducing the flow, then how was it that a force that was powerful enough to destroy the party system remained powerless to follow up and realise its policy goal? The traditional answer is that nativism, as an organized political force, itself quickly foundered on the sectional issue. But this is not a sufficient explanation. In the short period between its apogee and its demise, the nativist movement scored a number of victories in the realm of immigration policy. However, at the critical moment, it was robbed of its triumph by the effective intervention of another, equally powerful, actor. For the 1850s was not only the high point of nativist fury and of sectional conflict; it was also a decade in which the economic transformations under way since the 1830s crystallized into a more advanced form of American capitalism. Immigration made possible the managerial revolution in American business, and it was this which in turn firmly kept the flood gates from being closed.

Chandler has suggested that 'Before the 1840's the relative scarcity of labor and the continuing use of traditional technologies [...] sharply limited the amount an enterprise was able to produce and the size to which it might grow' (Chandler 1977: 63). Although the lack of coal, which held back the development of factory production, was overcome in the 1830s, the revolution did not occur until the railroad and the telegraph simultaneously transformed the processes of distribution. At this point, 'These changes in production and distribution reinforced one another'. They caused entrepreneurs to integrate and subdivide their business activities and to hire salaried managers to monitor and coordinate the flow of goods through their enlarged enterprises (Chandler 1977: 77). Chandler thus attributes the rise of modern business enterprise, engaged in mass production, mostly to 'the almost simultaneous availability of an abundant new form of energy and revolutionary means of transportation and communication' (Chandler 1977: 78, also 244ff.). It should be added, however, that immigration also simultaneously reduced the scarcity of labour and that this important change in the character of the labour supply reinforced the other processes, since the revolutionary reorganisation of enterprise enabled the leading sectors of American capital to take advantage of the availability of an unlimited pool of cheap European labour.

The revolution was under way when the European economy went into depression. The period 1849–56 was one of nearly continuous boom in the U.S. interrupted by only brief slumps in the latter half of 1851 and again the fall of 1854 (Holt 1973: 325). Foreign investments, which had declined sharply after 1839, returned massively, so that net liabilities of the U.S. to foreigners reached $384 million in 1859, a 66 percent increase over the previous historical maximum attained in 1839.

The railroad both contributed to the revolution of American capitalism and was its leading manifestation. It follows that the railroad industry rapidly emerged in the policy arena as a major actor favouring a high level of immigration on several grounds. The European flow not only supplied the huge pool of low-wage construction workers necessary for its rapid development, but also increased its passenger clientele, especially in newly developing regions, where railroad companies also sold land to Americans and newcomers.

Albeit less affected by the managerial revolution, the shipping industry also underwent a spectacular expansion. American ship construction surged forth in the middle third of the century. Concentrated in the period 1847–1857, the boom entailed not only the construction of more ships, but of much larger ones as well; average capacity grew from 400 tons in 1820 to 1,250 by 1854 (Jones 1973: 13f.). The jewel of the American merchant marine was the sleek and fast packet-ship, which achieved toward the end of the era of sail a near-monopoly of fine freight and cabin-passenger trade; but its mainstay consisted of combination traders, full of line and much slower, designed to carry cotton bales to Europe and from three hundred to six hundred immigrants in the 'tween decks on the westbound voyage. Packets turned to the emigrant traffic when their monopoly began to be challenged by steam. The vessels launched at the height of the boom 'were designed for emigrants, as carriage of emigrants had become the greatest single source of revenue for owners' (Jones 1973: 14f.). Concomitantly, American shipping companies also developed an extensive network of recruiting agencies in Europe (Abbott 1924: 27f.). Mid-century efforts to restrict immigration thus had to contend with a shipping industry that was both more powerful and economically more dependent than ever before on the maintenance of an open door policy. At the height of nativist fervour, railroads, factory-owners, and shippers, formed a stalwart alliance in defence of immigrationism.

To this camp should be added the western states, viewed here both as a sectional interest within the national legislative arena, and as institutional actors in relation to the immigration process. The West had long favoured immigration, supporting incentives and opposing barriers; but, at about this time, the western states also began to intervene more actively to stimulate the flow and direct its course by appointing Commissioners of Emigration with funds to advertise on the East Coast and abroad.

Responses to the tidal wave were quick in the making. Paralleling what had occurred a decade earlier, shipper-engineered challenges to the constitutional validity of state regulations restricting entry of persons likely to become public charges were again pending in the courts at the very moment that conditions fostered efforts to close loopholes by replacing selective bonds with generalized head taxes, and by enforcing regulations on those entering by land or sea from British and North America. The Senate and the House again began gathering information from American consuls on the process whereby undesirables were being shovelled out (Klebaner 1958: 323; Abbott 1924: 129f., 142f.). At the same time, however, there was movement in another direction. In January, 1847, the Common Council of New York City requested from the Almshouse Commissioner's office a report on the numbers received since the previous September (Abbott 1924: 27f.). Describing the dreadful conditions of those seeking assistance, the report suggested that the cause was to be found less in the state of affairs in Europe, but in the fact that many who were enticed by alluring descriptions 'of the blessed state of American life' became ill and physically undermined by the nefarious experience of travel itself. One month later, the legislature of New York State enacted a concurrent resolution, which urged that the state's representatives and senators work to secure a more humanitarian passenger law (Abbott 1924: 28; Hansen 1961: 253). Documents such as the Almshouse Commissioner's report were communicated to the Congress along with petitions from the state, the city, and charitable organisations.

Quickly passed and without divisions in either house, the resulting Passenger Act of February 22, 1847, was the first national measure dealing directly with immigration since 1819. It imposed, in addition to the established minimum volume requirement of 2.5 tons per passenger, a space requirement expressed in 'superficial feet'. Designed in relation to two-deck ships, it set this at 14 feet for the upper 'platform' – increased to 20 if the ship passed through the tropics – and at 30 feet for the bottom 'orlop' deck. Children under the age of one were not counted, and those between one and eight-years-old were reckoned as half-passengers. Penalties were set at $50 as well as up to one year of imprisonment for each violation, with the possibility of seizure in case excess passengers numbered over twenty. The new regulations were scheduled to come into effect on May

31 of the same year, as soon as they could be communicated to European embarkation points. On March 2 the law was rendered even more severe by providing that children over one year of age be counted as full passengers.

Incidentally, a law of January 21, 1848, exempted ships removing blacks on behalf of the African Colonization Society from all of the above requirements (Minot 1862: 127f., 149, 210). The same problems of interpretation arise with this as with the 1819 act, since humanitarian and nativist objectives overlapped in some respects. It cannot be gainsaid that this was a humanitarian measure. At the same time, the law would have the effect of lowering incoming numbers by reducing the carrying capacity of the existing fleet, in accord with nativist objectives. In combination, the new state and federal laws probably did act as a deterrent. Since they came into effect after the beginning of the 1847 season, their full impact was not appreciable until 1848; however, new passenger regulations, discussed below, came into effect in mid-June of the latter year. As it was, the number of recorded landings rose from 154,416 to 234,968 in 1847; and although conditions in Europe deteriorated further in the winter of 1847–48, arrivals in 1848 decreased slightly to 226,527. The statistics thus point in the appropriate direction; it must be acknowledged, however, that the evidence they provide is inconclusive.[5]

In retrospect, the federal passenger law of 1847 was a pyrrhic victory for whatever combination of humanitarian and nativist concerns had led to its speedy enactment. Even as seaboard states struggled to cope with the growing influx, among whom undoubtedly an unusually large proportion were destitute or ill and in need of immediate relief, the shippers, alarmed by the diversion of traffic to British North America, prevailed upon the Secretary of the Treasury to interpret the new regulations loosely (Hansen 1961: 255). Meanwhile, the congress again took up the issue of passengers. The result was an act 'to provide for the Ventilation of Passenger Vessels and for other Purposes', signed into law on May 17, 1848, and scheduled to go into effect with respect to the Atlantic thirty days later (Minot, 1862; 30th Congress, Sees. 1, Chap. XLI: 220–3).

The new law represented a signal victory for the shippers (Hansen 1961: 260). It abolished the minimum volume requirement altogether. The 'superficial' requirement was maintained; but whereas the 1847 act distinguished between two decks, the present measure related the requirement to distance between decks. The net consequence was to increase the legal carrying capacity of immigrant ships.[6] That the shippers had gained the upper hand is confirmed by the enactment of yet another passenger law in 1849 – the first one referring to Pacific as well as Atlantic traffic – which liberalised regulations concerning mandatory provisions and dropped the requirement of additional passenger space for ships passing through the tropics (Minot, 1862; 30th Congress, Sees. II, Chap. CXI: 399f.).

Meanwhile the confrontation came to a head also with respect to the welfare burden. Although the Miln decision had sustained bonding of those liable to become public charges as a legitimate exercise of police power by the states, shippers naturally persisted in their attempts to minimize the impact of such regulations. To avoid forfeiting the bonds in case immigrants became ill or destitute, the shipping industry sponsored the construction of cut-rate commercial hospitals and poorhouses, in which individuals were incarcerated under conditions considered dreadful even by the generally low standards of contemporary philanthropic or public establishments. Consequently, the shipping industry's camp was reinforced by the emergence of builders and institutional operators who shared their interests in forestalling enactment of more stringent regulations. Another problem was that many of these inmates were later surreptitiously unloaded into public facilities as long-term residents rather than as recent arrivals.

Hence the states searched for more reliable income in the form of head taxes and health fees, to be collected from shippers prior to landing and from all immigrants, usually in combination with additional bonds for those who appeared likely to become public charges: often referred to at this time as 'defectives'. New York, which had required payment of a hospital fee ever since 1797, established a $1.00 general head tax in 1847, together with a $300, five-year non-commutable bond for 'defectives'. At the same time, the state took responsibility for the care of poor immigrants out of the hands of the city's Almshouse Commissioners and bondsmen, placing it into the hands of a newly created State Board of Commissioners of Immigration, which included the mayors of New York City and Brooklyn, ex officio, as well as the heads of the leading Irish and German immigrant societies (Erickson 1976: 270ff.). Massachusetts had already enacted a $2.00 head tax in the wake of the 1837 immigration crisis, with a $1,000 ten-year bond for 'defectives'; in 1848, the bond was extended to life. Louisiana and Texas established similar head taxes when they became ports of entry in 1842–44 (Klebaner 1958: 274; Hansen 1961: 256; Tuerk 1951: 13f.).

The response of American and European shippers to these new developments was as anticipated. Fees and head taxes imposed

on entire shiploads as a condition for landing were more difficult to evade than selective bonds and other such regulations;
and although the cost could be passed on in the form of higher
fares, acute competition for the immigrant trade rendered this
inexpedient (Hansen 1961: 260). Hence the shippers turned once
again to the courts. In 1841, George Smith, master of the British
vessel *Henry Bliss*, refused to pay the New York health fees; and,
in a similar vein, James Norris, master of the British vessel *Union
Jack*, entered a suit in Boston to recover head taxes he had paid
under protest to a city official. Persisting after their defeat at the
hands of the judiciary of the respective states, Smith and Norris
brought their cases before the U.S. Supreme Court. Argued in
various terms beginning in 1846, Smith v. Turner and Norris v.
City of Boston were decided together on February 7, 1848, in
what came to be known as the 'Passenger Cases' (7 How. 283,
1849; Warren 1922: 171–282; Hames and Sherwood 1957: 152f.).

As with Miln, the significance of the 'Passenger Cases' in American constitutional history transcends the sphere of immigration.
Contemporary comments by participants indicate a clear understanding that the New York and Massachusetts immigrant laws
paralleled enactments whereby southern states prohibited the
landing of free Negroes in their ports, so that the outcome of the
'Passenger Cases' would also determine the validity of the latter.
To what extent such considerations affected the outcome,
however, cannot be ascertained. As it was, in a five to four split,
the Supreme Court declared the New York and Massachusetts
laws interfered with immigration and thereby infringed upon
federal authority in the sphere of interstate and international
commerce.

The arguments advanced on behalf of the states left no doubt
that the measures under consideration were designed to serve as
instruments of a restrictionist immigration policy. The substantive aspects of the matter were concomitantly emphasised by the
other side as well, in a manner which confirms the validity of the
present interpretation.

With respect to constitutional law, the decision in the Passenger Cases was quite clear: it was a move away from state rights.
In effect, the Supreme Court qualified the Miln doctrine regarding the exercise of police power by the states to protect
themselves against undesirables, be they foreign paupers or free
Negroes, by prohibiting them from excluding such persons
outright or from doing so indirectly by taxing entries. With
respect to its consequences for immigration policy, however, the
decision was ambiguous. While declaring head taxes in this form

unconstitutional, it did sustain the exercise of police power to enact financial measures to alleviate burdens ensuing from the entry of destitute or 'defective' immigrants. In effect, the states were allowed to impose bonds on categories of persons considered likely to become public charges or even on entire shiploads, and to require detailed reports from masters or even to dispatch inspectors on shipboard, so long as the financial transactions involved were conducted after the passengers were landed.

The clarification prompted the seaboard states to quickly design and enact a modified system of bonds and commutation fees that was as effective as head taxes or hospital fees with respect to the generation of revenue. The system could obviously also be used to reduce immigration by raising bonds and concomitant commutation fees to prohibitive levels. What kept this from occurring was that, as in the past, state immigration policy remained governed by pressures to pursue conflicting objectives. In response to the mid-century flood, most of the seaboard states did indeed raise the costs of immigration; but even before it had receded, many of them retreated as a consequence of competition among ports of entry to maximize business (Klebaner 1958: 281). These vacillations, which paralleled those of Congress with respect to passenger legislation, further confirm the nature of the confrontation and its nationwide character.

As the tidal wave continued in the early 1850's, the 'visible hand' not only intervened time and again to keep the floodgates open, but reached out beyond them to beckon for more. The consequences exceeded the catastrophic vision conjured up by the Native Americans in 1845. In relation to total U.S. population, 1854 remains the historical record year for immigration. Arrivals amounted to an increment of 1.6 percent, the equivalent of what would be produced today by an immigration of the order of 3.5 million people in a twelve-month period, three times the highest estimates – legal and undocumented – for the most recent years. Even leaving aside the Chinese who were beginning to land in larger numbers on the West Coast, most of the immigrants were alien in religion, language, or both; of the white total in 1854, less than one in seven was of 'founding stock'. Whatever their origins, the massive influx also had a significant impact on the American labour market. The decade of the 1850's was an inflationary one because of the California gold strikes and the vast influx of foreign capital; but whereas the cost of living went up by 12 percent, money wages rose by only 4 percent, so that real wages in fact declined (Morris 1976: 764). The squeeze affected more people as a larger proportion of the population – native Americans as well as immigrants – were now wage workers; and as the boom years were punctuated by slumps, more of them experienced unemployment as well. Compounding such fluctuations were disruptive changes associated with the revolution in American business. In particular, the railroad and telegraph altered the location of commercial and manufacturing centers, as well as fostering greater elasticity of the labour supply, founded on the physical mobility of workers within an enlarged spatial domain (Holt 1973: 325–8). Overall, the nexus of economic and social changes amounted to an American version of the Great Transformation.

The association between massive immigration, the rapidly increasing participation of foreigners in politics, and the disruptions which have just been delineated, contributed to 'the politics of impatience' which lay at the root of the spectacular rise of the 'Know Nothing' movement at this particular time rather than at some other (Holt 1973: 322, 325; Holt 1978; Knobel 1996: 88–115). In short, the revolt of the rank and file against the old parties was brought about by a broad 'uneasiness about the powerlessness of the people to control the meteoric social and economic changes transforming their environment and threatening their most cherished values' (Holt 1973: 322).

Ever since the early 1830s, the conflict over immigration had been kept within bounds by the operation of the American party system; now, however, that system was being severely tested by the growing sectional rift over slavery, and the conflict over immigration itself hastened its demise. The independent contribution of the immigration issue to the central political crisis of American politics has been recognised only recently.

By the time they entered into the electoral arena, the bulk of the Irish and German newcomers had developed a strongly Democratic partisan orientation. The growing 'impatience' of the Whig rank-and-file in the face of a business-minded, and therefore immigrationist, leadership, is understandable. The rift between them contributed to the emergence of the Know Nothings, a trans-sectional party, alongside a new Republican party in the North.

As of mid–1854, when ships were dumping unprecedented numbers in American ports of entry, it appeared likely 'that the Catholic or immigrant question might replace the slavery question as the focal issue in American political life' (Potter 1976: 250). The new party's rapid ascent was probably stimulated further by the business recession induced by summer drought, punctuated by a panic on the New York Stock Exchange in the fall even as the new arrivals crowded into the labour market. Over the next few months, Know Nothings scored 'astonishing successes' in various municipal, state, and congressional elections.

These developments provided the political setting within which Congress, in 1854, once again took up immigration policy by way of a reconsideration of passenger regulations. Senator Hamilton Fish of New York secured the appointment of a Select Committee, headed by himself, on Sickness and Mortality on Board of Emigrant Ships. A New York City Whig and former Governor, Fish had long been concerned with immigration, and was among those urging congressional action in 1844–45 against the dumping of paupers and convicts (Garis 1927: 44). The Committee reported on August 2, 1854. They advocated a law which left the details of passenger arrangements to be determined by shippers themselves, but which would induce them to safeguard passengers by making unsanitary ships unprofitable. To this effect, the Fish Committee proposed fining carriers for deaths incurred in the course of passage (Abbott 1924: 41). Given mortality rates amounting to as much as 20 percent on a bad voyage, this would have the effect of an incentive to reject as passengers all persons deemed ill or weak, surely a substantial proportion of those leaving Europe at this time.

New York merchants quickly arrayed themselves against the bill and sent a protest delegation to Washington. In the midst of all this, the Treasury began to seize ships under a surviving clause of the 1847 act providing for such seizures when excess passengers numbered over twenty. The reasons for this abrupt departure from hitherto lax enforcement practices cannot be ascertained. Given evidence of subsequent collaboration between the Treasury and the shippers in drafting new regulations, it may have been a ploy by the Pierce Administration to render the shippers more amenable to some departure from the permissive status quo, a change necessitated by the Know Nothings challenge in an election year. As emerged from subsequent congressional debates, Fish then agreed to provide for remission of penalties incurred by shippers under the existing law, in exchange for their consent to his proposal. Although the bill was referred to the Committee on Commerce for further action, consideration in the remaining months of 1854 was delayed owing to Fish's ill health. By the time the second session of the 33rd Congress opened in January, 1855, the financial panic and the nativist victories had intervened. But given the problem of state rights, if the open door policy were to be modified by congressional action, it must occur by way of passenger legislation.

It is at this point that the role of the business community in countering restrictionist efforts at the very height of the nativist furore emerges most visibly. On February 15, the Senate's Committee on Commerce reported out a passenger bill which differed significantly from the measure initiated by the still absent Fish. As modified, the bill no longer pertained to 'the better protection of life and health on board of passenger ships', but was instead a measure with the more limited aim of 'regulating the carriage of passengers in steamships and other vessels'. However, a bill tailored exclusively to the preferences of the shipping industry evidently had no chance of passage in a congress attuned to the nativist surge. The proposal drafted by the Treasury in collaboration with the New York merchants was sent back to committee, which reported out a measure incorporating aspects of both the Fish and Treasury proposals. The bill was speedily enacted by both houses in the remaining days of the session without further debate or division, and signed into law on March 3.

A consideration of the detailed provisions of the act suggests that it was, nevertheless, a victory for restriction, the most significant one to date at the national level. The most striking aspect of the law – and the least noted by historians of the subject – was its comprehensiveness as a regulatory instrument. Repealing all previous passenger legislation, the act covered all traffic under both sail and steam, in every conceivable type of vessel, plying the Pacific as well as the Atlantic; and it covered outbound ships operating on behalf of the African Colonization Society as well. Minimal requirements pertaining to passenger comfort were considerably raised. With respect to space, the act reinstated the 1847 system combining both volume and superficial feet, and specified as well minimum distances between decks.[7] This would of course reduce crowding, as humanitarians in Britain and in the U.S. advocated; but, as indicated previously, it would also have the effect of lowering the carrying capacity of ships and of raising fares, thereby reducing the incoming tide by selecting out the poorest immigrants. Despite the shippers' vehement objections, the law also provided for payment of $10 for every person above the age of eight who died of disease in the course of passage. The proceeds of this death tax were to be allocated to boards established by the various states for the care of immigrants. Nativist concerns surfaced explicitly in the form of a clause prohibiting the distribution of such funds 'to any board, or Commission, or Association, formed for the protection or advancement of any particular class of emigrants, or emigrants of any particular nation or creed'.

And yet doubt lingers with respect to the measure's true intent. Its effectiveness as an instrument for restricting immigration and protecting passengers depended on vigorous enforcement. Would this occur? The standard fine remained at $50 for each excess passenger, as established in 1847 and 1848; but the maximum discretionary prison term was reduced from one year to six months, and non-payment of the formidable 'death tax' was sanctioned by a fine only. Most important, the controversial 1847 clause, providing for outright seizure in case excess passengers numbered over twenty was repealed along with the act in which it was contained. Out of kilter with the comprehensive and severe passenger regulations, the sanction side of the law suggests the measure as a whole was designed as a palliative. The restrictionist triumph was hollow.

The outcome of this episode can be viewed as a stand-off. But the confrontation was hardly over and its outcome still uncertain since the full impact of the nativist surge would be felt only in the next Congress. However, in the nine-month interim between the end of the 33rd Congress and the beginning of the 34th in December 1855, the configuration of political and economic factors relevant to the determination of immigration policy continued to evolve rapidly, and there was also a very dramatic change of situation with respect to immigration itself.

The recession that began in the latter half of 1854 lingered on through the early months of the following year, after which the American economy again surged forward. It was stimulated by the unusually high European demand for U.S. products, induced by the Crimean War, which among other things kept Russian wheat from the market. But the bad conditions in the months preceding 1855 undoubtedly dissuaded many from embarking for the United States. The recently enacted state and federal legislation had a deterrent effect, as did the nativist surge. On the European side, the direct and indirect consequences of the Crimean War tended to reduce exit. Moreover, emigrants from the United Kingdom now had the additional alternative of going to Australia, where gold was discovered in 1851, while continentals were being wooed very actively by a number of Latin American countries. The tidal wave receded as abruptly as it had come. This turn of events probably affirmed the immigrationist posture of the shipping industry. Although such programmes hardly constituted policy, local and state governments, controlled by Know Nothings – perhaps one fourth of the states now had

'American' governors – or attempting to forestall the new party's further electoral progress by pre-emptive moves, initiated ever more vigorous efforts to reduce the entry of undesirables and also launched a war against the enemy within. In the absence of a federal measure to prohibit the entry of criminals, paupers, and 'defectives', Massachusetts, for example, armed itself with a law authorizing any Justice of the Peace, upon complaint, 'to cause any pauper to be removed to his place of last abode beyond the seas' (Abbott 1924: 160f.).

It is the more puzzling, in the light of this, that the heavily nativist 34th Congress, whose term ran from December 1855 to March 1857, contributed nothing further to the redirection of American immigration policy. How did such inaction come about? The major part of the explanation lies in the disarray of partisan politics: 'The Democrats...had lost control of the House, but the opposition could not be consolidated into a majority under the Know-Nothing, anti-Nebraska, or any other, label'. It took two months and 133 ballots to elect a Speaker, and even then by a plurality only (Potter 1976: 255).

In the emerging alliance between the two movements in the north, however, the Republicans were gaining the upper hand. By mid-1856, if nativism continued to flourish throughout the country, Know Nothing would be moribund as an organized force in the national legislative arena. Its last success was the long-awaited bill prohibiting the entry of foreign paupers and convicts. Authored by Rep. Fuller of Maine, the same who had steered the passenger law through the House the previous year, it was reported out by the Committee on Foreign Affairs on August 16, 1856 (34th Congress, 1st Sess., H. of R., Report No. 359, August 16, 1856). The 152–page document reprinted evidence of dumping from as early as 1832 and restated all the familiar themes.

On the issue of deportation, the report countered a communication from the government of Württemberg denying the right of the U.S. to return paupers once they had been admitted, with the assertion that this was founded on the right of self-defence under the laws of nations: 'the power exists somewhere either in the states, or in the general government, or in both of them'. (Report No. 359: 23). But where, exactly, remained problematic. Granting differences of opinion as to the power of Congress, the report emphasized that each level of government must act in its own sphere. In the Committee's view, Congress 'can and ought to exert its authority to prevent the further introduction of those who exercise such influence upon society [...] but beyond this it can accomplish but little'. Advocating the passage of a law to this effect, the Committee then went on to recommend more vigorous action by the states, which were saddled with the main burden, but which 'with a few exceptions [...] have been as remiss as congress in the discharge of their duties on the subject' (Report No. 359: 26).

In their view, deportation of undesirables was a proper exercise of state police powers, as stated in Miln, and in more recent cases involving runaway slaves. Beyond this, reflecting much of what was already going on at the state and local level, the committee's recommendations adumbrated a comprehensive program of political management for a country which had been transformed beyond recognition into a nation of immigrant urban wage-workers as well as of mostly native "mechanics" and farmers: the states must equip themselves to maintain law and order under the new circumstances, and conduct a vigorous policy of enforced Americanisation.

Referred to the Committee on the Judiciary, the recommendation for prohibiting the landing of foreign criminals, paupers, and 'defectives' was subsequently reported out as a bill. But this did not proceed beyond the Committee of the Whole on the State of the Union; revived in the next session, the attempt failed in 1857 as well. In the absence of direct evidence, it is reasonable to surmise that in 1856–57, as in 1854–55, the gate was kept open by a combination of strange bedfellows: business-minded immigrationist northerners, be they still Whigs or already Republicans; and southerners, be they Democrats or South Americans, for whom the paramount issue was to forestall any federal encroachment in the sphere of state rights.

The organisational collapse of Know Nothing and the defeat of its legislative programme at the national level should not be taken as an indicator of the demise of nativism. Republican efforts to co-opt Know-Nothing voters were vastly facilitated as the decade wore on, by the ebbing of the immigration wave. Channelled into the Republican party, the nativist sensibility, founded on a defence of the traditional cultural order, was offset within its fold by the commitment of the party leadership to the vigorous development of American capitalism (Knobel 1996: 155–234).

## Notes

1. For a vigorous contemporaneous defence of this perspective, by a lawyer long associated with the American Jewish Committee, see Kohler 1936. This compendium includes articles published as far back as the early 1900s.

2. For an elaboration of this theoretical perspective see Zolberg and Long 1999.
3. See, for example, the article by A. H. Everett reprinted in Abbott (1926): 440–7.
4. The above figures are total recorded arrivals, minus Asians. Arrivals from Asia were recorded throughout the period, but obviously inaccurately. They hovered between 2 and 11 from 1841 to 1852, and reached 47 in 1852. The first count we can take seriously is 1854, with 13,100.
5. The decline pertained entirely to arrivals from continental Europe, whose totals for the three successive years were 72,894, 99,937, and 69,455. Under the circumstances, however, it is impossible to distinguish the deterrent effects of American laws from those of revolution in France and Germany, which probably fostered a desire to emigrate but also temporarily disrupted shipping. In those same years, arrivals from the United Kingdom rose from 73,932 to 128,838 and then 148,095; although there was an increase in 1848, it occurred at a much lower rate.
6. The superficial requirement remained at 14 feet in the uppermost deck; beyond this, the requirement was raised to 16 feet should the distance between decks be between 5 and 6 feet, and to 22 should it be less than 5 (as against 30 for the unventilated 'orlop' in two-deck ships).
7. Although the minimum volume was now only two tons per passenger (as against 2.5 from 1819 to 1848), the law imposed the new requirement of a minimum distance of six feet between decks, and increased the allotment of superficial feet aboard three-deckers from 14 (as it was since 1848) to 16. They were also detailed provisions concerning ventilation, food, and water.

## References

Abbott, Edith, 1924, *Immigration: Selected Documents and Case Records*, Chicago.

Abbott, Edith, 1926, *Historical Aspects of the Immigration Problems*, Chicago.

Anbinder, Tyler, 1992. *Nativism and Slavery: The Northern Know-Nothings and the Politics of the 1850s*. New York.

Bridges, Amy B., 1984, *A City in the Republic: Antebellum New York and the Origins of Machine Politics*, Cambridge.

Chandler, Alfred D., 1977, *The Visible Hand. The Managerial Revolution in American Business* Cambridge, Mass.

Erickson, Charlotte (ed.), 1976, *Emigration from Europe 1815–1914. Select Documents*. London.

Garis, Roy, 1927, *Immigration Restriction: A Study of the Opposition to and Regulation of Immigrants Into the United States*, New York.

Hames, Charles, and Foster Sherwood, 1957, *The Role of the Supreme Court in American Government and Politics, 1835–1864*, Berkeley.

Hansen, Marcus Lee, 1961 [orig. published 1940], *The Atlantic Migration, 1607–1850*, New York.

Higham, John, 1994, *Strangers in the Land. Second Edition, Revised*, New Brunswick.

Holt, Michael F., 1973, 'The Politics of Impatience: The Origins of Know-Nothingism', *Journal of American History*, 60.

Holt, Michael F., 1978, *The Political Crisis of the 1850's*, New York.

Howe, Daniel Walker, 1979, *The Political Culture of the American Whigs*, Chicago.

Jones, Maldwyn, 1973, 'The Background to Emigration from Great Britain in the Nineteenth Century', *Perspectives in American History*, 7.

Klebaner, Benjamin J., 1958, 'State and Local Immigration Regulation in the United States Before 1882', *International Review of Social History* 3: 269–359.

Knobel, Dale T., 1996. *America for the Americans: The Nativist Movement in the United States*. New York.

Kohler, Max J., 1936, *Immigration and Aliens in the United States: Studies of American Immigration Laws and the Legal Status of Aliens in the United States*, New York.

Minot, George (ed.), 1862, *Statutes at Large and Treaties of the United States of America*, vol. 9, Boston.

Morris, Richard B. (ed.), 1976, *Encyclopedia of American History*, New York.

Neuman, Gerald L., 1996, *Strangers to the Constitution: Immigrants, Borders, and Fundamental Law*, Princeton.

Potter, David, 1976, *The Impending Crisis, 1848–1861*, New York 1976.

Thomas, Brinley, 1973, *Migration and Economic Growth. A Study of Great Britain and the Atlantic Economy*, Cambridge.

Tuerk, Edward F., 1951, 'The Supreme Court and Public Policy: The Regulation of Immigration, 1820–82', MA Thesis, Department of Political Science, University of Chicago.

Warren, Charles, 1922, *The Supreme Court in United States History*, vol. 1, Boston.

Zahler, Helene S., 1941, *Eastern Workingmen and National Land Policy, 1829–1862*, New York.

Zolberg, Aristide R., 1999, 'Matters of State: Theorizing Immigration Policy", in *The Handbook of International Migration: The American Experience*, eds Charles Hirschman, Philip Kasinitz, Josh De Wind, New York pp. 71–93.

Zolberg, Aristide R, and Litt Woon Long, 1999, 'Why Islam is Like Spanish: Cultural Incorporation in Europe and the United States', *Politics and Society*, Spring.

# Chapter 14

# Hamburg and the Transit of East European Emigrants

*Katja Wüstenbecker*

In the 1890s, the senate of the city of Hamburg changed its migration policy from a liberal policy to a restrictive one within three years. There were several reasons for this development. The growing influx of emigrants made it necessary for an important port like Hamburg to control and organise emigration more effectively. Whereas most city officials preferred to keep emigrants out of the city as much as possible in order to lessen the risk of diseases and disorder, economic interests also had to be taken into consideration: boarding-houses, restaurants, shops and, of course, the shipping companies, were all eager to get their share of the emigration business. The city, therefore, had to find a way to reconcile these economic interests with its need for security. The solution that was eventually found had a major impact on the future transit of East European emigrants. In order to understand what happened in the summer of 1892 and why city and state officials reacted so strongly, we need to consider the developments that led to these events.

## Hamburg's Society for the Protection of Emigrants and its Information Centre

Up to the 1850s, the German states had only few laws concerning the safety of emigrants. It was due to private initiative that the Society for the Protection of Emigrants was founded in Hamburg in 1851. Although it did not have any official authority and suffered from the lack of financial means, it was soon very successful in its efforts.[1] The main task of the society's members[2] was to restrict the work of so-called 'runners': locals employed by innkeepers, whose job it was to wait for the arrival of emigrants at the railway station and to direct them to over-priced lodgings. The society, therefore, set up an information centre which provided prospective emigrants with information on the usual prices of lodging, food, travel essentials, exchange rates and travel routes, free of charge. The centre's employees also distributed material on the emigrants' destinations and the addresses of the German Aid Societies and consulates in the United States. Moreover, the information centre succeeded in inducing local innkeepers to accept contracts, which committed them to charge fixed prices and not to overcrowd their rooms. The innkeepers were in turn assured of being placed on the centre's list of recommendable accomodation. As it was generally known that the information centre was impartial, most of the emigrants stopped there for advice. Because of the huge number of callers, a second centre was opened in the railway station a year later.[3] In 1854, the society even succeeded in banning all persons, except the station officials and the employees of the information centre, from the railway station upon arrival of an emigrants' train. The 'runners' were thus completely kept at bay.[4]

The senate of Hamburg reacted to the growing influx of emigrants by founding the Committee on Emigration in 1855. This committee, whose members were also in the senate or in the chamber of commerce, cooperated with the police to control the enforcement of existing laws.[5] The information centres were now controlled by this new committee, which had the advantage that donations from private citizens were no longer required to finance such services.[6] The information centres' employees were now authorised to mediate in disputes between emigrants and innkeepers. Furthermore, the information centres were respon-sible for making unannounced monthly checks on inns to ensure that the innkeepers fulfilled their obligations. Those found in breach of contract were no longer recommended by the centres. As soon as emigrants arrived at the railway station, they were given a leaflet stating the following information in several languages: 'Emigrants can get protection and advice free of charge at the information centres of Hamburg's Committee on Emigration'. The centres' employees recommended inns, tried to solve problems, looked for lost baggage, took ill emigrants to hospitals, and gave further information on all parts of the journey. The establishment of these information centres added to Hamburg's already good reputation as emigration port.

At the end of the nineteenth century, the German ports of Hamburg and Bremen had overtaken all other European competitors. The North German Lloyd Line soon became the leading shipping company in Bremen. Its main competitor in Hamburg was the Hamburg-Amerika-Packetfahrt-Actien-Gesellschaft (Hapag), also known as the Hamburg-America-Line from 1891.[7] The emigrants had more alternatives, owing to the development of railways and shipping companies, and this created fierce competition between companies. In order to defuse economic conflict the North Atlantic Steamship Association was established in 1892 by Hapag, Lloyd, the Holland-America-Line and the Belgian Red Star Line. English companies joined the Association later on.

## Transit to the German ports

When a strong emigration movement from eastern and south-eastern European countries started in the 1880s, the emigrants could embark for North America from one of six major ports: Hamburg, Bremen, Liverpool, Antwerp, Rotterdam, and Le Havre. Of course, the two German shipping companies Hapag and Lloyd were interested in gaining new customers. They built up a far-reaching network of agents in Eastern Europe in order to guide this new mass emigration into 'their' ports. This effort was supported by the good reputation that the two Hanseatic cities had gained in caring for emigrants. Liverpool was the least expensive port, but the East European emigrants could expect better legal protection in the German ports. Few emigrants used the Russian port Libau, although this route was subsidised by the state. There were only a limited number of ships going to America and Libau could not be used in winter. Hapag had the advantages of having good railway connections to the eastern borders and an active network of agents.

## The flight of Russian Jews in 1891

When Russia tightened the so-called 'May laws', pogroms occurred, which caused a mass emigration of Jews. The German aid committees along the borders helped the emigrants with problems of language and passports, gave information on possible routes, and often even paid for the stay of impoverished refugees. In July 1891, the city of Hamburg dispatched an

official to the Russian border to prompt the establishment of
more aid committees. He was also to ensure that not too many
poor Jews emigrated.[8] The German Central Committee for
Russian Jews (founded in 1881) was joined by other aid societies, which took care exclusively of Russian-Jewish emigrants.
These aid societies were situated at the border stations, along
the transit route, and in the ports.[9] The senate of Hamburg sent
a letter to the Imperial Chancellor in August 1891, requesting
'that those impoverished Jews who do not have the prospect of
support by the Jewish Committee are to be kept back at the
borders'.[10] Hamburg wanted to prevent too many poor Jews
from being stranded in the city and subsequently becoming
public charges. The Imperial Foreign Ministry did not react to
Hamburg's request until January 1892, when it decided to let
only those impoverished emigrants pass who could produce
guarantees that an aid society would assist them. The official
Prussian explanation for this was that it was trying to prevent
diseases from entering the country. Christian emigrants from
Russia, however, were not stopped at the borders. Senator
Hachmann, chairman of Hamburg's police department, called
this procedure absurd and instead supported the health committee's proposals[11] to conduct medical examinations at certain
locations along the Prussian-Russian border. Destitute emigrants
who were healthy should be allowed to pass if the German
Central Committee for Russian Jews accepted liability for their
expenses.[12] This proposal was finally accepted in May 1892.

As the number of East European emigrants arriving in
Hamburg had reached such proportions that it was no longer
possible to lodge all of them in inns and hotels, the city had
given Hapag a strip of land close to the so-called America quay
under the condition that the company built hostels for the
emigrants there. The city officials saw an additional advantage
in building accomodations outside the centre of town, because
it would restrict the spread of diseases. The emigration hostels
were opened on 20 July 1892. Emigrants' trains now travelled
directly to the America quay instead of stopping in the city.
When, shortly after the opening of the hostels, cholera broke
out in the city, the authorities immediately ordered the
emigrants to be put into quarantine.[13] Emigrants from Russia
and Galicia were kept under strict surveillance for six days, but
first and second class passengers did not have to undergo this
procedure.[14] During the medical examinations at the hostels
doctors not only looked for signs of cholera infection but also

for smallpox or inflammation of the eyes,[15] which were also reasons for the rejection of immigrants by the United States.

## Cholera in Hamburg

With the outbreak of cholera in Hamburg in the middle of August 1892, the situation for East European emigrants changed dramatically. The epidemic had already been noted in July in various regions of Russia and the population of Hamburg had, therefore, concluded that Russian emigrants had brought the disease into the city. Robert Koch, the physician who had discovered the cholera pathogen in the 1880s, came to survey the situation in Hamburg and also attributed the epidemic to the Russian emigrants.[16] Theodor Deneke, who as a young doctor had participated in fighting the cholera in Hamburg, contradicted this assumption in an essay which he wrote fifty years later:

> The distance between Odessa/Moscow and Hamburg is 1,700 km/1,800 km, respectively. I do not know of any example in the history of the cholera where the germ of this disease has travelled through strongly populated areas without causing an infection.

Deneke assumed that the cholera germ had been brought to Hamburg by a sailor from the French port of Le Havre, where the epidemic had also been noted in July. Another possibility that he considered was that a ship coming from Le Havre had dumped its sewage into the harbour. The germ would then have reached all households, since there was no sufficient water treatment at the time. This was, however, not a point discussed by contemporaries, most of whom held Russian emigrants responsible for the outbreak of cholera. The city was severely hit by the disease. When the epidemic finally subsided in November, it had claimed more than 8,000 lives.[17]

On 26 August, the Hamburg Senate applied for the closure of the eastern borders of Germany for Russian emigrants. The Prussian government willingly complied with Hamburg's request and issued a decree on 29 August, which was sent to the Senate by telegraph:

> the passage onto prussian territory is prohibited for those russian emigrants who are en route to america and who either do not own a ticket at all or only a third-class ticket. this is a telegraphic order from the prussian departmental minister on the 26th of the month. prussia counts on hamburg to transport those emigrants who are on their way to the port.
>
> the chancellor = p. p. nieberding[18]

It was in Hamburg's interest to get rid of the emigrants, who had arrived from Russia, as soon as possible. For this reason, many people were already on board ships when the disease broke out. The port of New York refused to allow the infected people to land and ordered them to remain on board for twenty days of quarantine. The Hamburg shipping companies were ordered not to carry any more Russian third-class passengers.[19] The North German Lloyd decided to follow this instruction as well.

## Hapag's and Lloyd's struggle for the re-opening of the eastern borders

It has already been mentioned that the borders with Russia and with Austrian Galicia were virtually closed when the cholera broke out in Hamburg. A complete closure of the frontier proved to be impossible. In fact, there was a noticeable increase in illegal crossings with the help of bribed Russian officials or forged passports. Employees of the German shipping companies were also involved in these transactions, as the companies suffered great financial losses from the closing of the borders. This was especially felt when German emigration declined around 1893 and East European emigrants, who could have filled the gap, were kept back at the frontiers. When it became evident that East European emigrants were arriving in Hamburg despite the border closure, the Senate decided 'to prevent the arrival of Russian emigrants in Hamburg by police force' from June 1893.[20] Hapag and Lloyd calculated their financial loss for the year 1892 at eight to nine million marks, and an additional two million marks were lost by the Prussian railway companies.[21] Hapag and Lloyd decided to cooperate in order to solve this problem. On 24 July 1893 they sent a petition to the Prussian Minister of the Interior, Count Eulenburg, and proposed the establishment of control stations at the borders, in which all emigrants would have to pass medical examinations and their baggage would be disinfected. Healthy emigrants would then be allowed to board special trains, which would take them directly to the German ports. The government in Berlin, however, based its consent on certain conditions. The shipping companies were to finance the erection and operation of these control stations. They were responsible for board, accomodation and medical care of the emigrants in these stations. Furthermore, they had to guarantee that all newcomers were in possession of a valid passport and had enough money for immigration into the United States.[22] Neither the German nor the American governments wished to have to care for impoverished persons. Those who did not have sufficient financial resources had to show a statement from one of the aid societies proving that they would receive assistance. The stations were to be built on the model of the one at Ruhleben, which had already been established in November 1892. This institution near Berlin had been set up, first, to ease the traffic at the railway stations in Berlin, and, second, to allow the medical examination of those emigrants who had been able to cross the borders despite the closures.

Hapag was in a worse situation than Lloyd as a result of Hamburg's closing its land and sea border with Prussia. Many of those East European emigrants who had been able to cross the Prussian borders chose the route via Bremen in order to avoid further complications at Hamburg. The blockade was only lifted by the Hamburg Senate after Hapag had threatened to move its business to Nordenham, close to Bremerhaven, in November 1893. The prospect of losing jobs and taxes caused a change of mind – the senators yielded.[23]

Representatives of the two German shipping companies met with Prussian ministers in Berlin on 4 May 1894. It took several additional petitions and meetings until the government in Berlin finally decided to accept the proposal of the shipping companies. They reached an agreement to set up five control stations along the Prussian-Russian border.[24] It was not until September, however, that the Minister of the Interior gave permission to start building the stations at Bajohren, Eydtkuhnen, Prostken, Illowo and Ottlotschin.[25] With this decree the two German shipping companies were given the monopoly of running the control stations: 'As the erection and operation of the control stations are exclusively financed by the two shipping companies, only those emigrants are allowed into the stations who intend to travel with the ships of these companies'. This effectively led to the exclusion of all competitors. Before the control stations were set up, about 41 percent of Russian emigrants chose the route via England to America; now, only 4 percent were considering this. The foreign companies' protests went unheard for a long time. The regulation was only modified in 1897 when those shipping companies who were partners of Hapag and Lloyd in the North Atlantic Steamship Association were included. The new control stations were completed in January 1895 and inspected and approved by Prussian officials.[26] The stations were run by the German shipping companies, but officially administered by the Prussian government.

## The control stations on the eastern borders

All control stations – the five already mentioned and four that were set up later at Tilsit, Insterburg, Ostrowo and Posen – were almost identical. Their measurements had been laid down in detail in the Prussian decree of 18 September 1894. They were located in those places where Prussian and Russian railway lines met. Every station consisted of four separate buildings: (1) the main building which was supposed to be 30 meters in length, 15 meters in width, and 4.5 meters in heigth; (2) a medical building for those who were feared to be ill; (3) a ward, and (4) toilets. Arriving emigrants were taken to the main building where they had to sit down in a waiting room while their papers and tickets were checked. Those who did not yet have a ticket had to buy one. Afterwards, they had to hand over their baggage. Next, emigrants were separated according to sex, had to undress, and take a shower in an adjoining bathroom. In the meantime, their baggage and clothes were disinfected. After a medical examination, the passengers were allowed to dress and to proceed to the so-called 'clean area' for the departure of their train. Those who appeared to be ill, however, had to stay under surveillance for five days in another building. Sick persons were either taken to the medical ward for treatment or were sent back immediately. Until 1907, taking a shower was compulsory for all passengers, afterwards only for those persons who were dirty or who seemed to be ill.[27] Cleaning and disinfecting cost two marks for passengers with tickets to America and four marks for those who held tickets to England. Family members were often separated because of the procedures in the main building. Healthy passengers were not allowed to remain in the control station and wait for those family members who had been selected for further medical examinations in the ward. They could only hope to find each other again at the port. The emigrants were then put in special trains and taken to Ruhleben.

All trains from the east stopped at Ruhleben. At this station, all procedures of the control stations were repeated in order to examine those emigrants who had passed the borders illegally. The treatment of the emigrants in the control stations as well as in Ruhleben was often rough, as large numbers of people were pushed through the rooms. Most emigrants experienced the situation as threatening, because nobody knew what was going to happen next. Mary Antin, a thirteen-year-old Jewish girl from Lithuania, who emigrated with her mother and siblings to America in 1894, gave a strong impression of her experience in Ruhleben in her autobiography:

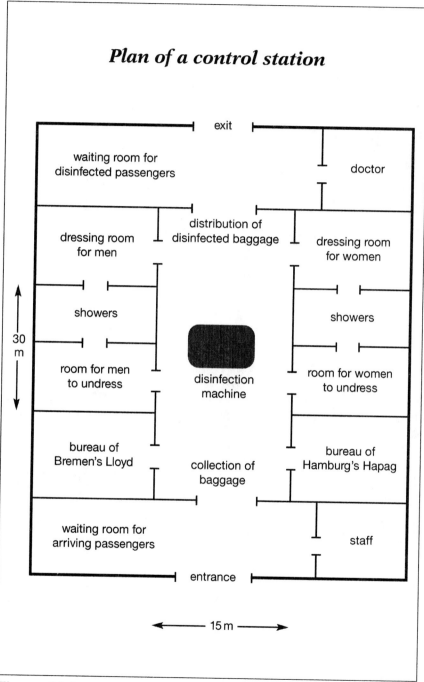

**Figure 14.1**

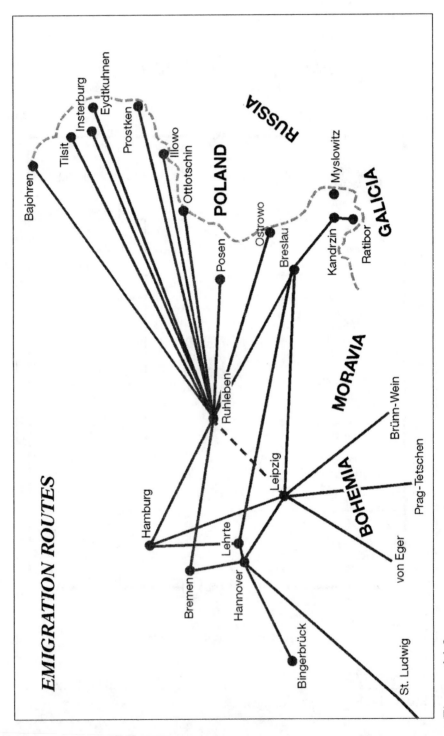

Figure 14.2

In a great lonely field, opposite a solitary house within a large yard, our train pulled up at last, and a conductor commanded the passengers to make haste and get out. He need not have told us to hurry; we were glad enough to be free again after such a long imprisonment in the uncomfortable car. All rushed to the door. ... . He hurried us into the one large room which made up the house, and then into the yard. Here a great many men and women, dressed in white, received us, ... baggage being thrown together in one corner of the yard, heedless of contents, which suffered in consequence; ... ourselves driven into a little room where a great kettle was boiling on a little stove; our clothes taken off, our bodies rubbed with a slippery substance that might be any bad thing; a shower of warm water let down on us without warning; again driven to another little room where we sit, wrapped in woollen blankets till large, coarse bags are brought in, their contents turned out, ... . We are forced to pick out our clothes from among all the others, ... ; we choke, cough, entreat the women to give us time; they persist, 'Quick! Quick! Or you'll miss the train!' Oh, so we really won't be murdered! They are only making us ready for the continuing of our journey, cleaning us of all suspicions of dangerous sickness. Thank God! (Antin 1912: 174f.)

The transit became even longer and more strenuous owing to these stops and examinations. Many emigrants had left home hastily. They arrived at the control stations in a state of physical or mental exhaustion and still had to pass various examinations. Afterwards, they were pushed into special trains and had to travel for about twenty-four hours until they reached Ruhleben, where they had to undergo the same procedures again. Finally, it took them another day in the train to get to their port of embarkation. There they were again isolated and examined. Only third class passengers had to endure all these strains: cabin passengers were exempt from the examinations. A journalist of the social-democratic newspaper *Vorwärts* pretended to be an East European emigrant in order to collect information on the unfair treatment of passengers. He soon realised that money protected from all these controls. He also criticised in his articles the fact that only those emigrants who wanted to travel to America with German ships were allowed to pass the stations. Some emigrants who owned tickets from other companies were even told that their tickets were not valid and that they had to buy new ones from the German shipping companies. He described the case of a young Russian who had intended to travel through Germany in order to visit a friend in Paris. This young man was stopped at the control station Prostken, because he did not have a railway ticket to one of the German ports. Since he had neither the money needed for immigration into the United States, nor was he able to buy a ticket to America, he was sent back to Russia despite his protests.[28]

## Conclusion

For most emigrants the shortest way to a port of embarkation was via the German Empire. The transit was regulated by the state in order to make sure that none of the emigrants remained in the country illegally or had to be supported financially. The major event that changed the course of East European emigration was the outbreak of cholera in Hamburg in 1892. The authorities of the port cities and Prussia, as well as the officials of the railways and shipping companies, were involved in the decision-making process after this event.

The shipping companies had been very successful in establishing an extensive network of agents even before the increase in emigration from Eastern Europe. These agents had to persuade prospective emigrants of the good accessibility of the German ports and the strict laws for the protection of emigrants. The shipping companies, on the other hand, had such a strong economic importance for the Hanseatic cities that they could exert their influence on the decisions made by the authorities. Requests, petitions, discussions, and threats, were all means used by the two major German shipping companies in dealing with officials of the port cities and Prussia. When Hamburg closed the borders with Prussia because of cholera, a large effort from Hapag was required to force them open again. The compromise with Prussia, which led to the establishment of the control stations, put the German shipping companies in a position of hitherto unknown power. After the control stations were set up, the whole transit of emigrants lay in their hands. What is more, the state even supported their monopoly against foreign companies.

Hamburg is a good example of the nexus of state and economic interests. The public need for control and safety and the shipping companies' demand for profit found its outlet in the control stations along the eastern borders. Within three years, state and company officials had found a better way to manage the huge amount of incoming emigrants, and to extend their share of the emigration business at the same time. Hamburg (and of course, Prussia) took all precautions to prevent East European emigrants from staying in the country once they had successfully crossed the border. Only those persons were allowed to pass the control stations who seemed to be healthy, well-equipped and not likely to become public charges.

## Notes and references

All translations into English are by the author.

1. 'First Report of Hamburg's Society for the Protection of Emigrants', 25 February 1852, State Archive Hamburg (StAH), Auswanderungsamt I, I E I 2, vol. 1.
2. Humanitarian motives must have played a role in founding this society, as many members did not profit from the emigration business. For a survey on the professions represented in the society see B. Gelberg, *Auswanderung nach Übersee. Soziale Probleme der Auswandererbeförderung in Hamburg und Bremen. Von der Mitte des 19. Jahrhunderts bis zum Ersten Weltkrieg*, Hamburg, 1973, 13f.
3. 'First Report of Hamburg's Society for the Protection of Emigrants', 25 February 1852, StAH, Auswanderungsamt I, I E I 2, vol. 1.
4. 'Fourth Report of Hamburg's Society for the Protection of Emigrants', 7 February 1855, StAH, Auswanderungsamt I, I E I 2, vol. 1.
5. 'Order concerning the appointment of a Committee on Emigration', 25 April 1855, StAH, Auswanderungsamt I, II A I 1.
6. The Society for the Protection of Emigrants disbanded in 1855 when it found its purpose fulfilled by the state. E. Baasch, 'Gesetzgebung und Einrichtungen im Interesse des Auswanderungswesens in Hamburg', in *Auswanderung und Auswanderungspolitik in Deutschland. Berichte über die Entwicklung und die gegenwärtigen Zustände des Auswanderungswesens in den Einzelstaaten und im Reich*, ed. Eugen von Philippovich, Leipzig 1892, 412.
7. The company kept its original name, but used the new 'catchy' name for its general transactions. See M. Just, *Ost- und südosteuropäische Amerikaauswanderung 1881–1914*, Stuttgart 1988, 71–73. K. Schulz, 'Von Anatevka nach Amerika – Stationen einer Reise', in *Hoffnung Amerika. Europäische Auswanderung in die Neue Welt*, ed. K. Schulz, Bremerhaven 1994, 122.
8. 'Report of Senator Hachmann to the Senate', 31 July 1891, StAH, Auswanderungsamt I, II E I 1 a 1.
9. There were branches of the Committee for Russian Jews in seventy-four cities of Prussia, Baveria, Württemberg, Saxony, Baden, Hesse, Brunswick, Saxony-Coburg-Gotha, Alsace-Lorraine, Hamburg, Bremen and Lübeck. See 'Executive Committee of the German Central Committee for Russian Jews', March 1892, StAH, Auswanderungsamt I, II E III P 24.
10. 'Letter to the Imperial Chancellor', 7 August 1891, StAH, Auswanderungsamt I, II E I 1 a 1. J. Sielemann, '"Haben Alle Passagiere Auch Geld?" Zur Geschichte der Auswanderung über den Hamburger Hafen 1892–1954', in *Hoffnung Amerika. Europäische Auswanderung in die Neue Welt*, ed. K. Schulz, Bremerhaven 1994, 84.
11. 'Statement of the Health Committee', 21 March 1892, StAH, Auswanderungsamt I, II E I 1 a 1.
12. 'Letter of Senator Hachmann to the Chief of Police in Berlin', 30 March 1892, StAH, Auswanderungsamt I, II E I 1 a 1.
13. 'Order of Senator Hachmann, Charmain of the Police Department in Hamburg', 22 August 1892, StAH, Auswanderungsamt I, II E I 1 a 2, vol. 1.
14. See 'Announcement of the Police Department', 11 July 1892, StAH, Auswanderungsamt I, II E III 10.

15. The contagious eye disease 'trachoma', which was widely spread in East Europe, was especially feared because it could lead to loss of sight.

16. Th. Deneke, 'Die Hamburger Choleraepidemie 1892', *Zeitschrift des Vereins für Hamburgische Geschichte* 40 (1949): 137. The thesis that Russian emigrants brought the cholera to Hamburg is still advocated by R. J. Evans, *Death in Hamburg*, New York 1987. Deneke, 'Choleraepidemie', 138.

17. Hamburg had a population of about 500,000. 16,596 persons became ill, of whom 8,605 died. Deneke, 'Choleraepidemie', 145.

18. 'Telegraph of Mr. Nieberding on the instructions of the Imperial Chancellor to Senator Hachmann, Chairman of the Police Department in Hamburg', 29 August 1892, StAH, Auswanderungsamt I, II E I 1 a 2, vol. 1.

19. 'Order of the Committee on Emigration to the shipping companies in Hamburg', 3 September 1892, StAH, Auswanderungsamt I, II E I 1 a 3.

20. 'The Fight against the Cholera (1886–1893)', StAH, Auswanderungsamt I, II E IV 1, vol. 1, p. 151.

21. 'Petition of Hapag and Lloyd to the Secretary of the Interior, Count Eulenburg', 24 July 1893, StAH, Auswanderungsamt I, II E IV 1, vol.2, p. 4.

22. The obligation for Russian emigrants to have a passport was repealed in 1895 to make sure that they no longer avoided the control stations because of fear of complications.

23. 'Letter of the Police Department to the shipping companies and agents', 22 December 1893, StAH, Auswanderungsamt I, II E I 1a 6.

24. 'Letter of Ballin to Senator Hachmann', 30 May 1894, StAH, Auswanderungsamt I, II E I 1a 7.

25. Ibid., 'Decree of the Secretary of the Interior for the erection of control stations', 18 September 1894.

26. 'Annual Report of the Administration for the year 1894: Report of the Committee and the Information Centre for Emigrants in Hamburg', StAH, Auswanderungsamt I, I E I 2, vol. 2, p. 2.

27. 'Order of the Department of the Interior', 19 April 1907, StAH, Auswanderungsamt I, II E I 1. M. Antin, *The Promised Land. The Autobiography of a Russian Immigrant*, Boston 1912, 174f. See Schulz, 'Amerika', p. 125.

28. Articles in the *Vorwärts*, 3 and 30 August 1904, StAH, Auswanderungsamt I, II E I 1. There was also criticism in other newspapers. See the article cited in Schulz, 'Jüdische Auswanderung', 472f.: 'Only those are allowed to go on, who have been declared free of diseases at the control stations. But the examinations follow strange methods otherwise unknown to physicians: Those who have a German ticket to America are absolutely immune, those who have money are bathed and disinfected until they buy a ticket, and those who do not have enough money or for some reason only want to buy a ticket to England are suspected of having cholera and turned back to Russia'.

# Chapter 15

# Labour Unions and the Nationalisation of Immigration Restriction in the United States, 1880–1924

*Catherine Collomp*

If, according to Patrick Weil's definition, the nineteenth century was the golden age of immigration, a time when migratory movements remained unrestricted and did not constitute an object of government regulation, the United States was the country of immigration *par excellence*. The nation's population had classically been formed out of the resettlement of European immigrants and, from the Civil War to the First World War, the nation's economic development called for a massive and hardly regulated immigration to develop the West and man the mines and mills of the developing industrial nation.

The national regulation of immigration to the U.S. was enacted between 1882 and 1924 through successive immigration laws which were eventually consolidated and combined with the quota system. It is not a coincidence that this time span also corresponds to the emergence of a strong national labour movement and to its eventual recognition or acceptance as a legitimate, if not yet legal, representative institution in the nation.[1] Indeed the main labour organisations played a central role in the establishment of the United States's immigration policy. Not only did they rank among the most vocal and most constant institutions to demand the restriction of immigration and a selection of immigrants, but that demand in itself was constitutive for their growth and of the definition of their role in the nation. Beyond the unions' desire for a protectionist control of the labour market, the demand for immigration regulation can be seen as a logical outcome of the trade-unionist structure of the main U.S. labour organisations, as well as a cultural and political factor helping their own national integration.

The nationalisation of the restriction of immigration is not independent from the nationalisation of the labour movement, which reached national dimensions in its scope and agenda. But before addressing the history of that progression it is necessary to point out that the American nation was itself still in the making. At the end of the nineteenth century it had barely completed its continental expansion, and it was embarking on an imperialist crusade in the Western hemisphere that changed the meaning of nationalism. The country's shift from a predominantly agricultural to an industrial economy caused it to undergo fundamental changes for which it was ideologically unprepared. The growth of the urban population, its predominantly foreign origin[2], and the continuity and ethnic diversification of immigration, all led to a revision of the meaning of citizenship. The U.S. population more than doubled from 50 million in 1880 to 118 million in 1920, four decades during which 25 million immigrants reached the United States, most of whom became part of the American labour force. They were now of more diverse origins than ever before: approximately 100,000 Chinese workers lived on the Pacific Coast in 1880, while the millions of 'new' immigrants to the eastern and the midwestern industrial heartland were likely to be of Slavic, Jewish or Mediterranean extraction. Thus we are confronted with two processes rather than one. The labour movement was seeking its national recognition by a nation that was being simultaneously transformed through immigration and industrialisation. It is in this context that the regulation of immigration was adopted.

## Nationalisation of the labour movement

The many labour unions that existed before the last quarter of the nineteenth century had remained local or short-lived before they eventually reorganised and formed federations on a more stable basis in the 1880s. They had sprung up at the city level, from craftsmen's desire to control their trades and to reduce their working time, but political dissensions or economic downturns often destroyed their programmes and even institutions. At the end of the Civil War, for instance, some thirty trade unions had a national scope, outgrowing their members' local demands to establish common rules concerning apprenticeship, wages, and access to the trades they organised (Ulman 1955). In addition, the creation of a first federation, the National Labor Union (NLU), in 1866, had reinforced the national and central links in a widely scattered and heterogeneous labour force. Yet, the NLU, and most of the national unions affiliated to it, were destroyed by the economic depression of the 1870s that shattered business and labour organisations alike. In the 1880s, however, the rise of the American Federation of Labor, of the Order of the Knights of Labor and of the national unions affiliated to them heralded the emergence of what was to become the United States's national labour movement and its stabilisation for decades to come.

The Noble and Holy Order of the Knights of Labor was the first broad working class movement to emerge. Between 1878 and 1886, the movement had soared to a membership of 700,000, thus becoming by far the nation's, and even the world's, largest union movement. It sought to organise all workers regardless of skill, trade, nationality or creed. Addressing itself to all 'producers', artisans as well as factory operatives, men and women, natives and immigrants, white and black labourers, the Order had a mixed membership. Because of the presence of skilled workers in its ranks, its membership therefore partly overlapped that of the trade-union movement which was also re-forming itself. The aftermath of the Haymarket events in 1886, however, as well as political and organisational feuds with the trade unions, brought about its gradual demise.[3]

At the same time, the American Federation of Labor (AFL, founded in 1886), headed by Samuel Gompers, grew out of its antecedent, the Federation of Organized Trades and Labor Unions (FOTLU, 1881–86). It federated the main national trades unions which were reappearing in the 1880s and establishing themselves on the more stable and centralised basis of the English amalgamated 'new model unionism'. By the turn of the century, the AFL, which had absorbed most of the skilled workers' unions formerly affiliated to the Knights, dominated the whole U.S. labour movement. However, unionisation remained marginal to most workers' lives, it reached barely one tenth of the whole labour force and, with the exception of the United Mine Workers, which organised all workers 'in and around the mines', labour organisation was mostly a skilled workers' phenomenon. Whole sectors of industry, precisely those that recruited labourers among the 'new immigrants' coming from the eastern and mediterranean parts of Europe, were hardly affected by unionisation at all.

The nationalisation of labour unions, that is their growth and institutionalisation in a national, and even international (many of them included Canadian branches) dimension, provided a new scale of intervention: they were now able to establish national, rather than local, wage scales and work-time regulations. They came to define what was the American standard of wages, and by the same token also imposed a national vision of the American workers' life style. They also established centralised decision-making and bureaucratic structures that placed them in a position to create a broad movement and publicise their demands. Motions passed on the floor of national conventions took effect nationally, amplifying local demands. Conventions, as well as national trade-union journals, now created a space and a medium through which local news was circulated and national agendas were established. In addition to the many local or regional labour papers, from the 1880s most unions had journals with a national circulation that conveyed the news from east to west, north to south and contributed to nationalising events happening in one corner of the country.[4]

For instance, while the anti-Chinese agitation had remained a purely Californian movement in the 1870s, once the local Californian shoe or cigar workers' unions were integrated into national unions, and these unions became part of the large federations, their demand for a boycott of Chinese-made goods, and for the suspension of Chinese immigration, became a national issue addressed to the working class at large as well as to the Federal Government. In 1880, one Californian delegate wrote in one of the very first issues of the Knights of Labor's *Journal of United Labor*:

> We are warning our brothers of the East to protect themselves against the Chinese that are starting to appear in their localities. We enjoin you to use your sense of self preservation, the Chinese bring nothing but degradation and misery. We know the beast and the competition it creates.

The admonition was followed by a lengthy description of the 'Chinese evil', a venomous story that became standard in national trade-union literature throughout the 1880's, and beyond.[5]

The nationalising labour movement did not only break the isolation of local working class communities. It also linked the individual to a collective identity that overcame many ethnic and local sources of fragmentation. For the new immigrant workers, whose main level of social organisation was provided by the ethnic community, the labour movement offered a median structure of integration that introduced the individual worker to another set of collective identities. Labour unions did not exactly supersede ethnic institutions as forms of social organisation – often they were themselves merely local and ethnic institutions– but, in as much as unions and their federations enlarged their scope to national dimensions, they helped workers overcome the trade, skill, religious, ethnic, or local divisions that separated them to eventually create a common class identity. The United States at the end of the nineteenth century was still a composite world of atomised religious, social, and ethnic communities that had only loose contact between themselves, let alone with the Federal Government whose bureaucratic functions were very limited.[6] Unionisation was one of the rare institutions that helped supersede the bonds created by these communities to give the workers a sense of universal brotherhood: 'Workers, remain English, Irish, Hottentot, American, what you wish, you can be Free-Traders, Protectionists, Christians or Jews, but be trade-unionists and support the eight-hour day', claimed the German leaders of the Bakers' Union who were trying to organise the English and Irish workers in the trade.[7]

At another level, unionisation was also a form of proto-citizenship for immigrant workers, and a reassertion of American identity for the native and naturalized ones. The difficult position of organised labour in the world of economic liberalism, and its own mainstream political traditions, led it to articulate the American character of the movement. In addition, organising a working class of predominantly foreign origin, was also a task implying civic integration similar to naturalisation.

> 'The labor movement takes the workman from the moment he lands on our shores and starts to make him a good citizen', Gompers claimed in 1909, 'and it is so far the most valuable and efficient agent that we have for this purpose. In fact it is about the only agent to do that work'.[8]

Organising did not simply mean gathering workers as union members and getting them to act collectively: it also implied integrating them into the body politic of the American nation. In the union hall, the foreign-born worker could learn the value of representative government and the workings of democracy. Trade union government itself borrowed its functioning from representative democracy (Glocker 1913). And the federative structure of the AFL was made to resemble the structure of the Federal Government:

> 'There are today before the American working people two forms of republican labor organization', Gompers claimed. 'The one adopting the French system, a grand centralized body, made of all classes, from which emanate all laws for all classes; the other is founded on the principles of the American Federal Republic. To the latter class belong the American Federation of Labor and the Federation of Railway Employees, the component parts of which being sub-organizations'.[9]

Indeed, the structural comparison between the AFL and the Federal Government was not inappropriate, however bold and patriotic the simile sounded. Gompers, certainly, behaved as a working class statesman. He also intervened as little in the life of the unions affiliated to the Federation as the Federal Government intervened in the states' internal politics and agendas. Until 1906, the AFL made practically no demands on the Federal Government.[10] There is one exception to this general statement, however: on the subject of immigration restriction, and of the exclusion of certain categories of immigrants, the AFL, its FOTLU antecedent and the Knights of Labor alike, constantly asked Congress to legislate. For labour leaders, immigration was seen as creating both internal and external problems. The agenda was twofold: the implicit aspect of it meant organising all workers in the U.S., natives and immigrants, a task that was left to the unions themselves and in which the AFL, as a federation, did not really intervene. But on the question of immigration regulation the Federation never stopped seeking the Federal Government's intervention (Collomp 1998; Mink 1986). The two functions of integration and exclusion, however, were not independent from one another. It is my contention that they were correlated factors of the integration of the labour movement in the nation.

## Inclusion and exclusion: two related functions of mainstream labour unions

The cultural Americanisation of foreign-born workers was a policy consciously encouraged by the leadership of the main federations and unions. While tolerating the publication of many union journals in German, Czech, and Yiddish, they emphasised the use of English as the main language of union literature. For instance, while one third of its members in the 1890s were German immigrants, the AFL did not allow the use of the German language on convention floors.[11] Similarly, while recognising the expedience and necessity of organising foreign-born workers in language locals, they encouraged the integration of these ethnic levels of organisation into larger English-speaking unions. The system of delegation of power of the language locals to the English-speaking leadership among the United Mine Workers, for instance, favoured the integration of the most diverse labour force in the U.S. in a strong national movement. Linguistic homogenisation also conveyed an image of political unity by identifying

American language and trade-union philosophy with mainstream political beliefs. Gompers's famous statement that he 'would have been a nihilist in Russia, a socialist in Germany, but in the United States he was a trade-unionist' conveys that meaning.[12] By 1910, the AFL had become a mostly English-speaking body of two million workers who were partly acculturated to the American nation, at least integrated into representative organisations whose voice was mainly expressed at the level of existing structures of political mediation or discussion.

Yet the continuity of immigration and its massive increase and diversification in the 1900s, meant that the labour organisations could at no time reflect the current composition of the labour force. At the same time as they organised workers, the unions, in a defensive position, also excluded, or simply did not or could not admit, others beyond their trade-union structure. As a reaction, they sought to exclude from the nation those workers deemed most 'undesirable' by demanding the enactment of laws restricting immigration. Such a reaction may seem classic, and predictable in any country with heavy immigration. But organised labour's reaction to immigration is not systematic: in the United States a direct link can be established between trade-unionism, the dominant but selective form of organisation, and the movement for the restriction of immigration from the nation at large (Collomp 1999). The most exclusive craft unions of skilled workers were also the most active advocates of restriction. Their vision of a national immigration policy mirrored the exclusive principles by which they restricted admissions to the union. Ideological factors are, of course, equally important but they were often linked to structural ones. The advocates of the more open form of industrial unionism were generally socialists, and opposed to the restriction of immigration.[13]

Indeed the position of the Industrial Workers of the World (IWW), the anarcho-syndicalist movement founded in 1905 was, in that respect as in all others, in direct opposition to the AFL. As a movement whose goal was to organise all industrial workers regardless of skill, race or ethnicity, the IWW had a broadly proletarian internationalist vision which stood in complete contrast to the trade-unions' exclusive membership as well as to their integration into mainstream politics. According to the IWW's political philosophy, unskilled immigrant workers, the most numerous and replaceable labour force of modern industry, constituted the vanguard of labour's struggle against capitalism. Thus the IWW never partook of the AFL's restrictionist venture. On the contrary, they sought to organise those workers whom AFL unions would not integrate; they were also very contemptuous of the AFL's political manoeuvring. The violent repression caused by their resonant critique of capitalism, and, eventually their opposition to U.S. entry into the First World War, made the Wobblies (as the IWW were called) physical and legal outcasts of the American nation.[14] In this brief survey, however, I will outline the main steps and significance of those organisations of labour that successfully campaigned for immigration legislation while pleading for their own legitimacy.

## Chinese exclusion

The anti-Chinese movement in California in the 1870's, and its subsequent national repercussions, is surprising to our modern sensitivities by its display of explicitly racial arguments. But racism had a function for the labour movement: (a) it helped define the common ground of an otherwise heterogeneous labour force; (b) it reinforced the otherwise evasive line that separated skilled from unskilled workers, craftsmen from factory operatives. Thus it was part and parcel of the definition of the trade and trade union jurisdiction. In California, the workers of German, Irish, English or American origin who had moved in from the East found a common denominator in their being Christian and of 'Caucasian origin'. Their anti-Chinese agitation provided the cultural vector of their unity. The Chinese immigrants thus were collectively described as 'pagans', 'dirty rat or rice eaters', stealing the welfare of American citizens and destroying the American wage standards by the low levels of pay they accepted (Sandmeyer 1973; Saxton 1971; Collomp 1998: 109–44, 263–311).White workers' unions literally adopted anti-Chinese restrictive clauses even when some of them, such as the building trades unions, had little to fear from Chinese competition. Those unions representing industries where the Chinese constituted a numerous labour force in San Francisco in the 1870s and 1880s (cigar- and shoe-making) adopted a narrow definition of the trade to exclude the Chinese workers who worked in mechanised manufactures. The introduction of the 'white label', and boycott of Chinese-made goods were launched by the Cigar Makers and the Shoe Workers' unions to protect the white craftsmen's trades against the invasion of mechanised industries manned by Chinese workers. This is why they monitored the national trade unions and the federations (Knights of Labor and FOTLU/AFL) to promote national legislation for the interruption of Chinese immigration. Both the Knights of Labor in 1880 and the FOTLU in 1881 formulated anti-Chinese clauses in their platforms. The 1882 law that suspended Chinese immigration for ten years was passed at the federal level to respond to the request formulated by Californians and by the fledgling national labour movement. In later years, the AFL became the guardian of that law by demanding its prolongation every ten years and finally obtained the integration of Chinese and Asian exclusion into the 1917 literacy test act and the integration of anti-Asian clauses into the quota laws of 1921 and 1924 (Collomp 1998: 109–44, 263–311).

## Anti-contract labour and other protectionist policies

The union movement to obtain legislation to ban the contract labour system, a quasi repetition of the anti-Chinese exclusion, also sprang from the combination of two sources of anxiety: protection of the trades and fear of displacement by 'alien workers'. The contract labour issue had become an ambiguous demand in the 1880s. Originally, according to the 1864 law that had introduced the practice during the Civil War, contract labourers were skilled workers directly recruited from Europe to develop the steel, coal, textile, and glass industries. By the 1880s, while still allowing the isolated recruitment of some English and Belgian workers in the glass industry, the practice had become obsolete. But many unskilled inexperienced Hungarian, Polish or Italian immigrants were recruited by mining operators or building entrepreneurs, if not always on a preliminary contract, at least in conditions devised to undermine the skilled American workers' efforts towards unionisation to raise their pay scales. Thus, organised American workers directed their action to obtain legislation that would repeal the contract labour system. The 1885 Foran Act was passed directly in response to that demand. Two elements were instrumental in the discussion of the bill. The contract labourers were described in derogatory terms that had previously been used to eliminate the Chinese. They were described as beasts of burden 'eating food that a Chinaman would not touch', whose level of civilization unfairly competed with the American standard of wages.[15] But the most decisive intervention was that of the skilled glass workers of Local Assembly 300, affiliated to the Knights of Labor. These workers were the only ones who had been able to bring the actual evidence of the recruitment of foreign workers directly from Europe to act as strike breakers against the local labour force. Their argument

convinced American law-makers of the existence of the practice
and led them to adopt the Foran Act in 1885 (Erickson 1957).

After Chinese exclusion, the 1885 anti-contract labour law
remained the second cornerstone of American immigration
policy. By outlawing the direct recruitment of European workers,
unionists believed that they had effectively stopped the source of
the so-called 'new immigration' of Eastern or Southern European
workers, who were described as 'undesirable' and more unskilled
than the 'old immigration' of English or German origin. However
erroneous, the vision had a long-lasting impact on all discussions
concerning immigration, from the 1890s onwards to the enactment of the literacy test. Finally, the anti-contract labour clause
was also included in the quota system.

To further protect themselves from the competition of immigrants, even when they were skilled and duly qualified, some
unions introduced specific clauses in their constitutions to bar
the admission of foreigners. Some unions were content with
demanding naturalization from the candidates seeking admission (this was the case of the socialist Bakers and Brewers, for
instance), but these aimed not at excluding but at promoting the
foreign workers' active participation in political life. But other
unions imposed differential conditions of admission for American and immigrant workers. All the unions of glass workers, for
instance, established exorbitant initiation fees for the admission
of immigrants to the union. These fees could range from $50 to
$500.[16] Only the most skilled workers' unions were able to
restrict membership in this manner without incurring the
competition of unorganised and therefore cheaper workers. They
were both the most centralised, and those that were in a position to control at least vast regional segments of the labour
markets (Glass Workers, Typographers, Machinists, Building
Workers). They were the most vocal in Knights of Labor or AFL
discussions of the immigration 'problem' and no doubt influenced these federations for the enactment of upstream federal
regulation of immigration.

When, in the 1890's, Senator Henry Cabot Lodge's project,
which consisted in restricting immigration by selecting only
those who were able to pass a literacy test, was discussed in
Congress, one glass worker could say 'we already restrict immigration by demanding a $50 initiation fee (to the union) for
foreigners while Americans are required to pay only $3'.[17] In a
similarly protectionist vein, one cigar-maker claimed that 'if
unions think they have a right to restrict the number of apprentices to the trade in function of the natural growth of the trade,

it is their right too to restrict immigration in function of the natural economic growth of the country'.[18] However, the cigar-makers pseudo economic position is revealed once one knows that the Cigar-Makers' International Union organised only the most traditional workmen who still worked by hand, and excluded the less skilled ones who worked with moulding machines, thus leaving the many Bohemian, and later Jewish, tenement workers outside the union. The lesser-quality cigars did not receive the union label that certified that the union cigars had been manufactured in the most traditional fashion.[19]

## The Literacy Test

Such union rules did not prevent the mainstream (i.e. non-social-ist) unions from actively pressing government for the literacy test as the most comprehensive method of immigration restriction and selection. Year after year, this demand was to keep them busy. More than two decades passed between the time when Samuel Gompers first echoed Senator Lodge's bill in 1891, when the AFL officially supported it in 1897, until its final enactment in February 1917, barely two months before the United States entered the First World War. The choice of the literacy test as a selective bias was not neutral. It was not so much a literate working class that the restrictionists wanted to obtain but the exclusion of those peoples whose rate of illiteracy was high: that is the Italians and Slavs of the 'new' immigration who were also predominantly unskilled workers. The AFL and its most craft-oriented trade unions were the active protagonists for the new legislation along with the patriotic and nativist societies such as Prescott Hall's Immigration Restriction League or the American Protective Association.[20]

Maintaining the debate in Congress on the literacy test, and arguing for the necessity of immigration restriction, gave the AFL a reason to modify its classic non-partisan approach in politics and eventually provided it with a form of political integration. During the 1900s, the AFL remained at the centre of the deci-sion-making process concerning immigration laws. It was constantly heard, and represented, from Congressional commis-sions to the National Civic Federation and finally to the U.S. Congress.[21] Eventually the bill containing the literacy test was adopted in Congress in 1912, and again in 1914 and 1916. Each time, however, it was vetoed by the President (President Taft in 1913 and Wilson in 1915 and 1917) until finally, in February 1917, Congress had enough time to override the last presidential veto and enact the much desired immigration restriction bill. The AFL's abandonment of its non-partisan attitude in the two-party system since 1906 and the *rapprochement* it operated with the Democratic party from 1908 onwards (Greene 1998), are partly responsible for its eventual legislative success. The bill was passed by Democratic majorities, and Woodrow Wilson's government was the first to address labour questions in a non-negative manner.[22] The 1914 Clayton Act was seen by Gompers as a sign of social and political recognition. And when the literacy test was finally enacted, Gompers claimed victory with a sense of great satisfaction, arguing that the last item on labour's *List of Grievances* had finally received the requested answer.[23]

It is significant, however, that the social and economic issues about which the AFL sought the Federal Government's intervention were limited in number and nature. Beyond its demand to obtain government's revision of its judicial attitude against strikes and strikers, immigration was practically the only social problem which the AFL addressed to the Federal Government and to which the latter responded. This is explicable by the fact that social policies were within the province of state governments but not of the Federal one. Economic liberalism also prevented government intervention in the sphere of social matters. But in 1876, a Supreme Court decision had established that immigration fell within the province of Federal Government regulation and not that of the states.[24] Organised labour, therefore, could and did address its pleas for immigration restriction to Washington and give paramount significance to the issue.[25] The restriction of immigration was a kind of general panacea meant to cure all labour's social and economic problems in the market place. It was a manner of social policy, or at least the only one that the Federal Government consented to legislate on until the New Deal. By participating in the definition of who could be accepted as future American citizens, the AFL had been at the core of the discussions concerning American national identity and citizenship. This criterion, rather than class solidarity, was therefore central to the AFL's own status in as much that it allowed its integration in the nation. 'America has not yet become a nation', Gompers pleaded in 1916, as a final argument to insist on the necessity of passing the literacy test.[26]

Two points can be stressed in conclusion. The arguments leading to immigration restriction were cultural rather than economic. They emphasised cultural differences to explain wage competition, rather than the problem of wage differences due to lack of unionisation or competition between employers. More generally, in the mainstream labour literature, it was the foreign immigrant (whose degrading influence was epitomized and most symbolically represented by the Chinese) who was designated as labour's arch-enemy rather than the capitalist system or even American economic liberalism. In addition, labour unions equally forcefully advocated immigration restriction during times of economic recession or periods of full employment and economic development. Year in, and year out, there was no relaxation of this demand from the labour unions. They clamored for racial, ethnic, and categorial selection of labour migrants rather than for a simple numerical limitation that would have been more in tune with labour market contingencies. Moreover, the racial exclusion established by the quota system closed the door mainly to unskilled labour, the category of workers most in demand in the modern U.S. factory system. To remedy the labour shortage created by the First World War, by the literacy test and by the quota system, employers now recruited unskilled African-Americans from the South, or agricultural migrants from Quebec or Mexico who came from other American countries outside the quota system.

The racial bias of the immigration selection process introduced by the successive laws and the quota system is well known and remained effective until 1965. Yet the laws governing the admission of foreigners to the nation contained labour qualifications that are often forgotten in the general analysis. The 1882 Chinese Exclusion Act and its prolongation in 1892 and 1902, as well as the 1885 anti-contract labour Foran Act, the 1917 act instituting the literacy test or the 1921 and 1924 quota systems all contained clauses that exempted non-labour migrants from their provisions. Students, merchants, artists, ministers of the various denominations, be they even Chinese, Japanese or from other Asian countries, were not denied access to the United States. It was not race or ethnicity of origin alone but social status and occupation that defined who could be admitted as an immigrant to the U.S.. At a later period, during the economic depression of the 1930s, this often overlooked technicality in the legislation allowed the entry of many intellectual refugees from Nazi controlled countries, who were admitted as non-quota immigrants, while non-intellectual occupations were denied that privilege (see for instance Fermi 1968; David 1947; Wyman 1968; Breitman and Kraut 1987). In the final analysis, the ethnic selection of immigration was therefore intended to shrink the resources of a world-wide labour market to suit the AFL's demand and it refelected its active intervention in that endeavour.

## Notes

1. Labour unionism was only given legal recognition during the New Deal by the 1933 National Recovery Act and more definitively by the 1935 Wagner Act. The 1914 Clayton Act hailed by AFL leader Samuel Gompers as 'Labor's Magna Carta' was a sign of labour's political recognition by the Woodrow Wilson government, yet it was only a step toward actual legalisation.
2. At the turn of the century, the foreign born population and that born in the U.S. of foreign born parents averaged between 70 and 80 per cent of the inhabitants of the major cities in the industrial East and Midwest: Ward 1971; Chudacoff 1981: 102.
3. The 1890s depression further contributed to a reorganisation of workers along the more solid but fragmented lines of trade-unionisation and therefore added to the eventual growth of the AFL. See Collomp 1987: 200–8.
4. *The Carpenter*, national organ of the Brotherhood of Carpenters and Joiners was founded, like the union, in 1881; *The Cigar Maker's Official Journal* started appearing in 1876; *The Furniture Workers' Journal*, organ of the International Furniture Workers' Union of America was first published in 1885; the Bakery and Confectionary Workers' International Union began publishing a journal in English,*The Bakers' Journal*, in 1888, prior to that date the union's journal was the German-language *Baecker Zeitung*; the publication of the *Monthly Journal of the International Association of Machinists* began in 1890; the Knights of Labor's organ, *The Journal of United Labor*, was published from 1880 to 1889, it was followed by the *Journal of the Knights of Labor* in 1890. *The United Mine Workers' Journal* was first published nationally in 1891. In 1894, the AFL established its own monthly organ, *The American Federationist*.
5. Quotation from *Journal of United Labor*, No. 4, August 1880: 1 and 39; on the anti-Chinese events in California, see Sandmeyer 1973; Saxton 1971. On the national repercussions of the anti-Chinese movement see Collomp 1998.
6. Wiebe 1967; Stephen Skowronek (1982) has described the nineteenth-century Federal Government as a government of parties and law courts.
7. *Bakers'Journal*, August 17, 1889.
8. Samuel Gompers, *American Federationist*, October 1909 : 866; see Collomp 1988.
9. *Cigar Makers Official Journal*, Nov. 1895, p. 2. It is not clear in the passage whether Gompers' reference to the French labour organisation was to the Confédération Générale du Travail founded in September 1895.
10. In 1906, abandoning its non partisan and anti-statist position, the AFL published a 'List of grievances'. This led it in 1908 to campaign openly for the Democratic Party in order to obtain redress on injunctions, immigration and a few other issues. Greene 1998: 107–80.
11. American Federation of Labor, *Proceedings of the 1890 Convention*: 27
12. American Federation of Labor, *Proceedings of the 1896 Convention*: 53.
13. Space is lacking to add nuances to this schematic vision. Some of the socialist led unions kept a trade-unionist structure: this was the case of the Brewers, the Bakers, or the Furniture Workers. Conversely, the United Mine Workers was structurally an industrial union, but ideologically it mirrored the AFL's 'pure and simple' political approach and its leader John Mitchell constantly seconded Gompers in his mission to restrict immigration.
14. The classic texts on the IWW are: Foner 1965; Dubofsky 1969.

15. See Knights of Labor Grand Master Workman T.V. Powderly's description of the Hungarian contract workers in the Connelsville mining town near Scranton, Pennsylvania: *Proceedings of the General Assembly of the Knights of Labor*, 1884, pp. 575–8; the text is reproduced in McNeill 1887: 419f. Collomp 1998: 145–75.
16. The IWW clearly denounced the exclusionist practices of the Glass Workers unions against immigrants: see *Founding Convention of the Industrial Workers of the World*, New York, 1905: 125. Wolfe 1912.
17. New York Bureau of Labor Statistics *Eighteenth Annual Report,* 1898: 1068.
18. *Cigar Makers' Official Journal*, Dec. 8 1897.
19. *Reports of the Industrial Commission*, vol. XV, *Immigration*, G.P.O., Washington DC, 1901: 369–85. The case was exactly the same with the United Garment Workers of America who refused to organise the more recent Jewish and later Italian immigrants to whom work was subcontracted in the tenement buildings of most big cities.
20. The AFL debated Senator Henry Cabot Lodge's bill at practically every convention since 1891 see : AFL, *Proceedings of Conventions*, 1891: 15; 1892: 39; 1893: 14; 1894: 12; 1895: 95; *American Federationist*, Dec. 1895: 173. After overcoming internal opposition it decided to support the Lodge bill in 1897 after it had just been defeated in Congress: AFL, *Proceedings of Conventions*, 1897: 51–53 and 97–98. Thereafter the AFL renewed its lobbying on Congress through party representatives and Congressional Commissions. On the AFL and the literacy test see Lane 1987: 75–94, 171–86.
21. Collomp 1998: 263–311. The AFL's position was taken into account in the *Reports of the Industrial Commission*, vol. XV, Washington, G.P.O., 1901, see esp. pp. II–IV, and John Commons' report in *Ibid*, pp. 293–723; The AFL views were published in the (Dillingham) *Report of the Immigration Commission*, Washington, G.P.O., 1911, esp. vol. 23, p. 369 and vol. 1, pp. 45–48. The AFL was also represented in the National Civic Federation's Committee on Immigration, see its reports in the *National Civic Federation Review*, Jan-Feb. 1906; July-Aug. 1906; Nov-Dec. 1906.
22. President Wilson however never personally favoured the literacy test. He was opposed to both the principle of restrictive legislation and to the method proposed by the literacy test, which 'through no fault of their own would exclude many willing immigrants and good laborers'. His December 1916 veto was overridden by the Democratic majority on February 5, 1917: see *Congressional Record*, 63rd Congress 3rd session, Jan. 1915, p. 2481; *Ibid.*, 64th Congress, 2nd Session, Jan. 29, 1917, p. 2212.
23. Samuel Gompers, 'Immigration Legislation Effrected', American Federationist, March 1917: 189–95.
24. The decision, in Henderson v. Mayor of New York, referred to legal precedents establishing that transatlantic transportation of travellers or immigrants was a question of commerce and therefore was within the province of Federal Government.
25. Apart from the question of back to work injunctions against labour that was superficially tackled by the 1914 Clayton Act, the other social issues within the realm of the Federal Government concerned federal employees or seamen: 'Labor's Bill of Grievances', *American Federationist*, May 1906: 294–95; *Ibid.*, Sept. 1906: 643–46, 689–90.
26. Samuel Gompers, 'Reasons for Immigration Restriction', *American Federationist*, April 1916: 253–6.

# References

Breitman, Richard, and Kraut, Alan, 1987, *American Refugee Policy and European Jewry, 1933–45*, Bloomington.

Chudacoff, Howard P.,1981, *The Evolution of American Urban Society*, Englewoods Cliff, N.J.

Collomp, Catherine, 1987, 'Les Knights of Labor et le syndicalisme de métier: structure et relations des deux types d'organisation', *Revue Française d'Etudes Américaines*, 32 (April): 200–208.

Collomp, Catherine, 1988, 'Unions, Civics, and National Identity: Organized Labor's Reaction to Immigration, 1881–1897', *Labor History*, 29: 4: 450–75.

Collomp, Catherine, 1998, *Entre classe et nation. Mouvement ouvrier et immigration aux Etats-Unis*, Paris.

Collomp, Catherine, 1999, 'Immigrants, Labor Markets and the State, A Comparative Approach: France and the United States, 1880–1930', *The Journal of American History*, 86:1 (June): 41–66.

David, Maurice, 1947, *Refugees in America : Report of the Committee for the Study of Recent Immigration from Europe*, Westport Conn.

Dubofsky, Melvyn, 1969, *We Shall Be All: A History of the Industrial Workers of the World*, Chicago.

Erickson, Charlotte, 1957, *American Industry and the European Immigrant*, New York.

Fermi, Laura, 1968, *Illustrious Immigrants: The Intellectual Migration from Europe, 1930–1940*, Chicago.

Foner, Philip, 1965, *History of the Labor Movement in the United States*, vol. 4: *The Industrial Workers of the World*, New York.

Glocker, Theodore, 1913, 'The Government of American Trade Unions', *Johns Hopkins University Studies in Historical and Political Science*, 31:2: 9–42.

Greene, Julie, 1998, *Pure and Simple Politics: The American Federation of Labor and Political Activism, 1881–1917*, Cambridge.

Lane, Andrew, 1987, *Solidarity or Survival : American Labor and European Immigrants, 1830–1924*, Westport, Conn.

McNeill, George, 1887, *The Labor Movement, The Problem of Today*, Boston.

Mink, Gwendolyn, 1986, *Old Labor and New Immigrants in American Political Development, 1875–1920*, Ithaca.

Sandmeyer, Clarence E., 1973, *The Anti-Chinese Movement in California* (1939) Urbana, Ill.

Saxton, Alexander, 1971, *The Indispensable Enemy, Labor and the Anti-Chinese Movement in California*, Berkeley.

Skowronek, Stephen, 1982, *Building the New American State: The Expansion of National Administrative Capacities, 1877–1920*, New York.

Ulman, Lloyd, 1955, *The Rise of the National Trade Union*, Cambridge, Mass.

Ward, David, 1971, *Cities and Immigrants. A Geography of Change in Nineteenth Century America*. New York.

Wiebe, Robert, 1967, *The Search for Order, 1877–1920*, New York.

Wolfe, F. E., 1912, 'Admission to American Trade Unions', *Johns Hopkins University Studies in Historical and Political Science*, 30:3:1–150.

Wyman, David, 1968, *Paper Walls: America and the Refugee Crisis, 1938–41*, Boston.

# Chapter 16

# Between Altruism and Self-Interest
## *Immigration Restriction and the Emergence of American-Jewish Politics in the United States*

*Michael Berkowitz*

At the heart of this paper is a paradox: that as Jewish immigrants to the United States were rapidly acculturating around the turn of the last century, they were not simply shedding their communal identity; it was being transformed. Part of what went into this process was Jews' collective safeguarding of what they deemed their present and future interests. Not the least of these was the right of their European brethren to follow them to the *goldene medinah*, the Golden Land of the United States. A smaller, but not insignificant part of what came to be a distinctly Jewish position stemmed from their sensitivity to the tribulations of other 'strangers',[1] fellow newcomers to the New World: such as immigrants from Asia. Although it is barely reflected in the historiography, Jews' encounter with Far Easterners, while not as pronounced and turbulent as their relationships with Irish, Italians, and Black Americans, influenced their politics and world-view. Even though Asians and Jews were usually not in direct contact, the Chinese and Japanese in America were not invisible to turn-of-the-century Jewry. Indeed, at some crucial junctures Jewish protest against immigration restriction converged with the Asian desire to maintain free entry. Both groups had been stigmatised as a supplier of prostitutes, supposedly menacing the health and well-being of the nation (Feffer 1999; Sachar 1992: 164–8), and were especially threatened by 'literacy tests' to determine eligibility for immigration (Sorin

1992: 57–62). These ties may have been a coincidence, but it indicates more than a passing oddity. The issue of immigration restriction and the Jewish immigrant generation deserves to be looked at as a distinct question: because it sheds light on underworked problems in labour and immigration history. It is hoped, as well, that this may contribute to an understanding of Jewish politics writ large, and ethnic politics and consciousness in the United States (Hollinger 1995).

The point of departure, to situate this problem historically and historiographically, is Irving Howe's classic, *The World of Our Fathers* (1976). This work is such a rich treasure that it will take generations of scholarship to tease out the articles and books it suggests. The problem, however, is that these potential subjects remain largely unexplored, because they reside within the realm of *yiddishkeyt* – not simply 'Jewishness', but the Yiddish language and its attendant secular culture – which is foreign to most scholars of labour and immigration history. This is significant, not simply because it means that a minority group is left out – but because one of the most vibrant segments of United States' organized labour, some 300,000 strong at its height, is ignored or otherwise muted in the historiography.

In part, this chapter builds upon and modifies one of Howe's insights, which is contained in a footnote. In discussing the intensification of Jewish unionisation and strikes beginning in 1909, Howe wrote:

As a central agency of the Jewish socialists in the unions, the United Hebrew Trades came in for severe attack from the leaders of the American Federation of Labor. In general, the tension during these early days between Jewish unionists of socialist inclination and the more conservative AF of L has been minimised by historians who respond to the leadership of the Jewish unions as it is now [that is, in 1976] and forget what it once was. A major point of contention was the immigration issue, with the UHT [United Hebrew Trades] favoring unrestricted immigration and most AFL unions restrictions of varying severity. In 1901 the AFL organizer Herman Robinson urged local unions not to affiliate with the UHT since it knew 'little or nothing about the trade union movement; its entire knowledge of unionism extends from East Broadway to Houston Street, and from the Bowery to Sheriff Street'. This kind of sparring continued for a good many years. In February 1918 the AFL Executive Council ordered all affiliates in New York to leave the UHT on the ground that it maintained close relations with the Amalgamated Clothing Workers and the Cloth, Hat and Cap Makers Union, both of which were independent unions led by immigrant Jews, many of them socialists, and both of which were in conflict with older, moribund AFL affiliates. It would take several decades before this clash between the Jewish socialist union leaders and the official AFL leadership came, not to an end, but at least to a point where it could be quietly contained (Howe 1976: 297).

Over twenty years since the publication of Howe's chronicle, there have been a number of scholarly works devoted to Jewish life and labour on the Lower East Side (Heinze 1990; Glenn 1990; Frankel 1981; Cassedy 1997), comparative historical treatments that aspire to include women, 'non-white', and 'off-white' ethnic groups in labour history (Brodkin 1998; Jacobson 1995 and 1998), and studies of relationships between labour and the state (Tomlins 1985; McCartin 1997). Yet this research has not greatly illuminated the issues and strife described by Howe. One objective of this paper is to investigate the relationship between the American Federation of Labor (AF of L) and the United Hebrew Trades (UHT). Is Howe's evaluation still accurate: that the tension between these bodies is absent in historiography? To what extent was the alienation of the pre-eminent body of Jewish labour, the UHT, from the AF of L, a factor of their opposing stances on immigration? Last, I wish to speculate on how the immigration-restriction question influenced Jewish labour and the formation of what was to become 'Jewish politics' in America. I will argue largely in favour of Howe's recognition of a tie between anti-immigration policies and sentiment (Archdeacon 1983: 143–72; Higham 1984: 29–70), and the emergence of a specifically ethnic-Jewish political constellation in the US from the period 1897 to 1939. The activities of the scions of the Lower East Side, Meyer London, Isaac Hourwich, and Abraham Cahan provide the main focus. Yet these individuals were not totally isolated, as Jews, in this battle. They were joined by some of the stalwarts from the United States' German-Jewish establishment, such as Max J. Kohler, Oscar Straus, Felix Adler, Jacob Schiff, and Louis Marshall (Kohler 1909). I propose, then, that it was not simply the phenomenon of Jewish mass immigration – with its accompanying demographic, geographic and vocational profile – that engendered the rise of Jewish politics in the United States. Jewish politics emerged, in part, out of a clearly articulated desire – arguably singular, among the United States' non-Asian ethnic groups – to keep the door of immigration open. Relatedly, the tension surrounding perceptions of a distinctive Jewish political style – with its emphasis on strikes and revolutionary rhetoric – cannot be separated from the Jews' understanding of immigration restriction. Their comprehension of the movement for curtailing immigration underscored both established Jewry's commitment to universal human rights, and immigrant Jews' connection to the majority of their co-religionists who remained in Europe. In total, these concerns made possible the crystallization of a Jewish lobby or special interest outside the labour framework per se, seeking to cultivate its own priorities and voice. I would qualify Howe's point, however, and say that the immigration issue was more subtle and complex than he infers, but nevertheless decisive. He was, I believe, more often right than wrong.[2]

Among mainstream historians, Thomas Archdeacon has argued that the transition 'from immigrants to ethnics', in which Jews are exemplary, occurred primarily in the 1920s, after the imposition of immigration quotas in the years between the wars (Archdeacon 1983: 174ff., 188f.). David Montgomery concurs that 'Closing the door to Europeans accelerated the stabilization of ethnic communities in industrial towns and cities (Montgomgery 1989: 462). I contend that the mobilization of American Jewry happened earlier, before the harsh measures of 1924 were implemented. To use the oft-quoted shorthand of David Hollinger, Jews creatively exercised their 'ethnic option' before being acknowledged for doing so (Hollinger 1995). In the second decade of the twentieth century, Montgomery remarks that at every AFL convention

> some black dockers, porters, hod carriers, or boilermakers' helpers challenged the racial exclusiveness of many affiliated craft unions, always without success. Despite the persistent difficulties they faced in securing a foothold in northern industry, however, black migrants were fashioning workplace and neighborhood networks of decisive importance of the next decade (Montgomery 1989: 460).

The historian does not remark, however, that Jews, too – especially women in the needle trades (Glenn 1990; Howe 1976: 297) – felt themselves separated from the AF of L, and that they also forged 'networks' of lasting importance.

It is no coincidence that up to 1897 the AF of L did not advocate immigration restriction. In that year, however, 'a majority of trade unions affiliated with the federation voted for the first time in favour of *a reasonable measure* of restriction' (emphasis added) (Lorwin 1933: 52f.). Also in that year, Abraham Cahan assumed editorship of the *Forward*, which animated the relatively radical Jewish labour movement, in particular, supplying the United Hebrew Trades with 'a new channel for publicity' (Finestone 1938: 19). In 1897 the branch of the Jewish Socialists was founded in New York. On the world stage, both the Zionists and Bundists held their founding conventions in 1897. These, too, would spur American-Jewish ethnic mobilization, but not necessarily immediately or directly.

It is crucial to bear in mind that 'the AF of L welcomed the quota law of 1924', as David Montgomery writes. 'From 1919 onward, the Federation had appealed for a halt to all immigration whatsoever, arguing that only if the influx of newcomers was prevented could the earnings of all American workers rise to the level of the 'living wage' demanded by the AF of L's reconstruction program' (Montgomery 1989: 461). Earlier studies of the AF of L were even more forthright in asserting that the Federation 'consistently and strongly urged legislation in its fight against the competition of the immigrant and especially of the Asiatic' (Carroll 1923: 118). 'On the question of immigration', beginning in 1917 there was a steep rise in the exclusionary posture of the AF of L. Before 1870, there had been significant lobbying, by organised labour, against the 'importation of Chinese as strikebreakers' (Barth 1964: 210) and 'in the early 1880's, the cigar makers' union', many of whose members and leaders were Jewish, 'finally succeeded in the virtual elimination of Chinese labour and Chinese sweatshops in manufacturing' (Chiu 1967: 126).

> Between 1919 and 1923 [the AF of L] demanded the abrogation of the 'gentleman's agreement' with Japan and the total exclusion of the Japanese. During these same years it also opposed the admission of Mexican laborers to the US and the importation of Chinese workers into Hawaii. In 1924 it supported the National Origins Law as a compromise, though it would have preferred a complete suspension of immigration for five years. Since 1925 the Federation has gone on record for applying the quota system to Mexico and Canada, despite the interrelations of the trade unions in these countries, for the exclusion of Hindus and Filipinos; for the reduction of immigration from the Eastern Hemisphere by fifty percent; for the strict enforcement of the deportation laws; and for similar measures which would extend the area of restriction and tighten the mechanism for enforcing the law (Lorwin 1933: 402f.).

In the current generation of scholars, the role of anti-immigrant, and especially anti-Asian sentiment, as a leading organising principle in the labour movement has been taken up by Gwendolyn Mink (Mink 1986) and modified by Julie Greene and Andrew Gyory (Gyory 1998). Greene, arguing that the AF of L was much more politicised that its legacy implies, states that immigration 'played a less central role than various other issues', in contrast to the thesis of Mink (Greene 1998: 10). Perhaps I can settle the difference between them: I believe that Greene is indeed correct, if one is looking at political activity per se, and Mink has a more plausible interpretation, if one wishes to discern workers' consciousness and account for solidarity between otherwise disparate groups (Brodkin 1998: 30). Greene recognizes that little effort had to be expended for the AF of L's to popularise its desire for restrictions, because the cause tended to be supported by the

vast majority of Americans. The organisation simply did not have
to work at it. For the most part this concurs with Gyory's assertion that the movement for Chinese exclusion was 'non-ideological'
(Gyory 1998: 6f.)

Mink, through her sensitivity to minorities, is one of few scholars, along with the little-cited Charles Lienenweber, Ira Kipnis
and Mel Dubovsky, to represent the bitterness of the AF of L
toward the UHT (Mink 1986: 201f.). Interestingly, however, she
quotes from an article of United Hebrew Trades' leader Morris
Hillquit, where he specifically calls for Asian immigrant restriction in 1907. His moderated view was embodied in a hotly
contested plank in a Socialist Party convention of 1910.

> The Socialist Party of the United States favors all legislative measures
> tending to prevent the immigration of strikebreakers and contract labor-
> ers, and the mass importation of workers from foreign countries, brought
> about by the employing classes for the purpose of weakening the orga-
> nization of American labor, and lowering the standard of life of American
> workers [...] [But] the party is opposed to the exclusion of any immi-
> grants on account of their race or nationality, and demands that the
> United States be at all times maintained as a free asylum for all men and
> women persecuted by the governments of their countries on account of
> their politics, religion, or race (quoted in Mink 1986: 232).

Mink infers that Hillquit, and by association, Meyer London and
the UHT overall, were obsequious to the animus against Asian
immigration (Mink 1986: 201, 230, 232).

Mink's thesis may be challenged by considering the careers of
some key players in the Jewish labour and immigration nexus.
Meyer London – a leading figure of the United Hebrew Trades
and its cultural arm, the Workmen's Circle (Arbeter Ring) – was
elected as a Socialist to the U. S. House of Representatives in
1914. Throughout his career, London refused to countenance
different treatment to minorities on the basis of 'race' or nationality. He believed that 'the doors of all countries must always
remain wide open to admit all people of all ranks who wish to
enter. In this London encountered opposition not only in the
conservative American Federation [of Labor] but his own Socialist Party'. In the US Socialist Party Congress in 1910, a resolution
was proposed to support restriction on Asiatic immigration, 'a
favourite measure of the Pacific Coast' and the AF of L. London
spoke against the motion:

> As a delegate representing a foreign-speaking National organization I
> desire to say that I participated in the formation of the first branch of the
> Social Democracy in America and that I had the honor of being a dele-
> gate to the national convention of the Social Democratic Party ten years
> ago. ... The majority report is faulty in this – it violates a fundamental

principle of socialism, which prohibits you from discriminating against a race. One of the painful things in life that I have been acquainted with is the murder of Chinese by thugs and ruffians. When you say, 'we will exclude people because they are Japanese and because they are Chinese and because they are Hindus you violate the Decalogue, one of the elementary principles of international Socialism. ... I do not speak on behalf of the Jewish immigrants, because we are not concerned. There are no restrictive laws against us. But I do speak in behalf of all oppressed races and I say that by adopting a resolution pointing to particular races, you have put upon the great mass of Japanese and Chinese the stamp of inferiority. This is your own act, and it is not in accordance with the ordinary principles of fair dealing and honesty or the principles of Americanism, as I understand them (Rogoff 1930: 172f.).

Although London claimed to detach himself from his immigrant cohort, instead casting himself as a socialist and American, he was in fact speaking for a significant share of his ethnic constituents. According to London's biographer, Harry Rogoff, when restrictions were being urged in Washington,

the Jewish immigrants watched every move with the deepest concern. They were vitally interested in defeating the bill for more than one reason. First, it cast a slur upon their race. It sought to bar out immigrants of certain countries and races, implying their inferiority to others, and Jews were included in the discriminated groups. Second, the Jews of this country could ill afford to have the doors of this country shut against them. Most of the immigrants here still had their nearest and dearest on the other side and their most earnest hope was to earn enough to be able to send for them. Any added hardship in the realization of their dream was dreaded as a great misfortune. There was, thirdly, the old problem of Jewish persecution in Russia and other European countries. Where would these unfortunate ones seek refuge if the doors of this country were barred? (Rogoff 1930: 174)

It has been noted that Jews saw the plight of the Negro in America as reflecting, or potentially related, to their own struggles (Davis 1999); much less has been said about Jewish perceptions of other groups. I believe that the Jews' stance toward those targeted groups was something of a rehearsal for defending their increasingly besieged co-religionists in Europe. Therefore, there is a tie between the immigration restriction movement and organized Jewry's polemics and activities in support of Jewish refugees, generally, and the Zionist project, specifically. Complementing his anti-restriction efforts in the U. S. Congress and Socialist Party, London furthermore argued that 'with the tide of immigration' there invariably followed 'industrial development and growth, and that those parts of the country that had forged ahead materially and in every other way had received the largest share of immigrants' (Rogoff 1930: 206). All immigrant restriction, he argued, was 'an assertion of that exaggerated nationalism which never appeals to reason and which has for its main source the self-conceit of accumulated prejudices' (Rogoff 1930: 205).

Another figure in the centre of the United Hebrew Trades and Arbeter Ring who was explicit and persistent in making the case for open immigration was Isaac Hourwich. As a journalist, scholar, attorney, and Russified Jew turned Yiddishist, Hourwich's opinions were based on an immersion in a wealth of raw and scholarly social-scientific data and the culture of the masses (Hourwich 1912). Hourwich was among the most important interpreters of political economy for the Jewish immigrants themselves. As an activist he 'belonged to a cohort of social scientists' that contended that hard-boiled social science must be allied with policy-making (Reiss n. d.: xxvii). Hourwich advanced a sophisticated, scholarly assessment of the Jewish immigrants' immediate past and present that showed them to be a hugely productive and vital part of the emerging economy. He expanded the horizons of this community through his oratory, official government duty, and translations of, among others, the works of Karl Marx into Yiddish.

In New York, along with Joseph Barondess and Meyer London, Hourwich 'formed the first unit of the Social Democratic party in New York in 1897' (Epstein n.d.: 165) while working as a labour lawyer. Hourwich subsequently went to Washington, where he spent many years as a government statistician and an expert on mining for the Bureau of the Census (Epstein n.d.: 258). As a result of his government-sponsored research he produced scores of articles and a weighty tome on the economics of immigration to the New World, *Immigration and Labor: The Economic Aspects of European Immigration to the United States* (1912). It remains an impressive polemic and piece of scholarship. He exposed the fallacy of accusations that immigrants were taking jobs away from so-called native Americans, that they were a drain on the economy, and that they exhibited an inferior moral constitution: such as a propensity to criminal behaviour (Hourwich 1912: 353–61). Hourwich argued that the immigrant masses were increasing the wealth and economic development potential of the nation exponentially; they were helping to provide for greater employment, rather than taking jobs away; and they were no more lawless or immoral in their behaviour than any previous generation of new immigrants. The notion that any one group might be 'unassimilable' was firmly dismissed. In fact, so-called 'new immigrants' constituted less of a social burden than earlier generations of immigrants (Hourwich 1912: 161–65).

Beginning around 1910, Hourwich enjoined a battle for greater workers' rights, eventually causing him to clash with Louis Brandeis, who is seen as a great champion of Jewish workers, as well as Zionists. It seems that the oblivion to which Hourwich's legacy has been consigned is due, in part, to this bitter fight with Brandeis over the 'Protocol of Peace'.

As 'Yitzhok Isaac' Hourwich began to write in Yiddish around 1897, after the *Forward* began publication under Abraham Cahan. Since he held a United States' government job, he could not openly write articles in socialist and anarchist papers; a pseudonym was indispensable. He picked a strange pen-name – Yitzhok Ben Arye Zvi Halevi – rife with poetic and animal allusions. In time, Hourwich learned Yiddish well, and became an important Yiddish publicist. Analysing and commenting on American economic and political institutions became his specialty. He wrote for the *Forward*, the anarchist *Freie Arbiter Shtimme*, the *Zukunft*, *Varhayt*, and *Der Tog*. It is not difficult to see why Hourwich entitled his unfinished autobiography *Memoirs of a Heretic*; it would be especially difficult to sustain his popularity, as he died in 1924, at the height of the isolationist hysteria that he fought to combat (Epstein n.d.: 267f.). Isaac Hourwich's ideas were certain to be seen as ill-conceived, or even threatening, to those wishing to rationalize an end to an open-door policy toward new immigrants.

Concerning the same Socialist Party National Conventions discussed by Mink, Hourwich also had a good deal to say. The issue of immigration restriction had first been raised at the International Socialist Congress in Amsterdam in 1904. Hourwich came down strongly on the side of forbidding restrictions. At the Stuttgart Congress of 1907, Hourwich said that Morris Hillquit's comrades did not find his case for selected exclusion convincing (Hourwich 1917: 137). Hourwich was appalled by the 'the position of American socialists to immigration'. Hillquit, he asserted, was pleading the 'American' case, as a member of the United States' delegation. Hourwich painted any such hindrance of immigration, like those attempted at the conventions in 1908 and 1910, as a betrayal of the principle of class solidarity; such resolutions rendered the socialists' so-called founding tenets a sham (Hourwich 1917: 140ff.).

Both Meyer London and Isaac Hourwich, however, were in the shadow of the gigantic figure of Abraham Cahan. Cahan awaits his definitive biography, as the task of comprehending and contextualizing his long and varied career is Herculean. It is widely accepted that Cahan 'seemed in many ways to incarnate the epic Jewish migration from Eastern Europe to America;'[3]

under his stewardship the *Forward* was hailed as 'the most eloquent expression' of the new Yiddish journalism.

> Cahan had come to New York in 1882 at the age of twenty-one, eager for freedom and determined to write. In the ensuing two decades he served an apprenticeship in American living that was to prepare him for his role as Editor of the nation's outstanding Yiddish daily. This perceptive Russian intellectual shared in all the experiences of his fellow immigrants: he was factory hand, lecturer, teacher of English, labor organizer, law student, and socialist preacher. But from the outset he cultivated literary ambitions (Rischin 1977: 124).

Cahan became the ultimate arbiter of both taste and politics. 'At its peak in the 1920s' the *Forward*'s circulation encompassed '11 local and regional editions, surpassed a quarter of a million and its influence extended to many times that number of people. The *Forward* defended the cause of labor, socialism, humanity, and distinguished Yiddish and other modern literature'.[4]

Concomitant to his role in the re-founding and life of the *Forward*, Cahan was also a prime mover in two central institutions in American Jewish life, the Arbeter Ring, or Workman's Circle, and the United Hebrew Trades. In 1936, the Workmen's Circle was 'the largest and wealthiest immigrant labor fraternal order, as well as the largest Jewish organization, in America' (Hurwitz 1936: 105–7). In addition to a shared ethos, both of these bodies came to be housed under the same roof as the *Forward*, giving the intersecting nexus of Jewish culture and politics a central address. 'It had a large auditorium for meetings and concerts. Built in 1908, it was an audacious project of the *Forward* manager Marcus Jaffee. The high cost of the building nearly wrecked the paper'.[5] It is not surprising, then, that the men identified and glorified as the moving spirits of the *Forward* were also major figures in the other organizations (Rogoff 1954). Although much of the historiography, such that it is, focuses on the quarrels, schisms, and breakdowns in relations between individuals and organisations, a point that is often eluded is that they were perceived as somehow belonging to each other, despite their differences.

The United Hebrew Trades was esteemed by Jews as their preeminent labour body, 'the mother organization of all Jewish trade unionists in the United States' (Vladeck 1938: 63). The 'power and prestige' of the UHT, with over 300,000 members in the late 1930s, could not be conceived as separate from the father figure of Abraham Cahan, as its fortunes were inextricably tied to the man and his newspaper (Feinstone 1938: 19). In recounting their history in 1938, Cahan loomed as the most formidable galvanizing force:

The Jewish trade union movement of New York may be said to date from July 27th, 1882. On that day, a young Russian intellectual, a former teacher and writer, Abraham Cahan, rose at a socialist meeting of the intelligentsia, and suggested that the Jews workers be addressed in Jewish [Yiddish], not Russian or German. The proposal astounded the intellectuals, who had remained cut off from the masses precisely because they had made no serious effort to bridge the linguistic gap between themselves and the workers. But Cahan's suggestion was followed, more perhaps in an experimental frame of mind than in conviction. Although the final fruits were not to come until 1888, when the UHT was established, the intervening six years were full of extraordinary activity, developing a whole movement towards what might be called popular education. The Jewish workers were addressed in their own tongue, in simple and unassuming manner, so that they gradually got over their understandable fear of the 'highbrow' ideas of the 'Deitsche' and 'Russische' intellectuals. Agitation for trade union and socialist principles was received with interest. A whole series of educational clubs and organizations was founded. In 1884, the Russian-Jewish Workers' Alliance was formed, its purpose being to hold lectures and meetings in Jewish for the spread of socialist thought. In 1885, the Labor Lyceum began sending out Jewish speakers. Another body set up at that time was the Jewish Workers' Alliance, an amalgam of the Russian, Hungarian and Galician Jews, established for the spread of socialist ideas and for the founding of a paper. The Jewish Workers' Alliance enjoyed an active but very short life, for two years later it was split by the old controversy over the place of politics in the trade unions. Of the two resultant wings, one became the Anarchists under Janowsky and Zolataroff, while the other became the powerful Branch 8 of the Socialist Labor Party. Cahan and Michael Zametkin were the leading spirits of Branch 8 (Feinstone 1938: 13f.).

As much as Cahan's advocacy prompted the rise of the United Hebrew Trades, he also helped define two seminal aspects of its programme: the aversion to communism, and the gradual warming to the Zionist movement. His visit to Palestine in 1925 became a legendary turning point for Cahan and the *Forward*. I believe it is no accident that Cahan sojourned in Palestine in 1925, soon after the 'golden door' to America was slammed shut. There is little possibility that the links forged between the central bodies of Jewish labour in the United States and Labour Zionism in Palestine, could have materialized without Cahan's change of heart. Of course this alliance was aided by the apparent coincidence of interests between Zionism, anti-fascism, and those dismayed by immigration restriction.

The 1938 annual of the Gewerkschaften of the United Hebrew Trades asserted that

The periodic attacks of anti-Semitism with which our history is punctuated only make it more imperative for the Jews in America, especially those in the trade unions founded by the United Hebrew Trades, to take stock of the advantages they have gained, and to frame a practical program for applying those advantages to fighting reaction and totalitarianism. ... We must realize our assets in order to marshal them against primitivism and unreason. The Jews of the world need our assistance–in Germany, in Central Europe, in Palestine. And we need them in order to assure the triumph of the principles for which we have fought these last fifty years (Lang and Feinstone eds 1938: 4f.).

The organisation made specific its perception, if not reality, of the convergence of interests of worldwide Jewish labour movements. Furthermore, it began to see Zionism as a solution to an immigration problem for East European Jewry. It therefore institutionalised, and highly publicized, its campaign to raise funds every year for the Histadruth, the Federation of Organized Jewish Workers in Palestine (Feinstone 1938: 26f.).

Leaving aside for a moment the immigration restriction issue per se: the tempestuousness in relations between the UHT and the AF of L has been ignored in most scholarly treatments of labour in general, and Jewish labour in particular, of the last dozen years, with the exception of the work of Robert Parmet (Parmet 1987: 100–5, 122f.). The seminal works of Irving Howe, Moses Rischin, Howard M. Sachar, and Ronald Sanders – which clearly show the friction between the UHT and the AF of L – do not seem to have influenced the master narratives and dominant interpretations (Rischin 1977; Sanders 1969). Even the recent *History of the Jewish People of America*, a multi-volume series intended to be the gold standard of historical scholarship, does not capture how the UHT went against the grain (Sorin 1992: 113f., 117, 120–4, 131). For the most part this follows the AF of L party line, which stressed that 'After some temporary maladjustments, [the immigrants who behaved and thought differently] absorbed the American point of view, which meant to them a desire for higher economic standards and more humane consideration' (Lorwin 1933: 105).

But even the AF of L's own record shows severe discord stemming from Jewish tactics. From 1909 to 1914,

Mass strikes, aggressive in character and often violent in form, swept the country, led by workers tasting industrial strife for the first time. As no strike statistics were published for these years, the total number of strikes and strikers is unknown. But the scope and intensity of many of them, such as that of the New York 'shirt waist girls' in 1909, the cloakmakers in New York, the men's garment workers' in Chicago in 1910...bore the imprint of deep social revolts. The unrest spread to the workers already organized in more skilled trades. Pressed by new immigrants and by employers unable to make economic concessions easily...these skilled workers showed a greater readiness to make common cause with the unskilled and to try new ideas and methods....The effects of these developments were spectacular. Small unions of a few thousand suddenly

became large organizations, with considerable funds and influence...A
number of unions reorganized on a wide trade and industrial basis...The
International Ladies' Garment Workers' Union, for instance, as a result
of the big strikes in 1909–10, became a semi-industrial or amalgamated
union combining all the workers within the industry but allowing the
separate crafts to retain a certain amount of craft autonomy (Lorwin
1933: 105f.).

Interestingly, it would be the International Ladies' Garment
Workers' Union which would be the last group to go on record
objecting to the extreme demands of the AF of L for curtailing
immigration in 1923 (Lorwin 1933: 403).

A retrospective of the career of Samuel Gompers, who was
well-known for his anti-Chinese position in the cigar-makers'
union, recalls the long-running feud with the United Hebrew
Trades. Ironically, Gompers had been among the founders of the
United Hebrew Trades but quickly separated himself from Jewish
concerns. Upon the establishment of the Amalgamated Clothing
Workers of America, the Executive Council of the AF of L ordered
the United Hebrew Trades 'to expel its locals aligned with the
seceders'. The UHT refused, asking instead to increase its efforts
at conciliation. When the AF of L later demanded the UHT to
'disaffiliate the seceding locals of the garment workers', the UHT
said that to do so would constitute a sacrifice of 'the very moral
foundation upon which our organization stands. We ask you no
more than would be expected of any body civic that sits in judgment, namely, to give the accused a chance to plead his case'.
Charges were made that 'seceders were being led by New York
Socialists, manipulated by the *Forward.* ... Following their
refusal to oust the seceding garment workers, unions affiliated
with the AF of L were required to withdraw from the UHT' (Taft
1957: 180). The issue was revived in 1915, and the Council's move
to stifle the UHT was upheld at its convention, with Gompers
apparently cutting short the debate (Taft 1957: 181).

In addition to differentiating themselves by condoning and
even glorifying strikes, and opposing immigration restriction,
Jews were separated from the Gentile majority. This began in
1910, in their vociferous opposition to the AF of L's linkage with
the National Civic Foundation. In the name of compromise
between employers and employees, the organisation was seen by
UHT stalwarts as a tool of employers to provide an appearance
of cooperation with workers, while actually giving them nothing
in return. The leading opponent of this trend was Morris Hillquit
(Taft 1957: 228). Hillquit characterized 'the game played by the
Civic Federation' as 'the shrewdest yet devised by employers of

the country. It takes nothing from capital, it gives nothing to labor and does it all with such an appearance of generosity, that some of the guileless diplomats of the labor movement are actually overwhelmed by it'. He said it comprised 'a subtle and insidious poison' which robbed the workers of their 'independence, virility and militant enthusiasm; it hypnotizes or corrupts its leaders, weakens its ranks and demoralizes its fights' (Taft 1957: 228). It was, in effect, an attempt to de-Yiddishize the movement.

These New York-based, East European Jews who headed the United Hebrew Trades, the Arbeter Ring, and the *Forward* were not alone, in the Jewish fold, in fervently resisting 'racial' immigration restriction. On the West Coast of the United States, 'a Polish Jew named Sigismund Danielewicz, a Socialist who worked as a barber and sailor', was the outstanding union organiser in California in the 1880s. Alex Saxton writes that Danielewicz would have been hailed as perhaps the greatest of labour leaders, 'except that he chose to stand for the principle of racial equality. The last reference I found to him indicates that he was out of work in the winter of 1910 and set out on foot for the East'. Saxton sees Danielewicz, unequivocally, as the foremost spokesman for 'humane and humanist radicalism in America' (Saxton 1971: x).

On the opposite end of the social spectrum, similarly dedicated to open immigration, were well-heeled German Jews such as Louis Marshall, who stood at the pinnacle of the institutional Jewish order; Felix Adler, the founder of the Ethical Culture Society and an international body based on the ideal of 'interracial friendship'; Simon Wolf, who had been instrumental in protecting Jewish immigration before the massive wave in 1881 (Selected Address 1926); Oscar Straus, Secretary of Commerce and Labor under President Theodore Roosevelt; and U.S. Attorney and legal scholar Max Kohler. Kohler was the grandson of Rabbi David Einhorn, who was one of the founding fathers of Reform Judaism in America, who forged his theology in opposition to that of Isaac Meyer Wise whom he saw as backtracking on the ideals of the movement. Max's father, too, Kaufmann Kohler, was a Reform rabbi, noted scholar, and President of the Hebrew Union College (Sachar 1992: 287f.). Max Kohler credited his father with instilling in him a consciousness of accountability for not only fellow Jews, but also for 'the stranger', as a part of the Judaeo-Christian tradition.

> My father ... called to my attention the circumstance that the Hebrew term for stranger, 'Ger', etymologically denotes 'protégé' or 'client' of God, evidencing the protection acquired by the alien through religious injunction, and the Biblical 'cities of refuge' in terms afforded asylum to the stranger, too. (Numbers XXXV, II.) It is primarily through the religious

appeal that the rights of the stranger have developed, and despite occasional differences between precept and practice, we may proudly point to Biblical commandments as paving the way for racial equality. Thus Leviticus XV 34 reads: 'The stranger that sojourneth with you shall be unto you as the home-born among you, and you shall love him as theyself, for ye were strangers in the land of Egypt'. Again, to quote Exodus XII 49: 'One law shall be to him that is home-born and unto the stranger that sojourneth among you' (Kohler 1909: 155).

Although it is usually easy to dismiss such religious rhetoric as hollow, in Kohler's case it reveals the thread that runs throughout his career: as he was clearly, and for the most part unheralded, an unparalleled champion of the rights of Asians and other racially-suspect groups. His grandfather, in fact, had been hounded out of his pulpit in Baltimore in 1861 for his strident abolitionist stand.

In an article entitled 'The Un-American Character of Race Legislation' (1909), as well as in several other articles and addresses, Kohler foreshadowed the rhetoric of Meyer London, albeit without a socialist dimension. Kohler railed against 'a constant reign of terror for all Chinese or alleged Chinese residents, laborers or non-laborers. Their liberty is constantly jeopardized by harsh and oppressive laws', and many contend 'that they are beyond the protection of our laws. Only one who, like the writer, has become familiar in practice with the injustice and barbarity of these laws in their actual practice and workings, can realize that such practices can exist amid our boasted American civilization' (Kohler 1909: 139). Although much of the historiography infers that the immigrant generation of East Europeans and German Jewry were totally separate, or only met in conflict, this issue may be the exception that proves the rule. In fact, both Isaac Hourwich and Max Kohler served on the U.S. Senate Committee on the 'Illiteracy of Jewish Immigrants and Its Causes', which served as a basis for relieving Jews from being scrutinized according to excessively biased criteria for a crucial decade before the Johnson Acts. Interestingly, although Hourwich seems to be the only 'downtown Jew' on the committee, the report appears to be largely his handiwork (Kohler 1909: 200–28). In several articles and briefs Kohler had used Hourwich's scholarship to buttress his claims (Kohler 1909: 81, 283, 291, 294).

Such was the general environment, then, that influenced the Jews' suspicious gaze at immigration restriction legislation. Over a period of decades, beginning in the last years of the nineteenth century, vocationally and class-based Jewish politics melded with the more expressly ethnic-national and political forms of Jewish politics, as class and language affiliation no longer bound Jews in the same way. The immigration-restriction movement must have helped to propel Jews who were previously not enamoured of Zionism, into its orbit by the late 1930s. Jews with experience in organised labour knew that the doors to their own country were locked; the fight was long lost. They also were aware that labour, overall, was set against relieving the bar on immigration. Furthermore, in that the Jewish settlement in Palestine was being led by the progressive-labour element in its midst, it was possible to transfer one's class loyalty to the dominant group in Zionism. Indeed, Zionism had long been equipped to recruit and sustain members whose ties to the movement were experienced vicariously.

As Jews became less working class and Yiddish-speaking, and as their status was threatened in Central Europe, Zionism was left as one of the more viable alternatives for an affirmatively Jewish, moderately politicised form of self-identification. The right to emigrate to America, to all intents and purposes, had vanished. Rather than 'stabilizing' the Jews, the U.S. government's '[c]losing the door to Europeans' (Montgomery 1989: 462) and Asians made them more anxious, and open to other means of alleviating the plight of their brethren who remained in Europe. In the decades before the 1930s and 1940s, American Jews in organised labour had been pioneering a new orientation in politics and culture that would come to be seen as the very hallmark of ethnic politics in the modern world. This emerged from a complicated matrix of perceptions and policies, beyond their inner-group dynamics and their own relationship with greater powers. At times they were moved by their view of those other 'Orientals' in the American concoction, an increasingly complicated mixture that would continue to sizzle and brew.

## Notes

1. Kohler 1909: 155. I wish to thank Ari Zolberg for directing me to this important source.
2. Cf. Alexander 1998, an attempted critical biography from a neo-conservative perspective which fails miserably as a biography and analysis of Howe's views.
3. Entry for 'Cahan, Abraham (1860–1951)', in *Encyclopaedia Judaica*, 14.
4. Entry for 'Cahan, Abraham (1860–1951)', in *Encyclopaedia Judaica*, p. 15.
5. Epstein 1971: 50; see Frankel 1981: 506f., for an amusing critical view.

# References

Alexander, Edward, 1998, *Irving Howe: Socialist, Critic, Jew*, Bloomington.

Archdeacon, Thomas J., 1983, *Becoming American: An Ethnic History*, New York.

Barth, Gunther, 1964, *Bitter Strength: A History of the Chinese in the United States*, Cambridge, Mass.

Brodkin, Karen, 1998, *How Jews Became White Folks and What that Says about Race in America*, New Brunswick, N.J.

Carroll, Mollie Ray, 1923, *Labor and Politics: The Attitude of the American Federation of Labor toward Legislation and Politics*, Boston.

Cassedy, Steven, 1997, *To the Other Shore: The Russian Jewish Intellectuals Who Came to America*, Princeton.

Chiu, Ping, 1967, *Chinese Labor in California, 1850–1880: An Economic Study*, Madison.

Davis, David Brion, 1999, 'Jews and Blacks in America', *The New York Review of Books*, December 2.

Epstein, Melech, n.d., *Profiles of Eleven*.

Epstein, Melech, 1971, *Pages from a Colorful Life*, Miami Beach.

Feinstone, Morris C., 1938, 'A Brief History of the United Hebrew Trades', in Lang and Finestone, eds, 1938.

Frankel, Jonathan, 1981, *Prophesy and Politics: Socialism, Nationalism, and the Russian Jews, 1862–1917*, Cambridge.

Glenn, Susan A., 1990, *Daughters of the Shtetl: Life and Labor in the Immigrant Generation*, London.

Greene, Julie, 1998, *Pure and Simple: The American Federation of Labor and Political Activism, 1881–1917*, Cambridge.

Gyory, Andrew, 1998, *Closing the Gate: Race, Politics, and the Chinese Exclusion Act*, Chapel Hill and London

Heinze, Andrew R., 1990, *Adapting to Abundance: Jewish Immigrants, Mass Consumption, and the Search for American Identity*, New York.

Higham, John, 1984, *Send These to Me: Immigration in Urban America*, revised edn Baltimore.

Hollinger, David, 1995, *Postethnic America: Beyond Multiculturalism*, New York.

Howe, Irving, 1976, *World of Our Fathers: The Journey of the East European Jews to America and the Life they Found and Made*, New York.

Hourwich, Isaac A., 1912, *Immigration and Labor: The Economic Aspects of European Immigration to the United States*, New York.

Hourwich, Isaac [A.], 1917, in *Oysgevhlte shriftn*, New York.

Hurwitz, Maximillian, 1936, *The Workmen's Circle: Its History, Ideals, Organization and Institutions*, New York.

Jacobson, Matthew Frye, 1995, *Special Sorrows: The Diasporic Imagination of Irish, Polish, and Jewish Immigrants in the United States*, Cambridge, Mass.

Jacobson, Matthew Frye, 1998, *Whiteness of a Different Color: European Immigrants and the Alchemy of Race*, Cambridge, Mass.

Kohler, Max J., 1909, 'The UnAmerican Character of Race Legislation', originally in *Annals of the American Academy of Political and Social Science*, 84,2 (1909): 275–93, reprinted in *Immigration and Aliens in the United States: Studies of American Immigration Laws and the Legal Status of Aliens in the United States*, New York, 1936: 131–38 (cited according to the reprint edition).

Lang, Harry, and Morris Feinstone, eds, 1938, *Gewerkschaften: Jubilee Book*, New York.

Lorwin, Lewis L., 1933, *The American Federation of Labor: History, Policies, Prospects*, Washington D.C.

McCartin, Joseph A., 1997, *Labor's Great War: The Struggle for Industrial Democracy and the Origins of Modern American Labor Relations, 1912–1921*, Chapel Hill.

Mink, Gwendolyn, 1986, *Old Labor and New Immigrants in American Political Development: Union, Party, and State, 1875–1920*, Ithaca.

Montgomery, David, 1989, *The Fall of the House of Labor: The workplace, the state, and American labor activism, 1865–1925*, Cambridge.

Parmet, Robert D., 1987, *Labor and Immigration in Industrial America*, Malabar, Fl.

Peffer, George, 1999, *If They Don't Bring Their Women: Chinese Female Immigration before Exclusion*, Urbana and Chicago

Reiss, Albert J., n. d., *Introduction to* On Cities *and* Social Life, by Lewis Wirth, Chicago.

Rischin, Moses, 1977, *The Promised City: New York's Jews, 1870–1914*, Cambridge, Mass.

Rogoff, Harry, 1930, *An East Side Epic: The Life and Work of Meyer London*, New York.

Rogoff, Hillel, 1954, *Der Gayst fun Forverts* [The Spirit of the Forward], New York.

Sachar, Howard M., 1992, *A History of the Jews in America*, New York.

Sanders, Ronald, 1969, *The Downtown Jews: Portraits of an Immigrant Generation*, New York.

Saxton, Alexander, 1971, *The Indispensable Enemy: Labor and the Anti-Chinese Movement in California*, Berkeley.

*Selected Address and Papers of Simon Wolf: A Memorial Volume, Together with a Biographical Sketch*, 1926, Cincinnati.

Sorin, Gerald, 1992, *A Time for Building: The Third Migration*, Baltimore.

Taft, Philip, 1957, *The AF of L in the Time of Gompers*, New York.

Tomlins, Christopher L., 1985, *The State and the Unions: Labor Relations, Law, and the Organized Labor Movement in America, 1880–1960*, Cambridge.

Vladeck, B. Charney, 1938, 'The Gewerkschaften Celebrates a Half-Century', in *Gewerkschaften: Jubilee Book*, eds Harry Lang and Morris Fieinstone New York.

# Chapter 17

# Races at the Gate
## *Racial Distinctions in Immigration Policy*
## *A Comparison between France and the*
## *United States*

*Patrick Weil*

The United States of America is a country where, throughout its history, the vast majority of citizens have been immigrants or descendants of immigrants. France is a 'country of immigration' where large numbers of foreigners have settled as permanent residents, but where (as in all European Union countries today) there is a dominant sense that the immigrants have joined a core, majority, population that has existed since time immemorial. Despite this difference, French and American immigration policies can be compared. France is the oldest country of immigration in Europe, which has received a significant number of immigrants since the middle of the nineteenth century and, like the U.S., faced a 'nationalisation' of immigration control at the end of nineteenth century. In fact, as this volume demonstrates, immigration control existed in Europe and United States throughout the nineteenth century. At points of entry into the U.S., severe state laws against convicts, paupers, aliens with contagious diseases and free black men were enforced (Neuman 1996: 19–43). But the main mechanisms of control remained social and economic, automatically imposed by the cost of transport and facilitated by the fact that boats and harbours were essentially the only way to enter U.S. territory. At the end of the nineteenth century, in response to the rapid increase of flows favoured by the decrease of transportation costs, the federal government took direct responsibility for immigration control.

A government agency was created: the name, organization and departmental affiliation of which changed over time. Today it is the Immigration and Naturalization Service, Department of Justice. During the same period, France also had various mechanisms designed to restrict and control immigration. Beginning in January 1887, France required newcomers to be recorded in a census, and in the following year all immigrants were asked to make themselves known to their local authorities. In 1893, the state imposed a specific census for all foreign workers – immigrants were required to register on a particular list at their town halls. Beginning a decade later with an agreement with Italy in 1904, France signed a number of conventions with various countries of emigration that further regulated immigration.

A debate on the mechanisms for implementing controls also took place in both countries. Roughly speaking, the debate was organized around two options: an 'egalitarian' or 'universalistic' selection based on individual qualifications (physical, mental, moral, and eventually educational), or a 'racialist' selection based on national or ethnic origin (Divine 1957: 5).

In the U.S., the racialist approach gained strength in the years following the end of the Civil War (1870 onwards) and officially dominated U.S. policy from the 1920s through to 1965.

In France, despite the strong attraction of the U.S. national and racial origin system for political leaders and policy-makers in the 1930s, and even after the Second World War, the racialist approach was eventually rejected in what still forms the basis of French immigration policy, the ordinance of October 18, 1945. Why did the U.S. choose the national origin system and France did not? Often, cultural predispositions – French republicanism versus American multiculturalism – are presented as the explicative variable, but this does not fit the facts. France was about to adopt the American model of national origin in 1945. General de Gaulle, who considered the need for a coherent immigration policy a priority, favoured such a system of selection. On the other hand, at the beginning of the century, Theodore Roosevelt considered implementing the 'French' approach. To develop a better understanding of what happened on both sides of the Atlantic, one must adopt a bottom-up perspective that carefully analyses the development of immigration selection through the institutionalisation, the legitimisation and the implementation of distinctions within the 'white race', in order to get a new understanding of what happened on both sides of the Atlantic. By studying this debate in France and in the U.S., one can try to understand the different outcomes.

## The United States

The creation and implementation of a 'list of races and peoples' by the Immigration Bureau played a major role in the victory of the racialist approach. While new arrivals had long been asked to report their country of origin, it was not until the end of the nineteenth century that authorities began to compile statistics classifying immigrants on explicitly ethnic grounds. The list of races and people, which provided the basis for the development of these racial statistics by the Immigration Bureau, was drafted by an internal committee led by Edward McSweeney, Assistant Commissioner of Immigration at Ellis Island and approved by the Commissioner of Immigration, Terence Powderly. It was implemented on July 1, 1898 and remained in effect until 1952. The list included: African (black), Armenian, Bohemian, Moravian, Bulgarian, Serbian, Montenegrin, Chinese, Croatian and Slovenian, Cuban, Dalmatian, Bosnian and Herzegovian, Dutch and Flemish, East Indian, English, Filipino, Finnish, French, German, Greek, Hebrew, Irish, Italian (north), Italian (south), Japanese, Korean, Lithuanian, Magyar, Mexican, Pacific Islander, Polish, Portuguese, Russian, Ruthenian (Russnik), Scandinavian (Norwegians, Danes & Swedes). After 1898, all aliens who had already had to answer a question about their country of origin now also had to indicate their 'race or people'.[1]

Prior to the creation of this list, racial discrimination against black immigrants had been removed in the aftermath of the Civil War. Yet, at the same time it was imposed against Asians: in naturalisation law by the Nationality Act of 1870, which ensured that Asian immigrants could not be naturalized; and in immigration law by the Chinese Exclusion Act of May 6, 1882 (22 Stat. 58). But with regard to other immigrants, mainly white Europeans, immigration selection was still based on the individual 'qualities' of newcomers. The Immigration Act of 1882 imposed a head tax of 50 cents on each immigrant and forbade the entrance of idiots, lunatics, convicts, and persons likely to become public charges.[2] In 1885, the contract labour law was approved to prevent the entry of cheap foreign labour. In 1891, polygamists, persons convicted of crimes involving 'moral turpitude' and those suffering contagious disease were excluded. An Omnibus Act of 1903 added epileptics, insane persons, professional beggars and anarchists.[3]

The creation of the list of races by the Immigration Bureau, working without the oversight of the U.S. Congress or any scientific authority, introduced for the first time in American history racial distinctions and statistics within the 'white race'. Soon after its creation, Congress was convinced of the 'value' of the list: in 1901, a Congressional committee, the Industrial Commission on Immigration and Education, concluded that 'the most important improvement since 1893 in the method of compiling statistics of immigration was introduced in 1899, when instead of the preceding classification of immigrants according to the countries or political divisions from which they came, they were classified according to the races to which they belonged. [...] For example it appeared that, in 1898, 40,000 Russians came to the United States, whereas the great majority of these were Poles or Jews, probably not over 200 being actually Russians'.[4] In March 1903, Congress approved this bureaucratic innovation, mandating classification by race of all aliens entering the U.S. (Act of March 3, 1903; 32 Stat. 1213). At this point, the list of 'races and peoples' started a double career.

On the one hand, it produced 'race-based' statistics, which legitimised a racial hierarchy of assimilation and was a major contribution to the victory of a new approach in American immigration policy. On the other hand, it became a discretionary tool that survived, despite criticisms, as an unofficial instrument of racial discrimination, when the law did not always permit such bias.

The list of 'races and peoples' provided nativists and eugenicists with evidence for their arguments (Fitzgerald 1996: 126). The list became the main tool used by the Immigration Restriction League, created in Boston in 1894 by three Harvard College graduates, Charles Warren, Robert DeCourcy Ward, and Prescott Farnsworth Hall with the legislative backing of Massachusetts Senator Henry Cabot Lodge. The league campaigned for immigration restriction by origin, which they suggested could be accomplished through the use of a literacy test. Prescott Hall, the executive secretary of the League, immediately endorsed the McSweeney system: 'the new classification is more valuable for many purposes than the old. ...../....While the average illiteracy of Austro-Hungarians last year was 25.2 percent, the Bohemians show only 3.3 percent and while the average illiteracy of all Italians was over 53 percent we find that of Northern Italians (i.e. those from Tuscany, Emilia, Liguria, Venice, Lombardy, Piemont, and natives resident in other countries) to be only 11.4 percent...../..... Although Russian Jews and German Jews differ from each other they differ more from the Russians and the Germans, and for the first time it is possible to tell the total Hebrew immigration' (Hall 1899: 183–85). In the following years, Hall systematically used the new racial statistics in the annual publications of its League in order to demonstrate the inferiority of certain races. For instance, in his book *Immigration and its Effects upon the United States* (Hall 1906), Hall relied extensively on the statistics that the Bureau of Immigration had published since 1899.

Later, in 1907, the Dillingham Commission, a Congressional Committee that had spent four years evaluating immigration and assimilation policies in the U.S., retained the entire 1898 list of 'races and peoples', only adding after the item 'West Indians', 'except Cuban'.[5] The Commission made extensive use of a list of 'races and peoples', publishing a list of principal races for countries of birth in order to aid the research of those working on the Commission's report. France appeared with French and Hebrew, England with English, Hebrew, Irish, Scotch and Welsh, Greece with Greek and Macedonian, Bulgaria with Bulgarian and Macedonian, Belgium with Dutch, Flemish and French, and so on.[6] These categories were used to collect an extraordinary amount of information on various aspects of immigration for the purpose of demonstrating the inferior capacity of certain races and peoples, primarily from Eastern and Southern Europe, to integrate into U.S. society (Fuchs 1990: 64). The influence of the forty-two volumes of the Dillingham Commission Report on the future course of immigration policy was enormous. As a result of the Commission's conclusions, further restrictions on Asian immigration were included in the Immigration Act of 1917. The 1917 Act also incorporated the literacy test, for which advocates of immigration restriction had worked so long and hard since it had first been suggested before the Senate in 1895 by the aforementioned Senator Cabot Lodge. The literacy test provision simply required that all adult aliens seeking admission as immigrants be able to read and write but the purpose of the test was to select immigrants on the basis of their 'race'. For example, the statistics on immigrants admitted during the year 1907 showed different illiteracy rates, according to 'racial' origin: 30 percent of Greeks, 37 percent of Croats and Slovenes, 47 percent of Russians, 45 percent of Serbs, Bulgarians or Montenegrins, 52 percent of Dalmatians, Bosnians and Italians (south), 34 percent of Romanians, 33 percent of Spanish, and 30 percent of 'Hebrew' applicants; compared to 10 percent of Poles, 7.1 percent of Germans, 2 percent of French, and 1.4 percent of English of fourteen years old and over.[7] It was soon adopted by both the House and Senate, but vetoed by President Grover Cleveland and all subsequent presidents until Wilson's veto was overridden by Congress in 1917. But the 1917 literacy test soon engendered

significant opposition by disrupting American labour markets:
Canadian and Mexican labourers who were previously able to
cross the border and work in the farms of Maine, Vermont, Texas,
Louisiana, and Arizona were suddenly submitted to this new test,
which the majority of them failed.[8] The new act was also a disap-
pointment to those who had adopted it for a different reason:
literacy rates among newcomers had increased since 1907, and
most immigrants of 'undesirable' origins were now able to pass
the test.

After the First World War, deteriorating economic conditions
and the increasing flows of immigrants contributed to the
passage first Quota Act in 1921 which represented the formal
introduction of a hierarchy of desirability within 'white Europeans', with Western Europeans' quotas ahead of those of
Eastern or Southern Europe. This Act had two goals: (1) for the
first time in U.S. history, a numerical limit was placed on the
total number of immigrants admitted per year, about 350,000; (2)
complementarily, the immigrants were selected by nationality: an
annual quota was assigned to each foreign state, calculated on
the basis of 3 percent of the number of this state's natives living
in the United States according to the 1910 census. In 1924, the
Johnson Reed Act, which remained in effect until 1965, provided
for the calculation of quotas on the basis of the national origin
of all Americans, thus creating higher quotas for the more 'desirable' immigrants since their 'co-nationals' represented a greater
portion of the American population.[9] This evolution was interesting. Under the first system of quotas, the U.S. was still
selecting 'foreigners'; under the second, they were looking for
'similars'. In fact, under the new legislation, which created the
most efficient and centralised system of restriction, candidates
not only had to fit into the confines of a national quota, but they
also had to fulfil two other conditions: belong to a race eligible
for naturalization (Asians were therefore eliminated) (Ngai
1999), and be deemed 'unlikely to be a public charge'.[10]

When it was adopted in 1924, the new legislative system represented a victory for the racialist approach in U.S. immigration
policy, to which those who made use of the list of 'races and
peoples' had contributed. This brings us to a second question:
why did the list remain in effect after the victory of the national
origin system, despite constant criticism, and why was it only
abandoned in 1952? As the list was maintained for more than fifty
years after its creation and for more than twenty-five years after
the restrictive legislation of 1924, I argue that it remained useful
to advocates of the racialist approach in American immigration

policy. One can find an indication of its purpose in the way the list was managed: after requests to alter the list, the Immigration Service adopted different strategies. They would now accept changes to the list only if these modifications would not merge 'desirable' and 'undesirable' races and peoples (more precisely Jews and non-Jews, Blacks and Whites) in the same category.

Immediately after the list was introduced in 1898, the majority of American Jewish Organisations disapproved of the creation of a Hebrew race. In a memo written in 1903, the Department of Labor and Commerce mentioned that while American Jews were divided on whether or not they constituted a race, they almost all agreed that they should not be classified as such by the Immigration Bureau. In fact, before the Second World War, the term race was frequently employed to mean a people or ethnicity. Yet, for Immigration officials, the justification of having 'Hebrews' among the list of races and peoples was that the Jews were not a people or an ethnicity but a race in a biological sense of the term. To justify this assertion, the Immigration Bureau often quoted Cyrus Adler who had written in the Jewish Encyclopedia: 'An even more delicate problem that presented itself at the very outset was the attitude to be observed by the encyclopedia in regard to these Jews who, while born within the Jewish community have for one reason or another abandoned it. As the present work deals with Jews as a race, it was found impossible to exclude those who were of that race, whatever their religious affiliation may have been'.[11] The Dillingham commission made good use of this quotation.[12] On several occasions, official answers reaffirmed that the Hebrews were a race and that even when converting to another religion, a Hebrew remained a 'Hebrew'.

After 1918, the list came under attack from foreign governments, successively Yugoslavia, Italy, Brazil, Mexico, Latvia, and so forth. When asked to add the Brazilian race to the existing list in 1925, William W. Husband, Commissioner-General of Immigration chose to stand firm in the defence of the list: 'The record of races or peoples, dating as it does from 1899 is by far the most valuable immigration data we have, and the Bureau feels very strongly that any change in the long established practice ought to be made only after the most careful consideration, and then only when it is of scientific value to our own statistical records, or at least is not detrimental to them'.[13]

Yet, on 11 September 1936,[14] the Albanian, Estonian, Filipino, and Latvian races were added to the list. North and South Italians were merged into one Italian race, and the 'African (Black)' became a Negro. The INS gave reasons for the latter change. The term 'African black' was not 'commonly used' anymore and 'very few aliens of this race come from or go to Africa. The vast majority of the number recorded come from the West Indies, it seems advisable to list them as "Negroes"'. The merger of the two 'Italian races' was done 'with respect to the Italian people',[15] probably under pressure from Benito Mussolini's government. And, in order to justify the addition of some European races, the INS took the creation of six new countries since the First World War into account. On 31 July 1937 the INS decided to classify 'Mexicans' as 'White', in order to satisfy the Mexican government's complaints about the 'Mexican' race. On 12 August 1937, following a request from the North American Manx Association asking for the inclusion of Manx in the list ('The Manx are Celtic, but distinct from the Irish, Welsh, Scotch and English [...] They are obliged to call themselves English which is not entirely accurate'), the 'Manx' race was added to the list.[16]

In the same year, the Brazilian authorities asked that Brazilian newcomers be called 'Brazilians'. This demand was rejected once again. The INS gave partial satisfaction to the Brazilian government only in March 1942[17]: Latin Americans replaced Spanish Americans.[18] With this modification, the Immigration Service permitted white, Portuguese-speaking Brazilians to be classified in a new way, while at the same time it avoided placing them in the same category as 'Blacks', which the creation of a 'Brazilian' race would have done.

The term Hebrew was finally removed on 8 November 1943[19] by Earl G. Harrison. Named INS commissioner on 20 July 1942, Harrison asked Dr. Henry B. Hazard, Director of Research and Education in the INS, to review the question of the Hebrew race on 17 September 1942.[20] The forty-six pages of the Hazard memorandum, given to Harrison on 5 November 1942, were very definite in their conclusions[21]: 'The enlargement of the classification of the groups of aliens coming to the United States to include "peoples" appears to have been made arbitrarily, possibly because of the difficulty in determining just what the term "race" might imply'. (p. 41) ..... the term "race" as such is not defined in either the immigration or nationality laws of the United States', although 'certain specified racial groups (not including the Hebrews) are debarred from immigration to and naturalization in the United States'. He proceeded to note that 'the scientists are in hopeless confusion and contradiction as to the criteria of "race" and what particular groups of persons constitute "races" and that 'there are no final and comprehensive judicial definitions of "race" and particularly not of the term "Hebrews"'. His final argument for removing the 'Hebrew race' from the list was political: 'The significance of racial differences [...] has lessened immeasurably [...] with peoples of innumerable origins now banded together in all quarters of the world fighting side by side with the United States for the establishment and maintenance of the Four Freedoms'.

If the term 'Hebrew race' was not repealed until late in the Second World War during 'a global battle against the dark forces of dictatorship, chaos, and destruction' (Hazard's memo) in which people of various ethnic origins throughout the world fought together as U.S. allies; and if the list of races and peoples continued to be maintained for several years after this epic war, with the explicit goal of having immigrants report their race,[22] one can only conclude that officials' selective response to pressure to alter the list had some 'policy' utility. Most of all, maintaining the racial categories within national origins permitted authorities to keep race-based records that could be used to justify separate management, discrimination, and exclusion on the basis of race rather than of national origin, most notably by claiming that certain races were especially likely to be a public charge (LPC).

Already at the beginning of the century, an Immigration Bureau study was used to demonstrate that, during the four years 1899, 1900, 1901 and 1902,

> the percentage [of Jews] debarred because of disease was nearly twice that of other races, and the percentage of those receiving treatment in hospitals after landing was two-thirds more than of other races. The Hebrews had but $8 per capita upon arrival, as against $16 for other races, and but 2% has been in this country before as against 13% of other races..../... By occupation, they also differ greatly, having proportionately about ten times as many tailors, tobacco manufacturers, shoemakers and persons of that class of vocation, with very few tillers of the soil. Thus it will be seen that the Hebrew comes to stay, and brings with him his family, and his children, which are numerous; that he is usually poor and often afflicted with disease and goes to the shops and trades of the large cities.[23]

The same kind of statistics produced in the 1930s could have justified the prejudice that the LPC clause applied to Jewish applicants for immigration more than to others. There were no written instructions to this effect, but in this area it was common to apply oral instructions. An American consul-general in Tirana (Albania) 'soon realized the obvious fact that the whole secret of the work lies in the interpretation of existing written law and regulations and that this interpretation can only be learned by word of mouth from other officers who have themselves been taught and had experience'. When a new instruction more favorable to Jewish immigrants was finally published in December 1936 after pressure from the Labor Department and American Jewish Organisations, it made him feel 'that all my interpretative training received since my arrival at this post is in almost every detail directly in contradiction with the policy of interpretation and decision expounded in the Department's instruction of December 30. I was taught among other things that "the public charge provisions should be stringently applied" since it is the Department's desire to keep immigration to a minimum in view of unemployment and that affidavits of relatives who could not be legally held for support were of very little value as evidence in rebuttal of the likelihood of L.P.C. I was told that "the department will support you to the limit in L.P.C. refusals"'.[24] National quotas were never filled in the 1930s, despite the needs of hundreds of thousands of European Jewish refugees escaping Nazi oppression (Breitman & Kraut 1987; Divine 1957). In 1933, 23,068 aliens were admitted to the U.S. (compared to 805,228 in 1921), the lowest level since 1831.

## France

At the end of the 1930s, a climate of economic crisis and the impending arrival of refugees brought France to the verge of adopting a national and racial quota policy also based on a list of 'races and peoples' built on a hierarchy of assimilability. Indeed, the U.S. approach was the main proposal of the two most renowned French immigration specialists of the period, René Martial and Georges Mauco.

Dr René Martial emerges as a figure of primary importance among the racist immigration specialists in France during this period.[25] Born in 1873, Dr Martial obtained his medical degree in 1900 and soon began specializing in public health matters. Beginning in 1909, in his capacity as director of the hygiene office of Douai, he took a keen interest in immigration. In this post, he had the opportunity to see and treat numerous immigrant workers who worked in and around the region's mines or who were in transit towards other destinations. During the First World War, he established an office of sanitation regulation for Spanish migrants who had come to work in France's Eastern Pyrenees. After the war, Martial spent three years as director of public health services in the city of Fez, Morocco. Responsible for the course on Immigration at the Hygienic Institute at the School of

Medicine in Paris, he published in 1931 a *Traité de l'immigration et de la greffe inter-raciale*, and then, in 1934, *La race française*.

Two principal aspects of the American method of selecting immigrants seemed appropriate him: the individual inspection of immigrants at entry points (principally Ellis Island at the entrance to New York), and the mechanism for selecting immigrants from the 'white race' according to ethnic and national origins through quotas. Martial proposed the creation of five 'land ports' of inspection for immigrants on the French border. However, he could not propose an exact replication of the American quota system in France. The American system was based upon calculating the proportion of each race or nationality in the U.S., but this was not possible for a country like France. However, in 1928, Martial believed he had found the solution for selecting immigration to France based upon ethnic origins.

For Martial, immigration was like a mixture or transfusion with the same effect on a people as on the blood of a person who had received a blood transfusion. He claimed that the 'blood affinity' was the essential criterion because 'categorization based on blood underpins psychology'. According to Martial, each people had a 'biochemical index' which was a function of the proportion of each blood group in the population and was calculated in the following manner:

$$\text{Proportion of people with blood types } \frac{A + AB}{B + AB}$$

Just as incompatibilities exist between individual donors and receivers – one does not transfuse the blood of someone with type A to someone with type 0 – Martial claimed that populations could not successfully assimilate immigrants if the biochemical compatibility between the receiving population and the immigrant population was not taken into account. The proportion of blood group B increased markedly in going from northwest to southeast Europe, and thus Martial's coefficients decreased in the same direction as follows: English, 4.5; Belgians, 4.4; Alsatians, 4.01; Swedes, 3.7; French, 3.2; Germans, 3.1; Dutch, 3.01; Scots, 2.7; Italians, 2.6; Danes, 2.4; Czechs, 2.4; Greeks, 2.25; Armenians, 2.01; Jews, 1.6; Arabs, 1.6; Russians, 1.4; Poles, 1.2; Negroes (American), 0.9 (Taguieff, 1999: 313).

According to Martial, the population mixing that resulted from immigration could not have a good result unless it took place between peoples with similar biochemical indices (Martial 1934: 306–307). Martial therefore supported racial selection of immigrants based upon this index. The decision to permit immigration and thus 'race mixing' must affect 'a very limited number of peoples, immigrant families should from now on be selected individually and in an ordered fashion based upon blood grouping to retain persons in categories 0 and A, to eliminate those in B, and to only keep those in AB whose psychological and sanitary examinations are favourable' (Martial 1935: 287–288).

Martial wrote a great deal, participated in numerous conferences, and was widely known and quoted. Nevertheless, he was not taken very seriously when he attempted to transform his ideas into concrete policy proposals. This official rejection did not affect Georges Mauco, who published a doctoral thesis entitled *Les Etrangers en France, leur rôle dans l'activité économique* in 1932, and who was soon considered the pre-eminent expert on immigration questions in France.[26]

In his thesis, Mauco described the evolution of migratory flows to France throughout recent years in great detail, as well as the distribution of immigrants in society according to their places of settlement, their professions, and their countries of origin. Evaluating migratory phenomena in the evolution of the French population, he analysed the 'assimilability' of immigrants according to their origins. In order to measure this assimilability, he re-examined a 'mini-survey' that had been carried out in 1926 with the assistance of the service directors of an important automobile construction company that employed 17,229 workers, of whom 5,074 were North African. A classification of the aptitudes according to nationality was thus created, 'the scores being given out of 10, the maximum, which applied to very good French workers'. Notations about the workers included their physical capabilities, the consistency of their work, their production, their level of discipline, and their comprehension of the French language. The composite score based on these criteria put the Arab workers at the lowest rung of the ladder, with a score of 2.9, then Greeks at 5.2, next Armenians, Poles and Spaniards at 6.3, 6.4, and 6.5 respectively, and finally the Italians, Swiss and Belgians, who came in the lead with scores of 7.3, 8.5, and 9. In 1932, Mauco was discreet in the expression of his beliefs.

During the Second World War, he openly began to express his racism and his anti-Semitism. On 3 September 1941, Mauco offered testimony before the Supreme Court of Justice sitting in Riom[27] to judge the leaders of the Third Republic, which he published almost verbatim in 1942 in *L'Ethnie française*, a journal directed by Montandon: 'The egalitarian tendencies of governments [during the Third Republic] prevented them from acting to ensure the ethnic protection of the country' (Mauco 1942: 6). Moreover, 'Of all the foreigners who arrive in France, refugees are the most undesirable. First, because this immigration is imposed, next because these immigrants pose the greatest problems from ethnic, sanitary and economic points of view' (PV Riom: 3). He also described the ethnic characteristics of Russians, Armenians and Jews that rendered them, in increasing order, less and less assimilable. 'All the particular disadvantages of immigration appear can be seen in considering Jewish refugees. Their physical health, morality, and character are all of diminished capacity.../....They have souls fashioned for great humiliations under servile conditions, where the hate they cannot express disguises itself as obsequiousness...../......Their character deficit ..../.... is grave because it is the product not only of the individual's education and social milieu, but in part due to heredity. Modern psychology – and especially psychoanalysis – has demonstrated that these traits, transmitted by the parents during the earliest years of the child, modify the child's unconscious and cannot be changed except after several generations under normal conditions that allow the subject to entirely escape the influence of the hereditary surroundings' (Mauco 1942: 14).

At the end of the war, Georges Mauco once again demonstrated a greater level of discretion. In the beginning of 1944, he joined the French Resistance and participated in the liberation of the quarter of Auteuil in Paris. When a High Population Council (HPC) was created in April 1945, Mauco was named its secretary-general, a position that he held until 1970. It is probable that his activities in collaborating with the Vichy regime were not known. In this post, which kept him in contact with Charles de Gaulle, the head of the government, Mauco was responsible for proposing a new policy of immigration and of naturalization.

Taking inspiration from the studies developed in 1944 within a Vichy government committee, in the course of collaboration between the French Foundation for the Study of Human Problems directed by Alexis Carrel and the General Delegation of National Activity, Mauco convinced the HPC to adopt a 'general directive' on 18 May 1945[28] that planned to subordinate the entry of individuals to the general interests of the nation based on 'ethnic, sanitary, demographic and geographic conditions'. The first criterion, that of ethnicity, revolved around an order of 'desirability' which was to be determined based upon the nationality of foreigners living in France in the censuses conducted between 1881 and 1891 (here, one cannot help think that the American law of 1921 was a determining influence). The first peoples in order of 'desirability' were 'the Nordics': Belgians, Luxemburgers, Dutch, Swiss, Danes, Scandinavians, Finns, Irish, English, Germans and Canadians. Their proportion of the immigrant population would be 50 percent. The second group on this ladder of desirability – who would account for 30 percent of immigration – would be people from the Mediterranean, provided they came from the North of each country: Spaniards from Austurias, Leon, Aragon and Galicia as well as Basques, Catalonians and those from Navarre; Italians from Lombardy, Piedmont, the Veneto, Liguria, Emilia and Tuscany; Portuguese from the region of Beira. Finally, Slavs – Czechoslovaks, Poles, and Yugoslavs would represent 20 percent of newcomers. The introduction in France of 'all immigrants of other origins' should be, according to Mauco, strictly limited to 'only individual cases presenting an exceptional interest'. Finally, in order to prevent all Jewish immigration, Mauco proposed major restrictions on refugees.

All that remained was for Mauco to put his ideas into official legislation. This seemed easy, since these ethnic preferences were part of the dominant climate at the time (Le Bras 1994: 128), and were shared by all those participating in the aforementioned meeting where Mauco presented his ideas. De Gaulle had himself demonstrated his support by signing on a letter of 12 June 1945, prepared by Mauco, to the minister of justice asking the minister to give priority to the naturalizations of Nordics, Belgians, Luxemburgers, Dutch, Swiss, Danes, Scandinavians, Icelanders, English, Germans, etc. Finally, during this particular period of the Liberation, a law could, in the absence of Parliament, be rapidly adopted 'by ordinance' according to a procedure that, after the approval of the government, merely required the approval of the Council of State. The writings of the principal actors in the development of French immigration policy during this period – including Mauco, Cassin,[29] Sauvy, Tissier, and Parodi,[30] – demonstrate that, except for Cassin, Vice-President of the Council of State, and for Parodi, Minister of Labour, all those concerned clearly expressed their support for creating an ethnic hierarchy of immigrants, albeit to different degrees and based upon different factors.

Alfred Sauvy, former student of *the Ecole Polytechnique*, entered public administration in 1922 with the responsibility of producing statistics about France, and he became interested in questions of population and immigration shortly thereafter.[31] In 1946, Sauvy wrote in *Des Français pour la France*, 'An influx of Orientals, Levantines, Balkanites, etc [...] is far from being as desirable as that of Belgians and Dutch, or even Spaniards and

Italians. There again, one need not suggest a racial objection, but instead to remember that these [former] individuals are too far away from our civilization, which risks to be modified itself by contact with them'. (Sauvy 1946: 231). During the Liberation period, beginning on 4 April 1945, Sauvy was the secretary general of Family and Population at the Ministry of Public Health and Population. In this position, he coordinated the activities of different administrations responsible for immigration policy.

Pierre Tissier was the only member of the Council of State, to which he had been appointed in 1926, who was in London with General de Gaulle in June 1940. There, he became de Gaulle's chief of staff, then, in June 1943, he presided over the Committee of Legal Cases of Free France, working closely within René Cassin, who received the presidency of the Judicial Committee at the same time (de Gaulle 1983: 26). In London in 1942, Tissier wrote, in English, *The Government of Vichy*, a book of propaganda for Free France, in which he developed his views regarding population and immigration problems. Notably, in that text, he wrote that: 'The Jewish problem exists, even in France. It is an undeniable fact, and no realistic policy can be blind to it. It is not enough to say that the problem of the Jews is the problem of the Armenians, the Slavs, or the Arabs, for this is to disregard an essential factor. The Jewish race constitutes an international community. Among [its members] there is an absolute unity of language, of traditions, of intellectual and moral education' (Tissier 1942: 155). In this text, Tissier also demonstrated that he was in favour of a eugenics policy for his country: 'France should not have children at any cost and of any and every kind. She must turn to eugenics and – it is no use to shrink from the words – to the practice of properly controlled sterilization. This amounts to saying that marriage must be permitted only between individuals who are completely healthy and capable of producing healthy children; those who do not satisfy this condition should be allowed to contract a marriage after sterilization' (Tissier 1942: 157). Upon Liberation, he became director of the cabinet of the Socialist Interior Minister Adrien Tixier[32] and in this function actively participated in the creation of new immigration legislation.

While the discussions that took place regarding the objectives of immigration policy indicate that Sauvy, Tissier, and perhaps even Parodi and Cassin, thought in terms of ethnic preferences, their thoughts were not reduced to such considerations: in contrast to Mauco who thought entirely in these terms. Alfred

Sauvy, for instance, also conceived immigration policy as part of a broader populationist policy. Conforming to a long national tradition of concern over the continuing decrease of the French population,[33] Sauvy hoped to reverse this trend by increasing the birth rate, lowering the mortality rate, and encouraging immigration. He believed that immigrants' origins were important, but he was not obsessed by this issue. He thought that individual qualities were more important than ethnic origins in terms of a newcomer's capacity to assimilate. In short, for Sauvy, increasing France's population was of primary importance, so while it was better to have Italian immigrants than Turkish or Arab ones, it was better to have Turkish or Arab immigrants than no immigrants. For Mauco, on the other hand, ethnic origin determined the level of assimilability to such a degree that, except in rare cases, it was preferable to have no immigrants at all rather than Jews, Arabs, or individuals from Eastern Europe. It was thus in going against Mauco's opinion that Sauvy promulgated an official objective of France welcoming 300,000 foreigners annually.

However, Sauvy and Mauco agreed that a new agency should be created, the *Office National d'Immigration* (O.N.I.), which would determine: (1) A list of places of residence authorized or forbidden for all or parts of the foreign population, and (2) the number of immigrants that should be admitted into metropolitan France based upon nationality and professional qualification. Moreover, on the basis of various statutes, quantitative immigration designed to fill various vocational roles in the economy would be authorized on a temporary basis, but such foreigners would be repatriated almost automatically after one year. Only 'qualitative' immigrants, selected on their ethnicity and professional skills, would have the right to prolong their stay. Even this latter category was to be subjected to stringent state regulations: before they even attained the right to work, they had to undergo sanitary and physical and mental health checks; later, the state would continue to monitor closely their employment, housing, and any changes in their residence.

Tissier, however, reacted against these proposals for excessive regulation. As discussed above, he had indeed favoured eugenics in 1942, but he had wished to practise it without ethnic discrimination: he was an egalitarian and non-racist proponent of eugenics. This non-racist egalitarianism was also apparent in his 1942 work, in the way it conceived of proper behaviour towards foreigners. Tissier favoured treating all foreigners equally and believed in the possibility of assimilating them regardless of their ethnic origins. Here is what he added to his analysis of the Jewish 'problem' referred to above: 'Jews who have only recently acquired French nationality and who are unassimilated, must be subjected to the same measures of restriction as French subjects of recently acquired nationality who are unassimilated. To obtain French nationality in the future they must fulfil the same conditions as other foreigners' (Tissier 1942: 155).

In 1945, Tissier fought against the overly detailed restrictions on foreigners proposed by his colleagues. He offered the following response to Mauco's idea of requiring foreigners to inform authorities of any change in their place of residence: 'It is a source of constant difficulties that overwhelm and disorganize regulatory efforts. It gives, furthermore, a foreigner the feeling that he is perpetually being pursued'. Tissier succeeded in obtaining the withdrawal of this proposal. Similarly, Tissier was able to help create an official policy that provided those individuals who had obtained a temporary resident permit with a means of obtaining a permanent one. Nevertheless, the text approved by the government maintained a policy of recruiting immigrants based on their national origins under the auspices of the O.N.I.

One additional problem remained in the debate on immigration policy: the issue of refugees. Before the end of the war, in December 1944, the Interior Minister instituted a particular protection for refugees as distinct from other types of immigrants. The Director for Foreigners' Affairs at the Interior Ministry suggested to the Interior Minister that he propose that the government should allow refugees to benefit 'from a benevolent statute' attributed to the Foreign Affairs Ministry that would provide refugees a 'right to be admitted to France' that would facilitate 'their complete and real assimilation'. On the other hand, in his proposals regarding this subject, Mauco's racism clearly showed in his extremely restrictive proposals regarding refugees, whom he labelled 'fugitives'.[34] He convinced the High Committee to adopt a policy of requiring approval of both the Interior and Labour Ministries before asylum seekers and stateless persons could gain entry to France. Moreover, Mauco proposed that '[t]hose refugees, those fugitives, those stateless persons who become undesirable but who cannot be forced to leave French territory should be directed to "supervised work camps"'. Parodi and Tissier reacted strongly against this proposition. Parodi suggested that it is 'dangerous to re-introduce in our rules the principle of a work camp that frankly recalls Vichy institutions'. For Tissier, 'It appears completely inopportune ... to create ... centres of permanent internment where foreigners would be virtually refugees for life. Independently of all its other downsides, this seems as though it would jeopardize France's international reputation' Finally, these restrictive elements proposed by Mauco were removed. The text that the government submitted to the Council of State proposed that refugees should be treated in a manner similar to other foreigners.[35]

The text was thus submitted to the permanent commission of the Council of State presided by René Cassin. It was this commission, which, after having consulted the ministers or their cabinet – i.e. Parodi and Tissier – rather than the HPC, suppressed all reference to ministerial powers to regulate the ethnic or geographic origins of foreign immigrants. This commission also removed every mention of the status of refugees from the final text. It subsequently decided to grant refugees not only equal treatment, but in fact a special protective status guaranteed by the Geneva Convention of 1951.

The final immigration law that emerged from these various proceedings, the 2 November 1945 Act, which still constitutes the framework of French Immigration Policy, favoured the immigration not only of workers but also of their families. It organized an egalitarian, individualist, and progressive system of issuing permits without ethnic criteria for selection. And even though practice was to differ – the government could, for example, favour the recruitment of Italians over Turks by locating a public National Immigration Office in Milan and not in Istanbul – the French authorities would formally pay no heed to an immigrant's ethnic origins and thus treat a Turk and an Italian equally. Yet, this formal neutrality permitted authorities to maintain their immigration policy that still resulted in de facto discrimination well into the post-war period, despite the increasing acceptance of egalitarian and antiracist values, whereas the American national origin system was not abolished until 1965.

## Conclusions

Thus in the two countries, France and the United States, a list of races and peoples was institutionalised to different degrees. In the United States, the list served at once as a statistical tool and as an instrument for the selection of immigrants. Furthermore, in the United States, the statistics provided by the list were legitimised by law and fostered the adoption of legislation based upon the national origins of immigrants, and the list was probably utilized in practice as a complementary tool for racial selection when the law did not authorize it. In France, a similar list simply provided certain provisional indications in 1945 about the selection of immigrants and of naturalizations, but it was given no role in either law or practice. These different policy outcomes can be explained:

– When the selection of immigrants became an important part of public debate at the end of the nineteenth century, with the rapid industrialization of both countries, unions played a major role in defining the solution to the 'problem' of mass immigration (Collomp 1998: 13). In the U.S. as in France, other solutions were implemented before the racialist approach was chosen. But in the U.S. the union solution failed in limiting immigration, whereas in France it succeeded, at least temporarily.

In the U.S., unions had played an important role in the fight against the pre-recruitment of low-paid Chinese 'strike breakers' (Sandel 1996: 168–200), which led to the adoption of the 1882 Chinese Exclusion Act. A few years later, the Knights of Labor, the main workers' organization in the 1880s, played a major role in convincing Congress to adopt the Contract Labor Law in 1885. Previously, based on procedures first authorized in 1864 during the Civil War, employers had possessed the right to recruit workers in Europe and to have their first salaries pay the cost of their transatlantic transportation, which was considered to favour the massive immigration of cheap labour coming from 'new immigration' countries, i. e. from Eastern and Southern Europe. The union, on the other hand, supported a system in which workers should theoretically be able to negotiate their salaries freely with their employers upon arrival in the United States, a system which was implemented as a result of the Contract Labor Law and which unions hoped would discourage the influx of cheap foreign labour. This restrictive strategy corresponded to the values and philosophy not only of the American polity but also of American workers' unions who considered wage-labour a new form of slavery. Wage-labour was to be a temporary status, and the model of an American worker was to be a craftsman and an entrepreneur, a free man, as opposed to a slave. Yet, the U.S. unions' strategy failed to 'protect' domestic labour as employers rapidly found ways of circumventing the law. The decrease of transportation costs and the invention of the system of tickets which could be bought in the U.S. and sent to relatives across the Atlantic meant that the new legislation did not prevent the massive arrival of labourers ready to accept low pay.

In France, while authorities simply deported many 'undesirable' African and Asian colonial workers back to their colonies, the unions attempted to impose equality of salaries for foreign

workers in order to restrict European immigration. Influenced by
Marxism, the unions could support their proposals by claiming
that they valued the dignity of the working class and its power of
collective action and negotiation. The claim of equality of wages
was backed by the countries of origin where French companies
wanted to open recruitment offices; it was therefore under this
principle of equality of salaries that conventions were reached
with Italy and Belgium in 1904 and 1906 respectively and, in the
1920s, with Poland and Czechoslovakia (Weil 1995: 28–29).

Not only did the employer have to pay equal salaries to foreign
workers, he also had to pay for the cost of transportation and
often for housing. Theoretically, this arrangement would render
domestic labour more attractive than its foreign counterpart; and
this egalitarian approach sufficed to regulate immigration until
the beginning of the 1930s.

In the U.S., it was soon apparent that the Contract Labor Law
had not succeeded in drastically reducing immigration from
Eastern and Southern Europe. Hence, in 1906, at the personal
request of Theodore Roosevelt, several investigations were
commissioned from selected envoys of the Immigration Bureau.
Among these envoys was the former Commissioner-General
Powderly, who, in October 1906, reported the full details of his
findings. President Roosevelt invited him to the White House.
After the meeting, he sent a written memo to the President with
his primary proposal: the selection of immigrants abroad. To this
end, representatives of the U.S. immigration service should be
stationed in countries of emigration, with the consent of foreign
governments. 'Through a governmental agency the exact industrial condition of every town in the U.S. should be ascertained
every week or at most every two weeks .... It should be easy to
gather this information and impart it to newly landed immigrants as well as to our own people'.[36] However, this new system
of immigration selection never received congressional approval,
which instead moved towards a race-based approach under the
influence of the unions. In the U.S., the failure of non-racist,
individual liberty-oriented policies of control left the unions, in
their view, without any other strategy of 'protecting' domestic
labour other than explicitly racist policies.

– In the U.S., too, the institutionalisation of the racialist
approach was facilitated by the fact that at the decisive time of
the national debate on the subject, the 'racists' were not the only
individuals who supported classifying immigrants by races and
peoples. Rather, certain important anti-racist figures, persons
whom one would today call multiculturalists, unintentionally

legitimised the list. The example of two of the list's authors, Dr Moses Victor Safford, a proponent of a racist immigration policy, and McSweeney, who opposed such an approach, illustrates this point. Dr Safford was the secretary of the committee in charge of creating the list, and he was the one who designed the categorization of races and peoples.[37] Safford was trained as a physician and was in charge of a hospital when he was recruited at the end of the 1890s to serve as a Surgeon General at the Marine Hospital in Ellis Island. His responsibilities included the examination of new immigrants; he also acted as an interpreter since he was able to speak four languages and had a working knowledge of several others.[38] He believed in his talents to deal with different human 'races' (Safford 1925: 6f.). He was also a member of the Immigration Restriction League, which at the beginning of April 1921 actively campaigned to have him designated as the Immigration Commissioner for Boston.[39] McSweeney, who supported Safford regarding the creation of the list in 1898, became a fierce critic when Safford supported the racialist immigration laws of the 1920s. McSweeney appeared then as he did in 1903: a defender of the existence of racial – one would say today, cultural – identities, and therefore a partisan of a race-basis classification, but for purposes of description, not of exclusion (McSweeney 1905: 1–27). In fact, McSweeney was an active advocate of Irish independence; he would later organise the sojourn and campaign of DeValera when he sought support for the Irish Free State in the U.S. In 1898, with the list of races and peoples, he wanted the Irish to be counted separately from the English. But later, McSweeney became one of the leaders of the battle against the national origin quotas law of 1924. As Vice President of the American Irish Historical Association, he campaigned against a law with the purpose of reducing immigration from predominantly Catholic or Jewish countries (McSweeney 1926: 223); as President of the historical commission of the Knights of Columbus, he acted in various ways to promote 'multiculturalism', publishing for example W.E.B. DuBois's *Gift of Black Folk, The Negroes in the Making of America* (1924). He also wrote the preface to the book and an introduction on 'The racial contributions to the United States'. In the preface, he emphasised the diverse contributions of different 'races' to America against 'thinkers who assume that the United States of America is practically a continuation of English nationality'. He emphasised 'Negroes'' distinctive assets 'without which America could not have been'. In some ways, he tried to organise a coalition of Blacks, Catholics and Jews, i.e. of all minorities, which later became a key element of support for the Democratic Party. In the U.S., the racism of the restrictionists was camouflaged. Their racism could be made to tie in with one important principle of the American republic, namely the recognition of cultural pluralism, which helped them win allies who unwittingly aided the push for a racialist immigration policy.

In France, twenty-five years later, in the context of the aftermath of the Second World War and a clear need for immigration, adopting a racialist approach was only supported by those who actually wished to achieve racist ends, while individual anti-racists (like Cassin or Parodi) and even eugenicists (like Tissier) opposed it, arguing that any legislation which explicitly mentioned national origins as criteria for the selection of immigrants would too closely resemble Nazi ideology.

– Finally, and perhaps most importantly, in both countries, key civil servants played a major role in the choice of policy:

In the U.S., the civil service was linked with the unions, connected with racism in academia and was 'specialized'. Representative of this were the civil servants who were involved in the establishment of the list of races and peoples. Among the three who played major roles – Terence V. Powderly, Edward F. McSweeney and Moses Victor Safford – two were former union leaders. Before being named by the new Republican President William McKinley as Commissioner-General of Immigration on 1 July 1897, Terence Powderly had been General Master Workman of the Knights of Labor from 1879 until 1893.[40] Edward McSweeney, Assistant Commissioner of Immigration at Ellis Island since his nomination by Democratic President Grover Cleveland in 1893, had previously been the leader of a local section of the AFL, and continued to maintain a strong link to Samuel Gompers, the famous AFL president.[41] In preparing his list, McSweeney read Prescott Hall's books and made Powderly read them too. In his letter of 3 June 1898 to McSweeney, Powderly also acknowledged receiving 'a copy of the Harvard Law Review containing Mr. Hall's paper' and confirmed his recent trip to New York, the only purpose of which was a visit to Colonel Lee, one of the leaders of the Immigration Restriction League, with whom he spent a long afternoon in discussion.[42]

To implement its new policy, the Immigration Bureau had to work with a specialized committee created in 1889 in the U.S. Senate (Committee on Immigration), and in the House of Representatives (Committee on Immigration and Naturalization) (Wurtz 1925: 11–12). These committees proved to be easily influenced by the self-proclaimed immigration 'specialists' trained by the Immigration Restriction League, who designed new race-based immigration legislation (Tichenor 2002).

In France, where policymakers later seriously considered developing a racist immigration policy, such a policy was opposed by key civil servants who were not immigration specialists but generalist legal scholars, and were not closely tied to the unions. Parodi, Tissier, and finally Cassin, who were all members of the French Council of State, opposed the race-based project, even though it was backed by de Gaulle. It was, finally, partly chance that reference to national origins was not included in the French immigration law. While Mauco and his supporters deeply objected to the egalitarian amendments added by the Council of State, they worried that trying to challenge these provisions would ensure that no immigration legislation was adopted before the first postwar Parliament convened, and they were worried that the left-wing majority of the new Parliament would develop an immigration policy that they would find even more distasteful.

In short, an examination of the history of American and French immigration policy clearly indicates that the specific historical context, the strategies of major actors such as unions, and the perspectives of key civil servants – rather than theoretical differences in political culture – were responsible for the United States' implementation of a racialist immigration policy for much of the twentieth century and France's use of a more egalitarian approach. Later on, after the racist approach became de-legitimised by the Nazi policies of the Second World War, and in the context of de-colonization, the United States Congress abandoned its racialist policies by repealing the national origins system in 1965. Had the wishes of France's leader Charles de Gaulle been followed in 1945, France would probably have been forced to follow the same path. This did not happen, for the reasons shown.

## Notes

The research which resulted in this paper would not have been possible without the Woodrow Wilson International Center for Scholars. Being a fellow at the Center for five months in 1995–96 gave me the opportunity to work in Washington DC, in particular at the National Archives, the Library of Congress and in the Immigration and Naturalization Service (INS) Archives. I am particularly indebted to the expertise and professional dedication of Marian Smith, historian at the INS. Constance Potter, the archivist at National Archives, guided my earliest steps in the research. Without the help of Professor David Martin, General Counsel of INS, I would not have had access to any INS file: he deserves a special thanks. Last but not least, Josh Gibson, my assistant at the Wilson Center, has become my most talented accomplice on the research front.

1. For a detailed reconstitution of the elaboration of the list see Weil, 2001.
2. Act of Aug. 3, 1882. U.S. Department of Justice, Immigration and Naturalization Service, *An Immigrant Nation: United States Regulation of Immigration, 1798–1991*, U.S. Government Printing Office, 1991, p.5.
3. Acts of Feb. 26, 1885, 23 Stat.332; March 3, 1891, 26 Stat. 1004; March 3, 1903, 32 Stat. 1213.
4. Reports of the Industrial Commission on Immigration and on Education, vol. XV, Washington, Government Printing, 1901, p. ix. See also vol. XIX, p. 960.
5. Letter from the Commissioner of Immigration, Ellis Island, to Former President Theodore Roosevelt, July 15, 1911, National Archives (henceforth: NA) Rg 85, Records of INS, Box 103, file 52363/25 A.
6. See *Reports of the Immigration Commission*, presented by Mr. Dillingham, vol. 2, Appendix A, pp. 685, 700, 713, 721, 726.
7. See *Annual Report of Commissioner-General of Immigration*, 1907, Chart III, page 8.
8. Letter from the Senator of Maine to the Secretary of Labor, May 25, 1917, NA, Rg 85, Records of INS, entry 9, file 54261/202 box 272.
9. The same quota system remained in place except that the 1890 census now formed the basis of calculation rather than the 1910 census.
10. The LPC clause was first included in the US legislation of 1882; from 1917 to 1952 the legal authority for LPC exclusion is founded on the Immigration Act of 1917.
11. Letter of W.W. Husband, secretary of the Immigration Commission to William R. Wheeler, Assistant Secretary of Commerce and Labor, December 15, 1908, NA Rg 85, Records of INS, Entry 9, file 52363/25.
12. *Reports of the Immigration Commission*, presented by Mr. Dillingham, vol.1, p. 19–20.
13. Memorandum for the Secretary of Labor, March 3, 1924, NA, Rg 85, Records of INS, Box 99, file 52332/7.
14. Circular Letter No. 28 of September 11, 1936.
15. Memorandum written the May 29, 1936, the Chief of the Statistical Division of INS, NA, Rg 85, Accession 85–58A734, file 55882/926.
16. NA, Rg 85, Accession 85–58A734, file 55882/926.
17. By a Central Office Instruction No. 48, March 12, 1942.
18. US Department of Justice, Immigration and Naturalization Service, Letter From Mr. Reitzel to Major Schofield, February 14, 1942, NA, Rg 85, Accession 85–58A734, file 55882/926.
19. Instruction No. 177 of November 8, 1943.
20. NA, Rg 85, Records of INS, Accession 85–58A734, file 55882/926.
21. Memorandum of Henry B. Hazard, Director of Research and Education, for Mr. Earl G. Harrison, Commissioner of INS, November 5, 1942, NA, Rg 85, Records of INS, Accession 85–58A734, file 55882/926.
22. Act of July 30, 1947, 61 Stat. 630.
23. NA, Rg 85, Records of INS, Entry 9, Box 103, file 52363/25.
24. Riggs to John Farr Simmons, March 3, 1937, NA, State Department Files, Rg 59, 150.062/ Public Charge 915 1/2.
25. For more information on René Martial (1873–1955) see Schneider 1990: 231–55, and Taguieff 1999: 306.
26. For more on Georges Mauco, see Weil 1999.
27. Archives Nationales 2W/ 66.

28. Archives Nationales, *cote CAC 770 623–68, projet d'instruction* of June 6, 1945, completed by an *instruction complémentaire* for the Ministry of Justice and its naturalization service on July 18, 1945.
29. A law professor, René Cassin was the French Representative to the League of Nations from 1924 to 1938. He rallied to the cause of Free France in June 1940 and became its chief legal council, afterwards the president of the judicial committee (August 1943 to July 1945). He was Vice-President of the Council of State from November 1944 to 1960.
30. Alexandre Parodi was appointed to the Council of State in 1926. In January 1939, he was named director general of Work and Manual Labour at this same ministry. In this role. He was responsible for statutes related to foreign workers. He refused to deport political refugees from Spain and Germany back to their countries of origin. He was thus stripped of his responsibilities in October 1940 and became one of the leaders of the Resistance. From September 1944 to September 1945, he was minister of Work and Social Security in the government of General de Gaulle. See *Alexandre Parodi (1901–1979)*. Gap, 1980.
31. He thus published, in 1927, 'La population étrangère en France et les naturalisations', *Journal de la Société de statistique de Paris*, No. 2, February 1927: 60–72 and No. 3, March 1927: 89–97.
32. Director of the International Work Office before the war, Adrien Tixier joined the Free France movement in 1940 and represented it in Washington between 1941 and 1943. Minister of Work and the Future of Society in the provisional government of the French Republic from 7 June 1943 – 9 September 1944, he became the Minister of the Interior between 9 September 1944 and 26 January 1946.
33. On this point, see the excellent work by Teitelbaum and Winter 1985, esp. chapter 2.
34. Archives Nationales, CAC 770 623–68.
35. Archives Nationales, F60/493. Lettre à G. Mauco, 28 juin 1945, Archives Nationales CAC 860269/0001 Archives Nationales CAC 860269/0007 art 28 of the final draft of the *projet d'ordinance*, Archives du Conseil d'Etat.
36. Copy of a letter sent to President Roosevelt, 8 December 1906, Library of Congress, *Knights of Labor Papers*, reel 71, published in *The Path I Trod*: 302–6.
37. Testimony of Safford, Reports of the Industrial Commission on Immigration and on Education, vol XV, Washington, Government Printing, 1901, p. 131.
38. Cf NA, Rg 85, Entry 7, Box 21, letters received, letter of Victor Safford to the Secretary of Treasury, December 31, 1897 and Victor 1925.
39. Boston Historical Society, Lee papers, box 3.
40. Born in 1849 at Carbondale Pa, Terence Powderly started working at 14 as a car examiner, came to Scranton at 17 as an apprentice, and worked in a locomotive shop at 20. He joined the Machinist and Blacksmith Union in 1871 and became president of this union in 1872. Mayor of Scranton from 1878 until 1884, he joined the Knights of Labor in 1876. Powderly, *The Path I Trod*. New York, 1940, Introduction.
41. Edward McSweeney, born in Marlboro, Mass, started working in his native town in a shoe factory at age 11 in 1864. At 19 he created the Lasters' Union and became its president in 1886. In 1890 he worked as the publicity manager for the second presidential campaign of the Democratic candidate Grover Cleveland. Knights of Columbus Supreme Council Archives, New Haven CT, SC-12-056.

42. Letter of McSweeney to Powderly, 2 June 1898, and response, 3 June 1898, *Knights of Labor Papers*, Library of Congress, reel 71.

# References

Breitman, Richard, and Alan M. Kraut, 1987, *American Refugee Policy and European Jewry*, Bloomington.
Collomp, Catherine, 1998, *Entre classe et nation, mouvement ouvrier et immigration aux Etats-Unis*. Paris.
De Gaulle, Charles, 1983, *Lettres, notes et carnets*. Paris.
Divine, Robert A., 1957, *American Immigration Policy, 1924–1952*. New Haven.
DuBois, W.E.B., 1924 *Gift of Black Folk, The Negroes in the Making of America*. New-Haven.
Fitzgerald, Keith, 1996, *The Face of the Nation. Immigration, the State and the National Identity*. Stanford.
Fuchs, Lawrence H., 1990, *The American Kaleidoscope, Race, Ethnicity, and the Civic Culture*. Hanover.
Hall, Prescott F., 1899, 'Statistics of Immigration', *Quaterly Publications of the American Statistical Association*, New Series, 48, vol. VI, December 1899.
Hall, Prescott F., 1906, *Immigration and its Effects upon the United States*. New York.
Higham, John, 1975, *Send These to Me: Immigrants in Urban America*. Baltimore.
Le Bras, Hervé, 1994, *Le sol et le sang*. La Tour d'Aigues.
Mauco, Georges, 1932, *Les Etrangers en France, leur rôle dans l'activité économique*. Paris. Mauco, Georges, 1942, *L'Ethnie française, no 3*. Paris.
Martial, René, 1934, *La Race Française*.
Martial, René, 1935, 'Politique de l'immigration', *Mercure de France*, 15 April.
McSweeney, Edward F., 1905, 'The Character of Our Immigration, Past and Present', *The National Geographic Magazine*, Vol. XVI, No. 1, January: 1–27.
MacSweeney, Edward F., 1926, 'The Immigration Act of 1924– Fallaciousness of the "National Origins" Theory', *Journal of the American Irish Historical Society*, 25.
Neuman, Gerald L., 1996, *Strangers to the Constitution, Immigrants, Borders and Fundamental Law*. Princeton.
Ngai, Mae M., 1999, 'The Architecture of Race in American Immigration Law: A Re-examination of the Reed-Johson Act of 1924', *Journal of American History*. July.
Safford, Victor, 1925, *Immigration Problems*. New York.
Sandel, Michael J., 1996, *Democracy's Discontent, America in Search of a Public Philosophy*. New York.
Sauvy, Alfred and Robert Debré, 1946, *Des Français pour la France*. Paris.
Schneider, William H., 1990, *Quality and Quantity, the Quest for Biological Regeneration in Twentieth Century France*. Cambridge.
Taguieff, Pierre-André, 1999, 'La "science" du Docteur Martial', in *L'antisémitisme de plume 1940–1944, études et documents*. Paris.
Teitelbaum, Michael S., and Jay M. Winter, 1985, *The Fear of Population Decline*. Orlando.
Tichenor, Daniel J., 2002, *Dividing Lines: The Politics of Immigration Control in America*. Princeton.
Tissier, Pierre, 1942, *The Government of Vichy*. London.
Weil, Patrick, 1995, *La France et ses étrangers, l'aventure d'une politique de l'immigration de 1938 à nos jours*. Paris

Weil, Patrick, 1999, 'Georges Mauco: un itinéraire camouflé, ethnoracisme pratique et antisémitisme fielleux', in *L'antisémitisme de plume 1940–1944, études et documents*, ed. by Pierre André Taguieff, Paris, pp. 267–276.

Weil, Patrick, 2001, 'Races at the Gate: A Century of Racial Distinctions in American Immigration Policy (1865–1965)', *Georgetown Immigration Law Journal.* Vo. 15, summer 2001, No. 4: 625–648.

Wurtz, Pierre, 1925, *La question de l'immigration aux Etats-Unis.* Paris.

# Part IV

---

# Provisional Conclusions

# Chapter 18

## Law and Practice
### *Problems in Researching the History of Migration Controls*

*Andreas Fahrmeir*

The essays in this volume illustrate the degree of state intervention in migration processes on either side of the Atlantic in the
nineteenth century. Some focus on general questions, others on
detailed case studies, but all of them implicitly or explicitly
suggest comparisons between different national experiences:
between 'liberal' and 'autocratic' states, or between countries of
immigration and countries of emigration. Finding a firm basis for
such comparisons involves certain difficulties. One of them is that
the type of sources on which research can be based is itself determined at least in part by the system of migration control in place.
This concluding essay will therefore seek to address some general
questions regarding the sources and their reliability.

The preceding chapters have described the practical implica-
tions of the new concept of citizenship introduced by the French
Revolution for migration movements. Passport and visa requirements gave state officials much greater power to intervene, which
grew as the nineteenth century progressed. For this reason, the
decade after 1800 has been described as the beginning of the era
of the 'documented citizen' (Spencer 1992: 19). On the European
Continent, the system of migration control introduced then
remained in operation until well after the revolutions of 1848. In
the later 1850s and 1860s, however, the (first) passport system
was dismantled. Visa requirements and routine passport controls
at frontiers were abolished, until they were re-introduced at the
beginning of the First World War. Some parts of this story
are clearer than others. The processes at the beginning of the

nineteenth century and at the beginning of the First World War
have been well researched (Burger 2000; Geselle 2000; Torpey
2000 and Torpey this volume), whereas what happened in the
1860s, 1870s, and 1880s is rather more controversial. Some historians have interpreted the reforms of these decades as an
introduction of practically unfettered freedom of movement
throughout Europe and the world (Noiriel 1991: 77–9); others
suggest that all that changed was the way in which control was
exercised (Fahrmeir 2000: 100–51); different contributions to this
volume also incline to different interpretations.

The emerging new narrative of the development of state
control of migration gives rise to some general questions.

- What was the actual impact of the new 'immigration laws'
  on patterns of migration?
- How were the prescriptions of passport and police laws put
  into practice in different countries?
- Was there a connection between migration control and
  processes of national unification in Italy and Germany, and
  moves towards national dis-unification in the United
  Kingdom, and were there fundamental differences between
  the way in which liberal and less liberal states regulated
  migration?
- What precisely went on during the 'liberal period' in the
  decades before the First World War? While preliminary
  controls designed to keep 'undesirable' people from entering
  a country were abolished, the deportation of such persons
  remained possible. Did a system of control by deportation
  develop, and – if so – was this really more 'liberal' than its
  predecessor, or did it disrupt migrants' lives even more?
- Finally, how did the nationalisation of immigration policies,
  which can be clearly observed by the end of the nineteenth
  century, come about?

In order to answer these questions, fairly detailed knowledge of
the practice of migration control is required. However, such
knowledge is difficult to obtain for a number of reasons.

## What Do Laws Mean?

In the nineteenth century, migration was regulated in legal texts:
laws, administrative directives, orders and ordinances of government ministers, regional and local officials. These texts are the
first port of call for historians trying to reconstruct the immigration policies of the eighteenth and nineteenth centuries.

Contemporaries did the same; at least from the 1830s onwards, official or semi-official handbooks on the 'droit des étrangers', or the 'gesetzliche Behandlung der Ausländer' were being published, intended for use by officials as well as foreigners who wished to acquaint themselves with the regulations to which they were supposed to conform (Okey 1831; Legat 1832; Müller 1841; Vesque von Püttlingen 1842). Without exception, these books summarise or print the relevant statutes and directives, and offer no comments on practice. They thus suggest that there was little difference between the letter of the law and the way it was applied. Of course, this is unrealistic: the truth probably lies somewhere between a very strict adherence to the law, and absolute disregard of it. Until recently, there was a fairly widespread consensus that, in early modern and modern Europe, neither extreme was likely to exist for long, for if a government was no longer able to enforce its laws at all, then surely it was on the verge of collapse.

A recent article by Jürgen Schlumbohm (1997) has, however, called this assumption into question for the early modern period. Summarising a wide range of recent research into various areas of governmental activity, primarily in early modern German territories, Schlumbohm concludes that not only were many laws openly flouted; in fact, governments made no serious effort to enforce them, because they were painfully aware that they did not possess the resources to coerce their subjects into obeying the numerous 'police' directives turned out by their chancelleries. He therefore suggests that the point of such ordinances was not to influence everyday life, but merely to ensure that 'good government' was seen to take place.

Schlumbohm believes that attitudes to the law changed decisively in the nineteenth century, and that the correlation between law and practice became much closer. On one level, this is doubtless true. The concepts of law and politics evolved in the course of the nineteenth century from the notion that the law was essentially immutable and given, so that parliaments or governments could only explain it or reform it by restoring it to an earlier, uncorrupted state, to the concept that the law itself could undergo substantial modification in response to, and even in anticipation of, social change (Steinmetz 1993). In Britain, where legal continuity was not interrupted by the promulgation of new civil and criminal codes which took place on the Continent, the literal interpretation of precedents and old, obsolete, statutes by the courts in the nineteenth century led to conclusions which would have surprised earlier generations of legal professionals. For instance, while it had been obvious to all contemporaries that the citizenships of Hannover and Britain were distinct during the period of personal union, the Court of Queen's Bench decided in 1886 that a common British-Hanoverian citizenship had existed until Queen Victoria succeeded to the British, but not the Hanoverian, throne in 1837 (Isaacson vs. Durant, 5 April 1886, *Law Reports, Queen's Bench Division*, 27 (1886): 54–9).

But on closer inspection a distinction between a nineteenth century where laws were meant to be enforced, and an early modern period where this was not the case, becomes more difficult to sustain. For instance, A. V. Dicey called attention to the fact that the savage provisions which threatened proselytising foreign Jesuits with transportation for life, as well as those imposing criminal penalties on converts to Catholicism, were only included in the British legislation emancipating Catholics in 1829 in order to secure approval for the bill in the Commons (Dicey 1914: 12). Some laws faded into oblivion fairly quickly even in the nineteenth century, regardless of whether or not they remained on the statute books. The 1819 Foreign Enlistment Act, which prohibited recruiting British subjects as mercenaries for foreign armies, was taken seriously enough to induce agents for South American governments involved in wars of independence to stop recruiting men and to start raising money on the financial exchanges, thus causing the 'first Latin American Debt Crisis' of 1822–1825 (Dawson 1990: 26). By 1854, when some British subjects who wanted to join the Austrian army enquired at the Home Office about the possibility of relinquishing their British nationality, it emerged that the licenses required by this act were routinely being granted by British ministers abroad in clear breach of the law.[1]

There are many examples of laws with a very brief life period in German states as well. In 1834, the Frankfurt Federal Diet decided to require more detailed verification of the identity documents of people travelling by mail coaches. Laws to this effect were passed in the roughly 40 member-states of the German Confederation in the course of the same year (*Protokolle der deutschen Bundesversammlung* (1834): 47f., 189f., 265f., 304f., 351f., 403, 476, 496, 522, 562, 588, 617, 842) but an enquiry in 1845 revealed that they were no longer enforced in many states.[2] Indeed, when the 1860s are described as a 'liberal era', it is implicitly assumed that the passport and registration laws of German states as a whole, not just the specific sections that were repealed, fell into disuse.

These examples (merely) confirm the fairly obvious insight that the letter of the law and its practice do not always coincide, and that it is risky to take laws at face value without a general indication of what practice was like. An ideal class of records for this purpose would be judicial files, but in some countries, notably in some German states, judicial documents were routinely destroyed after a fixed period (Temme 1996: 95).

Legislation on its own can thus be misleading in establishing a chronology of migration policies. Nevertheless, it remains plausible to assume a close resemblance between migration control and the laws on the subject. This assumption is confirmed by travel guides, which could hardly afford to lead their purchasers directly to gaol for infringement of immigration or passport regulations. However, the strictness of migration control probably depended substantially on the general political and economic situation of a country. The wide berth immigration regulations gave to the officials charged with their execution meant that it was not necessary to change the law every time immigration policies were liberalised or tightened.

The general premise on which legislation relative to aliens was based in German states, for instance, was that foreigners had no rights not granted to them by explicit laws. This was of crucial importance when it came to deciding whether individual aliens should be allowed to enter a state or to remain there. Until they obtained the citizenship of the state where they resided, their 'residence permit' (in fact a brief entry in a passport or even an oral agreement) could be revoked by the police more or less at will. Even though individuals who received an expulsion order could ask officials on the next step on the administrative ladder to reconsider it,[3] there was no judicial right of appeal. From the point of view of the police, most of the aims laid down in immigration regulations, e. g. keeping foreigners from entering certain professions, from engaging in political activity, or from embarking on dubious business ventures, could all be resolved by issuing expulsion orders or by refusing to extend residence permits. Because this was a realm where police authority was almost absolute, there was little prospect of such cases coming before courts of law, whose decisions would probably have been reported in newspapers, discussed by legal professionals, and thus been more predictable than those arrived at in the chaotic world of police stations. This makes it difficult, for instance, to compare the pre-1871 German situation with that in countries such as Belgium or the Netherlands, where the judiciary handled some types of deportations, and where records are therefore more complete and systematic.

The regulations relative to foreigners guided police officers in the use of their discretion by naming certain groups which should not be allowed to enter a country, and by specifying others whose travels should not be interrupted by intrusive police controls. But this did not amount to more than very general rules of conduct. The 1823 Hesse-Kassel regulations concerning the establishment of the *Landdragoner* (an equivalent of other countries' *Gendarmerie*) ordered them to enforce the passport regulations on the main roads. They were to request to see passports of 'suspicious' foreigners, and to present foreigners without passports to the next judicial official. 'Honest' business was not to be hindered, and the *Landdragoner* were explicitly prohibited from using excessive force. The only part of the instructions which achieved a certain level of clarity was a list of persons who were *also* to be treated as 'vagrants', presumably in addition to those immediately recognisable as such: quacks, unknown peddlers without a licence or apparent means of support and servants who had been out of work for more than six months. It was thought necessary to point out to the officers that travellers with several passports in different names, who did not fit the personal description on their passport, or who carried passports, which had obviously been tampered with, were 'suspicious' (*Sammlung von Gesetzen, Verordnungen, Ausschreiben und sonstigen allgemeinen Verfügungen für die Kurhessischen Staaten* (1820): 99f., §§46–55).

In Britain, where the legal protection of the rights of foreigners was usually quite stringent, the form of the laws restricting immigration between 1793 and 1826[4] was similar. The Alien Acts did not place any restrictions on the immigration of foreigners to Britain, but they allowed any 'principal secretary of state' to order any alien to leave the country. No specific reasons had to be given, and there was no right of appeal. There is a further parallel: even though illegal or clandestine immigration was considered a crime both in German states and in Britain, the matter was only referred to the courts in the case of a second offence.[5]

To sum up: if all officials had stuck to the letter of the law at all times, this would still leave us, if not in the dark, then in twilight, about what the epithet 'undesirable' meant. Did it refer to people convicted of crimes, to people who could not support themselves, all people considered likely to become criminal or poor, or simply anybody whose looks officers did not like? Were certain social, religious, ethnic or linguistic groups automatically considered 'undesirable'? Most likely this depended on the particular conditions in a locality or country. If there was demand for foreign labour, then presumably even servants who had not worked for six months got the benefit of the doubt. If unemployment was high, this was less likely to be the case. Unless there was no co-ordination of policy at all, some of these facts ought to emerge from administrative correspondence. Such correspondence is, however, unlikely to mention prejudices, which were widely shared. It would therefore be better if direct evidence of how individual officers acted in individual cases could be found.

## Problems of Examples

The most readily accessible source about nineteenth-century migration controls are individual travel accounts. They exist in great numbers and they document a wide range of experiences people had with migration controls at various times and places. For instance, Elizabeth Rosanna Gilbert, better known under her stage name Lola Montez, a British subject posing as a Spanish dancer, was apparently able to tour Europe without proper travel documents in spite of drawing police attention to herself by routinely attacking gendarmes before 1847. Even though she was officially created Countess Mansfeld by king Ludwig I of Bavaria in 1849, she found it impossible to obtain papers for a journey from Britain to Spain later that year (Seymour 1996: 53ff., 259). A Mr. Phillips, travelling from Brussels to Frankfurt in 1851, was not sanctioned when he disobeyed an order to depart from Prussia immediately which was entered into his passport at Aachen.[6] By contrast, a Captain Macdonald, a member of the British royal household, was gaoled and fined for an altercation with a railway guard in Bonn in 1860 (Urbach 1999: 108f.). These examples indicate the difficulties such sources present. First, records of unusual situations are much more common than descriptions of standard practice. Incidents which were particularly noticeable, annoying, or funny have a much greater chance of entering diaries or travel accounts than those which were routine. Second, such texts are not representative. More reports survive which emanate from middle- or upper class travellers than from members of the lower classes, who were probably much more affected by migration controls. Third, deducing general observations from such sources is fiendishly difficult: for every text that suggests one interpretation, there is usually another one that proves the opposite.

For instance, constructing a hierarchy of the severity of passport controls in various European countries, based on the experience of travellers who visited more than one, and recorded their impressions, appears to be a relatively simple and straight-forward task. In the 1820s and 1830s, on the route between Britain and Italy via the German states, migration controls seemed to increase in intensity as one travelled south. British travellers reported surprise at the intrusiveness of controls in German states (Chambers 1839: 71), travellers from German states singled out Austrian measures as having been particularly strict (Förster 1887: 191–9), and people from Lombardy remarked on the comparative freedom from control north of the Alps (Phillips-Matz 1993: 213). So far, so good: unless these statements turn out to reflect national preconceptions or an oblique form of political commentary. At least one pair of Prussian travellers, representatives of the Cologne Handelskammer who visited Britain in 1829, complained about the length of time it took to clear immigration and customs on entering Britain: four hours, which is more than the three-hour delay reported on entering Prussia (Schumacher 1968: 154, 310f.; Chambers 1839: 47). This is curious, because both the law and condescending British comments about European passport fanaticism suggest that entry into Britain was unchecked. Of course, the Prussian travellers did not distinguish between delays imposed by customs and immi-gration restrictions, but then neither did the British, because in practice both examinations frequently took place at the same spot. Furthermore, the Swiss consul general in London sent a number of scathing reports to the Home Secretary in 1827, which alleged widespread corruption and abuse of power by Alien Office employees. An enquiry by the Home Secretary could not confirm most of the charges, but some of the complaints were upheld.[7]

Likewise, Mr. Phillips's easy escape at Aachen contrasts sharply with another account of the same border crossing at roughly the same time by a former Prussian judge who had fallen into disgrace in 1848. He describes travellers being herded like cattle into small rooms where their papers were subject to prolonged and detailed scrutiny, thus 'unmasking' Prussia as the lawless police state as he had experienced it (Temme 1996: 270). It is not entirely unfair to dismiss these remarks as an obsession with detail. But answers to more general questions depend on our interpretation of such details.

One such point is the issue of class. In *ancien régime* societies, nationality was of secondary importance for migration control. Whether or not obstacles to migration existed depended largely on the travellers' rank. Judging from the texts of the relevant laws, this changed decisively in the nineteenth century. In the

1850s and 1860s, different European states' entry visa require-ments were abolished by country, not by rank: British peers, just like British labourers, had to obtain a visa before entering Bavaria prior to 1862, and did not have to do so thereafter.[8] Some commentators nevertheless remarked that rank remained the most important factor in determining who was subject to migra-tion controls until well into the 1850s (Mohl 1834–43: 375; Duthie 1865: xiif., xxviii; Lüdtke 1993: 40). This was, of course, partly due to the fact that travellers staying in grand hotels were less likely to be placed under police surveillance than those sleep-ing in dodgy hostels: a Nassau regulation specified that only landlords of the lower class of boarding houses had to forward the passports of all their guests to the police, while other estab-lishments could merely pass on entries in their registers.[9] The social divide between lowly police officers charged with enforc-ing immigration regulations and noblemen or members of the upper middle classes placed limits on police powers. This did not always prevent police officers from taking action against their social superiors – as scores of aristocrats detained at borders could have affirmed (e. g. Ridley 1970: 362) –, but it frequently did. The interesting question is when the importance of rank began to decline decisively: during the revolutionary upheavals of the 1830s? Or the 1840s? In the course of the 1850s and 1860s? In the aftermath of the Franco-Prussian War? Or only with the First World War? Or was it, as seems most likely, a gradual process, which was accelerated in times of political crisis?

To answer these questions, we would need some insight into what went on in nineteenth-century police stations. What propor-tion of travellers of different classes was subject to control, how many were sent back, how many were imprisoned for immigra-tion offences? How many foreigners were deported, to which countries? Such numbers are usually not available, but even if they are, it will have to be examined carefully whether such infor-mation cannot be supplied from other sources, which would not require the analysis of thousands and thousands of entries in ledgers.

The nineteenth century was a century of substantial and ever increasing mobility. People travelled frequently and went further afield as travel became swifter, more pleasant and easier to afford. This means that the passport system produced an enormous amount of paperwork. There are 283,958 counterfoils of declara-tions made by foreigners in Brighton, Dover, Folkestone, Hull, London, and Ramsey on arrival in the United Kingdom between 1836 and 1858, a period when the requirement to register was hardly enforced. Passport officials are known to have checked an average of 188,000 *Wanderbücher* (journeymen's papers) at Munich each year between 1830 and 1833, and 36,000 papers at Dresden in the first three quarters of 1836 (Giebel 1967: 60; Rupieper 1977: 333). Even samples of migration control procedures over an extended period of time in more than one location would usually involve very high numbers of cases and are feasible only in the context of larger research projects; if the aim is to trace travellers' movements, in a methodology reminiscent of 'family reconstruction', the workload becomes next to impossible to master.

Moreover, the limited importance of the individual decisions in immigration cases saw to it that many such records disappeared almost immediately. When the British Alien Office was closed in 1836, most of its files were destroyed shortly afterwards.[10] In German states' archives, few passport registers survived.[11] In Britain, the Passport Office files contain periodic lists of fees received for passports issued, but no registers.[12] Decisions on visaing individual passports may have been recorded in visa registers, but there is a strong possibility that they were only noted on the back of the passport, and there is evidence that some decisions, up to and including deportation orders, were made orally in some German states until the 1830s (Küster 1995: 124f.). There are some systematic collections of passports, for instance of *Wanderbücher* of journeymen who settled permanently in nineteenth-century Chemnitz (Bräuer 1982), but, once again, in German states such collections seem to be rare. In France, the quality and quantity of relevant material appears to be much better (Vialdenc 1971; Grandjonc 1975).

But what of statistics that were prepared at the time – do they provide any answers?

## The Unreliability of Statistics

There are many questions which statistics can answer. However, this type of source material also has its problems. State government apparently did not attempt to monitor the actions of their police forces by collecting comprehensive statistics on their activity. Criminal statistics tend to be selective. Bavarian statistics list only deportations for vagrancy, but not for other reasons, for the period between 1836 and 1850 (*Beiträge zur Statistik des Königreichs Bayern*, 2 (1853): 48–56). Accounts covering the cost of deportations in Hesse-Darmstadt were limited to cases where the state treasury was responsible for the expense incurred by municipalities.[13]

A final problem is that the statistics may not themselves be reliable. This is not only to say that they are subject to the ordinary problems of data collection and compilation.[14] They may have been drawn up mainly to prove to the central state governments that its instructions were being obeyed. One prominent example of inaccurate statistics are the records on emigration from nineteenth-century German states. Theoretically, all would-be emigrants had to complete a formal emigration procedure. State officials were to enquire whether there were any unresolved criminal or civil enquiries against the applicants; whether all dependants were properly cared for; whether all debts and taxes had been paid, military service had been completed if they were eligible for conscription, if all state scholarships they might have received had been repaid, and so on. The files drawn up in the course of these processes have served as the basis for a number of important studies of emigration from German states (e. g. Lubinski 1992).

It has long been recognised, however, that not everyone who left completed this procedure. It is possible to calculate this by comparing the, usually triennial, censuses with the information on births and deaths, immigration and emigration. If one assumes, as some statisticians did, that any errors can be explained entirely through unrecorded emigration, then only a minority of emigrants stuck to the letter of the law, sometimes as little as 10 per cent in Prussia's eastern provinces (Markow 1889: 125–33). Seeing the error entirely in terms of clandestine emigration is problematic, however, because, at least in Bavaria, the population calculated from the last census by adding births and immigrants and subtracting deaths and emigrants could be higher than the next census, as one would expect if clandestine emigration took place, but it could also be substantially lower (*Beiträge zur Statistik des Königreichs Bayern*, 13 (1865): 27). Bavaria also counted the incidence of illegal emigration directly, suggesting that some 25 per cent of emigrants left Bavaria without completing the proper formalities, and thus illegally (*Beiträge zur Statistik des Königreichs Bayern*, Heft 8 (1859): 240f.). Yet a study of emigration from the Bavarian Palatinate, the province of the country adjacent to France, has found that the official figures for illegal emigration substantially underestimated reality (Faltin 1987: 144, 189f., 250). There are two possible explanations for this: either migration controls were inadequate; or there was some degree of complicity between local officials and emigrants when it came to disregarding the formalities (Heinz 1989: 225; Faltin 1987: 263–6). Unless future studies are able to disprove this interpretation, then the statistics on emigration, one of the most powerful arguments for the inefficiency of migration controls in nineteenth-century German states, must be considered to be problematic. It almost appears as though the sources that appear most objective have to be treated with most caution.

Research into nineteenth-century migration policy is faced with formidable difficulties, because the question of the effectiveness of control is so crucial. The point of evading migration controls is to stay out of the bureaucratic paper trail, and thus out of most sources. Estimating how easy it was to escape migration control can easily become a matter of guesswork, and it may be impossible to arrive at definitive conclusions. The importance of sources produced by state institutions, which cannot always be crosschecked against contemporary newspaper accounts or travel guides, is another potential difficulty. For this reason, international comparisons are of particular importance. Different national experiences, which produced different types of documentation, may suggest ways of overcoming deficiencies in sources, and provide some basis for reasonable estimates. This is feasible because, as the papers in this volume show, all countries in Europe and North America were part of the same system of migration control. The study of different national experiences within the context of this system should therefore bring us closer to reaching conclusions on some of the questions outlined above.

## Notes

1. Public Record Office, London (henceforth: PRO), HO 45/8829.
2. Replies received 26 June 1843 to 17 February 1845, Hessisches Staatsarchiv Marburg (henceforth: StAMa) 16/VII 8/2 Bd. II.
3. Cf. e. g. the files in StAMa 19h/275.
4. 33 Geo. III, c. 4 and the acts which regularly prolonged it.
5. For Hesse-Kassel, where the 1820 and earlier police regulations had still assumed that foreigners about to be arrested or deported would be given the right to state their case before a 'judicial official', this was altered in the 1823 *Sicherheitsverordnung, Sammlung von Gesetzen, Verordnungen, Ausschreiben und sonstigen allgemeinen Verfügungen für die Kurhessischen Staaten* (1823): 57–68, §7.
6. Mr. Phillips to Viscount Palmerston, Royal Exchange, 25 March 1851, PRO, FO 612/8.
7. Memorandum by A. L. Prevost summarising a previous conversation, dated Clapham Common, 23 July 1827; observations on Mr. Prevost's letter, 25 July 1827; remarks on cases communicated by Mr. Prevost, no 7, 23 July 1827, PRO, HO 3/102; F. Spring Rice to Consul General of the Swiss, Alien Office, 24 July 1827, PRO, HO 5/21, fols. 41–4, and circular, fols. 46f.

8. Bavarian Embassy London to Foreign Office, 25 March 1862, PRO, FO 612/27.
9. *Sammlung der landesherrlichen Edicte und anderen Verordnungen, welchen vom 1. Julius 1816 an, im ganzen Umfang des Herzogthums Nassau Gesetzeskraft beigelegt worden ist* (4 vols. Wiesbaden, 1817-[1846]), vol. 2, 157, §9.
10. See e. g. Benetto Devotto to Home Office, 23 July 1853, and minutes, PRO, HO 45/4932.
11. See e. g. Hessisches Staatsarchiv Darmstadt G 15 Büdingen Q31.
12. See PRO, FO 612, *passim*.
13. Regierung Starkenburg circular, 5 July 1831, StADa G 15 Alsfeld Q 70; Kreisamt Dieburg to clerk, Groß-Umstadt, 26 March 1831, Stadtarchiv Groß-Umstadt XVIII/3 Kosten.
14. Cf. e. g. the very different estimates of the number of Germans in Paris in the nineteenth century in Grandjonc 1975: 216f., 227f., 291f., or Noiriel 1991: 77f. and Jeanblanc 1994: 9, which are based on different assessments on whether census figures were reliable.

# References

Bräuer, Helmut, 1982, *Gesellenmigration in der Zeit der industriellen Revolution: Meldeunterlagen als Quellen zur Erforschung der Wanderbeziehungen zwischen Chemnitz und dem europäischen Raum*, Karl-Marx-Stadt.

Burger, Hannelore, 2000, 'Paßwesen und Staatsbürgerschaft', in *Grenze und Staat. Paßwesen, Staatsbürgerschaft, Heimatrecht und Fremdengesetzgebung in der österreichischen Monarchie (1750–1867)*, eds Waltraud Heindl and Edith Saurer, Vienna, pp. 3–172.

Chambers, William, 1839, *A Tour in Holland, the Countries on the Rhine, and Belgium in the Autumn of 1838*, Edinburgh.

Dawson, Frank Griffith, 1990, *The First Latin American Debt Crisis. The City of London and the 1822–25 Loan Bubble*, New Haven.

Dicey, A. V., 1914, *Lectures on the Relation Between Law and Public Opinion in England During the Nineteenth Century*, 2nd edn, London.

Duthie, William, 1865, *A Tramp's Wallet; Stored by an English Goldsmith during his Wanderings in Germany and France*, 2nd edn, London.

Fahrmeir, Andreas, 2000, *Citizens and Aliens: Foreigners and the Law in Britain and the German States, 1789–1870*, New York.

Faltin, Sigrid, 1987, *Die Auswanderung aus der Pfalz nach Nordamerika im 19. Jahrhundert: unter besonderer Berücksichtigung des Landkommissariates Bergzabern*, Frankfurt/Main.

Förster, Ernst, 1887, *Aus der Jugendzeit*, Berlin and Stuttgart.

Geselle, Andrea, 2000, 'Bewegung und ihre Kontrolle in Lombardo-Venetien', in *Grenze und Staat. Paßwesen, Staatsbürgerschaft, Heimatrecht und Fremdengesetzgebung in der österreichischen Monarchie (1750–1867)*, eds Waltraud Heindl and Edith Saurer, Vienna, pp. 347–518.

Giebel, Hans Rainer, 1967, *Strukturanalyse der Gesellschaft des Königreichs Bayern im Vormärz 1818–1848*, Diss. phil. Munich.

Grandjonc, Jacques, 1975, 'Éléments statistiques pour une étude de l'immigration étrangère en France de 1830 à 1851', *Archiv für Sozialgeschichte*, 15: 211–300.

Heinz, Joachim, 1989, *"Bleibe im Lande, und nähre dich redlich!" Zur Geschichte der pfälzischen Auswanderung vom Ende des 17. bis zum Ausgang des 19. Jahrhunderts*, Kaiserslautern.

Jeanblanc, Helga, 1994, *Des Allemands dans l'industrie et le commerce du livre à Paris (1811–1870)*, Paris.

Küster, Thomas, 1995, *Alte Armut und neues Bürgertum: Öffentliche und private Fürsorge in Münster von der Ära Fürstenberg bis zum Ersten Weltkrieg (1756–1914)*, Münster.

Legat, B. J., 1832, *Code des étrangers, ou Traité de la législation française concernant les étrangers*, Paris.

Lubinski, Axel, 1992, *Entlassen aus dem Untertanenverband. Die Amerika-Auswanderung aus Mecklenburg-Strelitz im 19. Jahrhundert*, Osnabrück.

Lüdtke, Alf, 1993, '"Willkürgewalt des Staates"? Polizeipraxis und administrative Definitionsmacht im vormärzlichen Preußen', in *"...nur für die Sicherheit da ..."? Zur Geschichte der Polizei im 19. und 20. Jahrhundert*, ed. Herbert Reinke, Frankfurt/Main, 35–55.

Markow, Alexis, 1889, *Das Wachsthum der Bevölkerung und die Entwicklung der Aus- und Einwanderungen, Ab- und Zuzüge in Preussen und Preussens einzelnen Provinzen, Bezirken und Kreisgruppen von 1824 bis 1885*, Tübingen.

Mohl, R[obert] von, [1834]–1843, 'Paßwesen', in *Staats-Lexikon oder Encyclopädie der Staatswissenschaften*, eds Carl von Rotteck, Carl Welcker, 15 vols, Altona, vol. XII, 370–9.

Müller, Alexander, 1841, *Die deutschen Auswanderungs-, Freizügigkeits- und Heimaths-Verhältnisse: Eine vergleichende Darstellung der darüber in den Staaten des deutschen Bundes besonders in Oesterreich, Preußen und Sachsen bestehenden Verträge, Gesetze und Verordnungen, zugleich mit literärischen Nachweisungen und Bemerkungen für die Gesetzgebungs-Politik. Zur Selbstbelehrung für deutsche und ausländische Staatsbürger jeden Standes*, Leipzig.

Noiriel, Gérard, 1991, *La tyrannie du national: le droit d'asile en Europe 1793–1993*, Paris.

Okey, C[harles] H[enry], 1831, *Droits, privilèges et obligations des étrangers dans la Grande-Bretagne. Deuxième édition, corrigée et augmentée, revue par N. M. Thevenin, Ancien Avocat aux Conseils d'État et à la Cour Royale de Paris*, Paris.

Phillips-Matz, Mary Jane, 1993, *Verdi: A Biography*, Oxford.

Ridley, Jasper, 1970, *Lord Palmerston*, London.

Rupieper, Hermann-Josef, 1977, 'Die Polizei und die Fahndungen anläßlich der deutschen Revolution von 1848/49', *Vierteljahrschrift für Sozial- und Wirtschaftsgeschichte*, 44: 328–55.

Schlumbohm, Jürgen, 1997, 'Gesetze, die nicht durchgesetzt werden – ein Strukturmerkmal des frühneuzeitlichen Staates?', *Geschichte und Gesellschaft*, 23: 647–63.

Schumacher, Martin, 1968, *Auslandsreisen deutscher Unternehmer 1750–1851 unter besonderer Berücksichtigung von Rheinland und Westfalen*, Cologne.

Seymour, Bruce, 1996, *Lola Montez. A Life*, New Haven.

Spencer, Elaine Glovka, 1992, *Police and the Social Order in German Cities: The Düsseldorf District, 1848–1914*, De Kalb, Ill.

Steinmetz, Willibald, 1993, *Das Sagbare und das Machbare. Zum Wandel politischer Handlungsspielräume. England 1780–1867*, Stuttgart.

Temme, J[adocus] D. H., 1996, *Augenzeugenberichte der deutschen Revolution 1848/49. Ein preußischer Richter als Vorkämpfer der Demokratie*, Darmstadt.

Torpey, John, 2000, *The Invention of the Passport: Surveillance, Citizenship, and the State*, Cambridge.

Urbach, Karina, 1999, *Bismarck's Favourite Englishman: Lord Odo Russell's Mission to Berlin*, London.

Vesque von Püttlingen, Johann, 1842, *Die gesetzliche Behandlung der Ausländer in Oesterreich nach den daselbst gültigen Civilrechts-, Straf-, Commercial-, Militär- und Polizei-Normen nebst einer einleitenden Abhandlung über die österreichische Staatsbürgerschaft*, Vienna.

Vialdenc, Jean, 1971, 'Une source d'histoire économique et sociale. Les passeports: problèmes d'utilisation, limites et lacunes', *Bulletin de la section d'histoire moderne et contemporaine*, fasc. 8: 187–202.

# Index